Lecture Notes in Computer Science   6141

Commenced Publication in 1973
Founding and Former Series Editors:
Gerhard Goos, Juris Hartmanis, and Jan van Leeuwen

Jan Vitek (Ed.)

Objects, Models, Components, Patterns

48th International Conference, TOOLS 2010
Málaga, Spain, June 28–July 2, 2010
Proceedings

 Springer

Volume Editor

Jan Vitek
Purdue University
Computer Science
West Lafayette, IN, USA
E-mail: jv@cs.purdue.edu

Library of Congress Control Number: 2010929256

CR Subject Classification (1998): F.3, D.2, D.3, D.1, C.2, D.2.4

LNCS Sublibrary: SL 2 – Programming and Software Engineering

ISSN	0302-9743
ISBN-10	3-642-13952-3 Springer Berlin Heidelberg New York
ISBN-13	978-3-642-13952-9 Springer Berlin Heidelberg New York

springer.com

© Springer-Verlag Berlin Heidelberg 2010
Printed in Germany

Typesetting: Camera-ready by author, data conversion by Scientific Publishing Services, Chennai, India
Printed on acid-free paper   06/3180

Preface

It is a pleasure to present the proceedings of the 48th TOOLS Europe Conference (TOOLS 2010) held in Málaga, Spain. The conference continues to serve a broad object-oriented community with a technical program spanning theory and practice. The program was rounded out with keynotes by Oege De Moor, Ivar Jacobson and Bertrand Meyer, and a banquet speech by Jean Bzivin. The proceedings include 16 papers selected from 60 submissions. The papers were reviewed in a single-blind process with 4-7 reviews per paper. The Program Committee (PC) discussions followed Oscar Nierstrasz' Champion pattern. PC papers had additional reviews and were held at a higher standard. For the first time this year, TOOLS had a PC meeting which combined in-person discussions and electronic presence.

TOOLS owes is success to the efforts of many. I would like to thank the authors for their submissions, the PC members and their subreviewers for their reviews, our General Chair Bertrand Meyer, Antonio Vallecillo for the overall organization; Richard van de Stadt for his invaluable help with Cyberchair, and Bertrand Meyer and Peter Müller for hosting the PC meeting at the ETHZ.

April 2010   Jan Vitek

Organization

The TOOLS 2010 conferences were organized by the Department of Computer Science of the University of Málaga, in co-operation with the ETH, Zürich.

Executive Committee

Conference Chair   Betrand Meyer (ETH Zürich and
                                           Eiffel Software)
Program Chair   Jan Vitek (Purdue University)
Organizing Chair   Osmar Santos (University of York)
Website   Petr Maj (Purdue University)

Program Committee

Uwe Assman	University of Dresden, Germany
Elisa Baniassad	Chinese University of Hong Kong, Hong Kong
Alexandre Bergel	University of Chile, Chile
Lorenzo Bettini	University of Turin, Italy
Judith Bishop	Microsoft Research, USA
William Cook	University of Texas Austin, USA
Sophia Drossopolou	Imperial College London, UK
Catherine Dubois	ENSIIE, France
Stphane Ducasse	INRIA Lille, France
Manuel Fahndrich	Microsoft Research, USA
Harald Gall	University of Zurich, Switzerland
Benoit Garbinato	University of Lausanne, Switzerland
Angelo Gargantini	University of Bergamo, Italy
Jeff Gray	University of Alabama Birmingham, USA
Kathryn Gray	University of Cambridge, UK
Thomas Gschwind	IBM Research, Switzerland
Matthias Hauswith	University of Lugano, Switzerland
Nigel Horspool	University of Victoria, Canada
Tomas Kalibera	Charles University, Czech Republic
Gerti Kappel	Vienna University of Technology, Austria
Doug Lea	State University of New York Oswego, USA
Shane Markstrum	University of California Los Angeles, USA
Peter Müller	ETH Zurich, Switzerland
Oscar Nierstrasz	University of Bern, Switzerland
James Noble	Victoria University of Wellington, New Zealand
Nate Nystrom	University of Texas Arlington, USA
Manuel Oriol	University of York, UK
Jonathan Ostroff	York University, Canada

Richard Paige	University of York, UK
Shaz Qadeer	Microsoft Research, USA
Awais Rashid	Lancaster University, UK
Vivek Sarkar	Rice University, USA
Doug Schmidt	Vanderbilt University, USA
Manuel Serrano	INRIA Sophia Antipolis, France
Peter Thiemann	University of Freiburg, Germany
Dave Thomas	Bedarra Research Labs, Canada
Laurence Tratt	Bournemouth University, UK
Mandana Vaziri	IBM Research, USA
Tian Zhao	University of Wisconsin-Milwaukee, USA

Table of Contents

Deep Meta-modelling with METADEPTH

Juan de Lara[1] and Esther Guerra[2]

[1] Universidad Autónoma de Madrid, Spain
Juan.deLara@uam.es
[2] Universidad Carlos III de Madrid, Spain
eguerra@inf.uc3m.es

Abstract. Meta-modelling is at the core of Model-Driven Engineering, where it is used for language engineering and domain modelling. The OMG's Meta-Object Facility is the standard framework for building and instantiating meta-models. However, in the last few years, several researchers have identified limitations and rigidities in such a scheme, most notably concerning the consideration of only two meta-modelling levels *at the same time*.

In this paper we present METADEPTH, a novel framework that supports a dual linguistic/ontological instantiation and permits building systems with an arbitrary number of meta-levels through deep meta-modelling. The framework implements advanced modelling concepts allowing the specification and evaluation of derived attributes and constraints across multiple meta-levels, linguistic extensions of ontological instance models, transactions, and hosting different constraint and action languages.

1   Introduction

Model-Driven Engineering (MDE) is a software development paradigm aiming at speeding up development times, while increasing quality and maintainability. MDE pursues these goals by treating models as the key assets of the process, being no longer mere documentation but used actively to (re-)generate code, as well as for validation and verification. Therefore, these activities demand computer-processable models with precise syntax. In MDE, models' syntax is defined through a meta-model that describes the set of valid models. Hence, meta-modelling is one of the pillars of MDE, being used for language engineering and domain modelling, and it is also at the core of other related approaches like product lines, feature-oriented development [6] and method engineering [12].

The OMG has proposed the Meta-Object Facility (MOF) [22] as the meta-modelling approach in the Model-Driven Architecture (MDA) [19], a particular incarnation of MDE. MOF has been adopted as a standard by many meta-modelling tools and frameworks, most notably by the Eclipse Modelling Framework (EMF) [24]. MDA proposes a four layer, linear meta-modelling architecture and a style of meta-modelling called *strict* in which an element of a meta-layer is the instance of exactly one element at the upper meta-level. Several authors

J. Vitek (Ed.): TOOLS 2010, LNCS 6141, pp. 1–20, 2010.

have pointed out limitations of this approach [4,5,11,12], in particular concerning the existence of only one kind of instantiation relation and the constraint of considering only two adjacent meta-levels at the same time. Two meta-levels are enough to cover the *linguistic* case, where an object is an instance of exactly one class, but cannot capture in addition *ontological* instantiation relations within a domain. Hence, engineers are often forced to squeeze into two meta-modelling layers concepts that would naturally span several layers, resulting in more complex and cluttered models [5]. Moreover, the lack of uniformity employed in the concepts at the different layers in most approaches (e.g. UML associations are structurally different from links) makes it difficult to treat in a uniform way meta-models and models, as well as to link models in different meta-levels (since "meta-" is a relative term and meta-models are also models).

Several solutions have been proposed to these problems [5,11,12]. Their common idea is to increase the flexibility of the meta-modelling architecture by allowing an arbitrary number of meta-levels. In [5] a mechanism called *potency* was proposed, so that one model can control the properties of models that are indirect instances of it. In [1,4] a dual ontological and linguistic instantiation is proposed, allowing an element to be a linguistic instance (e.g. be an instance of Class in the upper linguistic meta-level) and also an instance of some domain concept (e.g. be an instance of ProductType in the upper ontological meta-level).

This paper presents METADEPTH, a new meta-modelling environment that allows modelling with an arbitrary number of ontological meta-levels. It implements the *potency* concept and permits a dual ontological and linguistic instantiation. It is distinguished from other similar frameworks [2,3] in that it supports advanced modelling concepts, like (OCL) constraints, derived attributes and transactions, and allows controlling whether ontological instance models can be linguistically extended. The purpose of the framework is to permit experimentation with this alternative way of meta-modelling, but at the same time provide a scalable, efficient system that permits its industrial use. Hence, METADEPTH can work in an interpreted mode, where a stack of models can be kept and worked with, and then allows compilation to obtain specialized code (in the line of JMI [25]) and optimized performance. The framework is integrated with the Epsilon languages [10], which permits using the Epsilon Object Language (EOL) [16] as an action language to define behaviour for meta-models, as well as the Epsilon Validation Language (EVL) [17] for expressing constraints. Both EOL and EVL are extensions of OCL. To the best of our knowledge, no framework with similar characteristics exists. Moreover, the interplay of potency with constraints, actions, multiplicities and association ends has not been properly addressed in the literature, nor have the mechanisms and benefits for controlling linguistic extensions. We also aim to contribute to the clarification of these issues.

Paper organization. Section 2 reviews multi-level meta-modelling and the concept of potency. Section 3 details the architecture of METADEPTH. Section 4 presents two examples that show the benefits of our approach. In the first one, we define a multi-level language through a unique meta-model. For example, one can think that in UML it is natural that Objects are instances of Classes, and hence should belong to a lower meta-level (so that an object diagram is an instance of a class diagram). Our framework naturally allows this, with the benefit of a less complex language definition. In the second case study, we solve the impedance mismatch arising when one needs to relate models at different meta-levels (a complicated technical issue in two-level frameworks such as EMF). Section 5 compares with related approaches and Section 6 concludes. A beta version of the tool can be downloaded from http://astreo.ii.uam.es/~jlara/metaDepth/

2   Deep Meta-modelling

Some authors have pointed out the limitations of considering only two meta-modelling levels at the same time [5,11], either for language engineering or for domain modelling. A common example is the item-description or the type object pattern [18], where one needs to design a language containing both *Product Types* (e.g. Books) and *Products* (e.g. the book "Moby Dick"). In the classical meta-modelling approach, one would propose a two-level solution like the one to the left of Fig. 1. Although this solution is valid, it has some drawbacks. First, the user has to manually maintain the type links between each instance of Product and its ProductType at the model level. These links are indeed a (manually maintained) form of ontological instantiation relation for which the system does not provide automatic conformance checks. Should we have inheritance between types at the model level, it would have to be emulated manually too. Hence, this solution squeezes three meta-levels into two.

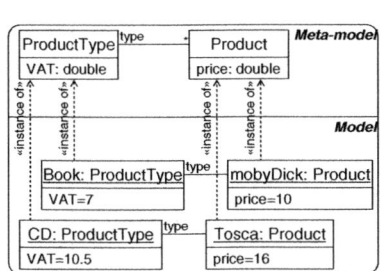 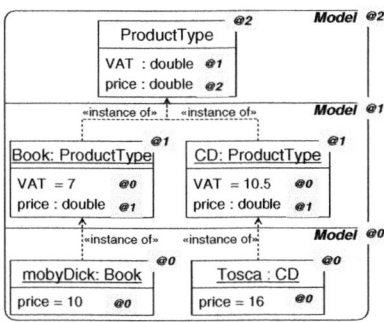

Fig. 1. A meta-model and a model including the *Type Object* pattern (left). The same system using deep meta-modelling (right), adapted from [18].

The solution to the right explicitly organizes the domain concepts into three levels. In this way, the ProductType is declared at the top-level, the different kinds of ProductTypes at the following meta-level, and the instances of these at the bottom level. This solution reduces accidental complexity, as one does not need the artificial class Product that the solution to the left introduced[1].

---

[1] One can still eliminate Product in the two-level solution by moving Book and CD to the top meta-model and setting them as subclasses of ProductType. However, this solution is not valid if we need to add new kinds of ProductTypes at run time.

Moreover, the instantiation of `ProductTypes`, `Books` and `CDs` is handled by the system thus enabling automatic conformance checks. Note that this pattern is ubiquitous in the definition of many languages, for example in UML (classes/objects), in web modelling languages (node types/node instances), role access control languages (user types/users) and so on. We call this style of meta-modelling, which considers more than two levels, *deep* or *multi-level meta-modelling*.

The solution meta-model to the left of Fig. 1 is able to control the attributes that instances of `Product` (`mobyDick`, `Tosca`) have. Hence, in deep meta-modelling we would expect the language designer to have the same level of control over *indirect* instances two or more meta-levels below. For this purpose, *potency* was proposed in [4] as a way to express how many times a property needs to be instantiated down the meta-levels before we get a *plain* instance and hence we have to assign it a value. The potency is a natural number that is assigned to properties, and which gets decremented each time we go down a meta-level. Hence, in our example, property `VAT` is assigned a value in the next meta-level, and `price` two meta-levels below. Not only properties can have potency, but also classes and associations. As we will see later, METADEPTH allows assigning potency to models, constraints and derived attributes as well.

Considering the solution to the right of Fig. 1, one realizes that the elements in the middle meta-level have both type and instance facets. This is so because they are instances of `ProductType` and, as they have potency bigger than zero, can be instantiated in turn. The term *clabject* was coined in [4] to refer to elements with a dual type/instance facet.

The ≪`instance of`≫ relation between the elements in different meta-levels is *ontological*, as this is a relation within the domain (i.e. `mobyDick` is a `Book` and this a `ProductType`). At the same time, as we have to use a modelling language to build the models, we can argue that `Book` is an instance of `Class` and `mobyDick` an instance of `Object` (if such concepts exist in the language). One way to support this duality is to introduce another instantiation dimension, called *linguistic*, and to have a meta-model that governs the linguistic constructions used by the models at the different meta-levels. While the

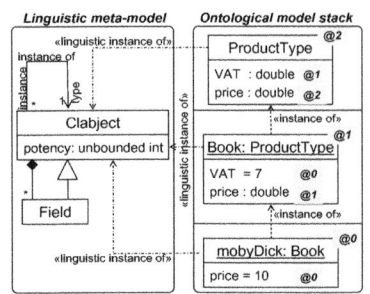

Fig. 2. Dual classification

ontological instantiation is a relation within a domain, the linguistic instantiation refers to implementation and provides the underlying modelling primitives. This situation is depicted in Fig. 2, where the linguistic meta-model contains concept `Clabject` with property `potency` to allow its instantiation in any meta-level. An important issue is that the union of the models in the three ontological meta-levels is a *strict* instance of the linguistic meta-model.

After having introduced the basics of deep meta-modelling, there are still missing details. For example, how could constraints be introduced in the different ontological models? Should these and other elements like association ends be given a potency? Finally, one may wonder whether, as elements `Book` and `CD` have a type facet, we could declare new attributes for them, or whether we could *linguistically extend* a certain ontological model by introducing new types, instances of elements of the linguistic meta-model. In other words, do we demand strictness of the ontological ≪`instance of`≫ relation? The next section introduces METADEPTH's architecture, and discusses these issues.

3   The Architecture of MetaDepth

METADEPTH is a new meta-modelling system that we started to develop in 2008, based on the experience we gained with AToM^3 [8] in previous years. AToM^3 is a Python-based tool for the definition of the syntax of visual languages by meta-modelling and their semantics by graph transformation. METADEPTH is a completely rebuilt kernel, written in Java, which uses the deep meta-modelling approach presented in Section 2. It can work in two ontological instantiation modes: *strict* and *extensible*, as shown in Fig. 3.

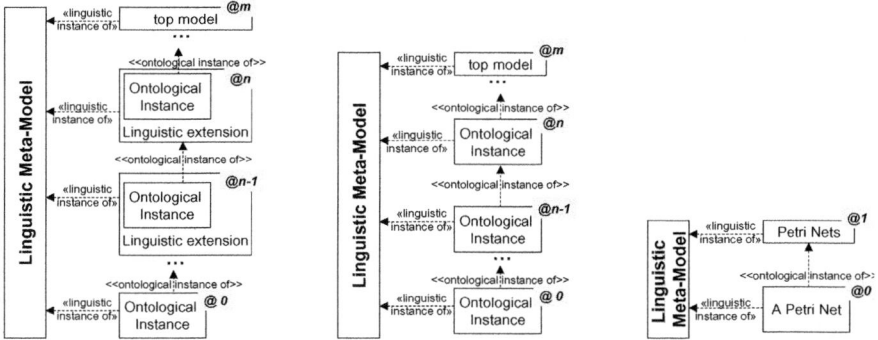

Fig. 3. METADEPTH instantiation schemes: extensible ontological instantiation (left) and strict ontological instantiation (center). Example of strict instantiation (right).

In the *extensible* case, each ontological instance model can be linguistically extended using the "horizontal" instantiation provided by the linguistic metamodel. Hence, instances of elements marked as `ext` can be extended with new attributes. A complete model can also be marked as `ext`, which means that new types can be added and that all its elements (except those explicitly marked as `strict`) can be extended. This situation is shown to the left of Fig. 3, which depicts how two models can be linguistically extended. In all cases strictness is kept for the linguistic instantiation dimension.

The *strict* case is closer to standard meta-modelling environments, where the top-level meta-model hard-codes all language concepts and can be subsequently instantiated ontologically, but such instances cannot be linguistically extended. This situation is represented in the center of Fig. 3. In this mode one could use the highest meta-level to describe the MOF meta-model with potency 2, such model could be ontologically instantiated to describe meta-models for languages at potency 1, which in turn could be instantiated to models of potency 0. Hence, the strict mode is similar to most meta-modelling environments (although without restrictions on the number of meta-levels). The right of the figure shows a simple case where the linguistic meta-model is directly used to define a meta-model for Petri nets, which is instantiated into a Petri net model.

Note that allowing linguistic extensions adds extra flexibility to this meta-modelling framework in two senses. First, at any potency bigger than zero clabjects retain its *type* facet, and hence can be allowed for linguistic extension (i.e. to define attribute types). On the other hand, it is often convenient to extend models by allowing the introduction of new linguistic elements, e.g. to adapt languages to particular usages, as we will see throughout the paper.

3.1   The Linguistic Meta-model

MetaDepth's linguistic meta-model took MOF as inspiration, but we have modified it to accommodate an arbitrary number of meta-levels, deep instantiation and potency. Fig. 4 shows a fraction of it, where the uncoloured concrete classes are those the designer typically instantiates when building a model (i.e. Model, Node, Edge, Field and DerivedField).

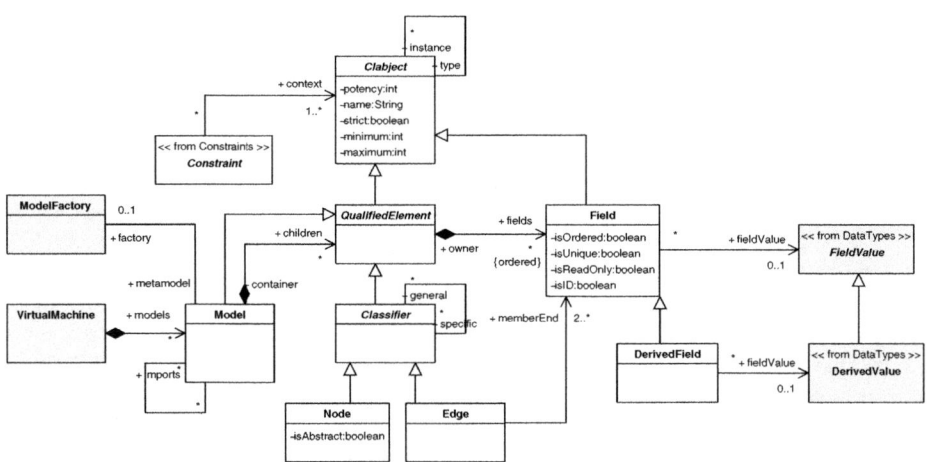

Fig. 4. MetaDepth's linguistic meta-model, partially shown

The root class Clabject takes responsibility of handling the dual type/object facet of elements. As such, it holds a potency value, as well as links to its type and instances. The potency can be unlimited, and in that case the instances of the clabject can have arbitrary potency (included unlimited). Clabjects also define a minimum and maximum multiplicity to control the cardinality of its instances within a given context. Constraints can be attached to clabjects, have a potency, and can specify on which events they should be evaluated (e.g. when creating or deleting the clabject). QualifiedElements are Clabjects owning some field. Models, Nodes and Edges are all QualifiedElements. Classifiers are a special kind of QualifiedElement that can form general/specific hierarchies, and are refined into Nodes and Edges. The latter have two or more association ends modelled as Fields. Finally, derived fields are fields of which their value is automatically calculated.

METADEPTH's modularity mechanism is based on the notion of Model, which can be nested, as shown by the composite pattern used. Models are QualifiedElements and hence can own Fields and have associated Constraints. Each model with potency bigger than zero has an associated ModelFactory in charge of instantiating the clabjects defined in the model. All working models are managed by a VirtualMachine container, which is a *singleton* object.

The framework supports the usual *atomic* data types, like integers, floating point numbers, strings, etc.; user-defined enumerations, as well as ordered and unordered collections with unique or non-unique elements.

3.2 Tool Support, Compiled and Interpreted Modes

METADEPTH models can be built through the provided Java API, or through a CommandShell and a textual syntax – similar to the Human Usable Textual Notation (HUTN) [21] – that we have built with ANTLR [23]. Loading and storing models is also done in this format. As an example, Listing 1 shows how the three models in Fig. 2 are defined with the textual syntax. The top-most model Store is assigned potency 2, which means it can be instantiated in the following two lower meta-levels. All elements defined inside Store have the potency of the container clabject, hence we only need to explicitly declare potencies different from 2 (field VAT in this case). Please note also that we give an initial value to the fields of ProductType. Although all elements in the listing are given an explicit name, this is not mandatory: we can declare *anonymous* clabjects like Book {price=10;} (i.e. the book is not given a name) and the system assigns them a unique UUID-based identifier.

The framework is fully integrated with Epsilon, a family of languages built on top of the Epsilon Object Language (EOL) [16], which extends OCL with expressions permitting secondary effects such as assignments and methods. The integration was possible because EOL communicates with the models through a connectivity layer. Thus, EOL can work with EMF models, but also with any other model technology that implements the interface of this connectivity layer. We implemented such an interface and provided support to make EOL aware of the multiple ontological levels. The solution is very practical as one can use EOL programs to build models as in Listing 2. The listing shows a typical interaction with the command line interpreter. In line 1 we enter in the context of model *MyLibrary* (we could have created a new model as well). In line 2 we begin writing the EOL program (which could be loaded from a file as well). Then the program inserts 1000 new books in the model and initializes their price.

```
1  Model Store@2 {
2    Node ProductType {
3      VAT@1 : double = 7.5;
4      price : double = 10;
5    }
6  }
7  Store Library {
8    ProductType Book { VAT = 7; }
9  }
10 Library MyLibrary {
11   Book mobyDick { price = 10; }
12 }
```

Listing 1. A simple METADEPTH three-model stack

```
1  context MyLibrary
   ::entering context MyLibrary
2  # EOL
   :: entering eol execution mode
3  for (i in Sequence{1..1000}) {
4    var b : new Book;
5    b.price := 10+i/500;
6  }
```

Listing 2. A simple EOL program to populate a METADEPTH model

We can use EOL not only for initializing models, but also to define their behaviour. As an example, Listing 6 shows a Petri net simulator we have built for Petri net models. Moreover, we can use the rest of the Epsilon languages with our METADEPTH models so that it is possible to transform models with the Epsilon Transformation Language [10].

Another feature of METADEPTH concerns undoability of actions. Using the *Command* pattern, all API calls are recorded in an event list, and each command provides an appropriate undo function. This allows undo/redo of any action on models, and permits integration with the transaction syntax of EOL.

By default, METADEPTH works in interpreted mode. This allows for flexible modelling and is useful for rapid prototyping of languages, as one can evolve models and meta-models at the same time. One can also create several independent models in the same VirtualMachine (i.e. models do not need to be related through instantiation). Once the meta-models are ready, they can be *compiled* if so desired. We have built a code generator that produces specialized classes inheriting from the classes in the meta-model of Fig. 4, as well as interfaces declaring getter, setter and creation methods that follow the JMI specification [25]. This enables interface compatibility with applications that handle JMI meta-data (like those of the EMF), and improves performance as we generate optimized code which improves, e.g., constraint evaluation, object creation and field access. However, compiled meta-models are less flexible because they can no longer be modified, even though all their properties are readily accessible. The compilation we have implemented is more complex than in normal two-level meta-modelling frameworks, since compiling a model with certain potency implies compiling all direct and indirect models above in the ontological meta-level hierarchy. The compilation also generates a specialized command shell that initializes the `VirtualMachine` with the compiled meta-models and allows their instantiation.

3.3 Constraints and Derived Attributes

Constraints and actions can be defined using Java or EOL. Constraints and derived attributes have an assigned potency that governs the meta-level at which they have to be evaluated. For example, Listing 3 modifies the running example by adding a few constraints and a derived attribute on the top-level model.

```
1  Model Store@2 {
2   Node ProductType@2 {
3    VAT@1      : double = 7.5;
4    price@2    : double = 10;
5    discount@2: double = 0;
6    minVat@1   : $self.VAT>0$
7    minPrice@2: $self.price>0$
8    maxDisc@2 : $self.VAT*self.price*0.01+self.price<self.discount$
9    /finalPrice@2:double=$self.VAT*self.price/100+self.price-self.discount$;
10  }
11 }
```

Listing 3. Constraints and derived attributes in METADEPTH

The previous listing adds property `discount` to `ProductType`, declares three constraints in lines 6, 7 and 8, and defines a derived field in line 9. Constraints are specified between two "$" symbols, preceded by their identifier, and can be declared inside the context of a clabject (as done in this case), or be declared outside and then explicitly assigned to one or more clabjects, promoting reusability. The constraint in line 6 has potency 1, therefore it will be evaluated in the next meta-level below. This constraint cannot access the value of fields with potency bigger than 1, like `price`, as these may not have a value[2]. The default language for constraints is EOL, but one can also use Java. For example, the equivalent Java code to the constraint in line 6 is `minVat[Java]@1:` $((Integer)self.getValue("VAT"))>0$, which is more verbose but permits interacting with external Java programs.

Constraint `maxDisc` is more interesting as it uses fields with potency 1 and 2. This is allowed as, from the point of view of action and constraint languages, fields whose value is given in a type are accessed in the same way as fields whose value is given in the instance. In our example, `mobyDick` interprets `VAT` like a static field for which its value was set at the upper meta-level. This feature simplifies writing constraints spawning several meta-levels.

---

[2] In our case `price` does have a value as it has been initialized with the value 10, but this is not the general case.

```
 1  Store Library {
 2    ProductType Book {
 3      VAT    = 7;
 4      title  : String;
 5      author : Author;
 6    }
 7    Node Author {
 8      name   : String;
 9      nonRep : $Author.allInstances().forAll(x|x<>self implies
 9                                        x.name<>self.name)$
10      books  : Book[1..*]{unique};
11    }
12    Edge writer (Book.author, Author.books) {
13      year : int;
14    }
15  }
```

Listing 4. Linguistic extensions and associations in METADEPTH

Finally, `ProductType` defines the derived field `finalPrice`. The declaration of derived fields is similar to the declaration of normal fields, but these are preceded by a backslash, and include a calculation function in EOL or Java that can use fields with equal or lower potency. Our current implementation calculates derived field values in a lazy way, whenever they are accessed by some getter function. This works well in textual modelling environments, but we foresee the need for a change propagation algorithm in case some exogenous observer (e.g. a graphical visualization) needs the value.

3.4   Controlling Linguistic Extensions

METADEPTH supports both *strict* and *extensible* ontological instantiation, the latter being the default. Linguistic extension is interesting to permit unforeseen extensions to Domain Specific Languages (DSLs) spawning more than one level, as our running example. In these languages, the top-most meta-model is usually highly generic, and hence extensions at lower levels are often required.

Listing 4 shows an extension of the running example, where an extensible instantiation of model `Store` is used to define a `Library`. In this usage scenario we are interested in associating an author to `ProductType` instances (i.e. to Books). Thus, we add to the library a new node `Author`, instance of `Node` in the linguistic meta-model. For the sake of illustration, `Author` is provided with the constraint `nonRep` that forbids replicating names. This shows that *allInstances* effectively returns all ontological instances of `Author`. As an alternative, we could have just assigned the modifier `{id}` to the field `name` to obtain the same behaviour. Please note that `Library` is still a strict instance of the linguistic meta-model.

Authors are related to one or more Books, which is modelled through their field `books`. The `{unique}` modifier ensures that a given `Author` is not related to the same Book twice. Other supported modifiers are `id` (ensures uniqueness

```
1  strict Model PetriNets@1{
2    abstract Node NamedElement { name : String{id}; }
3    Node Place : NamedElement {
4      tokens    : int = 0;
5      outTrans  : Transition[*] {ordered,unique};
6      inTrans   : Transition[*] {ordered,unique};
7      minTokens : $self.tokens>0$
8    }
9    Node Transition : NamedElement {
10     inPlaces  : Place[*] {ordered,unique};
11     outPlaces : Place[*] {ordered,unique};
12   }
13   Edge ArcPT(Place.outTrans,Transition.inPlaces){ weight : int = 1; }
14   Edge ArcTP(Transition.outPlaces,Place.inTrans){ weight : int = 1; }
15   minWeight(ArcPT, ArcTP) : $self.weight>0$
16   minPlaces : $Place.allInstances()->size()>0$
17 }
```

Listing 5. A meta-model for Petri nets

of values among all clabjects in the same context), `ordered` (retains the order of elements) and `readOnly` (forbids changing the value).

Associations can be provided with fields (i.e. similar to association classes) by explicitly defining an `Edge` between their association ends. An example is shown in lines 12–14 of Listing 4, where the `Edge` relating books and authors includes the year in which the book was written. As in UML, declaring such an `Edge` has the effect of allowing the navigation from an `Author` to all its edges through `self.writer`, while the direct navigation from an `Author` to its Books is done by `self.books`. In the context of the `writer` edge, it is possible to navigate to the `Author` and Books through the `author` and `books` ends.

In the example we have made reference to the ontological types `Author` and `Book` to declare associations. However, in specific situations, it is useful to refer to linguistic types, like `Node`, when defining association ends. This makes sense if

```
1  while (Transition.allInstances()->exists(t |
1                             t.enabled() and t.fire())) {}
2  operation Transition enabled() : Boolean {
3    return self.ArcPT->forAll(arc | arc.inPlaces.tokens>=arc.weight);
4  }
5  operation Transition fire() : Boolean {
6    for (arc in self.ArcPT)
7      arc.inPlaces.tokens := arc.inPlaces.tokens-arc.weight;
8    for (arc in self.ArcTP)
9      arc.outPlaces.tokens := arc.outPlaces.tokens+arc.weight;
10   return true;
11 }
```

Listing 6. A simulator for Petri nets defined with EOL

we want to specify that a certain association end is to be taken by any (linguistic) instance of `Node`. As the next section will show, this is very useful if we want to relate models of different potency.

Listing 5 shows an example of *strict* meta-modelling. It is a meta-model for Petri nets containing `Places` and `Transitions` (both inheriting from `NamedElement`), as well as weighted arcs. All these elements inherit the *strict* modifier from their container model. In the example, `NamedElement` and its children have the same potency 1, but METADEPTH also allows clabjects in a hierarchy to define different potencies. A clabject keeps the biggest potency of all its ancestors.

The Petri net meta-model defines several constraints. In the context of the model, `minPlaces` restricts nets to have at least 1 place (line 16). Most meta-modelling approaches do not allow global constraints; however some constraints (like `minPlaces`) are inherently global and do not fit in the context of any class in the meta-model. As all METADEPTH elements have built-in cardinalities (see Fig. 4), we can obtain the same restriction as `minPlaces` by replacing line 3 with "`Node Place[1..*] : NamedElement {`". Constraint `minWeight` is also defined globally, but it is assigned to both kinds of arcs to enforce a positive weight (line 15). This has the advantage of promoting reusability as the constraint does not have to be defined twice.

For the sake of completeness, Listing 6 shows a simulator for Petri nets specified through EOL. This language allows adding operations on meta-classes, and we have used this feature to define the operations `enabled` and `fire` on node `Transition`. The first one contains pure OCL code, which checks if the transition is enabled. For this purpose it iterates through all incoming arcs checking that the number of tokens in the pre-place is bigger or equal than the arc's weight. Operation `fire` has secondary effects: the removal and addition of tokens to the pre- and post-places of the transition. The main simulation loop is defined in line 1, which iterates on all transition instances while there is some enabled, and then fires it.

4   Examples

This section presents two examples that show the usefulness of METADEPTH and help to illustrate some of its distinguishing features, such as the use of linguistic types or the interplay of potency, multiplicities and association ends.

4.1   Defining Multi-level Languages

The first example shows the use of deep meta-modelling for defining DSLs spawning more than one meta-level. This is the case of many languages that implement the *Type Object* pattern. For example, UML defines class and object diagrams as two different structural diagrams. However, UML defines both in the same meta-level, with the drawback that one has to maintain explicit relations between objects and their classifiers and ensure that they remain consistent. Instead, one can use deep meta-modelling to simplify the language definition and to automate the maintenance of consistency between classes and objects.

Listing 7 shows how a simple language containing class and object diagrams is defined in META DEPTH. The idea is to specify a three-level meta-modelling architecture where the top-most level contains the definition of class diagrams and potency 2 (Model ClassDiagram in Listing 7). In this way, in the next meta-level we can build class diagrams (e.g. Zoo in Listing 8), and in the bottom meta-level we can build object diagrams and the built-in meta-modelling infrastructure of META DEPTH handles the type checking with respect to the class diagram that the object diagrams instantiate. In this way, a stack of two languages is defined with just the model in Listing 7. This model is *strict* to avoid the creation of new linguistic types in class and object diagrams, and permit only the creation of Classes and Assocs. On the contrary, classes and associations are *extensible* to allow their instances to define new fields in them. Node Class contains field isAbstract to designate whether the class is abstract or not, and constraint noAbsObjects ensures that object diagrams (two levels below) do not contain objects whose class is abstract. The constraint is evaluated two levels below, on all indirect instances of Class, because the constraint has potency 2 (as it is not explicitly specified, it receives the potency of the owner clabject).

```
1  strict Model ClassDiagram@2 {
2    ext Node Class {
3      isAbstract@1 : boolean = false;
4      in           : Class[*];
5      out          : Class[*];
6      noAbsObjects : $self.isAbstract=false$
7    }
8    ext Edge Assoc(Class.out, Class.in);
9  }
```

Listing 7. A meta-model for class and object diagrams (meta-level 2)

Listing 8 shows an instance of ClassDiagram, namely a class diagram named Zoo which declares two classes and one association. Class Person declares one field (name) and one association end (pet). The field name has been added as a linguistic extension to Person (that is, name is not an instance of any feature in the upper ontological meta-level). The association end pet is an ontological instance of the association end out defined for Class in the upper meta-level. This fact is indicated with modifier {out} in line 4 of Listing 8. The listing also shows an instance (i.e. an object diagram) of the defined class diagram called myZoo.

Revisiting our language specification in Listing 7, we can see that fields in and out have an (unbounded) multiplicity. This multiplicity constrains the meta-level immediately below, and hence one can have an unbounded number of instances of them in a class diagram. These instances can declare their own multiplicity, which affects their instantiation in object diagrams. However, please note that

```
1  ClassDiagram Zoo {
2    Class Person {
3      name : String {id};
4      pet  : Animal[*] {out};
5    }
6    Class Animal {
7      kind  : String {id};
8      owner : Person[1..*] {in};
9    }
10   Assoc hasPet (Person.pet, Animal.owner) { since : int; }
11 }
12 Zoo myZoo {
13   Person p { name = "Juan"; }
14   Animal a { kind = "monkey"; }
15   hasPet(p,a) { since = 2010; }
16 }
```

Listing 8. A class and an object diagram (meta-levels 1 and 0, respectively)

```
1  Model Graphics@2 {
2    abstract Node Figure {
3      x : int;
4      y : int;
5      rotation : double = 0;
6      scale    : double = 1;
7      refersTo : Node;
8    }
9    Node Rectangle : Figure {
10     width@1  : int;
11     height@1 : int;
12   }
13 }
```

Listing 9. The Graphics meta-model

association ends in and out have potency 2 and are also available in object diagrams, storing the content of all their instances. For example in Listing 8, p.out evaluates to [a] because p.pet evaluates to [a]. This shows that the instantiation semantics for fields is coherent with the way of handling indirect instances of all other elements, like Nodes and Edges, as e.g., both p and a are indirect instances of Class.

4.2 Relating Models at Different Meta-levels

Next we illustrate how to relate models at different meta-levels in METADEPTH. This is of practical importance as, in standard approaches like in EMF, models cannot be meta-models at the same time. In EMF, models can be treated as meta-models by passing through a transformation called *promotion*, thus making it difficult to link elements of models with elements of meta-models. As an example we show a multi-level language to define the graphical concrete syntax of meta-models. The purpose of the example is not to show advanced concrete syntax concepts, nor to discuss how instances would be graphically rendered, but only show how models can be naturally put in relation with meta-models. In order to keep the example simple we restrict our discussion to the visual representation of Nodes as rectangles.

Listing 9 shows the meta-model for the two-level language called Graphics. When instantiated in the next meta-level it allows defining visualizations for a meta-model M. Then, by instantiating it again we obtain instances with the rendering information about the instances of M. This situation is depicted in Fig. 5, which shows that Graphics models are associated to the definition of a language, and the rendering information to models of this language. The Graphics definition contains an

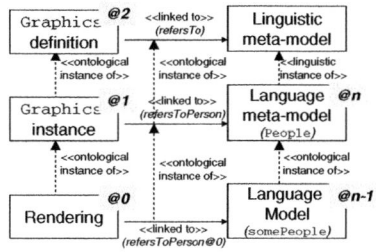

Fig. 5. Scheme of the example

abstract clabject Figure with fields x and y that store the absolute position of instances of figures two meta-levels below, as well as their rotation and scaling. Figures also contain field refersTo to point to the Node that the figure is representing. A real-world model for concrete syntax would include several types of figures (circles, text, etc.) that could be composed to form the visual concrete syntax of a Node. In our case, for space constraints, we consider just Rectangles which can be configured with their dimension.

```
1  Model People@1 {
2    Node Person { name : String; }
3  }
4  Graphics ConcreteSyntax imports People {
5    Rectangle iconPerson {
6      width  = 15;
7      height = 10;
8      refersToPerson: Person{refersTo};
9    }
10 }
```

Listing 10. Defining the concrete syntax for a language meta-model

Consider the simple language defined by the meta-model People in Listing 10. We can instantiate the Graphics meta-model to define a visual representation for Person in the language meta-model. This is possible because we have defined association end refersToPerson in line 8, which instantiates the association end refersTo. Association end refersToPerson points to Person, which is a linguistic instance of Node, hence being type compatible with the definition of refersTo in line 7 of Listing 9. Moreover, since meta-model Graphics is generic,

```
 1  People somePeople {
 2    Person e {
 3      name = "Esther";
 4    }
 5  }
 6  ConcreteSyntax concreteSyntax01 imports somePeople {
 7    iconPerson {
 8      x = 10; rotation = 90;
 9      y = 10; scale = .5;
10      refersToPerson = e;
11    }
12  }
```

Listing 11. Instantiating the meta-model and its concrete syntax

we can also define a visualization for the class diagram Zoo in Listing 8 by just replacing "People" by "Zoo" in line 4 of Listing 10. This shows the flexibility of METADEPTH to relate models at different potencies and meta-levels, and the advantages of treating uniformly models at different meta-levels.

Finally, we can instantiate the People meta-model and its associated concrete syntax as shown in Listing 11.

5   Related Work

There are two main lines of related research: those works following a MOF-like way of meta-modelling, where only two adjacent levels are considered at the same time, and those following a deep meta-modelling approach.

Regarding the first group, MOF [22] is the OMG's language to specify meta-models and the most adopted approach in practice. The MOF specification is divided in two parts: a basic one called Essential MOF (EMOF), and a more advanced one called Complete MOF (CMOF). The specification claims that it can be used with as many meta-levels as users demand. However, there are conceptual problems, e.g. when one needs to introduce data type instances, as the basic data types would have to be replicated across the different meta-levels. Moreover, current implementations only allow handling two levels at the same time. Even though MOF specifies a set of reflective services, the specification neglects that considering three or more meta-levels at the same time requires some entities to simultaneously have both type and object facets. The main implementation of MOF is integrated within EMF [24] and is called *Ecore*. It forces a tree-based edition of models, and only supports EMOF, therefore lacking useful constructs like a proper concept of association enabling the definition of associative classes. Neither EMOF nor CMOF specify how to define constraints or actions to calculate derived attributes.

Many current meta-modelling research efforts revolve around MOF. For example, KM3 [14] is a DSL to specify meta-models based on MOF. KM3 has a textual front-end for meta-modelling frameworks, and as such can be compared to the textual notation we have developed for METADEPTH, but does not introduce new meta-modelling concepts. Kermeta [15] is another textual language whose purpose is to specify behaviours for EMF meta-models. Hence, its role for EMF meta-models is equivalent to our use of EOL to specify behaviour. In [9], Smalltalk is used to implement a reengineering framework based on EMF, which allows using Smalltalk also as an executable meta-language.

XMF [7] is a complete MDE framework which allows language-driven development. Hence, XMF permits defining the abstract and concrete syntax of languages (both textual and diagrammatic), their semantics as well as transformations. In XMF, behaviour is expressed by means of XOCL, an extension of OCL with imperative constructs in the line of EOL. XMF has meta-modelling facilities supporting an arbitrary number of meta-levels, a meta-object protocol and a language for expressing mappings between meta-models. However, even though XMF permits an arbitrary number of meta-levels, it lacks constructs (like potency) to control the structure of deep instances of a model, making it difficult to define deep languages with it.

Concerning deep meta-modelling, several efforts can be recently found directed to a practical test of the seminal ideas of Atkinson and Kühne [4]. For example, DeepJava [18] is an extension of Java with the concept of potency and, as such, it cannot be considered a meta-modelling framework. It provides methods with potency, but has to use special keywords to navigate up the type hierarchy in order to find attribute values. On the contrary, our constraints and computations for derived attributes can access type fields in a uniform way. This is similar to considering that a type attribute value is like a *static attribute* with respect to an instance, and has the advantage that one does not need to know exactly how many meta-levels up the given field was given a value, and facilitates the integration with constraint and action languages.

The work in [3] is another recent proposal for deep meta-modelling. The tool is currently being developed, based on *Ecore*. They consider multi-level constraints, and propose extending OCL to cope with multiple ontological meta-levels. This is similar to our approach, but we assign *potency* to constraints, making them easier to define. This is so because potency layers constraints, and hence they do not have to explicitly invoke *allInstances()* a predefined number of times, it is enough to implement in the OCL interpreter the ability to recognise indirect ontological instances of clabjects, and to interpret fields of ontological types similar to static attributes in Java. Another difference concerns relations, as they do not consider association ends, but add this information inside the relation class itself. The main motivation for this is graphical visualization in concrete syntax and uniformity of structure between ontological meta-levels. On the contrary, the design of our framework was not driven by concrete syntax issues, as we foresee building systems supporting graphical syntax as well as a more sophisticated textual syntax, probably posing different challenges. We retain association ends (similar to MOF and UML), as this allows us to reuse the multiplicity semantics of structural features. Most importantly, it makes easier the practical integration with navigation languages like OCL. We also agree on the importance of uniformity of relations at the different levels, and hence we retain association ends (i.e. fields) at all levels. Finally, [3] does not consider linguistic extensions, transactions, derived attributes, nor an action language, whereas we can use the Epsilon languages, which enable manipulation and transformation of models. Our dual working scheme of interpretation/compilation allows rapid prototyping of languages, and enables the generation of stand-alone, efficient domain-specific tools.

Nivel [2] is a deep meta-modelling framework based on the weighted constraint rule language (WCRL). It implements the concept of potency and the dual linguistic/ontological classification. It brings some interesting ideas from conceptual modelling, like the possibility of several classes to implement an association role. Nivel's semantics is given by its translation into WCRL, which allows some form of automated reasoning, but the kind of reasoning and its usefulness was not shown in [2]. The language lacks constraints and action languages (except WCRL itself), which hinders its use in practical MDE.

Other works that have influenced METADEPTH include Amulet [20], whose prototype/instance concept is similar to our linguistic clabject extensions.

6   Conclusions and Future Work

In this paper we have presented METADEPTH, a novel framework for deep metamodelling. The tool supports the concept of potency, allowing an arbitrary number of ontological meta-levels. It provides advanced features like multi-level constraints, derived attributes and linguistic extensions at lower meta-levels. The framework can work either in interpreted or compiled modes, favouring flexibility or efficiency. The current implementation offers a textual syntax, inspired by HUTN, and is integrated with the Epsilon languages. In particular, we have shown the use of EOL for specifying actions and EVL for constraints.

Concerning future work, we will continue improving METADEPTH in the near future. For example, we would like to allow the framework to run in client/server mode, so that the kernel can be accessed through web services. We would also like to build a system to support a graphical concrete syntax, in the spirit of the old AToM^3 [8], but allowing interaction through the web navigator. Even though we can use ETL now, the plan is to incorporate a formal model transformation language into it, and for this purpose we are working on an implementation of our pattern-based transformation language [13]. It could be interesting to study the implications of deep meta-modelling for model transformation, and for this we would need a formalization of the framework. Finally, we believe that deep meta-modelling allows improving the current practice of MDE. We are currently exploring idioms, and identifying good practices and patterns for deep meta-modelling and multi-level language engineering.

Acknowledgements. This work has been partially sponsored by the Spanish Ministry of Science and Innovation, under project "METEORIC" (TIN2008-02081), and mobility grants JC2009-00015 and PR2009-0019, as well as by the

R&D programme of the Community of Madrid, project "e-Madrid" (S2009/TIC-1650). The authors are grateful to the five anonymous reviewers that helped in improving the paper, as well as the research group of Prof. R. Paige at the University of York, and Prof. H. Vangheluwe for their comments and discussions.

References

1. Álvarez, J.M., Evans, A., Sammut, P.: Mapping between levels in the metamodel architecture. In: Gogolla, M., Kobryn, C. (eds.) UML 2001. LNCS, vol. 2185, pp. 34–46. Springer, Heidelberg (2001)
2. Asikainen, T., Männistö, T.: Nivel: a metamodelling language with a formal semantics. SoSyM 8(4), 521–549 (2009)
3. Atkinson, C., Gutheil, M., Kennel, B.: A flexible infrastructure for multilevel language engineering. IEEE Trans. Soft. Eng. 35(6), 742–755 (2009)
4. Atkinson, C., Kühne, T.: Rearchitecting the UML infrastructure. ACM Trans. Model. Comput. Simul. 12(4), 290–321 (2002)
5. Atkinson, C., Kühne, T.: Reducing accidental complexity in domain models. SoSyM 7(3), 345–359 (2008)
6. Batory, D.S.: Multilevel models in model-driven engineering, product lines, and metaprogramming. IBM Systems Journal 45(3), 527–540 (2006)
7. Clark, A., Sammut, P., Willans, J.: Applied Metamodelling: A Foundation for Language Driven Development, 2nd edn., Ceteva (2008), http://itcentre.tvu.ac.uk/~clark/Publications.html
8. de Lara, J., Vangheluwe, H.: AToM³: A tool for multi-formalism and meta-modelling. In: Kutsche, R.-D., Weber, H. (eds.) FASE 2002. LNCS, vol. 2306, pp. 174–188. Springer, Heidelberg (2002)
9. Ducasse, S., Girba, T., Kuhn, A., Renggli, L.: Meta-environment and executable meta-language using Smalltalk: An experience report. SoSyM 8, 5–19 (2009)
10. Epsilon (2009), http://www.eclipse.org/gmt/epsilon/
11. González-Pérez, C., Henderson-Sellers, B.: A powertype-based metamodelling framework. SoSyM 5(1), 72–90 (2006)
12. González-Pérez, C., Henderson-Sellers, B.: Metamodelling for Software Engineering. Wiley, Chichester (2008)
13. Guerra, E., de Lara, J., Orejas, F.: Pattern-based model-to-model transformation: Handling attribute conditions. In: Paige, R.F. (ed.) ICMT 2009. LNCS, vol. 5563, pp. 83–99. Springer, Heidelberg (2009)
14. Jouault, F., Bézivin, J.: KM3: A DSL for metamodel specification. In: Gorrieri, R., Wehrheim, H. (eds.) FMOODS 2006. LNCS, vol. 4037, pp. 171–185. Springer, Heidelberg (2006)
15. Kermeta, http://www.kermeta.org/
16. Kolovos, D.S., Paige, R.F., Polack, F.: The Epsilon Object Language (EOL). In: Rensink, A., Warmer, J. (eds.) ECMDA-FA 2006. LNCS, vol. 4066, pp. 128–142. Springer, Heidelberg (2006)
17. Kolovos, D.S., Paige, R.F., Polack, F.: On the evolution of OCL for capturing structural constraints in modelling languages. In: Abrial, J.-R., Glässer, U. (eds.) Rigorous Methods for Software Construction and Analysis. LNCS, vol. 5115, pp. 204–218. Springer, Heidelberg (2009)
18. Kühne, T., Schreiber, D.: Can programming be liberated from the two-level style? – Multi-level programming with DeepJava. In: OOPSLA'07, pp. 229–244. ACM, New York (2007)

19. Mellor, S.J., Scott, K., Uhl, A., Weise, D.: MDA Distilled. Addison-Wesley Object Technology Series (2004)
20. Myers, B., McDaniel, R., Miller, R., Ferrency, A., Faulring, A., Kyle, B., Mickish, A., Klimovitski, A., Doane, P.: The Amulet environment: New models for effective user interface software development. IEEE Trans. Soft. Eng. 23(6), 347–365 (1997)
21. OMG. HUTN (2009), http://www.omg.org/cgi-bin/doc?formal/2004-08-01
22. OMG. MOF 2.0 (2009), http://www.omg.org/spec/MOF/2.0/
23. Parr, T.: ANTLR (2010), http://www.antlr.org
24. Steinberg, D., Budinsky, F., Paternostro, M., Merks, E.: EMF: Eclipse Modeling Framework, 2nd edn. Addison-Wesley Professional, Reading (2008), http://www.eclipse.org/modeling/emf/
25. Sun. Java Metadata Interface, http://java.sun.com/products/jmi/index.jsp

A Generic Meta-model-Based Approach for Specifying Framework Functionality and Usage

Fabian Christ[1,2], Jan-Christopher Bals[2], Gregor Engels[1,2],
Christian Gerth[2], and Markus Luckey[2]

[1] s-lab - Software Quality Lab
fchrist@s-lab.upb.de
[2] University of Paderborn, Warburger Str. 100
33098 Paderborn, Germany

Abstract. Enterprise software development is based on the usage of frameworks. However, well-established concepts to specify framework functionality and how to use it can hardly be found. As consequence, there are poor framework documentations. Various problems arise from this, e.g. a high effort for learning a framework and therefore the need of framework specialists. Existing framework description languages (FDL) focus on parts of the problem but do not cover all aspects of specifying framework functionality and usage. In this paper, we present a generic approach for specifying all aspects of framework functionality and usage. We collected requirements to identify relevant aspects and defined a generic meta-model for FDLs. The generic meta-model is the base for defining concrete FDLs while guaranteeing that all relevant framework aspects are covered. Particularly, due to its generic character, parts of the meta-model representing specific framework aspects can be instantiated by existing or newly defined languages.

1 Introduction

Enterprise software development is based on the usage of frameworks. The used frameworks range from application frameworks for user interfaces over frameworks for component-based software development to frameworks for service orchestration in a service-oriented architecture [1]. Most current middleware technologies in enterprise environments like Sun's Java Enterprise Edition (JEE) [2] or Microsoft's .NET framework are largely affected by framework concepts. The reason for the success of these frameworks is that this technology is one key to reduce software development costs.

Frameworks are a technique to provide efficient reuse of software. Once developed, the framework can be reused in numerous development projects and, therefore, reduce development time and costs in such projects. If the framework is available as open source, even the development costs for the framework itself are omitted.

Framework development is known to be a difficult task [3] but also the correct use of a framework is often not trivial. Large frameworks offer complex APIs

J. Vitek (Ed.): TOOLS 2010, LNCS 6141, pp. 21–40, 2010.
© Springer-Verlag Berlin Heidelberg 2010

and require a deep understanding of the framework [4]. This may even yield to situations where the effort for learning a framework is as high as developing the needed functionality from the scratch. It is a trade-off between learning a framework and developing the needed functionality. The result is an increased need for framework specialists by the industry. Surprisingly, well-established concepts for specifying the functionality and correct use of a framework hardly exist. Either existing documentation does not cover all aspects of the framework usage or the documentation is not focused on the framework's use but rather specifies its implementation.

We have gained experience in using open source frameworks by carrying out several industrial project. The goal was to integrate different JEE [2] related frameworks into so-called software stacks. Currently, we are working on this topic in an integrating project part-funded by the European Commission called "Interactive Knowledge Stack"[1] [5]. The IKS will provide an open source software stack [6] for semantic Content Management Systems. One of the biggest problems in these projects is to retrieve the needed information about the frameworks in order to use and integrate them properly. The absence of useful framework documentation having been created by using some framework description language (FDL) is the main reason for this.

To the best of our knowledge existing FDL approaches, like "Motifs" [7] or "UML-F" [8], do not cover all aspects of specifying framework functionality and use. They mostly focus on specific aspects only, like the description of *hooks* [9] which will be described later, and have hardly succeeded in the market. Unfortunately, the used description techniques today are often a generated API documentation combined with some basic examples or tutorials. To get more information developers search the web for specific problems about how to use the framework. The next source of information are books about the framework that claim to be more complete than the available documentation. The last way out to receive more information is to examine the framework's source code if available and try to understand the framework by reverse engineering.

To improve the situation, we developed an approach to describe frameworks for developers who want to use the framework. Our contribution is a generic modelling approach, which defines an extensible meta-model for FDLs. This framework description meta-model (FDMM) defines all relevant aspects that have to be considered by any FDL. The meta-model allows the integration of existent and new description languages for different framework aspects. The FDMM is a reference model for framework documentation and allows us to evaluate existing documentations. Future FDLs which are based on the FDMM will provide better framework documentation focused on the developer.

This paper is structured as follows: In the next section, we give a motivating example which demonstrates the basics of framework usage. Then we describe the features which are realized by our FDMM in section 3. The FDMM is defined in section 4 and applied using our motivating example in section 5. Then we take

---

[1] This work has been part-funded by the European Commission under grant agreement FP7-ICT-2007-3/ No. 231527 (IKS - Interactive Knowledge Stack).

a look at related approaches for specifying framework functionality and usage in section 6 and present the conclusion and future work in section 7.

2   Motivating Example

To demonstrate the state-of-the-art framework usage process and the deficiency of existing framework descriptions, we use a concrete example and take a closer look at the *Apache Axis2* [10] web services framework. The process for using a framework starts with the vendor who implements and documents the framework. Then a developer must understand the options to use the framework, implement an appropriate custom extension, bind the new extension and deploy it within the framework. We will give an example how to use a framework from the perspective of a developer which is the framework user.

Axis2 is an open source framework that can be freely used and downloaded from the web [10]. Axis2 is just one representative for frameworks with similar documentation problems. The available documentation at the website consists of a generated API documentation and user guides which aim to illustrate the features of Axis2 by simple examples. The user guide exists in two versions – one for novice users and an advanced version for more experienced users. Both seem to be incomplete and rather short compared to the complexity of Axis2. They only briefly describe some features of Axis2 and do not follow any structural concept. It is more of a collection of articles without any overall concept. The most referenced document for "more" information is the API document which means a Javadoc page.

The Axis2 framework was designed to implement web services. By using Axis2 we don't have to deal with SOAP message parsing, network socket handling, and so on. Axis2 takes over these tasks and allows to focus on the implementation of the web service functionality by offering several options to implement it. One option is to implement a POJO and to deploy it as a web service in Axis2. A POJO is a Java class which does not rely on any component architecture which is not part of the Java Runtime Environment. In particular, a POJO is not an Enterprise Java Bean. We choose this option. Axis2 defines that the public methods of such a POJO can be accessed via web service calls by the convention that the service's operation names match the method names.

Our `AuthorizedService` will have one operation called `isAuthorized` which gets a user name and password as parameters and returns `true` in case the combination is valid, otherwise `false`. The implementation is done in a class called `AuthorizedServiceImpl` and is rather simple. It just compares the user name and the password and returns `true` if they match lexically.

The next step is to tell Axis2 which class corresponds to which web service calls. We call this step *binding*. Without any binding the framework would not have any knowledge about the existence of our service. The binding is done by writing an XML configuration file called `service.xml` (see Listing 1.1). The part of interest is the parameter `ServiceClass` which gets the fully qualified class name of our implementation as value. By doing this, the framework

maps any web service calls for `AuthorizedService` to our implementation class
`AuthorizedServiceImpl`. The last step is to deploy our service into the Axis2
environment. The details of this step are not of interest for our example, thus
we will omit them.

Listing 1.1. service.xml

```
<service name="AuthorizedService" scope="application">
  <description>
    Checks whether user name and password are correct.
  </description>
  [...]
  <parameter name="ServiceClass">
    de.upb.services.AuthorizedServiceImpl
  </parameter>
</service>
```

The point we make here is that it is not difficult to use a well-designed framework when you know how to use it. But the information that is needed is most
often not available in a structured way. Instead of that, developers have to guess
that the framework might offer a mechanism to control some behaviour, have to
read books about it that are not shipped with the framework, or have to search
the web in the hope that other people might have had similar problems and have
written about their solutions. Last chance in case of open source frameworks is
to directly contact the developers via a mailing list. From our experiences with
industrial partners we argue that this is the standard process for enterprise application developers to collect information about a framework.

We will demonstrate this observation by refining our example. The first implementation of `AuthorizedServiceImpl` was rather simple. It just checked
whether the user name equals the password. But what has to be done to compare
the values with entries from a database? First, we need to establish a database
connection. For performance reasons this should only be done once when the service is created, not every time the service is called. So the database connection
code should not be part of the `isAuthorized` method. But unfortunately, the
Axis2 documentation does not provide any example for this particular problem.
Finally, we found a solution by reading a book about Axis2 and asking a web
search engine.

Our solution is the `DBAuthorizedService` class which is illustrated in Listing 1.2. The `DBAuthorizedService` class implements two hook-methods which
control the lifecylce of a web service: `init` and `destroy`. These hooks are defined in the interface `Lifecycle` of the Axis2 framework. The `init` hook-method
is called by the framework when the service is constructed. After the connection is established, it can be used by the `isAuthorized` method. The `destroy`
hook-method is called when the service is destructed.

This example points out the problem that information, like the `Lifecylce`
interface, are often not available. One might argue that a lack of documentation
is a common problem of open source software but our observation is that this is

not true for popular and widely used frameworks. Even the open source projects start to invest a high effort in extensive documentation. Unfortunately, those documentation are often unstructured, do not reflect the framework concepts, focus on the specification of the framework – not on its usage, and miss the right level of abstraction for describing the framework use. The reasons for this are inadequate established methods and the absence of a reference about how to document framework use.

Our approach is to improve the situation by defining a meta-model for all framework description languages (FDLs), called FDMM. It contains elements to describe all relevant framework aspects which have to be reflected by a framework description. Any framework which is described using an FDMM-based language won't be missing such important information as seen in the example. Additionally, the FDMM can be used e.g. as a reference to evaluate the quality of existing documentations, or to help framework vendors to document their implementation in an adequate manner. We show how a concrete FDMM-based FDL may look like and present an improved framework description for our example.

Listing 1.2. DBAuthorizedService.java

```
import org.apache.axis2.service.Lifecycle
public class DBAuthorizedService implements Lifecycle {
  private Connection con;
  public void init(ServiceContext sctx) {
    this.con = DBDriverManager.getConnection();
  }
  public boolean isAuthorized(String user, String pass) {
    Result rs = this.con.exec(SELECT pass FROM usrs
                              WHERE username = user);
    if (rs.getValue().equals(pass))
      return true;
    else
      return false;
  }
  public void destroy(ServiceContext sctx) {
    this.con.close();
  }
}
```

3   Features

In this section, we describe the features of our FDMM and concrete FDLs, respectively. The features are based on requirements that were gathered using three different sources. First, our experience in integrating frameworks gained in industrial projects about the integration of open source frameworks. Second, we evaluated popular open source frameworks in the domain of JEE application development and analysed their documentation. Additionally, we examined existing framework description approaches taken from the literature.

Different frameworks require slightly different description languages. Frameworks can be differentiated into system infrastructure frameworks, middleware integration frameworks, and enterprise application frameworks [11] where each requires a specialised description language. Additionally, different framework aspects, require specific description techniques, i.e. domain specific languages (DSL).

The FDMM supports the integration and therefore the reuse of existing approaches. For example, the FDMM allows to reuse the UML-F approach to mark the framework's hot spots. Another example is to use UML Protocol State Machines [12] to specify the protocol between framework and hot spot. The FDMM as the meta-model for all FDLs reflects all relevant aspects which have to be described by a framework description. We hereby ensure that any FDMM-based FDL will consider these aspects. Fig. 1 depicts some of the aspects which are described hereafter.

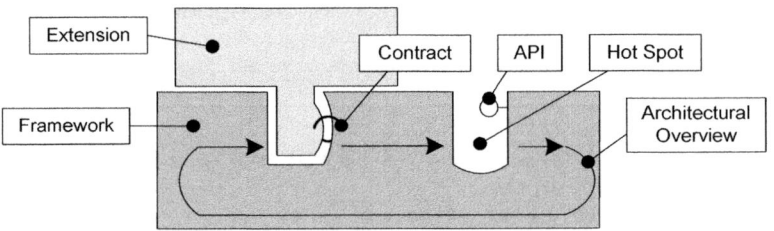

Fig. 1. Framework Aspects

Architectural Overview. A developer has to understand the architectural structure and the framework's purpose. These are relevant framework aspects mentioned by framework definitions from Johnson [13] [14]. It is required that structure and purpose are documented using abstract architectural overviews (see Fig. 1). This enables a developer to get a helpful overview of the framework before starting to use it in detail.

This feature reflects the idea of a structured framework documentation [15] which follows the pyramid principle. This principle splits a problem into sub-problems, these sub-problems into sub-sub-problems and so on. A developer starts to learn the framework by abstract views and specifically refines his knowledge by looking deeper into the framework details.

Therefore, the overview must combine the abstract view at the framework with markers that point out the framework's hot spots. The FDMM groups similar hot spots into so called hot spot groups. These hot spot groups are then linked from the architectural overviews. With regard to our motivating example, an architectural overview may be described using an UML Activity Diagram. As an example, the diagram in Fig. 2 expresses the SOAP request flow and states out where hot spots belonging to certain hot spot groups are invoked.

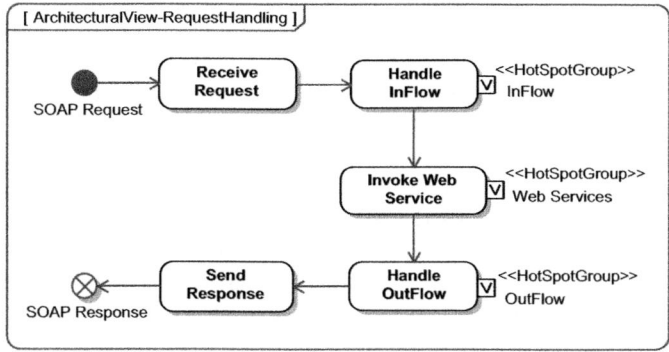

Fig. 2. Architectural views on Axis2 process flows

Hot Spot: Description. Further definitions of frameworks, e.g. [16] and [17] focus on the aspects that a framework transports a reusable design and can be customized by an application developer. The customization is done by using the offered hot spots [18]. The implementation which uses a hot spot is called an *extension* for a hot spot. See Fig. 1 for hot spot and extension.

Hot spots are the central concept in framework design. Therefore, the FDMM forces the hot spot description and groups all hot spots in hot spot groups. An undocumented hot spot must be interpreted as non-existent because a developer cannot be sure that an undocumented hot spot will be maintained.

In Fig. 2 the activity "Invoke Web Service" is linked to the `HotSpotGroup` "Web Services". This group contains a hot spot called "POJO-WS" which stands for the opportunity to implement an Axis2 web service using a POJO. A developer who wants to implement an extension for POJO-WS has to follow the instructions described by the hot spot, e.g.

1. Implement a new POJO `WsClass` with a default constructor.
2. Implement a `public void` method which will be invoked by the service call.

Hot Spot: Variants. Often, a hot spot offers different alternatives for its use. The developer may choose between several options that depend on his needs. Furthermore, hot spots are often modular in the sense that a developer can implement a basic variant of a hot spot and then add further features. The result is a more advanced variant of the extension for the same hot spot. The FDMM supports this by a generalization concept between hot spots.

As an example, the POJO-WS hot spot is the basic variant for implementing a POJO web service. An extended variant called "ExtPOJO-WS" implements the `Lifecycle` interface, additionally. The `Lifecycle` interface controls the initialization and destruction of a web service's instance. As a result, the extended variant uses the hook methods `init` and `destroy` which are defined by ExtPOJO-WS.

Hot Spot: Binding and Deployment. After implementing an extension it has to be bound to the framework and deployed in the framework environment. Binding is the process of making the extension public to the framework. An FDMM-based FDL describes how the binding mechanism is realized and how a developer has to use it.

Additionally, the FDMM specifies the units of deployment and the deployment process for extensions. The deployment defines the packaging format and how these packages are installed inside the framework. Binding combined with deployment ensures that a framework uses an extensions.

As seen in the motivating example the binding of a POJO-WS is realized by creating a service description in a `service.xml` file, see Listing 1.1. The binding description has to define the XML schema and which elements have to be used to describe the service. Additionally, Axis2 uses the Axis Archive (`*.aar`) file format for deployment. The `aar` format defines that the `service.xml` file has to be in a subdirectory called `META-INF`. The archive also contains the compiled Java classes and is compressed using the ZIP algorithm. For deployment, the aar file is placed into the `services` directory of the Axis2 installation. This information is described by deployment and description languages as part of the FDMM.

Hot Spot: Examples. Examples or case studies are important aspects in order to describe programming problems [19]. An FDMM-based FDL reflects this by using concrete examples to depict the framework use. An example often depicts specific details more clearly than keeping a hot spot in perspective and examples are often used in today's framework descriptions. Tutorials fall in the same category and can also be included by the FDMM.

Hot Spot Contract Description. Frameworks use the inversion of control (IoC) communication paradigm to communicate with the hot spot's extensions. For this, each extension has to fulfil a contract that is defined by the hot spot which binds hot spot and extension together as depicted in Fig. 1. Such a contract describes four aspects of the hot spot usage: *hooks*, *recommended interfaces*, *constraints*, and *protocols*. The details are described in the following paragraphs.

Contract: Hooks. A hot spot is used through its *hooks* [9] whereby, according to [20], hooks are the building blocks of hot spots. The framework uses the IoC principle to communicate with the extension through the predefined hooks. According to [21], a hook is a method which is called by the framework. The framework methods which call the hooks are referred to as template-methods.

The ExtPOJO-WS hot spot from our previous example implements the `Lifecycle` interface which implements the hook methods:

```
public void init(ServiceContext)
public void destroy(ServiceContext)
```

The hook description of an FDL identifies the interface which has to be implemented or the class which has to be subclassed and the methods which have to be implemented/overwritten.

Contract: Protocols. Most often, frameworks implement a protocol that defines when each hook is called. The FDMM reflects this by describing the hook protocol of a hot spot. A major application of such a protocol is to specify the lifecycle of an extension from construction to destruction. From the ExtPOJO-WS example we have seen how a framework may control the lifecycle by hooks for `init` and `destroy` actions. The protocol can be described by UML Protocol State Machines as depicted in Fig. 3.

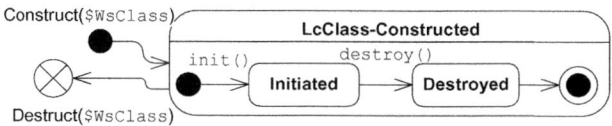

Fig. 3. Hook Protocol

Contract: Recommended Interface. A developer gets access to the framework API offered by the hot spot (see Fig. 1) while implementing the hooks. The FDMM connects hooks with API documentation to specify direct links to the API which may be used by a specific hook. The API documentation may be given using state-of-the-art techniques like Javadocs. We call this the *recommended interface* regarding a hook which is a subset of the whole framework API. Technically, a developer may be able to access the whole framework API from a hook but often this is not intended by the vendor. Because of this, an FDMM-based FDL is able to define which parts of the framework API are recommended to be used by an extension.

Having a look at the ExtPOJO-WS hot spot the hooks `init` and `destroy` allow access to the framework API using the parameter of type `ServiceContext`. The recommended API may allow usage of some API parts and forbid the usage of others. The use of placeholders known from regular expressions can be used to describe a set of API functions, like

```
FROM HOOK init(ServiceContext)
   ALLOW  ServiceContext.getAxisService().get*
   FORBID ServiceContext.getConfigurationContext().terminate()
```

Contract: Constraints. The hook interfaces often carry functional constraints like value ranges for parameters, objects that may not be `Null`, or return values that must ensure some condition. But constraints may also be non-functional like performance requirements, real-time constraints, or the allowed binding of external resources by an extension. A constraints may be a restriction or some assurance like an invariant which is always valid. Using the FDMM constraints can be connected to hot spots itself and to hooks.

Constraints may be expressed in various ways and different complexity. With respect to our example we define two trivial constraints in terms of assurances:

```
Hook init(ServiceContext): ServiceContext IS NOT NULL
Hook destroy(ServiceContext): ServiceContext IS NOT NULL
```

4   The Framework Description Meta-model (FDMM)

The framework description meta-model (FDMM) is divided into six packages. These packages and their import relationships are depicted in Fig. 4.

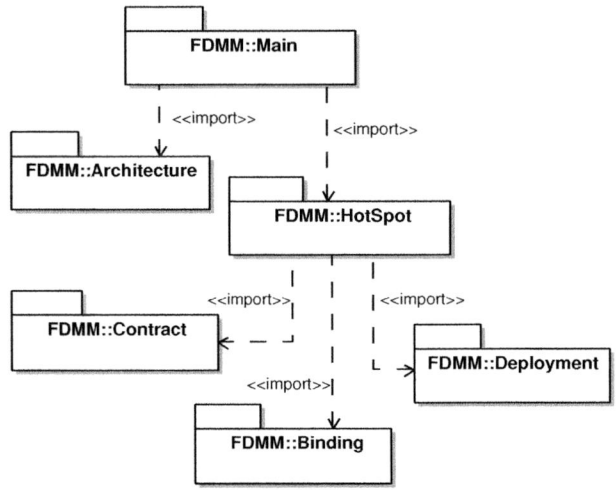

Fig. 4. Framework Description Meta-Model (FDMM) – Package View

The *Main* package contains the whole meta-model by importing everything from the other packages. The sub-packages are named accordingly to the features listed in Section 3. The *Architecture* package contains elements for describing the architectural overview, the *HotSpot* package has all elements for describing the different parts of a hot spot. These parts are described in three sub-packages: The *Contract* package consists of elements for describing the extension's contract. Apart from this, the packages *Binding* and *Deployment* contain elements to describe how to publish an extension. The FDMM is modelled as an UML [12] Class Diagram, which is depicted in Fig. 5 and implemented as an EMF [22] model.

The root class for a framework description is the *Framework* class, which holds all *HotSpotGroups* and *ArchitecturalViews*. The *ArchitecturalViews* provide an overview of the framework with links to available *HotSpotGroups*. By looking at an *ArchitecturalView* a developer knows where the framework can be adapted using the mentioned *HotSpots*. A framework is documented by combining several *ArchitecturalViews* to describe parts of the framework.

Each *HotSpot* belongs to at least one *HotSpotGroup* to provide a better overview of all *HotSpots*. For example, a *HotSpotGroup* may be used to group all variants of one *HotSpot* together. Variants of *HotSpots* can be modelled by using the *Generalization* relationship. When one *HotSpot* is a *Generalization* of another *HotSpot*, the specialized *HotSpot* inherits all properties of the general one. A property may be any element of the FDMM which is related to a *HotSpot*,

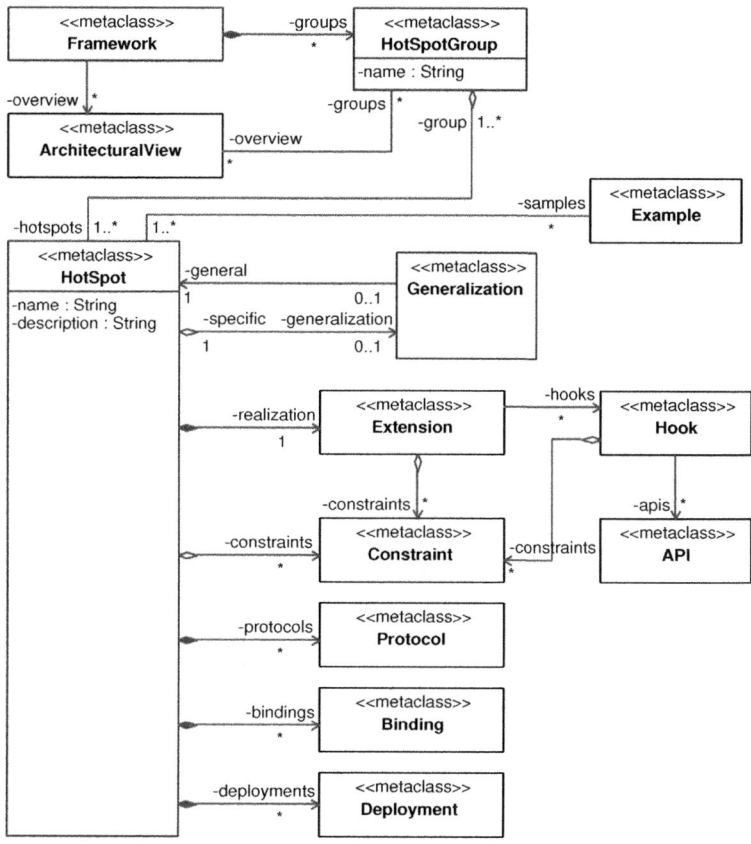

Fig. 5. Framework Description Meta-Model (FDMM)

e.g. some *Constraint.* The semantic of this *Generalization* is that a *HotSpot* inherits all properties of its parent *HotSpot* if the property is not overloaded by the specific *HotSpot.*

The feature of the hot spot contract is fulfilled by the class *Extension* together with its associated classes. The *Extension* class plus *Hook* and *API* classes describe details of the implementation. A developer gets the information which *Hooks* must be implemented and how to use the framework *API.* This can be refined by defining further *Constraints* for the *HotSpot,* the *Extension,* or the *Hooks.* Additionally, the *HotSpot* defines a *Protocol* about how to communicate with *Extensions.* Such a *Protocol* may also describe the *Extension's* lifecycle.

Bindings and *Deployments* can be described by using the corresponding classes. At last, the FDMM allows to document examples for concrete problems and their solution by using the *Example* class which is associated with *HotSpots.*

The idea of the FDMM is to use it as an parametrized meta-model which can be instantiated with different languages for the different aspects. The details of this parametrization are not in the scope of this paper and are therefore omitted.

Conceptually, we are using an approach called language-parametrized language. The language defined by the FDMM is parametrized using other languages, e.g. state machines, hook description languages, constraint languages, etc. The ability to reuse and include other languages makes the FDMM highly adaptive and allows the definition of specific FDLs for specific frameworks.

5   Applying the Approach

Before using the FDMM in a concrete scenario two steps are required:

1. Instantiate the generic aspects of the FDMM with concrete languages. For example, an aspect like the hook description has to be bound to a hook description language.
2. Tools have to be designed to support developers to document the framework under development during the framework development process. Ideally, tools for existing languages can be reused.

Both steps are not really in focus of this paper as we are describing the basics of FDMM-based FDLs. Anyway, during the first step an FDL designer has to decide which concrete languages should be used. Perhaps new DSLs have to be designed to meet the requirements for a specific framework. Each generic aspect of the FDMM is formalized by a so called intentional model which expresses the intention of the required language. For instance, the intention of a protocol description language is to express hook protocol states and the transitions between these state in terms of hook calls. Such an intention can be expressed by an intentional model for protocol description. This model can then be mapped to concrete meta-models, e.g. the UML meta-model for Protocol State Machines. As an example, Fig. 6 shows the intentional model for protocol description.

The tool support can be realized using model-driven engineering techniques and the Eclipse Modeling Framework (EMF) [22]. We have implemented the FDMM and the intentional models using EMF. This allows us to reuse existing EMF based editors, e.g. for UML diagrams like state machines.

The rest of this section demonstrates how to use the FDMM to create a concrete framework description language (FDL) and shows how the Axis2 framework should be documented using our motivating example.

The architectural view at the component structure of a framework may be modelled by using UML Component Diagrams. Additionally, behavioural details can be modelled using UML Activity Diagrams which we use in this example. The architectural view at the Axis2 behaviour of *Request Handling* was already shown in Fig. 2.

A SOAP request sent by some client is received by the Axis2 framework and at first handled by a collection of *InFlow* handlers. The pins with stereotype *HotSpotGroup* at some activities indicate hot spots which are executed when this activity is applied. E.g. the activity *Handle InFlow* which executes the hot spots of the group *InFlow*. The activity *Invoke Web Service* allows us to add our

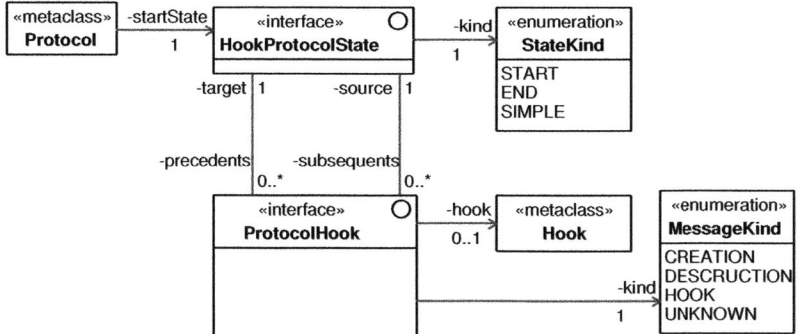

Fig. 6. Hot spot protocol intention

own web service implementation by using a hot spot of the group *Web Services*. After the web service was invoked the response is handled by some *OutFlow* handlers and in the end a generated SOAP response with the results is sent back to the client.

The architectural view provides the developer with the basic information needed to understand what happens when Axis2 processes requests. In addition, the architectural view provides information about available hot spots and when they are invoked. To implement a web service the developer has to look at the available hot spots of the group *Web Services*. The available hot spots of this group are shown in Fig. 7.

We decided to visualize a hot spot in this concrete FDL as a rectangle in the style of UML classes. The hot spot rectangle consists of five sections: a header section on top, then sections from top to bottom for describing the extension, the protocol, the binding, and the deployment.

The hot spot's name and its group is placed in the header section. The extension lists the hooks which have to be implemented together with information about the recommended framework API. These aspects can be expressed by using DSLs which may have existed before or are newly defined for this purpose. For example, we use the existing UML Protocol State Machines to describe a hot spot's protocol on the one hand and define a new DSL to express the extension's details on the other. Fig. 7, for example, illustrates the hot spots POJO-WS and its specialization ExtPOJO-WS.

The hot spot POJO-WS is the base variant of how to implement a web service. This variant was used in the beginning of our motivating example. This hot spot does not define any hooks and therefore any protocol. We just had to implement a POJO and create binding and deployment. In our motivating example, we have described the problem to identify how to realize the database connection for our web service. The solution was to use the Lifecycle interface. This solution is now described by a hot spot which is a more specialized variant of the POJO-WS.

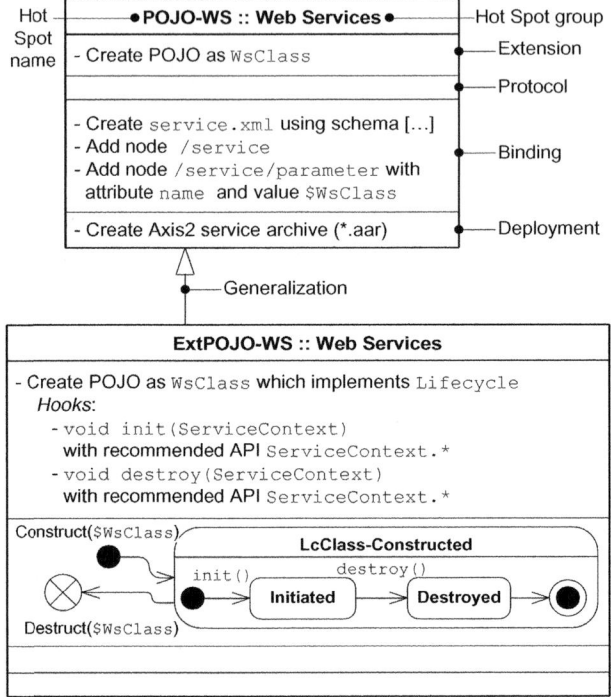

Fig. 7. Hot spot descriptions of POJO-WS and ExtPOJO-WS

The big advantage is that all those variants can be easily expressed using an FDMM-based FDL.

The extended version of POJO-WS is ExtPOJO-WS. Inheritance is visualized using an arrow between two hot spots similar to inheritance in UML Class Diagrams. By inheritance ExtPOJO-WS reuses all parts of the hot spot description of POJO-WS which are not described in ExtPOJO-WS. Hereby, the specialized hot spot ExtPOJO-WS does not have to describe the binding and deployment, because it has already been described by the super hot spot. But ExtPOJO-WS describes hooks which have to be implemented and it defines a protocol using the UML Protocol State Machine language. Such a protocol description is easy to understand for a developer who gets all information he needs to implement the extension accordingly.

This simple example illustrates how the FDMM ensures that the framework description contains all necessary information. Additionally, the FDMM determines the structural relation between this information. The result is a framework description, which directly supports the developer in learning and using the framework.

In the next section, we will discuss existing approaches to document frameworks and show the relation between these approaches and our generic FDMM.

6   Related Work

In this section, we have a closer look at existing approaches for framework documentation and at the established methods which are used e.g. by open source frameworks.

In case of open source frameworks the source code of sample extensions in combination with an API document is the usual way to demonstrate the framework use. Samples often have the problem to be either too simple or too complex. Nevertheless, examples are a way to demonstrate the functionality of a framework and how to use specific hot spots [19]. This can be useful to understand the framework as mentioned in [23]. Therefore, the FDMM supports this technique by linking hot spots with examples.

Another approach which makes use of examples is to structure them like a cookbook with recipes for different problems. This structure allows to search for a solution if a developer has a concrete problem.

These ideas were also applied by an approach of Johnson [24] who uses patterns to describe frameworks. Each pattern describes a problem that consistently arises in the domain of the framework. A similar approach is used by Meusel et al. [15]. This approach combines the idea of structured documentation which follows the already mentioned pyramid principle. The approach uses this principle to document the framework use in terms of "Application Patterns" which describe a problem and its solution, whereby the solution may reference underlying problems. The approach of "Active Cookbooks" [25] combines the cookbook approach with a graphical development environment. "Smartbooks" [26] [27] go one step beyond and try to support the developer by describing tasks that guide the developer. Tools monitor the compliance of the tasks while the developer is implementing an extension.

All these approaches focus on the description of a problem that a developer might have. The solution is described at the level of hooks without mentioning aspects like protocol and binding. However, a specific usage problem of a developer might not be contained in the cookbook. The FDMM combines both worlds by using architectural views to describe the overall structure and purpose of the framework with links to hot spots. The hot spots description contains all needed information and can be linked to concrete examples. A developer will use the architectural views to identify the available hot spots and select the ones which may help to solve the problem.

One concept for documenting frameworks is well-known beyond frameworks but has its roots in the design of frameworks. Design patterns [28] are a widely used concept to document and reuse solutions for architectural problems. Frameworks heavily make use of design patterns to implement the mechanisms that are needed to bind and use extensions. Design patterns are documented by describing the design problem to solve, its context, the solution, and some examples. They can help to document the framework's hot spots [29] but focus more on the implementation of a hot spot itself and not on its use – the implementation of an extension. Therefore, design patterns are not sufficient to describe the framework use [30].

A combination of the patterns used by Johnson and design patterns by Gamma et al. is the "Motif" approach [7]. A Motif is a pattern which describes a situation in which the framework is used. Thereby, Motifs are ordered from abstract to concrete which allows a developer to learn the framework from an abstract top level to more fine grained problems. Motifs document basic concepts, the framework use, and examples – the framework design is documented via contracts and design patterns. This approach demonstrates that a generic framework description approach like the FDMM must be a combination of different techniques to describe the different aspects of the framework use. But compared to the FDMM the Motif approach does not consider aspects like binding and deployment and it is not extensible as the FDMM.

Pree et al. developed an approach to document the hook- and template-methods of a hot spot [18]. This is done by annotating the methods of framework classes whether they are intended to be implemented by an extension (hook-method) or are methods which call a hook (template-method). This approach was formalized in the language "UML-F" [8] [31], an UML profile for framework architectures. The UML-F does not provide abstract views on the framework to support the developer finding the hot spot to use. Moreover, this approach does not describe any protocol or constraints for the hooks.

The UML is used by further approaches for framework design [32] and description, like the "UML-FD" profile [33] which is similar to UML-F. Both use UML stereotypes to annotate classes, interfaces, and methods of hooks. Another example is the framework design language "F-UML" [34].

Each considered approach may be used as part of an FDMM-based language but none covers all aspects of framework documentation. The advantage of any new FDMM-based FDL is that it covers all aspects of framework documentation and not only parts of the problems. We have summarized this analysis in a tabular overview shown in Fig. 8.

This table shows which features that were identified in section 3 are considered by other approaches. It is a simple yes or no matrix where a "yes" means that it may be possible to support the feature using the approach. A "no" means that the feature is not mentioned by the approach and it is unlikely from our point of view that the approach would support it.

An interesting observation is that approaches which use samples and tutorials are able to express most of the aspects if used properly. The main problem is that this kind of documentation mainly focus on some samples and tutorials for some use cases of the framework. The FDMM was designed to structure the documentation and to describe the whole framework – not only parts of it. Too much details are often left out by tutorials or are only implicit available. The framework user learns by playing around with the example using the unwanted try and error approach.

Our FDMM in contrast makes all these features explicit and defines their relationships. An FDMM-based FDL is forced to use specific description languages for the different aspects. Information is not hidden somewhere in a tutorial or only visible as part of an example. Framework developers get a clear

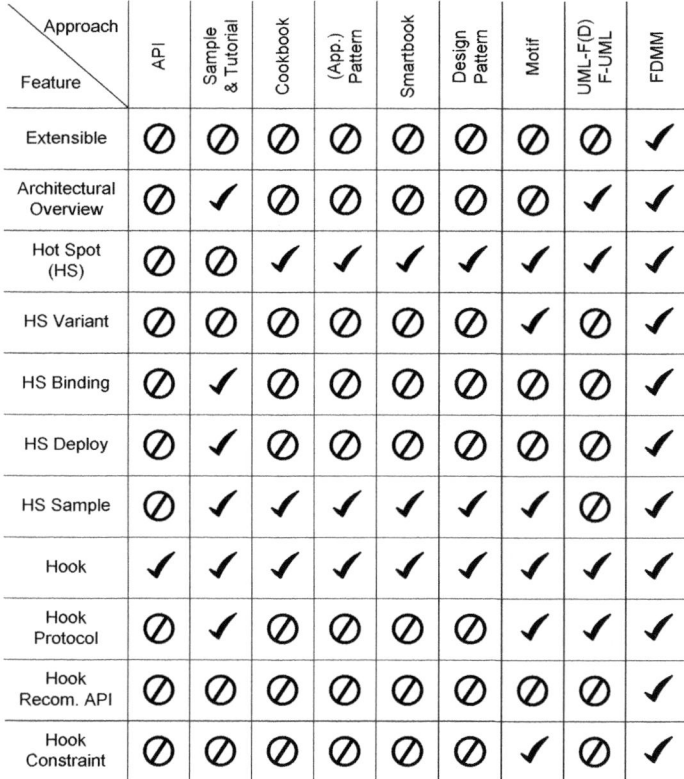

Feature \ Approach	API	Sample & Tutorial	Cookbook	(App.) Pattern	Smartbook	Design Pattern	Motif	UML-F(D) F-UML	FDMM
Extensible	⊘	⊘	⊘	⊘	⊘	⊘	⊘	⊘	✓
Architectural Overview	⊘	✓	⊘	⊘	⊘	⊘	⊘	✓	✓
Hot Spot (HS)	⊘	⊘	✓	✓	✓	✓	✓	✓	✓
HS Variant	⊘	⊘	⊘	⊘	⊘	⊘	✓	⊘	✓
HS Binding	⊘	✓	⊘	⊘	⊘	⊘	⊘	⊘	✓
HS Deploy	⊘	✓	⊘	⊘	⊘	⊘	⊘	⊘	✓
HS Sample	⊘	✓	✓	✓	✓	✓	✓	⊘	✓
Hook	✓	✓	✓	✓	✓	✓	✓	✓	✓
Hook Protocol	⊘	✓	⊘	⊘	⊘	⊘	✓	✓	✓
Hook Recom. API	⊘	⊘	⊘	⊘	⊘	⊘	⊘	⊘	✓
Hook Constraint	⊘	⊘	⊘	⊘	⊘	⊘	✓	⊘	✓

Fig. 8. Comparing Approaches

understanding of what has to be documented and, most important, the completeness of documentation becomes measurable.

7   Conclusion and Future Work

In this paper, we presented the FDMM, a generic framework description meta-model for defining concrete framework description languages (FDLs). One advantage of the generic FDMM approach is that it allows to reuse existing description languages which often focus on a specific aspect of framework description only, like the description of hooks. The FDMM does not focus on one particular aspect but defines all relevant aspects which have to be considered by any FDL. Therefore, the FDMM is a reference model for framework documentation. The FDMM's design ensures that documentation principles, as they are mentioned by related work, like the pyramid principle, are also addressed. FDMM-based FDLs will improve the quality of framework documentations as these documentation will be well-structured and consider all relevant framework aspects. Additionally, the FDMM can be used to evaluate the quality of existing and future framework descriptions.

The next important step is to improve the tool support for our approach. Framework documentation will be embedded into the framework development process and tools, like code analyser, are used to extract as much information from the framework implementation. On the basis of this information a developer is supported to easily fill in missing parts of the documentation. An integrated tool support in development environments like the Eclipse IDE connects implementation and documentation without changing the environment. Having a strong tool support offers the opportunity to validate the approach by documenting a wider range of frameworks, e.g. the ones used as part of the mentioned Interactive Knowledge Stack project.

Future work will focus on further application possibilities which evolve from this approach. One example is to use the well-defined and processable information from a framework documentation which is expressed by using an FDMM-based FDL, to test whether an extension is compatible to the framework according to its documentation. The software quality can be improved by better tests for extensions, which can automatically be derived from the FDL, using model-based testing approaches [35]. A more constructive approach would be to support a developer in creating an extension by generating as much code for an extension as possible by automatic code generation.

In summary, due to its generic properties combined with its well-defined structure and upcoming tool support the FDMM opens up a range of application areas to improve the software development in the field of enterprise application development.

References

1. Assmann, M., Engels, G.: Service-Oriented Enterprise Architectures: Evolution of Concepts and Methods. In: Proc. of the 12th IEEE International Enterprise Distributed Object Computing Conference 2008 (EDOC'08), Munich, Germany, September 2008, pp. 37–43. IEEE Computer Society, Los Alamitos (2008)
2. Sun Microsystems, Inc.: Java(TM) Platform, Enterprise Edition (Java EE) Specification, v5 (May 2006)
3. Bosch, J., Molin, P., Mattsson, M., Bengtsson, P.: Object-oriented framework-based software development: problems and experiences. ACM Comput. Surv. 32(1es) (2000)
4. Thomas, D.: The API Field of Dreams - Too Much Stuff! It's Time to Reduce and Simplify APIs! Journal of Object Technology 5(6), 23–27 (2006)
5. Interactive Knowledge Stack (IKS): Homepage (December 2009), http://www.iks-project.eu/
6. Christ, F., Sauer, S.: Open source stacks. In: Asche, M., Bauhus, W., Seel, B.K. (eds.) Open Source: Kommerzialisierungsmöglichkeiten und Chancen für die Zusammenarbeit von Hochschulen und Unternehmen, pp. 133–154. Waxmann Verlag (2008)
7. Lajoie, R., Keller, R.K.: Design and Reuse in Object-Oriented Frameworks: Patterns, Contracts, and Motifs in Concert. In: Proceedings of the Colloquium on Object Orientation in Databases and Software Engineering (COODBSE'94), May 1995, pp. 295–312. World Scientific, Singapore (1995)

8. Fontoura, M., Pree, W., Rumpe, B.: UML-F: A Modeling Language for Object-Oriented Frameworks. In: Proceedings of the European Conference on Object-Oriented Programing (ECOOP 2000), Sophia Antipolis and Cannes, France (June 2000)
9. Froehlich, G., Hoover, H.J., Liu, L., Sorenson, P.: Hooking into object-oriented application frameworks. In: Proceedings of the 19th International Conference on Software Engineering (ICSE'97), pp. 491–501. ACM Press, New York (1997)
10. Apache Axis2: Homepage (December 2009), http://ws.apache.org/axis2/
11. Fayad, M.E., Schmidt, D., Johnson, R. (eds.): Building application frameworks: object-oriented foundations of framework design. John Wiley and Sons, Chichester (1999)
12. OMG: Unified Modeling Language (OMG UML), Superstructure, V2.1.2 (November 2007)
13. Johnson, R.E., Foote, B.: Designing reusable classes. Journal of Object-Oriented Programming 1(2), 22–35 (1988)
14. Johnson, R.E.: Components, frameworks, patterns. In: ACM SIGSOFT Symposium on Software Reusability, pp. 10–17 (1997)
15. Meusel, M., Czarnecki, K., Köpf, W.: A model for structuring user documentation of object-oriented frameworks using patterns and hypertext. In: Aksit, M., Matsuoka, S. (eds.) ECOOP 1997. LNCS, vol. 1241, pp. 496–510. Springer, Heidelberg (1997)
16. Deutsch, L.P.: Design reuse and frameworks in the Smalltalk-80 system. Software reusability 2, 57–71 (1989); Published in Software Reusability: vol. 2, Applications and Experience
17. Fayad, M., Schmidt, D.C.: Object-oriented application frameworks. ACM Commun. 40(10), 32–38 (1997)
18. Pree, W.: Design Patterns for Object Oriented Software Development. Addison-Wesley, Reading (1995); Erste Auflage 1994
19. Linn, M.C., Clancy, M.J.: The case for case studies of programming problems. ACM Commun. 35(3), 121–132 (1992)
20. Pree, W.: Hot-Spot-Driven Framework Development. In: Fayad, M., Schmidt, D., Johnson, R. (eds.) Building Application Frameworks: Object-Oriented Foundations of Framework Design. Wiley & Sons, New York City (2000)
21. Pree, W., Pomberger, G.: Framework component systems: Concepts, design heuristics, and perspectives. In: Bjorner, D., Broy, M., Pottosin, I.V. (eds.) PSI 1996. LNCS, vol. 1181, pp. 330–340. Springer, Heidelberg (1996)
22. Steinberg, D., Budinsky, F., Paternostro, M., Merks, E.: EMF - Eclipse Modeling Framework, 2nd edn. Addison Wesley, Reading (2009)
23. Gangopadhyay, D., Mitra, S.: Understanding frameworks by exploration of exemplars. In: Proceedings of the International Workshop on Computer-Aided Software Engineering (CASE'95), pp. 90–99 (1995)
24. Johnson, R.E.: Documenting frameworks using patterns. In: Conference on Object-oriented programming systems, languages, and applications (OOPSLA'92), pp. 63–76. ACM, New York (1992)
25. Schappert, A., Sommerlad, P., Pree, W.: Automated support for software development with frameworks. In: Proceedings of the Symposium on Software reusability (SSR '95), pp. 123–127. ACM Press, New York (1995)
26. Ortigosa, A., Campo, M., Moriyn, R.: Enhancing framework usability through smart documentation. In: Proceedings of the Argentinian Symposium on Object Orientation, Buenos Aires, Argentina, pp. 103–117 (1999)

27. Ortigosa, A., Campo, M.: Smartbooks: A step beyond active-cookbooks to aid in framework instantiation. In: Proceedings of the Technology of Object-Oriented Languages and Systems (TOOLS'99), Washington, DC, USA, pp. 131–140. IEEE Computer Society, Los Alamitos (1999)
28. Gamma, E., Helm, R., Johnson, R.E., Vlissides, J.: Design Patterns. Elements of Reusable Object-Oriented Software. Addison Wesley, Reading (1995)
29. Silva, A.R., Rosa, F.A., Goncalves, T.: Framework description using concern-specific design patterns composition. ACM Comput. Surv. 32(1es), 16 (2000)
30. Richner, T.: Describing framework architectures: more than design patterns. In: Bosch, J., Bachatene, H., Hedin, G., Koskimies, K. (eds.) Proceedings of the European Conference on Object-Oriented Programming (ECOOP '98) Workshop on Object-Oriented Software Architectures, University of Karlskrona (1998)
31. Fontoura, M., Pree, W., Rumpe, B.: The UML Profile for Framework Architectures. Addison-Wesley, Reading (2002)
32. Ben-Abdallah, H., Bouassida, N., Gargouri, F., Ben-Hamadou, A.: A UML based Framework Design Method. Journal of Object Technologie 3(8), 97–119 (2004)
33. Lopes, S., Silva, C., Tavares, A., Monteiro, J.: Describing Framework Static Structure: promoting interfaces with UML annotations. In: Reussner, R., Szyperski, C., Weck, W. (eds.) Advances in Component-Oriented Programming - Proceedings of the 11th International Workshop on Component Oriented Programming (WCOP'06), July 2006, pp. 54–61. Universität Karlsruhe - Fakultät für Informatik (2006) ISSN 1432 - 7864
34. Bouassida, N., Ben-Abdallah, H., Gargouri, F., Hamadou, A.B.: Formalizing the framework design language F-UML. In: Proceedings of the First International Conference on Software Engineering and Formal Methods (SEFM'03), September 2003, pp. 164–172. IEEE, Los Alamitos (2003)
35. Güldali, B., Mlynarski, M., Wübbeke, A., Engels, G.: Model-Based System Testing Using Visual Contracts. In: Proceedings of Euromicro SEAA Conference 2009, Special Session on Model Driven Engineering, pp. 121–124. IEEE Computer Society, Los Alamitos (2009)

Loosely-Coupled Distributed Reactive Programming in Mobile Ad Hoc Networks

Andoni Lombide Carreton*, Stijn Mostinckx,
Tom Van Cutsem**, and Wolfgang De Meuter

Software Languages Lab
Vrije Universiteit Brussel, Pleinlaan 2 1050 Brussel, Belgium
{alombide,smostinc,tvcutsem,wdmeuter}@vub.ac.be

Abstract. Pervasive applications running on mobile ad hoc networks
have to be conceived as loosely-coupled event-driven architectures because of the dynamic nature of both the underlying network and the
applications running on top of them. Such architectures can become tedious to develop and understand when the number of events and event
handlers increases. The reason is that the control flow of the application
is driven by event handlers or callbacks which are triggered independently and are scattered throughout the application code. In this paper,
we propose a number of language constructs that reconcile the elegant
processing of events of a reactive programming system with the loose
coupling of a publish/subscribe system that is required to cope with the
dynamic nature of mobile ad hoc networks.

Keywords: reactive programming, publish/subscribe, event-driven programming, mobile ad hoc networks.

1 Introduction

Pervasive applications running in mobile ad hoc networks cannot be structured
as monolithic programs which accept a fixed input and compute it into some
output. Instead, to allow responsiveness to changes in the dynamically changing
mobile ad hoc network, programming paradigms targeting pervasive applications
propose the adoption of event-driven architectures [1,2,3,4].

The traditional way of conceiving an event-driven system in a setting where
producers and consumers change at runtime is by adopting a publish/subscribe
architecture, where event producers publish events and event consumers subscribe and react to events, either using a topic-based or content-based subscription [5,6]. In mobile ad hoc networks, where devices dynamically join and leave,
and where network connections can be broken at any point in time, the coupling
between producers and consumers should be very loose to prevent that network

---

* Funded by a doctoral scholarship of the "Institute for the Promotion of Innovation
through Science and Technology in Flanders" (IWT Vlaanderen).
** Postdoctoral Fellow of the Research Foundation - Flanders (FWO).

J. Vitek (Ed.): TOOLS 2010, LNCS 6141, pp. 41–60, 2010.

partitioning breaks the system when both parties are disconnected from one another. Furthermore, in such a setting without a fixed infrastructure such as naming servers, event producers should be able to notify event consumers without prior knowledge about their location and identity. This decoupling in space and time is what makes publish/subscribe so well suited to a dynamic environment such as a mobile ad hoc network [7,2] and both properties are needed to support application components that act as publishers and subscribers on *roaming devices*.

Eventually, the application layer should react to the events detected by the publish/subscribe layer. In most cases, this requires the programmer to bridge the gap between the underlying event notification system and the application layer. First, many event communication systems operate only on specific data types (e.g. event structs without methods) which lack some of the expressive power typically conveyed by high level programming languages. Consequently, application data types that correspond to events must adhere to additional criteria to allow mapping application data to events and vice versa. Furthermore, by adopting such an event-driven architecture, the application logic becomes scattered over different event handlers or callbacks which may be triggered independently [8]. The control of the application is no longer driven by an explicit control flow determined by the programmer, but by external events. This is a phenomenon known as *inversion of control* [9]. Control flow among event handlers has to be expressed implicitly through manipulation of shared state. E.g. unlike subsequent function calls, code triggered by different event handlers cannot use the runtime stack to make local variables visible to other executions (*stack ripping* [10]), such that these variables have to be made instance variables, global variables, etc. Finally, in more complex systems it is not always clear in which order different event handlers will be triggered, which can be critical in programming languages that allow side effects. In short, most publish/subscribe middleware lack a *seamless integration with a high level programming model* [11]. This is why in complex systems such an event-driven architecture can become hard to develop, understand and maintain [12,13].

In this paper, we propose a set of language constructs that enable the following:

1. **No inversion of control.** It should be possible to generate, combine and react to events all in the same programming language in an expressive way without inverting the control of the application and without introducing extra synchronization issues.
2. **Support for roaming.** Distributed application components notifying each other of events in an environment that exhibits all the characteristics of pervasive applications and mobile ad hoc networks mentioned above. This requires decoupling of event producers and consumers in both space and time.

Concretely, reactive programming techniques are used to build event-driven systems without inversion of control. Furthermore, we introduce *ambient behaviors*, a language abstraction built on top of publish/subscribe middleware which permits distributing event-driven applications over mobile ad hoc networks. The expressive power of the language construct is subsequently illustrated by its use in a non-trivial collaborative application deployed on a mobile ad hoc network.

In the next section, the key technologies on which our approach is based, namely the programming language AmbientTalk and ambient references, are briefly explained. In section 3, we discuss reactive programming in AmbientTalk/ R and introduce some event notification language constructs that support roaming and do not suffer from an inversion of control. Section 4 discusses a small pervasive application that we have implemented using our novel language constructs and subsequently in section 5 we point out the limitations of our approach. In section 6 we discuss some existing systems that permit building a similar kind of distributed event-driven systems by providing programming language support for one or more of the required features we pointed out above. Finally, section 7 concludes this paper.

2 Preliminaries

The *ambient-oriented* programming paradigm [14] is specifically aimed at pervasive applications running in mobile ad hoc networks. For this reason we chose to incorporate our language constructs in an existing ambient-oriented programming language. Ambient-oriented programming languages should explicitly incorporate potential network failures in the very heart of their computational model. Therefore, communication between distributed application components should happen without blocking the execution thread of the different components such that devices may continue doing useful work even when the connection with a communication partner is lost. Ambient-oriented languages also deal with the dynamically changing network topology in mobile ad hoc networks. The fact that in such networks devices spontaneously join with and disjoin from the networks means that the services these devices host cannot be discovered using a fixed, always available name server, but instead require dynamic service discovery protocols (e.g. broadcasting advertisements to discover nearby services).

2.1 AmbientTalk

AmbientTalk [15,16] is a distributed programming language embedded in Java[1]. The language is designed as a scripting language that can be used to compose Java components which are distributed across a mobile ad hoc network. The language is developed on top of the J2ME platform and runs on handheld devices such as smart phones and PDAs. Even though AmbientTalk is embedded in Java, it is a separate programming language. The embedding ensures that AmbientTalk applications can access Java objects running in the same JVM. These Java objects can also call back on AmbientTalk objects as if these were plain Java objects.

The most important difference between AmbientTalk and Java is the way in which they deal with concurrency and network programming. Java is multi-threaded, and provides either a low-level socket API or a high-level RPC API

---

[1] The language is available at `soft.vub.ac.be/amop`

(i.e. Java RMI) to enable distributed computing. In contrast, AmbientTalk is a fully event-driven programming language. It provides only event loop concurrency [17] and distributed objects communicate by means of asynchronous message passing. Event loops deal with concurrency similar to GUI frameworks (e.g. Java AWT or Swing): all concurrent activities are represented as events which are handled sequentially by an event loop thread.

AmbientTalk offers linguistic support to deal with the fluid topology of mobile ad hoc networks.

1. In an ad hoc network, objects must be able to discover one another without any infrastructure (such as a shared naming registry). Therefore, AmbientTalk has a service discovery engine that allows objects to discover one another in a peer-to-peer manner (by broadcasting UDP advertisements).
2. In an ad hoc network, objects may frequently disconnect and reconnect because of network partitions. Therefore, AmbientTalk provides fault-tolerant asynchronous message passing between objects: if a message is sent to a disconnected object, the message is buffered and resent later, when the object becomes reconnected. Other advantages of asynchronous message passing over standard RPC is that the asynchrony hides latency and that it keeps the application responsive (i.e. the event loop is not blocked during remote communication and is free to process other events).

2.2   Event-Driven Programming in AmbientTalk

AmbientTalk uses a classic event-handling style by relying on closures to function as event handlers. This has two advantages: closures can be used in-line and can be nested and closures have access to their enclosing lexical scope. Event handlers are (by convention) registered by a call to a function that starts with when. Events are always processed sequentially within the same event loop and event handler closures always run to completion before the next scheduled event handler is invoked, hence providing atomic execution of event handlers within the same event loop.

Throughout the rest of this paper we will use an example mobile application that assists visitors of a concert or other kind of event to trade tickets with other users. The following code snippet illustrates how AmbientTalk can be used to discover a `TicketVendor` object representing a user selling a ticket. Once discovered, the remote object is sent a message to retrieve its current location.

```
when: TicketVendor discovered: { |ticketVendor|
  when: ticketVendor<-getLocation() becomes: { |location|
    // Update user interface with the location.
  }}
```

The above code consists of two event handlers. The first event handler, registered by means of the `when:discovered:` control structure, is invoked when the language runtime discovers a `TicketVendor` object. Here, `TicketVendor` refers to a

Java interface. The discovered object is accessible via the `ticketVendor` variable, which denotes a remote AmbientTalk object that wraps a Java component implementing the ticket vendor. The syntax `obj<-msg()` denotes an asynchronous message send and is used here to query the `TicketVendor` object for its latest location. When the query message is processed by the remote `ticketVendor` object, that object's `getLocation` method is invoked. The return value of this method is used as the reply to the query. The caller is notified asynchronously when the reply has been computed. The `when:becomes:` control structure is used to install an event handler that can process this reply. The return value is passed to this event handler (cf. the `location` variable in the example).

As can be seen from the above example, service discovery and replies of remote queries are represented in AmbientTalk as events that trigger the appropriate event handlers, causing an inverted control flow. Furthermore, if the location of the ticket vendor has to be refreshed, the code shown above has to be executed periodically (e.g. in a loop). In the following section, we show how the events of discovering new and detecting lost services can be made implicit, by means of ambient references [18].

2.3   Language Abstractions for Roaming

When writing AmbientTalk code to query nearby services for data (e.g. all users selling a ticket) using the language features discussed in the previous section, one often writes a recurring pattern of code to deal with the discovery and loss of nearby services while a query is executing, and to deal with gathering the replies from all respondent services. To ease the writing of multicast queries, AmbientTalk introduces ambient references [18]. Ambient references represent a collection of nearby services of the same type. This collection is constantly kept up-to-date with the proximate physical environment: newly discovered services are added to the collection, while unreachable services are removed from it. This synchronization with the environment must no longer be done manually by the programmer, but is instead done by the ambient reference itself.

Sending a message to an ambient reference causes this message to be multicast to all services in the collection. A message can also be annotated with an expiration period (in milliseconds). If a message has an expiration period, it will not only be multicast to all services in the ambient reference's collection at the time the message is sent, but also to any services discovered at a later point in time, until its expiration period has elapsed. Consider the following example query:

```
def werchterVendors :=
  ambient: TicketVendor where: { |tv| tv.event == "Rock␣Werchter" };

whenAll: werchterVendors<-getLocation()@Expires(5.seconds) becomes: {
  |locations|
  // Update the map GUI with the locations
}
```

The keyword `ambient:` allows one to create an ambient reference given a Java interface. Additionally, an optional `where:` clause can be specified that allows to filter on properties of the discovered objects to allow content-based publish/subscribe. The variable `werchterVendors` contains an ambient reference that refers to all nearby `TicketVendor` objects that are selling tickets for an event named `"Rock␣Werchter"`. The message `getLocation()` is asynchronously multicast to these services with an expiration period of 5 seconds. This implies that the message may be received by all proximate ticket vendors at the time it is sent, as well as to all additional ticket vendors discovered within the next 5 seconds. The `whenAll:becomes:` control structure allows the programmer to install an event handler that can be used to gather the results of the query. Within this event handler, `locations` refers to an array containing the locations of the ticket vendors that replied. The event handler is triggered when the message's expiration period has elapsed.

The above example shows how ambient references relieve the programmer from having to deal explicitly with the events of discovery and loss of nearby services: ambient references transform these events into additions to or removals from their encapsulated collection. The programmer only has to specify an intensional (topic-based or content-based) description of the services that have to be discovered. The programmer must still capture the replies to the query by means of the `whenAll:becomes:` callback, leading to an inverted control flow. Furthermore, if the user interface showing the locations of the ticket vendors has to be kept up to date with the physical environment, the query has to be repeatedly executed in a loop. Eliminating both phenomena is the topic of the next section.

3   Reactive Programming in AmbientTalk/R

Reactive programming is a programming paradigm employed for various purposes such as animation [19], real time systems [20] and robotics [21]. Originating in Haskell, it has been successfully introduced in various other languages such as Java [22] and Scheme [23]. Reactive programming revolves around the use of time-varying *reactive values* or *behaviors*. While evaluating a reactive program, the interpreter implicitly constructs a directed acyclic *dataflow graph* [24] which mirrors the call graph of the program. Reactive values form the nodes of the graph, while the directed edges represent data dependencies. In this section, we briefly describe AmbientTalk/R, an extension of AmbientTalk with support for reactive programming.

As a first introduction to reactive programming in AmbientTalk/R, consider the following example: assume that the user interface of the ticket trader application introduced in the previous section sports a user interface which includes a map that shows the position of ticket vendors. The user can use this map to seek out a vendor and purchase one of the tickets being offered. To facilitate navigation, the map must be centered on the user's current position. Hence, whenever the position of the user changes, the user interface should be updated. The code excerpt below illustrates that using reactive programming, such behavior can be achieved without registering event handlers or suffering from inversion of control.

```
gui.centerOn(GPS_Location.latitude, GPS_Location.longitude);
```

In the above code excerpt, it is assumed that GPS_Location is a reactive value that represents the user's current location. Later in this section, we will illustrate how to construct such a reactive value by means of a built-in GPS location sensor. Given the GPS_Location, dependent reactive values are created implicitly when accessing its latitude and longitude fields respectively. These reactive values will be recomputed (i.e. the respective fields will be read anew) automatically whenever the GPS_Location is updated. In turn, the reactive values representing the user's current latitude and longitude are used as arguments to the invocation of the centerOn method. This method invocation will be lifted by the interpreter, resulting in the construction of a reactive value which depends on both reactive arguments. Hence, when either one of the arguments changes, the method will be invoked anew with the updated arguments. The dataflow graph that is constructed by evaluating this code snippet is shown in figure 1.

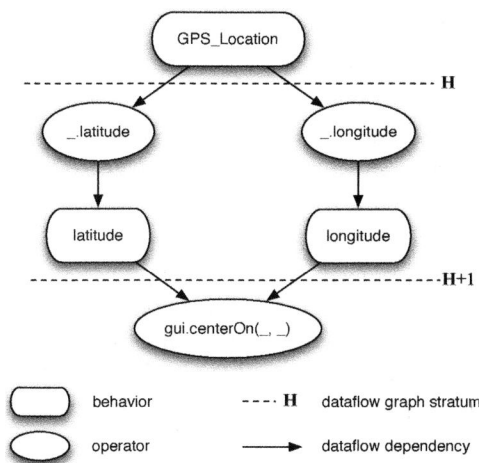

Fig. 1. Dataflow graph for centering the map in the ticket trader application

The graph shows the reactive value GPS_Location which acts as the *progenitor* for two dependent reactive values which represent the latitude and longitude. In turn, these reactive values are the progenitors for the reactive value that - as a side-effect - centers the user interface on the user's current location. Furthermore, figure 1 shows how the dataflow graph is partitioned into different layers or *strata* such that a reactive value only depends on reactive values situated in a lower stratum. This stratification (first proposed in [23]) is used when propagating the updates to ensure that a reactive value is recomputed only when all of its progenitors have been updated. For instance, when the user's current position changes, the interpreter will first update both the `latitude` and the `longitude` reactive values before the `centerOn` method will be invoked anew.

Having illustrated how dependent reactive values are created implicitly by the interpreter in a reactive program, we now describe how to create new reactive values *ex nihilo*. For this, AmbientTalk/R introduces the `makeReactive` construct which creates a reactive value based on the object it is passed. In the code example given below, we define a `Coordinate` object[2] which represents a GPS location. In addition to its fields, `Coordinate` objects also define two methods, to wit `distanceTo` and `update`.

```
1   def Coordinate := isolate: {
2     def latitude := 0;
3     def longitude := 0;
4
5     def distanceTo(anotherCoordinate) {
6       /* Compute via the Haversine formula */
7     };
8
9     def @Mutator update(newLatitude, newLongitude) {
10      latitude := newLatitude;
11      longitude := newLongitude;
12    };
13  };
14
15  def GPS_Location := makeReactive(Coordinate.new());
16  GPS.addLocationObserver: { |lat, lng| GPS_Location.update(lat, lng) };
```

When passing an object to the `makeReactive` construct, a clear distinction should be made between accessor methods which only read the state encapsulated by the object (e.g. `distanceTo`) and mutator methods which can change the object's internal state (e.g. `update`). Therefore, all mutator methods must be explicitly tagged with an `@Mutator` annotation. This requirement stems from the fact that the semantics for invoking both kinds of methods on a reactive value differs significantly:

Accessor methods. When invoking an accessor method (or reading a field) on a reactive value, a dependent reactive value is created which depends on the receiver and additionally on any reactive values that were passed as arguments. Hence, if the reactive value is updated, these dependent computations will be performed anew.

Mutator methods. When invoking a mutator method (or writing a field), no dependency on the receiver is recorded. In other words, if none of the arguments

---

[2] The object is created by means of the `isolate:` AmbientTalk language construct. This simply constructs a special kind of object that has no surrounding lexical scope and thus can be easily copied over the network, instead of having it to pass by reference as is done for regular objects.

of the method invocation are reactive values, the method is simply performed once. If at least one reactive value was passed as an argument, a dependent reactive value is created which ensures that the mutator method is invoked anew whenever the reactive arguments change. However, changes to the receiver are simply disregarded. Furthermore, the interpreter ensures that whenever a mutator method has been invoked, all dependents of the receiver are notified that their progenitor has been updated.

This semantics is used in line 16 of the code example to register a location observer with the GPS device, which will be invoked whenever the user's position has to be updated. At this point in time, the mutator method `update` is invoked upon the reactive object `GPS_Location`. This mutator method is invoked once (since its arguments are ordinary numeric values), updating the coordinates to reflect the most recent sensor values. Afterwards, all reactive values which implicitly depend on `GPS_Location` will be notified that the location has changed. This may result for instance in an update of the user interface, such that the map is centered on the user's updated position. Note that mutator methods do not need to be atomic to guarantee correctness: the stratification explained earlier in this section of the dataflow graph constructed by the interpreter in combination with all updates that are scheduled in a single event loop according to this stratification prevent local concurrency control problems and ensure that the ordering of updates to reactive values mirrors the call graph of the program (which is critical when reactive updates trigger side effects).

3.1 Loosely-Coupled Distributed Reactive Programming

The reactive programming system described in the previous section only deals with events in a single, local event loop. In many cases, distributed application components are interested in events coming from other devices (and thus event loops) in the mobile ad hoc network. In this section, we introduce a language construct called *ambient behaviors* that allows the loosely-coupled propagation of events to reactive values hosted on different event loops by means of publish/subscribe. The transition from local reactive values to ambient behaviors needs some special consideration in order to uphold the ambient oriented programming characteristics mentioned in section 2. First of all, because of the dynamic nature of mobile ad hoc networks, one cannot assume a stable dataflow graph as is constructed on the local interpreter level, such as explained in the previous section. Instead, the dependencies between different distributed computations should be encoded in such a way that the ambient-oriented programming characteristics are upheld. When we rename behaviors to event producers and dependent computations to event consumers, this means that there should be a very loose coupling between event producers and event consumers. In classic publish/subscribe systems, event publishers do not have explicit knowledge about their subscribers and vice versa. In mobile ad hoc networks, the binding between consumers and producers must happen in the absence of any infrastructure, such as a centralized broker network. In this section, we describe a publish/subscribe system where event producers and consumers, denoting reactive application components, find each other in the mobile ad hoc network by means of *intensional descriptions* that are broadcasted using UDP to allow *decentralized and spontaneous discovery*. The difference with an extensional approach (e.g. a list of registered subscribers) is that one merely states the conditions that the properties of a producer or consumer must satisfy to establish a loosely-coupled binding between the two.

Ambient Behaviors. We will continue the ticket trading example introduced earlier. Recall that ticket vendors have a behavior that denotes their current location by means of GPS coordinates. What we actually want to achieve is to discover ambient behaviors made available by other devices that signal the events in which we are interested, in this example a behavior that represents the GPS coordinates of the location of the ticket vendor. Publishing such a behavior happens as follows, on the ticket vendor's device:

```
exportBehavior: GPS_Location as: TicketVendorLocation
 to: { |buyer| buyer.interestedIn == "Rock␣Werchter" };
```

By exporting this behavior, applications running on other devices can subscribe themselves on the events that are signaled by this behavior. This happens as follows:

```
def vendorLocation := ambientBehavior: TicketVendorLocation
  where: { def interestedIn := "Rock␣Werchter" } @One;
```

The `ambientBehavior:` construct is used to create a local reactive value which is bound to one or more behaviors exported by other event loops. In the example given above, the `@One` annotation is used to indicate that `vendorLocation` should denote the location of a single ticket vendor, rather than a collection of vendor locations. Once an exported behavior can be found that matches the intensional descriptions given by the programmer (which can be either topic-based or content-based), the exported behavior will transparently start propagating update events to `vendorLocation`. Note that multiple applications could be subscribed to the `TicketVendorLocation` topic. The group communication required to notify all these subscribers is internally handled by the M2MI framework [1]. These events trigger an update in the reactive value which may result in further reactive computation in its own event loop. For instance, the `vendorLocation` could be used to update the location of the ticket vendor on the map in the graphical user interface:

```
GUI.showLocationOnMap(vendorLocation);
```

The point here is that while the ticket vendor roams the environment and his GPS device signals updates to all subscribed behaviors, the maps on the user interfaces of the (reachable) interested parties are transparently updated with the new locations without resorting to callbacks. Furthermore, if an ambient behavior is disconnected from the exported behavior it was bound to, the ambient behavior will attempt to match with another exported behavior in the ad hoc network. Finally, since ambient behaviors are treated as regular behaviors by the interpreter, they can be used in local reactive code as if they were behaviors that depend solely on local changes. On the other hand, applications that export the GPS_Location do not have explicit knowledge to which event consumers they propagate events, nor do they keep an explicit list of event consumers. This loose coupling between event producers and consumers is necessary to reflect the dynamic nature of mobile ad hoc networks and to support roaming of devices.

Reactive Queries in Mobile Ad Hoc Networks. The mechanism described above can only be used if there are ambient behaviors published in the network. Otherwise, one has to obtain ambient behaviors by querying the network for relevant information oneself. For this the programmer is provided with an abstraction that allows creating a behavior that autonomously queries the network to update itself. This abstraction is an integration of ambient references (which allow querying the network by sending messages) with the reactive programming language facilities of AmbientTalk/R (which allow reacting to and processing events without inversion of control). The example below shows the creation of a behavior by querying the network using a reactive ambient reference.

```
def werchterVendors :=
  ambient: TicketVendor where: { |tv| tv.event == "Rock␣Werchter" };

def locations := werchterVendors<-getLocation()@Refresh(5.seconds);
```

Note that the getLocation() message is annotated with @Refresh, which implies that the result of the message is accumulated in a reactive value. Hence, the locations variable contains a reactive value which initially denotes an empty array. The @Refresh annotation implies that the annotated getLocation message is sent every 5 seconds to all nearby ticket vendors offering a ticket for Rock Werchter[3]. The resulting locations behavior is updated every five seconds and contains an array of all responses from the ticket vendors in range. Since locations is a behavior, it can be passed on to other functions or methods as a normal value, as done below to update the map in the user interface of the user with *all* locations:

```
locations.each: { |coordinates| GUI.showLocationOnMap(coordinates) };
```

---

[3] In addition to the @Refresh annotation, one can add annotations to the message that specify the message sending semantics. By varying these annotations, one can decide to send the message to all objects in range like in the example, which will result in a changing array of results, or send the message to just one of the objects in range, resulting in a behavior containing a single value.

Note that by making use of a reactive query, the programmer does not have to explicitly poll the environment in a loop any more.

To conclude, integrating ambient references with reactive programming allows the results of queries over the network to be collected into a behavior that is automatically synchronized with the environment. Ambient references provide an abstraction over the events of appearance and disappearance of services in the network, while the reactive programming system provides an abstraction over the events generated by the reception of results of asynchronous queries. Reactive queries can be regarded as the dual language construct of ambient behaviors, offering pull-based instead of push-based communication.

4   The Ticket Trader Application

In previous sections, we have used the dynamic discovery of ticket vendors and their location as a running example to explain the various features of AmbientTalk/R and ambient behaviors. This section presents a slightly more elaborate version of the application, which matches ticket vendors with prospective clients. In publish/subscribe terminology, ticket vendors *publish* the offers for tickets they are willing to sell, while their prospective clients *subscribe* to events concerning tickets being offered in their vicinity. Clients are able to identify which ticket offers are relevant to them by specifying which events they want to attend, the price they are willing to pay for the ticket and the maximal allowed distance between themselves and the ticket vendor. The latter filter requires that both vendors and clients have access to a GPS device, such that their GPS coordinates can be used to compute the distance.

Note that different ticket vendors can offer tickets for the same event (possibly for a different price) and that different clients can be interested in the same ticket. Furthermore, both vendors and clients roam the environment, can cancel their offers, change the price of their offers, and announce new offers. The different instances of the application on the different devices should all respond to these changes.

Before turning our attention to the implementation of both parties in the system, we will show the implementation of a very simple object representing a ticket offer:

```
def TicketOffer := isolate: {
  def eventName := nil;
  def price    := 0;
  def location := nil;

  // Constructor
  def init(anEventName, aPrice) {
    eventName := anEventName;
    price     := aPrice;
  };
};
```

The object contains three slots: the event the ticket provides access to, the price at which it is currently being offered and the vendor's current location. During the course of the application, the latter two values may change: the vendor may roam and decide to adjust the price at which the ticket is being offered. Typically, the price can be reduced if interest is low or if the event is about to start.

To determine the vendor's current position, we reuse the `GPS_location` abstraction, which was defined previously as follows:

```
def GPS_Location := makeReactive(Coordinate.new());
GPS.addLocationObserver: { |lat, lng| GPS_Location.update(lat, lng) };
```

The following code excerpt defines an AmbientTalk type (which corresponds to a Java interface type) that will be used as the topic under which ticket offers are published.

```
deftype TicketOfferT;
```

Having described the necessary abstractions, we can now describe how ticket offers are published by the vendor:

```
1   def TicketVendor := object: {
2     def offeredTickets := HashMap.new();
3
4     // Offer a new ticket.
5     def offerTicket(eventName, price) {
6       def ticketOffer := makeReactive(TicketOffer.new(eventName, price));
7       ticketOffer.location := GPS_Location;
8       offeredTickets.put(eventName, ticketOffer);
9       exportBehavior: ticketOffer as: TicketOfferT;
10    };
11
12    // Change the price of a ticket on offer.
13    def setTicketPrice(eventName, newPrice) {
14      (offeredTickets.get(eventName)).price := newPrice;
15    };
16  };
```

Tickets are offered to all nearby prospective clients by invoking the `offerTicket` method. In it, a reactive `TicketOffer` object is created (line 6). Because the object is reactive, the vendor is guaranteed that whenever the offer changes, these changes will be automatically propagated to all prospective clients. One way in which the offer might change is if the location of the vendor changes. Note that in line 7, the location associated with the offer is set to the vendor's `GPS_Location`. Due to the fact that `GPS_Location` is a reactive value and due to the semantics of mutating reactive values (see section 3), the `location` field of the `ticketOffer` will be set anew whenever the `GPS_Location` is updated. In turn, this update will be propagated to reactive values which depend on `ticketOffer`.

In this particular case, this includes all prospective clients that are currently in range. The fact that these prospective clients can detect the offer, stems from the fact that it is published using the `exportBehavior:as:` construct in line 9.

Additionally, vendors keep track of the various events for which they offer tickets in the `offeredTickets` map. This map is used to update the price at which tickets are being offered. The `setTicketPrice` method uses the mapping to find a particular reactive ticket offer, in order to update its price. Due to the semantics of mutating reactive values, setting the price causes an update to be propagated to all prospective clients in reach.

The following code excerpt shows the `findOffers` function, which permits prospective clients to detect ticket offers that have been exported by nearby vendors by means of the `ambientBehavior:` construct.

```
1   def findOffers(event, maximumPrice, maximumDistance) {
2     // Subscribe to TicketOffers
3     def allNearbyOffers := ambientBehavior: TicketOfferT @All;
4
5     // Filter out interesting TicketOffers
6     allNearbyOffers.filter: { |offer|
7       (offer.eventName == event).and: {
8         (offer.price <= maximumPrice).and: {
9           GPS_Location.distanceTo(offer.location) <= maximumDistance }}};
10  };
11
12  def werchterTicketVendors := findOffers("Rock␣Werchter", 200, 500);
13  gui.updateWithOffers(werchterTicketVendors)
```

The ambient behavior `allNearbyOffers` will be bound to a collection that contains all ticket offers made by nearby vendors. This semantics is due to the fact that the `@All` annotation is used, rather than the `@One` annotation that was showcased earlier. In other words, `allNearbyOffers` is a reactive value denoting an array of exported ticket offers. This size of this array evolves as ticket vendors go in and out of range.

The reactive collection `allNearbyOffers` is subsequently filtered to produce a selection of ticket offers that are relevant to the client (lines 6-9). An offer is deemed relevant if it provides access to the correct event, its price does not exceed the maximum set by the client and if the distance to the client's current location does not exceed a given maximum. Since `allNearbyOffers` is an ambient behavior, the invocation of its `filter:` method (an accessor method) creates a dependent reactive value, which is the return value of the function. This reactive value is updated when vendors go in and out of range, but also if one of the previously detected offers change (i.e. the vendor has moved or the price has been updated). Furthermore, it is important to note that the condition to determine whether an offer is relevant also depends on the location of the prospective client. In line 9, the vendor's location is compared to the current location of the client. This implies that an offer can suddenly become relevant as the client is roaming.

In the code snippet, the `findOffers` function is called to find ticket offers to attend Rock Werchter, which cost less than 200 euro and whose vendor is less than 500 meters away. The resulting collection is passed as an argument to the `updateWithOffers` method of the user interface. This method expects an array of ticket offers (which all contain their last location) and draws them on the map. Since the `werchterTicketVendors` collection is a reactive value, this method will be invoked anew whenever the collection is updated.

Evaluation. Notice that ticket vendors and their prospective clients are loosely coupled to one another. They discover one another by means of a topic-based publish/subscribe architecture (which uses a common Java interface to denote the type of events that are exchanged). Parties that are disconnected from each other (e.g. by network partitioning of the mobile ad hoc network) are automatically discarded while newly connected parties dynamically discover each other and start exchanging events.

Furthermore, the publication of new events is integrated closely with the imperative object-oriented programming style of the host language. Provided that mutator methods are properly identified, any object can be used to create a reactive value. Once such a reactive value has been published, it suffices to write one of the object's fields or invoke one of its mutator methods to implicitly emit events notifying all reachable subscribers of the change.

Finally, the subscriber can trivially indicate which events it is interested in receiving (by means of a topic-based subscription) and can handle incoming events without resorting to a complex network of event handlers. In the ticket trader example, two sources of events are considered, to wit `allNearbyOffers` and `GPS_Location`. Changes to the former are the result of the appearance and disappearance of vendors (which result in the addition and removal of certain offers) as well as updates to the offers themselves (i.e. price and/or location updates). Changes to the latter are the result of roaming clients, and affect the number of offers reported to the user as they affect the distance between the vendor and the prospective client. The interplay between these different event sources are handled implicitly by the AmbientTalk/R interpreter.

5   Limitations and Future Work

As a first issue, it is clear that the reactive programming system of AmbientTalk/R comes with an overhead in terms of computational resources compared to the plain AmbientTalk interpreter. More (dataflow) events are scheduled in the different event loops of an application and more memory is being consumed to keep track of the different dataflow dependencies in a local application. Although in the near future we will investigate to which extent this is the case, we also observe that, with respect to pure processing power, AmbientTalk and AmbientTalk/R are targeted towards highly networked applications where the network will be the performance bottleneck instead of the interpreter.

Some of the limitations stem directly from the hardware characteristics of mobile ad hoc networks. Because of both the unreliability of the connections between the different devices and the unpredictable delays on the arrival of messages at remote parties, our system cannot provide real-time guarantees on the processing and reacting to events. Furthermore, when a message is sent from one device before a different message is sent from another device, the underlying AmbientTalk virtual machines do not guarantee that these messages will arrive at their destination in that same order. Providing such guarantees would involve keeping a global clock over all the distributed virtual machines (an assumption that is for example made in the GEM event monitoring language [25]) to time-stamp events, which is impractical in this setting. The programmer has to take this into consideration if causality between events has to be inferred. However, our system focuses on applications that work with a human time scale (e.g. seconds, minutes), so slightly drifting distributed clocks are tolerable.

Currently, there is no way for an event consumer to tell its event producer to limit the events that it wants to receive: an ambient behavior publication or subscription can only be cancelled. Afterwards, the subscription can be re-established. We have to investigate whether this can lead to network congestion or performance issues on the device that acts as event consumer. We might look for inspiration in some of the systems mentioned in section 6 which incorporate load balancing.

Finally, the naming and discovery of services happens via Java interfaces. We make the underlying assumption that the name of such Java interfaces represents a unique service and is known by all participating services. This discovery mechanism also does not take versioning into account explicitly. For example, if the `TicketVendor` from the example in section 2.1 is updated, older clients may discover the updated service, and clients that want to use only the updated service may still discover older versions. Clients and services are thus themselves responsible to check versioning constraints.

6   Related Work

Solar [26] is a graph-based abstraction for collecting, aggregating and disseminating context information targeting mobile, pervasive applications. The abstraction models context information as events, which are produced by *sources*, flow through a directed acyclic graph of event-processing *operators*, and are delivered to subscribing applications. Applications describe their desired event stream as a tree of operators that aggregate low-level context information published by existing sources into the high-level context information needed by the application. The *operator graph* is thus the dynamic combination of all applications' subscription trees. Solar assumes centralized, reliable components to process the subscription requests from applications (which may dynamically join and leave the network) and deploys operators onto appropriate nodes as necessary. These centralized components render Solar unsuitable for mobile ad hoc network applications.

Flask [27] is a functional reactive programming language embedded in Haskell that uses Haskell as a meta-language to generate node-level code fragments in a subset of Haskell called Red. Red is intended to run on resource-constrained sensor nodes and is stripped from language features such as closures and recursive data types to eliminate arbitrary allocation. Just like our approach, Flask constructs a distributed dataflow graph, but in this case at compile-time instead of run-time using the Haskell meta-language, which causes Red code fragments to be deployed on the distributed nodes. To cope with a dynamically changing network topology in mobile ad hoc networks we require the nodes to be deployed at runtime instead of at compile-time.

Opis [28] is a functional reactive extension to Objective Caml for developing event-based distributed systems. An Opis protocol description consists of a reactive function (called event function) describing the behavior of a distributed system node. Opis is very related to our approach in the sense that it both applies reactive programming as a paradigm to implement event-based distributed applications and uses a peer-to-peer overlay protocol to disseminate the events between distributed application components. However, Opis focuses on wide-area networks where nodes are fixed and hence does not support roaming.

SpatialViews [29] is an extension to Java designed to query wireless sensor networks. SpatialViews allows the specification of virtual networks of which the nodes are discovered dynamically with user-specified (physical) location and time constraints and execute mobile code that constitutes to the global query. SpatialViews might as well be a suitable building block to implement the language constructs presented in this paper and the location and time constraints that can be placed on nodes can enhance these constructs with similar features.

A similar idea exists in Location-based Publish/Subscribe (LPS) [30] in which publishers and subscribers are not only bound by means of a topic-based or content-based subscription, but also by taking into account external context such as the physical location of the different parties. However, such external context is provided in LPS by centralized infrastructure, whereas our approach does not assume any infrastructure. The ticket trader example application used in section 4 is strongly expired by the examples used to illustrate LPS.

Finally, the language constructs proposed in this paper are integrated in a distributed, imperative object-oriented scripting language. There exist dedicated languages for event processing, such as Aurora [31]. Aurora is a centralized stream processor that uses the popular *boxes* and *arrows* paradigm found in most process flow and workflow systems. Tuples flow through a loop-free, directed graph of processing operators (i.e., boxes) which the programmer has to specify using a graphical user interface. Aurora was afterwards extended to Aurora* and Medusa, which make decentralized event processing possible and additionally allow high level load balancing and load shedding policies to be expressed using specialized middleware. These systems however, focus on internet-scale application running in a reliable network.

7   Conclusion

We have presented a number of language constructs that reconcile the loose coupling of a distributed publish/subscribe architecture and the elegant event processing of a reactive programming language, AmbientTalk/R. Concretely, the dataflow graphs constructed by the AmbientTalk/R interpreter to keep track of dataflow dependencies can now be seamlessly distributed by means of ambient behaviors, which is a new language construct added to the language. The distributed dataflow dependencies are implemented on top of a decentralized publish/subscribe architecture to achieve a very loose coupling between the dependents (event consumers) and their progenitors (event producers). Hence, event producers can be dynamically replaced at run-time when they become unreachable due to network partitions. By adopting the reactive programming paradigm, the reception of events can be represented as (external) updates to a reactive value. Such updates are propagated implicitly to all relevant parts of the application. Hence, it is possible to react trivially to external events without the inversion of control that would result from having to resort to the use of explicit callbacks.

References

1. Kaminsky, A., Bischof, H.P.: Many-to-many invocation: a new object oriented paradigm for ad hoc collaborative systems. In: OOPSLA '02: Companion of the 17th annual ACM SIGPLAN conference on Object-oriented programming, systems, languages, and applications, pp. 72–73. ACM, New York (2002)
2. Meier, R., Cahill, V.: Steam: Event-based middleware for wireless ad hoc networks. In: ICDCSW '02: 22nd International Conference on Distributed Computing Systems, Washington, DC, USA, pp. 639–644. IEEE Computer Society, Los Alamitos (2002)
3. Murphy, A., Picco, G., Roman, G.C.: Lime: A middleware for physical and logical mobility. In: Proceedings of the The 21st International Conference on Distributed Computing Systems, pp. 524–536. IEEE Computer Society, Los Alamitos (2001)
4. Grimm, R.: One world: Experiences with a pervasive computing architecture. IEEE Pervasive Computing 3(3), 22–30 (2004)
5. Carzaniga, A., Rosenblum, D.S., Wolf, A.L.: Achieving scalability and expressiveness in an internet-scale event notification service. In: PODC '00: Proceedings of the nineteenth annual ACM symposium on Principles of distributed computing, pp. 219–227. ACM Press, New York (2000)
6. Cugola, G., Nitto, E.D., Fuggetta, A.: The jedi event-based infrastructure and its application to the development of the opss wfms. IEEE Trans. Softw. Eng. 27(9), 827–850 (2001)
7. Meier, R., Cahill, V.: Taxonomy of distributed event-based programming systems. In: ICDCSW '02: 22nd International Conference on Distributed Computing Systems, Washington, DC, USA, pp. 585–588. IEEE Computer Society, Los Alamitos (2002)
8. Chin, B., Millstein, T.: Responders: Language support for interactive applications. In: Thomas, D. (ed.) ECOOP 2006. LNCS, vol. 4067, pp. 255–278. Springer, Heidelberg (2006)

9. Haller, P., Odersky, M.: Event-based programming without inversion of control. In: Lightfoot, D.E., Szyperski, C. (eds.) JMLC 2006. LNCS, vol. 4228, pp. 4–22. Springer, Heidelberg (2006)

10. Adya, A., Howell, J., Theimer, M., Bolosky, W.J., Douceur, J.R.: Cooperative task management without manual stack management. In: USENIX Annual Technical Conference, pp. 289–302. USENIX Association, Berkeley (2002)

11. Verissimo, P., Casimiro, A.: Event-driven support of real-time sentient objects. In: 8th IEEE International Workshop on Object-Oriented Real-Time Dependable Systems, Guadalajara, Mexico (January 2003)

12. Levis, P., Culler, D.: Mate: A tiny virtual machine for sensor networks. In: International Conference on Architectural Support for Programming Languages and Operating Systems, San Jose, CA, USA (October 2002)

13. Kasten, O., Römer, K.: Beyond event handlers: programming wireless sensors with attributed state machines. In: IPSN '05: 4th international symposium on Information processing in sensor networks, Piscataway, NJ, USA. IEEE Press, Los Alamitos (2005)

14. Dedecker, J., Van Cutsem, T., Mostinckx, S., D'Hondt, T., De Meuter, W.: Ambient-Oriented Programming. In: OOPSLA '05: Companion of the 20th annual ACM SIGPLAN conference on Object-oriented programming, systems, languages, and applications. ACM Press, New York (2005)

15. Van Cutsem, T., Mostinckx, S., Gonzalez Boix, E., Dedecker, J., De Meuter, W.: Ambienttalk: object-oriented event-driven programming in mobile ad hoc networks. In: Proceedings of the XXVI International Conference of the Chilean Computer Science Society (SCCC 2007), pp. 3–12. IEEE Computer Society, Los Alamitos (2007)

16. Van Cutsem, T., Mostinckx, S., De Meuter, W.: Linguistic symbiosis between event loop actors and threads. Computer Languages Systems & Structures 35(1) (2008)

17. Miller, M., Tribble, E.D., Shapiro, J.: Concurrency among strangers: Programming in E as plan coordination. In: De Nicola, R., Sangiorgi, D. (eds.) TGC 2005. LNCS, vol. 3705, pp. 195–229. Springer, Heidelberg (2005)

18. Van Cutsem, T.: Ambient References: Object Designation in Mobile Ad Hoc Networks. PhD thesis, Vrije Universiteit Brussel, Software Languages Lab (May 2008)

19. Elliott, C., Hudak, P.: Functional reactive animation. In: ACM SIGPLAN International Conf. on Functional Programming, vol. 32(8), pp. 263–273 (1997)

20. Wan, Z., Taha, W., Hudak, P.: Real-time FRP. In: International Conference on Functional Programming, ICFP'01 (2001)

21. Peterson, J., Hudak, P., Elliott, C.: Lambda in motion: Controlling robots with haskell. In: Gupta, G. (ed.) PADL 1999. LNCS, vol. 1551, p. 91. Springer, Heidelberg (1999)

22. Courtney, A.: Frappé: Functional reactive programming in Java. In: Third International Symposium on Pratical Aspects of Declarative Languages (March 2001)

23. Cooper, G.H., Krishnamurthi, S.: Embedding dynamic dataflow in a call-by-value language. In: Sestoft, P. (ed.) ESOP 2006. LNCS, vol. 3924, pp. 294–308. Springer, Heidelberg (2006)

24. Johnston, W.M., Hanna, J.R.P., Millar, R.J.: Advances in dataflow programming languages. ACM Comput. Surv. 36(1), 1–34 (2004)

25. Mansouri-samani, M., Sloman, M.: Gem: A generalized event monitoring language for distributed systems. IEE/IOP/BCS Distributed Systems Engineering Journal 4, 96–108 (1997)

26. Chen, G., Kotz, D.: Context aggregation and dissemination in ubiquitous computing systems. In: WMCSA '02: Fourth IEEE Workshop on Mobile Computing Systems and Applications, Washington, DC, USA. IEEE Computer Society, Los Alamitos (2002)
27. Mainland, G., Morrisett, G., Welsh, M.: Flask: staged functional programming for sensor networks. In: 13th ACM SIGPLAN international conference on Functional programming, pp. 335–346. ACM, New York (2008)
28. Dagand, P.E., Kostić, D., Kuncak, V.: Opis: reliable distributed systems in ocaml. In: TLDI '09: Proceedings of the 4th international workshop on Types in language design and implementation, pp. 65–78. ACM, New York (2009)
29. Ni, Y., Kremer, U., Stere, A., Iftode, L.: Programming ad-hoc networks of mobile and resource-constrained devices. In: ACM SIGPLAN conf. on Programming language design and implementation, pp. 249–260. ACM, New York (2005)
30. Eugster, P.T., Garbinato, B., Holzer, A.: Location-based publish/subscribe. In: NCA '05: Proceedings of the Fourth IEEE International Symposium on Network Computing and Applications, Washington, DC, USA, pp. 279–282. IEEE Computer Society, Los Alamitos (2005)
31. Cherniack, M., Balakrishnan, H., Balazinska, M., Carney, D., Çetintemel, U., Xing, Y., Zdonik, S.: Scalable distributed stream processing. In: CIDR (2003)

Understanding the Impact of Collection Contracts on Design

Stephen Nelson, David J. Pearce, and James Noble

Victoria University of Wellington
Wellington, New Zealand
{stephen,djp,kjx}@ecs.vuw.ac.nz

Abstract. Java provides a specification for a user-defined general purpose equivalence operator for objects, but collections such as Set have more stringent requirements. This inconsistency breaks polymorphism: programmers must take care to follow Set's contract rather than the more general Object contract if their object could enter a Set. We have dynamically profiled 30 Java applications to better understand the way programmers design their objects, to determine whether they program with collections in mind. Our results indicate that objects which enter collections behave very differently to objects which do not. Our findings should help developers understand the impact of design choices they make, and guide future language designers when adding support for collections and/or equality.

1 Introduction

Designing good software is hard. Designing good programming languages is harder still. Modern programming languages have evolved to include numerous high-level constructs, and to provide vast libraries of reusable code. Inheritance, polymorphism, collections and first-class regular expressions are just a few examples. Many of these constructs have subtle and important effects on the way software is designed.

In this paper we consider the effect of one particular feature of Java on program design. Java's Object class provides a specification for defining general purpose object equality. However, Java Collections such as Set and Map require stronger contracts on the implementation of object equality than the Object specification provides.

This paper addresses the question, *how do programmers satisfy equality contracts?* We examine the behaviour of objects in running Java programs, comparing objects in different Collections and outside Collections to identify differences in their design. In particular, we compare objects which enter equality collections such as Set, non-equality collections such as ArrayList, and objects which do not enter a collection at all.

The contributions of this paper are:

1. A set of object characterisations, based on equality and state mutability, which can be measured at runtime.
2. Design and implementation a runtime profiler, called *#Profiler*, that observes the way objects behave when they are and are not in collections. #Profiler employs AspectJ to intercept field reads/writes, constructors and calls to collections.

J. Vitek (Ed.): TOOLS 2010, LNCS 6141, pp. 61–78, 2010.

3. Results from examining 30 real-world Java programs using *#Profiler*. Our results indicate:
   - Objects which do not enter collections do not change their equality;
   - Objects which enter non-equality collections are much more likely than other objects to change their internal state;
   - Objects which enter equality collections are much less likely to change internal state than objects which enter other collections;
   - Objects which enter equality collections and do change their state are no more likely to change their equality than objects which enter non-equality collections.

The rest of this paper is organised as follows: Section 2 discusses various contracts imposed on equality implementations by Java, particularly those imposed by Collections, and outlines our approach to categorising objects according to the way they address these contracts; Section 3 discusses how the object categorisations are measured with our profiling tool, #Profiler; Section 4 presents our experimental results looking at the behaviour of objects across 30 open source Java applications; Section 5 covers related work and, we summarise our findings in the conclusion. An extended version of this paper is available as a technical report [1].

2   Equality for Collections

Every object is inherently distinguishable by its location in memory and many languages, like Java, expose this using an equivalence operator. However, it can be useful for objects to define their own equivalence relation for comparing internal state. In addition to reference comparisons, Java provides equals(..) — a method defined on the root of the class hierarchy which subclasses can override to implement their own equivalence relations. The documentation provided for this method states that it must be an equivalence relation, but also that it is consistent — that is, it will return the same result for multiple calls so long as the information it uses does not change [2].

Java also provides the Java Collections API, a group of collections for programmers to use. Almost all of these collections are capable of storing Objects directly, without any additional type information, yet several require contracts on equals() which are stronger than the requirements imposed by Object on the equals method. For example, documentation for java.util.Set states:

> *"Note: great care must be exercised if mutable objects are used as set elements. The behavior of a set is not specified if the value of an object is changed in a manner that affects equals comparisons while the object is an element in the set. A special case of this prohibition is that it is not permissible for a set to contain itself as an element."* [2]

As there is no type constraint to prevent mutable objects from entering a Set, programmers must take care that they obey this contract or they may encounter subtle bugs in their programs. This paper attempts to discover how much programmers use mutable objects in collections and, if they do, how they avoid violating the additional constraints that some collections impose. We begin by discussing the collections contracts in more detail, then introduce two categorisations for objects based on equality and state, respectively. We conclude this section by discussing a unified categorisation for objects based on both equality and state which is used for the remainder of the paper.

2.1 Collection Contracts

The Java Collections API provides four main interfaces: List, Set, Map and Queue. There are also implementations provided and, in some cases, there are several each with different properties.

The Set interface imposes a particularly strict contract on the objects it contains: they cannot change while they are in the collection. Map requires the same of key objects, but not of value objects. Lists do not have additional requirements on the objects they contain, but they also have a related note of caution:

> *"Note: While it is permissible for lists to contain themselves as elements, extreme caution is advised: the equals and hashCode methods are no longer well defined on such a list."* [2]

This aside is because Lists, unlike Queues, implement Java's equals() and hashcode() methods which depend on the list's contents, recursively calling equals or hashcode on each member. While they do not directly impose a contract on their members, programmers must be aware that if the list is stored in another collection which does impose a contract it will transitively apply to the list's contents.

In the rest of this paper we will refer to objects entering *equality* and *non-equality* collections. Equality collections require that the equality of objects does not change while they are in the collection. These include subclasses of Set, and the key-sets of Map and HashTable subclasses. Non-equality collections are Lists, Queues, and the value-sets of Maps and HashTables.

2.2 Measuring Changes to Equality

An object following the contract for equality outlined by Object may change its equality at any point in its existence. If it is in a Collection, however, this could be an error. To determine which strategies programmers use to avoid these errors, we track objects throughout their lifetime to determine when they do change. We have identified three measurable stages in the life-cycle of an object which we can use to classify objects based on when they change their equality:

Construction: When an object is created the constructor is invoked to initialise the object. Even otherwise immutable objects will assign to fields in this phase, as Java allows objects to write to final fields during the constructor; so the first stage we consider ranges from the beginning to the end of the constructor.

Initialisation: After an object is created and the constructor has run, there may still be additional initialisation performed on the object which could change its equality. So long as this happens before the object enters a collection it will not violate any equality

Type of Object	Constructor	Initialisation	Post-Collection
Identity as Equality			
Initialised Equality	x		
Late-initialised Equality	x	x	
Reindexing	x	x	x

Fig. 1. Four types of objects distinguished by their different behaviours in various parts of their life-cycle. x denotes possible changes to equality during that phase.

contracts, so our second phase is from the end of the constructor until the object first enters a collection. Some objects will never enter a collection and thus never leave the 'initialisation' phase.

Post-Collection: After an object has entered a collection we consider it to be fully initialised; any further changes to its hash code could violate the internal consistency of the collection. A programmer would have to consider the implications of changing an object which is in, or could still be in a collection. The post-collection phase ends when the object is garbage collected or the program terminates.

These three measurable phases of an object's life-cycle lead to the following four categorisations of objects based on their changes to equality, which are also presented in Figure 1:

- **Identity as Equality:** objects in this category do not define a hash code method. They rely on reference equality for participation in equality-based collections.
- **Initialised Equality:** these objects define a hash code, but it does not change after the constructor has completed.
- **Late-initialised Equality:** late initialisation objects are distinguished by changes to their hash code after the constructor has completed but before entering a collection. They may also change their hash code during the constructor.
- **Reindexing:** finally, objects which change their hash code after entering a collection are called reindexing objects. Examples of reindexing objects are: objects which leave a hash-based collection, change their hash code, then re-enter a collection; and, objects stored in collections which do not use equality and change at will. Potentially, there are also objects which violate collection constraints and, hence, are erroneous.

These categories of objects are names for distinguishable groups of objects based on the observation points we have defined. Unless there is a reason to distinguish them, we will group these categories based on whether they change their equality after the constructor. *Identity as Equality* and *Initialised Equality* are referred to as *Immutable Equality* objects. *Late-initialised Equality* and *Reindexing* are referred to as *Mutable Equality* objects.

2.3   Measuring Changes to State

Objects are free to define their equality based on any or all of their reachable state, so it is interesting to see whether objects change state that is not used by equality when they are in collections. This will give us further insight into the techniques programmers use to satisfy the Collection contracts by showing whether the decision to make an object's equality mutable is made with the implementation of the object in mind.

- **Immutable State.** Objects do not change their state after the constructor ends. This may be because it does not have any state, or all of its state is final, or there are no accessor methods for changing state, but it could also be coincidental — none of the state happened to change.
- **Mutable State.** Objects can be observed to change state after the constructor. This could be any field of that object or another object which is reachable from fields of the object.

2.4   Classifying Objects

State and Equality measurements together will give us the four broad categories of objects listed below:

		Equality	
		Immutable	Mutable
State	Immutable	Immutable	Mutable Equality
	Mutable	Mutable State	Fully Mutable

- **Immutable** is by far the simplest approach to ensuring the collection contracts are preserved. In this case, the programmer simply ensures that the state of any object placed into an equality-dependent collection never changes during its lifetime.
- **Mutable State** requires that an object's equality never changes after the constructor, but allows other state to change. This is simple to implement if the object uses *Identity as Equality*, but more challenging to maintain if the object uses *Initialised Equality*: one strategy would be to use immutable objects to determine equality and annotate the fields containing them as final.
- **Mutable Equality** would occur if the object changed its equality but not its state. This cannot occur because the equality is based on state.
- **Fully Mutable** objects change their state and their equality after the constructor. These objects must still obey collection contracts, so this category includes *Late-initialised Equality* and *Reindexing* objects, both of which satisfy the contracts for equality collections, though each requires more care on the behalf of the programmer than objects with immutable equality.

The collections library itself provides examples of each of the three valid categories: `Sets`, `Lists` and `Maps` are Fully Mutable, while `Queues` are typically Mutable State objects. With appropriate care, `Collections.unmodifiableSet()` can provide an Immutable set.

In this paper, we are interested in exploring how these strategies are used in practice. We have implemented a profiling system designed to examine the way in which real programs operate and, hence, give insight into this issue. The next section discusses the profiling system and its implementation.

3   #Profiler

Detecting direct changes to object equality at runtime is difficult. Equality is inherently a binary operator, so changes to the equality of an object can only be detected by invoking the equals() method with another object which was previously equal. Detecting that equality has not changed would require comparing with all other objects, or knowing all possible execution paths and reachable objects, which are not feasible for a runtime profiler.

Instead of using the equals() method to detect changes to equality, we use hashCode() as a proxy. The hashCode() method is a unary operator which can be called without reference to other objects. This is a compromise because Java does not enforce any relationship between hashCode() and equals(). Java's documentation for developers does however specify that if two objects are equal then they must have the same hash code:

> "If two objects are equal according to the equals(Object) method, then calling the hashCode method on each of the two objects must produce the same integer result."[2]

That is, if the hash code of a correctly implemented object changes then the equality of that object to other objects has changed also. There are tools available to developers to ensure that they do this correctly [3].

Even if it is correctly implemented, the hash code is not a perfect proxy for equality. It is possible that a change to an object will cause its equality to change but not affect its hash code. However, this is unlikely in practice because good hash code methods are designed to avoid this kind of collision. Thus, hash code serves as a good lower-bound measure of equality changes.

3.1   Detecting Changes to Hash Code

Our strategy for detecting changes to an object's hash code has two parts; computing and recording the previous value, and tracking changes to objects which could cause the hash code to change. First, we compute the object's hash code. We track all method calls during this invocation, and record the objects on which methods have been invoked. This gives us a set of dependencies for computing the object's hash code. Once the hashCode() method completes we record the value returned.

Detecting changes requires calling the hashCode() method again to see whether the returned value has changed. We track all field and array writes, and when they occur we re-compute the hash code of each object which depends on the object which contains the field or array. If the hash code has changed we record the change, and if re-evaluating hashCode() invokes methods on objects which haven't already been encountered by that object we register the objects as dependents.

3.2   Detecting Changes to State

In addition to tracking changes to hash code, we also track changes to objects' fields and arrays. Tracking changes to an object's hash code requires that we monitor changes to fields and arrays, so we mark objects whose fields and arrays change after their constructors have completed. Classes for which all instances do not change are recorded as having immutable state. The detected immutability is not deep immutability, which would require traversing all reachable objects (which is beyond the scope of our profiler); a class marked as immutable state is simply shallow-immutable for the set of instances and the run of the program that we encountered.

As a consequence, it is possible that *Mutable Equality* objects will be incorrectly detected. That is, objects which appear to change their equality but not their state. This is because a change to an object's deep state may occur without triggering the profiler's mutability detection. We detect and report this when it occurs.

3.3   Profiler Implementation

Our profiler is implemented using the AspectJ load-time weaver to add code around method calls, field accesses, and array accesses. In addition, we have implemented replacement classes for common Java collections which are backed by the standard implementations, but record more information than would be possible using woven versions of the standard collections.

AspectJ is not able to add code to the standard libraries, so changes that occur within the standard libraries are not recorded (except in the case of collections, which we replace with our own implementations), but standard library objects are still observable when used in user code. For this reason we provide results both including and without standard library classes. We are also unable to profile certain applications which use their own class loaders (like Eclipse) or applications which are close to the limit on method size: AspectJ does not support breaking up methods to avoid overflowing method size limit, and as our profiler adds a lot of tracking code, this can result in invalid class files.

4   Results

To test our hypotheses we ran our profiler on a sample of applications from the Qualitas Corpus developed at Auckland University, NZ [4]. The Qualitas Corpus brings together a large number of open source Java applications to aid empirical research on Java. However, as the corpus was designed primarily for static analysis, not all of the applications could be profiled. Some were libraries or platforms which could not run independently, while others could not be profiled due to limitations in the profiler (Section 3.3). Of the 100 projects in the Qualitas Corpus, we chose a sample population of 30 which could be profiled relatively easily. These included compilers, command-line utilities, graphical tools, sample applications for libraries, and test suites. The complete list of applications profiled, with a short description of each, is presented in Figure 2.

4.1   Experimental Method

Each Java program was run within a standard Java HotSpot(TM) Server VM (build 1.5.0_15-b04, mixed mode) on an Intel machine running NetBSD 5.0_RC2. The programs were loaded using AspectJ's class-loader which weaves our profiler code written

Application	Synopsis
ant	Ant is a Java build system. Benchmarked building ant, included javac.
antlr	Antlr is a compiler-generator. Tested compiling Java grammar.
aoi	Art of Illusion, a 3D editor with raytracer. Built a simple model and rendered it.
columba	Java mail client. Connected to an imap server, browsed mail and sent a message.
derby	Java database. Ran tutorial on in-memory DB.
drawswf	SWF animation editor. Generated a small animation and exported to SWF.
fitjava	Testing framework. Ran tests distributed with framework.
freecs	Chat server. Ran server and connected several clients.
ganttproject	Graphical tool for task management.
hsqldb	Database tool. Created in-memory database and run various test scripts.
itext	Collection of tools for PDFs. Ran several tools.
jFin_DateMath	Date math library. Ran tests.
jasml	Java assembly compiler. Bootstrapped.
javacc	Java Compiler Compiler. Compiled JavaCC grammar.
jchempaint	Graphical molecule editor. Created and edited simple molecules.
jedit	Text editor. Created Java class, edited, searched, saved etc.
jfreechart	Graphical tool for creating charts. Tested UI.
jgraph	Library for drawing graphs. Ran several examples.
jgraphpad	Uses jgraph for drawing graphs. Created small graphs.
jgrapht	Views graphs, uses jgraph.
jhotdraw	Graphics framework. Tested sample application.
jmoney	Personal finance. Created sample accounts. Tested import/export, saving, editing, and reporting.
nekohtml	HTML parser. Ran samples.
pmd	Source code analyser. Tested on various projects.
pooka	Java email client. Tested connecting to IMAP server, reading mail, sending mail.
velocity	Templating engine. Ran sample application.
weka	Data mining tool. Ran sample application.
xalan	XSLT processor. Ran some examples.
xerces	XML parser. Ran some examples.
xmojo	JMX implementation. Ran sample application.

Fig. 2. Profiled applications. A selection of 30 applications from Qualitas Corpus release 20080603 [4]. Where multiple application versions were available the most recent was used. Where relevant, the table lists the application behaviour that was profiled.

in AspectJ into the classes as they are loaded. For each application we chose a suitable set of input designed to exercise as much functionality as possible, but without consulting source code or profiling coverage. For compilers, build tools and similar we tried to use samples distributed with the application or the application itself, while for GUI tools we run simple workflows, and attempted to use all available features, within reason. The profiler introduces significant overhead to the applications, so some interactive programs were difficult to use, while some autonomous programs ran for several hours.

On termination, the profiler output dumps were captured and stored. The raw results were then run through various scripts to extract the results presented in this section. Additional results are available in the technical report version of this paper [1]. The raw profiler output, and the profiler itself can be obtained by contacting the authors.

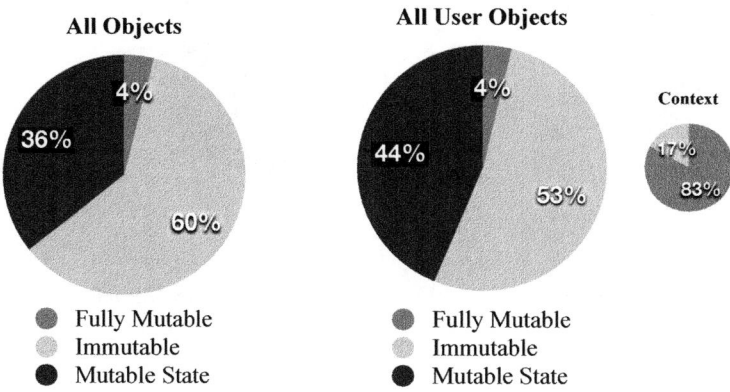

Fig. 3. An overview of all of the objects profiled. These are shown split into three categories: objects which change their equality and their state (*fully mutable*), which never change their state (*immutable*), and objects which don't change their equality but do change their state (*mutable state*). The large chart on the right shows the same distribution excluding Java standard library classes, and the small chart indicates how many of the objects in the chart on the left are also in the chart on the right (83%). This figure summarises 8,140,239 objects in 5,577 classes and 30 applications.

4.2   Experiment I: General Observations

This experiment provides a general overview of the objects profiled in the 30 sample applications. Figure 3 presents a summary of all objects encountered split into the categories defined previously: *fully mutable, immutable* and *mutable state*. These graphs account for the incorrectly detected *mutable equality* objects discussed in Section 3.2 by adding them to the fully mutable segment. See the error section below for a discussion.

The graph on the left of Figure 3 reports the data for all objects profiled, while that on the right only considers *user-defined* classes (i.e. excluding those from the standard libraries). The smaller pie-chart indicates what proportion of objects were user-defined (e.g. 83% of all profiled objects were user defined).

Discussion. Our conclusions from the data in Figure 3 are fairly straightforward: very few objects change their equality at all, and there are more objects with immutable state than mutable. This is fairly consistent between user-defined objects and the standard library objects which were profiled.

Error. Each segment of the charts in Figure 3 may include an extremely small error due to some objects which have immutable state (shallow) and mutable equality (deep). As we could not determine the exact number of objects in this category from the raw results, we included the error in the fully immutable segment and calculated an upper bound for the error using the breakdown of classes by program. For all the results presented in this paper, this error never reached one hundredth of a percentage point (197 objects of 5403518 total in the worst case).

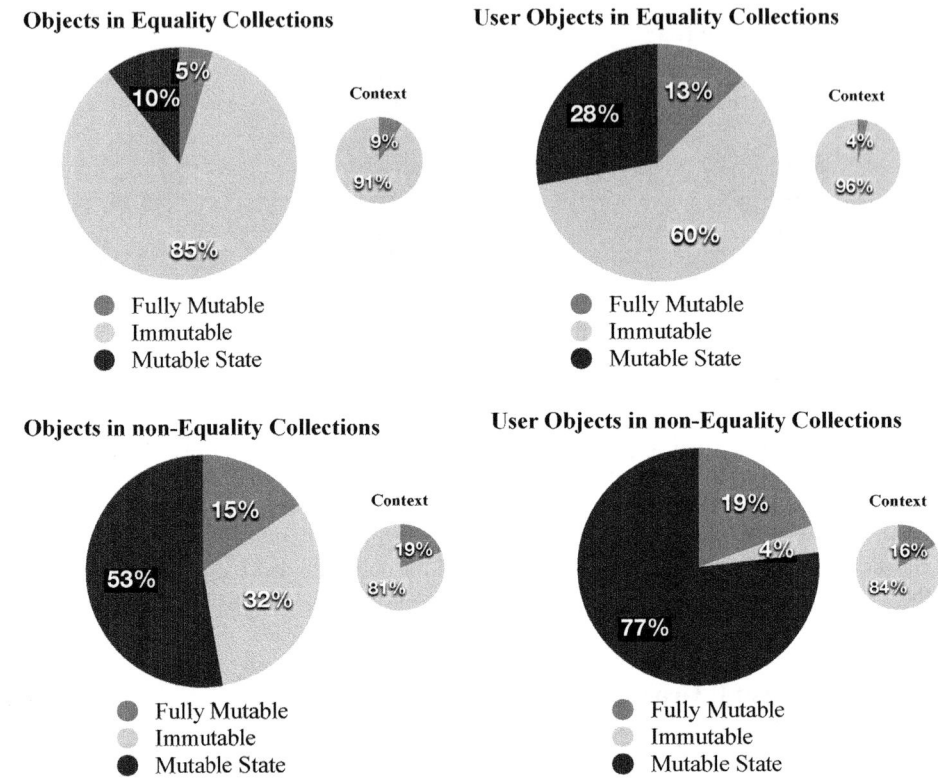

Fig. 4. An overview of all of the objects profiled, split into those which enter equality-dependent collections and those which enter non-equality dependent collections. Again, each chart splits into three categories: objects which change their equality and their state (*fully mutable*), which never change their state (*immutable*), and objects which don't change their equality but do change their state (*mutable state*). Equality collections include hash and tree sets, and the key-sets for maps and tables. Non-equality collections include lists, vectors, and queues, as well as value-sets for maps and tables.

4.3   Experiment II: Collection Contracts

This experiment examines the behaviour of objects which enter collections, comparing equality collections such as Set with non-equality collections like List. Figure 4 provides the same categorisations as before for these two categories. The top row of the figure illustrates data for those objects which do enter equality dependent collections, while the bottom row shows data for those which do not. Again, the smaller pie-charts illustrate the relative proportion to all objects (respectively, all user-defined objects). Thus, we see that only 9% of all objects enter an equality-dependent collection. Likewise, only 4% of all user-defined objects enter an equality-dependent collection.

Discussion. The results from Figure 4 demonstrate a clear difference between the behaviour of objects which enter equality collections and those that enter non-equality collections. We surmise that programmers prefer to use immutable objects in equality collections, even though the Collections contract permits them to change fields which do not affect the equality of the object. In particular, there is a large distinction between the number of immutable objects from standard libraries and user code. Further analysis of the results shows that most of these are `Integer` or `String` objects.

When we consider only user-defined objects, the bias towards immutable objects in equality collections is much lower; closer to the proportion in the whole population. This was surprising because these objects are a very small percentage of the whole population, and we expected most of them to be immutable, to easily satisfy the Collections contracts. While this is not the case further analysis of the results showed that objects did not change their equality at all after entering an equality collection. This is not so surprising, but this leads us to conclude that almost all Fully Mutable objects are actually the Late-initialised Equality strategy outlined in Section 2. This could pose a problem for researchers developing type systems for immutability: they will need to support late initialisation, or demonstrate that it can be removed without substantial burden to programmers. There were no broken objects — no objects changed their equality while in a collection.

Objects in non-equality collections show very different characteristics to the general population. The vast majority are not immutable, particularly when standard libraries are excluded, and there are a surprising number which both define and change their equality. The correlation between the relatively large number of objects changing their equality may indicate that programmers make a decision to define equality based on whether an object enters a collection at all, rather than whether the object will enter an equality collection specifically.

4.4   Experiment III: Objects in Collections

This final experiment contrasts objects which enter a collection with objects which do not. Figure 5 presents objects which enter a collection on the top row, and objects which do not on the bottom row. Again, the left column contains all objects, while the right column excludes standard library classes, and the small charts indicate the number of objects in each category as a fraction of the whole program.

Discussion. These figures show even more clearly the distinction between objects which enter collections and those which do not. The number of immutable objects in the no-collection set is close to the proportion in the general population, while the number of objects which modify their equality disappears completely. This was a very surprising result for us because we expected to see at least some types of objects defining equality unnecessarily. Note that the 1% of mutable state objects in the non-collection graph on the left does not appear on the right; further inspection of the raw results revealed that these are almost exclusively collection objects which define their equality recursively on their contents.

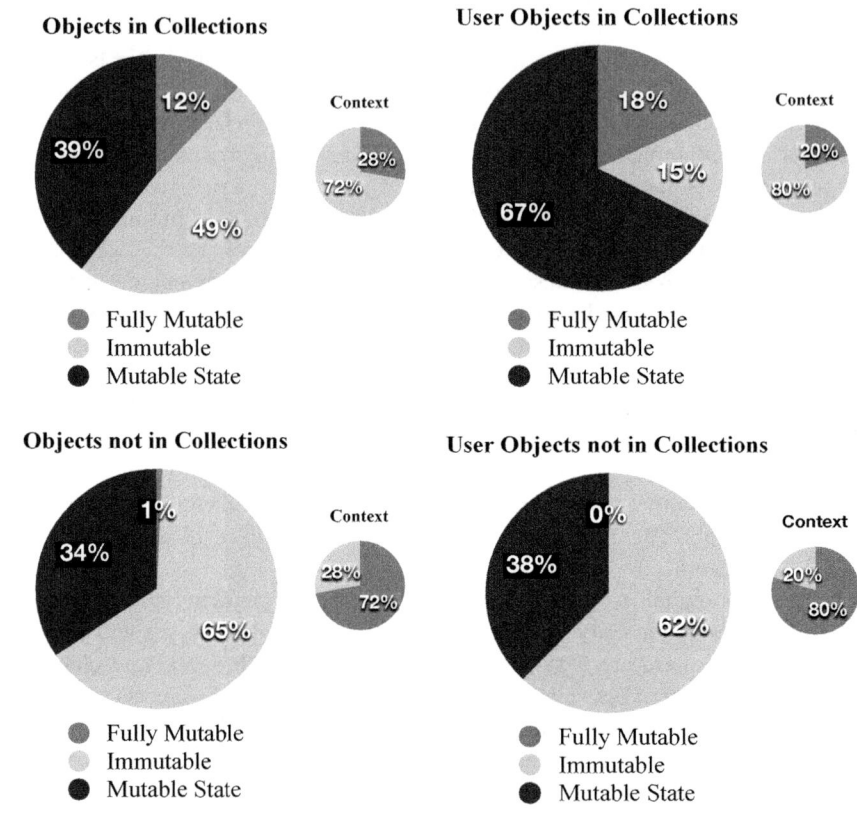

Fig. 5. An overview of all of the objects profiled, split into those which enter any collection and those which never do. Again, each chart splits into three categories: objects which change their equality and their state (*fully mutable*), which never change their state (*immutable*), and objects which don't change their equality but do change their state (*mutable state*).

The conclusion that we draw from these results is that programmers design their objects differently when they are going to enter a collection. This does not seem to be related to the contracts imposed by collections, because the trend is much more pronounced in non-equality collections. We do not have a clear understanding of why this should be. It is possible that the sample of applications has introduced some bias, for example a large proportion of objects were contributed by non-interactive programs like Ant. It would be interesting for future work to split applications by type to see whether the trend is consistent. Even so, programming language designers might consider ways to indicate that particular objects are designed for use in collections, as there seem to be large differences in the way they are used. Authors of optimising compilers could use these results to implement caching policies: the likelihood of an object in a collection changing is much higher than the full population, while objects which do not enter collections are extremely unlikely to change their equality, if they define it at all.

5   Related Work

We will now discuss various works of relevance to this paper, split into those relevant to object equality, and those related to profiling.

5.1   Object Identity and Equality

Object identity and equality has been studied since the first OOPSLA conference [5]. In the beginning, SIMULA provided only support for identity comparison [6], written ==, while Smalltalk provides two operators to compare objects: == (identity comparison) described as testing "whether two objects are equal", and = (equality) described as testing "whether two objects represent the same component" [7]. Smalltalk's == is generally not overridden by programmers while = certainly can be overridden. These two operators have survived essentially unchanged as Java's == and `equals()` — leading to all the issues we have identified earlier.

MacLennan [8] first described the distinction between values and objects in programming languages: that objects have identity and mutable state, while values are immutable and any identity they possess is merely an implementation detail. Khoshafian and Copeland [5] then provided one of the earliest definitions of object identity, shallow equality, and deep equality. Aiming to encompass databases as well as programming languages, their definitions explicitly incorporate sets and tuples.

Baker [9] presents a very comprehensive conceptual discussion of equality in imperative languages: although phrased in terms of Lisp his discussion is directly relevant to all object-oriented programming languages. Common Lisp, of course, has at least five different equality functions: eq, eql, `equal`, `equalp`, =, along with a range of type specific functions such as `char-equal`, `string-equal`, and `tree-equal` [10]. Baker suggests replacing all these separate notions of equality with single EGAL predicate, which is a recursive equality for immutable state terminating with identity comparison for mutable objects.

Grogono and Sakkinen [11] discuss equality in conjunction with object-copying in a C++ like language. There is clearly a relationship here that we have not addressed: a copy of an object should be equal to the object from which it was copied. Grogono and Sakkinen survey equality operations across a range of language and propose four different equalities: identity; shallow (one-level) equality; infinite deep equality; and a structural equality that distinguishes between cycles and their unfoldings as trees.

Vaziri et al [12] describe Relation Types, special kinds of classes whose equality and hash codes are automatically computed based on their "key" fields, which must be final. Relation Types use hash-consing to ensure that each of their instances are unique as far as values for these key fields are concerned. The resulting equality operation is quite similar to Baker's EGAL: objects are equal up to mutable state.

Hovemeyer and Pugh [3] show how very straightforward checks can detect Java equality bugs (such as an incorrect covariant signature for `equals` or a missing definition of `hashcode`) along with many other types of bugs, and report the results of an automatic static study of six Java applications. Rupakheti and Hou [13] present an observational study of the use of equality across five Java applications. Working within the existing Java equality contract (and generally not considering issues of mutability) they identify a number of recurring problems in the definition of equality. The study presented in this paper is both significantly larger, and focused explicitly on the mutability aspects of Java's equality contracts.

5.2   Object Initialisation and Immutability

Various OO languages have support for immutability via, for example, *final* or *const* fields. CLU [14] also supports immutable versions of primitive data structures — although clusters (classes) are always mutable. A similar design has been adopted in Scala, where the library provides mutable and immutable versions of most collections [15].

More recently, Zibin's IGJ language [16] provides explicit support for both object and class level immutability, and allows code to be parameterised in mutability. So for example, an IGJ map class can require its keys to be immutable, but could permit its values to be either mutable or immutable, and these restrictions will be statically enforced by a generic type system. Östlund et al. [17] use an ownership type system to obtain similar flexibility.

Immutable objects must be initialised before they can be used. Fähndrich and Xia's Delayed Types [18] use dynamically nested regions in an ownership-style type system to represent this post-construction initialisation phase, and ensure that programs do not access uninitialised fields. Haack and Poll [19] have shown how these techniques can be applied specifically to immutability, and Leino et al. [20] show how ownership transfer (rather than nesting) can achieve a similar result. Qi and Myers' Masked Types [21] use type-states to address this problem by incorporating a list of uninitialised fields ("masked fields") into object types. Gil and Shragai [22] address the related problem of ensuring correct initialisation between subclass and superclass constructors within individual objects. Given that our profiling has shown that the initialisation phase of an object is not bounded by the execution of its constructor, these kinds of type systems should be of benefit to real programs.

Rather than concentrating on whole object immutability, Unkel and Lam [23] consider individual fields: a Stationary Field is one where all writes precede all reads — that is, where a field is initialised (perhaps multiple times, during or after the constructor) but is not modified thereafter. They present a static corpus analysis study of 26 Java applications, backed by a dynamic analysis of 9 programs, and find that 40-60% of Java fields are stationary. Earlier, Porat et al. [24] conducted a similar analysis looking for "deeply immutable" fields (where neither the field itself nor any object reachable from that field is modified after the object's constructor completes) and found that around 60% of `static` fields were immutable. These results compare with our (dynamic) profile finding that a large fraction of Java objects are immutable after full construction.

Finally, Joshua Block [25] advises programmers to "prefer immutability", that is to use immutable objects wherever possible, and to ensure constructors create objects fully initialised. While we found many immutable objects in our study, we also found many objects whose life-cycle includes a post-construction initialisation stage, which breaches the letter (if not the spirit) of these guidelines.

5.3 Profiling

Numerous works have focused on profiling object lifetimes for pretenuring in virtual machines (e.g. [26,27,28,29]). Hirzel *et al.* studied a suite of benchmarks and concluded that object connectivity correlates strongly with object lifetime [30]. Contrasting with this, others have shown how stack state at the point of object allocation correlates with object lifetime [31]. Singer *et al.* studied a small benchmark suite in an effort to identify good predictions of long-lived objects [29]. Chen *et al.* consider the lifetime of object fields, rather than whole objects, since a field may not be active for the duration of its enclosing object's life; thus, fields with disjoint lifetimes can occupy the same memory, thereby reducing object footprint [32]. Similar work studied field lifetimes for the SpecJVM98 benchmark suite, and found on average a 14% reduction in heap space was possible [33]. Shankar *et al.* profiled Java programs in an effort to identify short-live objects suitable for stack allocation [34]. Dieckmann and Hözle performed a detailed study of the allocation behaviour of the SpecJVM98 benchmarks [35]. Pearce *et al.* evaluated AspectJ as a profiling platform by considering different case studies [36]. They considered profiling execution time, heap usage, object lifetime and more.

Röjemo and Runciman introduced the notions of *lag*, *drag* and *use* to describe the lifetime of objects during execution [37]. Under this terminology, *lag* is the time between creation and first use, *drag* is that between last use and collection, while *use* covers the rest. They focused on improving memory consumption in Haskell programs and relied upon compiler support to enable profiling. Building on this, Shaham *et al.* looked at reducing object drag in Java programs [38].

Perhaps the most relevant work to this paper, is that of Marinov and O'Callahan who considered object equality profiling [39]. Essentially, their aim was to expose situations where two identical objects could be reduced to one, thereby saving memory by avoiding redundant objects. To do this, their tool profiles the heap activity of a program, and then applies a post-mortem analysis once execution is complete. This analysis essentially examines the object graph, searching for sub-graphs which are structurally equivalent (i.e. isomorphic). They applied their tool to several programs from the SpecJVM benchmark suite, and found that several exhibited large numbers of equivalent
objects.

Mitchell presented a novel approach to compacting the typically huge amounts of data generated during profiling [40]. His approach exploits the dominates relation for objects in the heaps. Finally, Potanin *et al.* used the JVMPI interface [41] to profile object graphs in Java programs, concluding that these exhibit the property of being scale-free [42]. In particular, they observed a power-law distribution for edge degrees in the object graph of large programs: some objects were very highly connected, whilst most had low connectivity.

6   Conclusion

ALL OBJECTS ARE EQUAL
BUT SOME OBJECTS ARE MORE
EQUAL THAN OTHERS

(after George Orwell, [43])

Every Java object, one way or another, must participate in equality: it must implement the `equals` and `hashcode` methods according to a relatively straightforward contract. Objects may either inherit the default behaviour from class `Object`, and use their identity as their equality, or can override these methods to provide a more rarefied notion of equality. Objects that will participate in equality dependent collections — in hash sets, as keys in hash maps, or in their close cousins the sorted collections — must fulfil a more arduous contract: that their equality, their hashcode, their comparability *must never change* while they are within such a collection.

In this paper, we present the results of a study of Java programs with respect to these contracts. We hypothesized that programers could adopt a range of approaches to fulfilling these contracts, from using equality as their identity; via full immutability; or equality immutability, or ensuring their equality is immutable after construction; or finally to removing and reinserting changed objects in their collections. To test these hypotheses, we built a dynamic analysis tool, #Profiler, that determines when and how objects are constructed, initialised, and how they fulfil these equality contracts.

Using #Profiler to investigate 30 applications, we discovered that objects' equality generally does not change: with a few exceptions, objects which do not enter collections either do not change or do not define their hash code. Of objects which do enter collections, 19% changed their hash code after the constructor completed.

Surprisingly, objects which enter collections exhibit a strong tendency to change fields which are not used to determine hash code: 77% of user objects do this. Combined with the objects which do change their hash code, only 4% of objects which enter non-equality collections do not change; a huge difference to the general population where well over half are immutable. It is heartening though to find that none of these objects change their equality while actually in an equality collection, as such a change would be a bug in the programs we studied!

Equality, then, does seem important to Java programmers. More to the point, programmers make good use of equality in collections, and (at least in our sample) generally navigate Java's equality contracts successfully: equality is generally based on fully initialised immutable state, and collections can safely rely on stable equality. Proposals such as Baker's EGAL [9], Relation Types [12], and the various schemes for managing object initialisation [18,20,21] may well provide good language support for objects which enter collections, so long as they can cope with the relatively high number of objects performing delayed initialisation; while objects which do not enter collections seem to be adequately served by object identity, as they do not change their equality.

The exception to this rule — oddly enough – seem to be the collection objects themselves, whose equality changes whether or not they are in collections. Collections, indeed, are simultaneously more equal than other objects — because they all provide a specialised definition of `equal` — and less equal — because they change more often.

Acknowledgements. Thanks go to the anonymous reviewers for TOOLS who provided valuable insights and comments. Thanks also to Victoria University VC's Strategic PhD Scholarship for supporting this research, and New Zealand's BuildIT for providing funding for the first author to present this paper.

References

1. Nelson, S., Pearce, D.J., Noble, J.: Understanding the impact of collection contracts on design. Technical Report 10-09, School of Engineering and Computer Science, Victoria University of Wellington, New Zealand (2010)
2. Chan, P., Lee, R.: The Java Class Libraries, 2nd edn., vol. 1. Addison-Wesley, Reading (1999)
3. Hovemeyer, D., Pugh, W.: Finding bugs is easy. In: OOPSLA Companion (2004)
4. Qualitas Research Group: Qualitas corpus release 20080603. The University of Auckland (2008), http://www.cs.auckland.ac.nz/~ewan/corpus/
5. Khoshafian, S.N., Copeland, G.P.: Object identity. In: Proc. OOPSLA (1986)
6. Birtwistle, G.M., Dahl, O.J., Myhrhaug, B., Nygaard, K.: Simula Begin. Studentlitteratur (1979)
7. Goldberg, A., Robson, D.: Smalltalk-80: The Language and its Implementation. Addison-Wesley, Reading (1983)
8. MacLennan, B.J.: Values and objects in programming languages. SIGPLAN Notices 17(12), 70–79 (1982)
9. Baker, H.G.: Equal rights for functional objects or, the more things change, the more they are the same. In: OOPS Messenger, vol. 4(4) (1993)
10. Steele, G.L.: Common Lisp the Language, 2nd edn. Digital Press (1990)
11. Grogono, P., Sakkinen, M.: Copying and comparing: Problems and solutions. In: Bertino, E. (ed.) ECOOP 2000. LNCS, vol. 1850, pp. 226–250. Springer, Heidelberg (2000)
12. Vaziri, M., Tip, F., Fink, S., Dolby, J.: Declarative object identity using relation types. In: Ernst, E. (ed.) ECOOP 2007. LNCS, vol. 4609, pp. 54–78. Springer, Heidelberg (2007)
13. Rupakheti, C.R., Hou, D.: An empirical study of the design and implementation of object equality in Java. In: Proc. CASCON, p. 9 (2008)
14. Liskov, B., Guttag, J.V.: Abstraction and Specification in Program Development. MIT Press/McGraw-Hill (1986)
15. Odersky, M.: Programming in Scala. Artima, Inc. (2008)
16. Zibin, Y., Potanin, A., Ali, M., Artzi, S., Kiezun, A., Ernst, M.D.: Object and reference immutability using Java generics. In: ESEC/SIGSOFT FSE, pp. 75–84 (2007)
17. Östlund, J., Wrigstad, T., Clarke, D., Åkerblom, B.: Ownership, uniqueness, and immutability. In: TOOLS, vol. (46), pp. 178–197 (2008)
18. Fähndrich, M., Xia, S.: Establishing object invariants with delayed types. In: Proc. OOPSLA, pp. 337–350 (2007)
19. Haack, C., Poll, E.: Type-based object immutability with flexible initialization. Technical Report ICIS-R09001, Radboud University Nijmegen (January 2009)
20. Leino, K.R.M., Müller, P., Wallenburg, A.: Flexible immutability with frozen objects. In: VSTTE, pp. 192–208 (2008)
21. Qi, X., Myers, A.C.: Masked types for sound object initialization. In: POPL, pp. 53–65 (2009)
22. Gil, J., Shragai, T.: Are we ready for a safer construction environment? In: Drossopoulou, S. (ed.) ECOOP 2009 – Object-Oriented Programming. LNCS, vol. 5653, pp. 495–519. Springer, Heidelberg (to appear, 2009)

23. Unkel, C., Lam, M.S.: Automatic inference of stationary fields: a generalization of Java's final fields. In: POPL, pp. 183–195 (2008)
24. Porat, S., Biberstein, M., Koved, L., Mendelson, B.: Automatic detection of immutable fields in Java. In: Proc. CASCON (1990)
25. Bloch, J.: Effective Java. Prentice Hall PTR, Englewood Cliffs (2008)
26. Cheng, P., Harper, R., Lee, P.: Generational stack collection and profile-driven pretenuring. In: Proc. of the ACM Conference on Programming Language Design and Implementation, pp. 162–173. ACM Press, New York (1998)
27. Agesen, O., Garthwaite, A.: Efficient object sampling via weak references. In: Proc. ISMM, pp. 121–126. ACM Press, New York (2000)
28. Jump, M., Blackburn, S.M., McKinley, K.S.: Dynamic object sampling for pretenuring. In: Diwan, A. (ed.) Proc. ISMM. ACM Press, New York (2004)
29. Singer, J., Brown, G., Lujan, M., Watson, I.: Towards intelligent analysis techniques for object pretenuring. In: Principles and Practice of Programming in Java, Lisbon, September 2007. ACM Press, New York (2007)
30. Hirzel, M., Henkel, J., Diwan, A., Hind, M.: Understanding the connectivity of heap objects. In: Proc. ISMM, pp. 143–156 (2002)
31. Inoue, H., Stefanovic, D., Forrest, S.: On the prediction of Java object lifetimes. IEEE Trans. Computers 55(7), 880–892 (2006)
32. Chen, G., Kandemir, M., Vijaykrishnan, N., Irwin, M.J.: Field level analysis for heap space optimization in embedded Java environments. In: Diwan, A. (ed.) ISMM'04 Proc. of the Fourth International Symposium on Memory Management, Vancouver, October 2004. ACM Press, New York (2004)
33. Guo, Z., Amaral, J.N., Szafron, D., Wang, Y.: Utilizing field usage patterns for java heap space optimization. In: Proc. of the conference of the Centre for Advanced Studies on Collaborative Research, pp. 67–79. IBM (2006)
34. Shankar, A., Arnold, M., Bodik, R.: Jolt: Lightweight dynamic analysis and removal of object churn. In: Proc. OOPSLA, pp. 127–142. ACM Press, New York (2008)
35. Dieckman, S., Hoelzle, U.: A study of the allocation behavior of the SPECjvm98 Java benchmarks. In: Guerraoui, R. (ed.) ECOOP 1999. LNCS, vol. 1628, pp. 92–115. Springer, Heidelberg (1999)
36. Pearce, D.J., Webster, M., Berry, R., Kelly, P.H.J.: Profiling with AspectJ. Software: Pracice and Experience 37(7), 747–777 (2007)
37. Röjemo, N., Runciman, C.: Lag, drag, void and use — heap profiling and space-efficient compilation revisited. In: Proc. ICFP, pp. 34–41. ACM Press, New York (1996)
38. Shaham, R., Kolodner, E.K., Sagiv, M.: Heap profiling for space-efficient Java. In: Proc. PLDI, pp. 104–113. ACM Press, New York (2001)
39. Marinov, D., O'Callahan, R.: Object equality profiling. SIGPLAN Not. 38(11), 313–325 (2003)
40. Mitchell, N.: The runtime structure of object ownership. In: Thomas, D. (ed.) ECOOP 2006. LNCS, vol. 4067, pp. 74–98. Springer, Heidelberg (2006)
41. Liang, S., Viswanathan, D.: Comprehensive profiling support in the Java Virtual Machine. In: Proc. of the USENIX Conference On Object Oriented Technologies and Systems, pp. 229–240. USENIX Association (1999)
42. Potanin, A., Noble, J., Frean, M.R., Biddle, R.: Scale-free geometry in OO programs. Communications of the ACM 48(5), 99–103 (2005)
43. Orwell, G.: Animal Farm. Secker & Warburg (1945)

Reasoning about Function Objects

Martin Nordio[1], Cristiano Calcagno[2,3,*], Bertrand Meyer[1],
Peter Müller[1], and Julian Tschannen[1]

[1] ETH Zurich, Switzerland
{Martin.Nordio,Bertrand.Meyer,Peter.Mueller,julian.tschannen}@inf.ethz.ch
[2] Monoidics Ltd
[3] Imperial College, London, UK
ccris@doc.ic.ac.uk

Abstract. Modern object-oriented languages support higher-order implementations through function objects such as delegates in C#, agents in Eiffel, or closures in Scala. Function objects bring a new level of abstraction to the object-oriented programming model, and require a comparable extension to specification and verification techniques. We introduce a verification methodology that extends function objects with auxiliary side-effect free (pure) methods to model logical artifacts: preconditions, postconditions and modifies clauses. These pure methods can be used to specify client code abstractly, that is, independently from specific instantiations of the function objects. To demonstrate the feasibility of our approach, we have implemented an automatic prover, which verifies several non-trivial examples.

1 Introduction

Object-oriented design makes a clear choice in dealing with the basic duality between data and operations: it bases system architecture on the object, more precisely the object types as represented by classes, and attaching operations to one such class. Functional programming languages, on the other hand, use functions as the primary compositional elements. The two paradigms are increasingly borrowing from each other: functional programming languages such as OCaml integrate object-oriented ideas, and a number of object-oriented languages now offer a mechanism to package operations (routines, methods) as objects. In the dynamically typed world, the idea goes back at least to Smalltalk with its blocks; among statically typed languages, C# has introduced *delegates*, Eiffel *agents*, and Scala *closures*.

The concept of agent or delegate is, in its basic form, very simple, with immediate applications. A typical one, in a Graphical User Interface system, is for some part of a system to express its wish to observe (in the sense of the Observer pattern [12]) events of a certain type, by registering a procedure to be executed in response:

---

* This work was done while visiting ETH Zurich.

J. Vitek (Ed.): TOOLS 2010, LNCS 6141, pp. 79–96, 2010.
© Springer-Verlag Berlin Heidelberg 2010

US_map. left_click . subscribe (**agent** *show_state_votes*)

This indicates that whenever a *left_click* event occurs on the map, the given procedure *show_state_votes* should be executed. The routine *subscribe* takes as argument a function object representing a procedure with two integer arguments. Since the function object is a formal argument, *subscribe* does not know which exact procedure, such as *show_state_votes*, it might represent; but it can call it all the same, through a general procedure *call* applicable to any function object, and any target and argument objects.

Function objects appear in such examples as a form of function pointers as available for example in C and C++. But they go beyond this first analogy. Firstly, they are declared with a signature and hence provide a statically typed mechanism, whereas a function pointer just denotes whatever is to be found in the corresponding memory address. Secondly, a function object represents a routine abstraction, and can be subject to dynamic dispatch when the receiver is an open argument[1].

Function objects have proved attractive to object-oriented programmers, but they also raise new verification challenges. To address these problems, we introduce a specification and verification technique. Our approach uses side-effect free (pure) routines to specify abstractly the pre- and postconditions of function objects. These pure routines can be used to specify client code independently from specific function objects. Using previous work on encoding pure routines in Boogie [8,22], these routines are encoded as mathematical functions, which represent the function object's pre- and postcondition. The basic idea is that to prove a property of a function object call, it suffices to prove that the abstract precondition of the function object holds before the invocation; then we can assume the abstract postcondition of the function object holds after its invocation.

The main contributions of this paper are: (1) a verification methodology for function objects, and (2) an automatic verifier for function objects. The verifier takes an Eiffel program, translates it to Boogie2 [16], and then proves the Boogie2 code using the Boogie verifier [2]. We demonstrate the practicality of our approach with a suite of examples, including one previously described as an open problem, and more function objects intensive programs which implement graphical user interfaces. Although we focus on Eiffel agents, we believe that the same ideas apply to similar mechanisms in other languages, such as C# delegates.

Outline. Section 2 presents example applications of agents and their verification challenges. Section 3 describes the verification methodology. This methodology is extended to framing in Section 4. Section 5 applies the methodology to the examples from Section 2. In Section 6, we show a set of examples that have been verified using the implemented automatic prover. Section 7 discusses related work; Section 8 summarizes the result and describes future work.

---

[1] An argument is *open* if it must be provided in the invocation of the agent.

2   Agent Examples and Their Verification Challenges

In this section, we present some typical applications of agents.

2.1   Formatter

The first example comes from a paper by Leavens et al. [20] and is recouched in Eiffel below. It is of particular interest since they describe it as a verification challenge beyond current techniques. The class *FORMATTER* models paragraph formatting with two alignment routines. The class *PARAGRAPH* includes a procedure to format the current paragraph:

```
class  FORMATTER
    align_left  (p: PARAGRAPH)              align_right  (p: PARAGRAPH)
      require                                 require
          not p. left_aligned                     not p. right_aligned
      do                                      do
          ... Operations on p ...                 ... Operations on p ...
      ensure                                  ensure
          p. left_aligned                         p. right_aligned
end
```

```
class PARAGRAPH
    format (proc: PROCEDURE [FORMATTER, PARAGRAPH ];
            f: FORMATTER)
      do
          proc. call  (f,  Current)
      end
end
```

For illustration purposes, the routines *align_left* and *align_right* require that the paragraph is not left aligned and not right aligned, respectively. The routines *left_aligned* and *right_aligned* are pure routines (side-effect free) defined in the class *PARAGRAPH*, and return *true* if the paragraph is left aligned or right aligned, respectively.

In Eiffel, the contracts of a class are its invariant, and the precondition and postcondition that can be attached to any routine, with the respective keywords **invariant**, **require** and **ensure**. Each such clause involves an assertion written out as a sequence of boolean expressions. An absent contract clause is equivalent to one specificying *True*. In the routine *format*, the signature *proc: PROCEDURE [FORMATTER, PARAGRAPH]*[2] declares an agent *proc* with two open arguments (the target of type *FORMATTER* and a parameter of type *PARAGRAPH*). The agent *proc* is invoked using the procedure *call* (**Current** denotes the receiver object, *this* in C#).

---

[2] This is a simplification of the Eiffel syntax; the Eiffel declaration is *PROCE-DURE[FORMATTER, TUPLE[PARAGRAPH]]*.

An example of the use of the *format* routine is shown in the routine *apply_align_left*:

> *apply_align_left*   (*f*: *FORMATTER*; *p*:*PARAGRAPH*)
> > **require**
> > > **not** *p. left_aligned*
> > **do**
> > > *p. format* (**agent** {*FORMATTER*}.*align_left* , *f*)
> > **ensure**
> > > *p. left_aligned*
> > **end**

The notation **agent** {*FORMATTER*}.*align_left* denotes a function object that represents the *align_left* routine of the class *FORMATTER*. The keyword **agent** is used to distinguish between the function object *align_left* and the invocation of the routine *align_left*.

The verification challenge in this case is to specify and verify the routine *format* in an abstract way, abstracting the pre and postcondition of the agent. Then, one should be able to invoke the routine *format* with a concrete agent, here *align_left*, and to show that the postcondition of *align_left* holds. If the *format* routine is called with another routine, say *align_right*, one should be able to show that the postcondition of *align_right* holds without modifying the proof of *format*. Another issue is framing; one should be able to express what the routine *format* modifies, but abstracting from the specific routines *align_left* and *align_right*. When the routine *format* is invoked using the agent *align_left*, we should be able to show that *format* only modifies the locations that *align_left* modifies.

2.2   Archive Example

This section describes the *archive* example presented by Leavens et al. [20] and proved by Müller and Ruskiewicz [23]. This example illustrates the application of agents with closed arguments[3].

Figure 1 presents the example encoded in Eiffel. The class *TAPE_ARCHIVE* defines a tape with a routine *store* which stores objects if the device is loaded. An application of agents is implemented in the routine *log* of class *CLIENT*, which calls the agent *log_file* with the string *s*. Finally, the class *MAIN* shows an example of the invocation of the routine *log*.

The invocation *log_file.call*(*s*) invokes the procedure *log_file* with the parameter *s*. The declaration *PROCEDURE[TAPE;ANY]*[4] indicates that *log_file* is an agent with closed argument of type *TAPE* and one open argument of type *ANY*. The target of the invocation is defined in the creation of the agent. In this example, the target object is *t* defined by **agent** *t.store*.

---

[3] Closed arguments are the arguments of an agent provided in the agent declaration.

[4] This is a simplification of the declaration in Eiffel. The declaration in Eiffel is *PRO-CEDURE[TAPE,TUPLE[ANY]]*..

```
class TAPE_ARCHIVE                    class TAPE
  tape: TAPE                            save(o: ANY) do ... end
  is_loaded: BOOLEAN                      -- other routines omitted
    ensure                            end
    Result = (tape /= void)
                                      class CLIENT
  make                                  log ( log_file :PROCEDURE[TAPE;ANY];
  do                                             s:STRING)
      create tape                         do
  end                                       log_file . call(s)
                                          end
  store (o: ANY)                      end
    require                           class MAIN
      is_loaded                         main (c: CLIENT)
  do                                      local
    tape.save (o)                           t: TAPE_ARCHIVE
  end                                     do
  -- other routines                         create t.make
  --   omitted                              c.log (agent t.store, "Hello World")
end                                       end
                                      end
```

Fig. 1. Archive example encoded in Eiffel

The verification challenge in this case is to verify the routine *log* in an abstract way, and being able to show that the precondition of the agent *store* holds before its invocation. In the routine *log*, the methodology has to assume that the target is closed but the exact target is unknown.

3   Verification Methodology

A verification technique should address both the specification of routines that uses function objects and the verification of invocation of function objects. Section 3.1 considers the first issue; the remainder of this section examines the second one.

3.1   Specifying Function Objects

The difficulty of specifying the correctness of agents is that while a variable of an agent type represents a routine, it is impossible to know statically which routine that is. The purpose of agents is to abstract from individual routines. The specification must reflect this abstraction.

What characterizes the correctness of a routine is its precondition and its postcondition. For an agent, these are known abstractly through the functions *precondition* and *postcondition* of class *ROUTINE* and its descendants. These functions enable us to perform the necessary abstraction on agent variables and expressions. The approach makes it possible for example to equip the routine *format* with a contract:

$format\ (proc:\ PROCEDURE\ [FORMATTER,\ PARAGRAPH\ ];$
$\qquad\qquad f:\ FORMATTER)$
   require
       $proc.\ precondition\ \ (f,\mathbf{Current})$
   do
       $proc.\ call\ \ (f,\mathbf{Current})$
   ensure
       $proc.\ postcondition\ \ (f,\mathbf{Current})$
   end

Note that the precondition of *format* uses the routine *precondition* to query the precondition of the procedure *proc*. Finally, we need to specify the routine *call* in the class *ROUTINE*. Its specification is the following:

$call\ \ (\ target:\ ANY;\ p:\ ANY)$
   require
      $\mathbf{Current}.precondition\ (target,p)$
   ensure
      $\mathbf{Current}.postcondition\ (target,p)$

3.2   Reasoning

This section describes the methodology to reason about agents with open arguments. This methodology is presented as a translation from Eiffel to Boogie2 [16]. The translation uses the basic Boogie2 instructions **assume**, **assert**, **havoc**, and assignment. In the following, we present the translation of agent initialization and agent invocation. The translation of other instructions such as assignments and routine invocation is similar to the translation applied in Spec#; for more details see [15]. The methodology is extended for closed arguments in Section 3.3; framing is handled in Section 4.

Agent Pre- and Postconditions. The methodology introduces two uninterpreted functions to model the pre- and postcondition of the agent. The function[5] *$precondition* takes three values (the agent, the target, and the parameter), and the current heap, and yields the evaluation of the agent's precondition. The function *$postcondition* takes a second heap to evaluate old expressions. The signatures of these functions are defined as follows[6]:

$\$precondition : Value \times Value \times Value \times Heap \rightharpoonup Bool$
$\$postcondition : Value \times Value \times Value \times Heap \times Heap \rightharpoonup Bool$

Invoking Agents. Given an agent a, a target t, and an argument p, the agent is invoked using the Eiffel routine *call*. The translation of the agent invocation

---

[5] We use the prefix $ for the mathematical functions to distinguish them from the Eiffel routines.

[6] $\rightharpoonup$ denotes partial functions.

$a.call(t, p)$ first asserts the precondition of the agent, and then assumes its postcondition. The proof obligations are the following:

assert $precondition(a, t, p, Heap)$
$h_0 := Heap$
havoc $Heap$
assume $postcondition(a, t, p, Heap, h_0)$

The current heap is denoted by $Heap$. The assignment $h_0 := Heap$ saves the current heap, then h_0 is used to evaluate old expressions in the postcondition of the agent. The **havoc** command assigns an arbitrary value to the heap.

Initializing Agents. The translation above asserts the abstract precondition of the agent. This abstract precondition could be any precondition of any procedure. Once the agent is initialized with a procedure pr, the methodology connects the abstract pre- and postcondition of the agent with the concrete pre- and postcondition of the procedure pr. Thus, if the precondition of pr holds, the prover will be able to show that the abstract precondition holds.

Given the agent initialization $a := \textbf{agent } pr$ where pr is a procedure[7], the methodology generates the following assumptions:

assume $\forall t, p : ObjectId; h_1 : Heap : \$precondition(a, t, p, h_1) = \$pre_{pr}(t, p, h_1)$
assume $\forall t, p : ObjectId; h_1, h_2 : Heap : \$postcondition(a, t, p, h_1, h_2) = \$post_{pr}(t, p, h_1, h_2)$

where $\$pre_{pr}$ and $\$post_{pr}$ denotes the pre- and postcondition of the procedure pr, t the target object, and p the argument respectively; we assume that the agent variable a is a fresh variable.

The translation of agents to Boogie2 is based on the translation of pure routines [8,22]. The novel concepts are the introduction of the functions $precondition$ and $postcondition$ to model the agent pre- and postcondition, and the generation of assumptions for the initialization of the agent, which relates the pre- and postcondition of the agent with the concrete pre- and postcondition of the procedure.

3.3   Reasoning about Closed Arguments

To model closed arguments, we define two uninterpreted functions: $\$precondition_1$ and $\$postcondition_1$[8]. These functions are similar to the functions defined in the section above but they take an agent with one closed argument (either closed target or closed parameter) and the heap(s), and yield the evaluation of the pre- and postcondition. The signatures are:

$$\$precondition_1 : Value \times Value \times Heap \rightharpoonup Bool$$
$$\$postcondition_1 : Value \times Value \times Heap \times Heap \rightharpoonup Bool$$

The translation for initializing agents, and invoking agents are similar to the section above; Figure 2 presents this translation.

---

[7] **agent** pr is an abbreviation for keeping all arguments open (including the target), as in **agent** $\{TYPE\}.pr(?)$.

[8] As a reminder, we assume that routines have only one parameter, although, the methodology can be extended easily.

Eiffel code	*Boggie2 code*
(A) $a.call(p)$	**assert** $precondition_1(a, p, Heap)$ $h_0 := Heap$ **havoc** $Heap$ **assume** $postcondition_1(a, p, Heap, h_0)$
(B) $a := \textbf{agent } t_1.pr$	**assume** $\forall p : ObjectId; h_1 : Heap :$ $\quad precondition_1(a, p, h_1) = pre_{pr}(t_1, p, h_1)$ **assume** $\forall p : ObjectId; h_1, h_2 : Heap :$ $\quad postcondition_1(a, p, h_1, h_2) = post_{pr}(t_1, p, h_1, h_2)$ where t_1 is the closed target, and pr a procedure
(C) $a := \textbf{agent } pr(p_1)$	**assume** $\forall t : ObjectId; h_1 : Heap :$ $\quad precondition_1(a, t, h_1) = pre_{pr}(t, p_1, h_1)$ **assume** $\forall t : ObjectId; h_1, h_2 : Heap :$ $\quad postcondition_1(a, t, h_1, h_2) = post_{pr}(t, p_1, h_1, h_2)$ where p_1 is the closed parameter, and pr a procedure

Fig. 2. Translation of Agents with Closed Arguments to Boogie2: (A) Agent Invocation with Closed Arguments; (B) Closed Target Initialization; (C) Closed Parameter Initialization

Note that Eiffel does not distinguish between an agent with open target and an agent with open parameter. Both agents are declared with the same notation. Thus, the methodology uses the functions $precondition_1$ and $postcondition_1$ to express the precondition and postcondition with closed target and closed parameter, and then it uses the assumptions generated in the initialization of the agent.

4   Framing

A necessary part of a routine specification is the modifies clause, which defines the locations that are modified by the routine. The problem of defining these locations is known as *frame problem*. The frame problem has been addressed for example using dynamic frames [18], ownership [6], separation logic [31,26], and regional logic [1]. However, this problem has to be solved for agents. This section presents a solution for framing agents based on dynamic frames. As future work, we plan to investigate the integration with other techniques such as separation logic.

In Section 2.1 we have specified the routine *format*, however, one needs to specify what locations this routine modifies. A candidate solution for this problem is to assume that *format* modifies all the locations than can be accessed from the target and the arguments of the agent *proc*. However, this assumption is too strong since *format* may only modify a few attributes of *proc*'s target. Note that *format* can be invoked with different routines, and each routine might modify different locations.

To address the frame problem for agents, we adapt dynamic frames. Instead of using a set of locations as in Kassios's work [18], we introduce a routine *modifies* (in the source language), which takes an agent *a*, its target *t* and argument value *p*, and returns the locations modified by the agent *a* with target *t* and argument *p*. This function abstracts from the specific locations that the agent modifies. Thus, the modifies clause of *format* can be defined as follows (pre and postconditions are omitted):

> *format* (*proc*: *PROCEDURE* [*FORMATTER*, *PARAGRAPH*];
>   *f*: *FORMATTER*)
>   **modify**
>   *modifies* (*proc*, *f*, **Current**)
>   **do**
>   *proc. call* (*f*, **Current**)
>   **end**

This modifies clause expresses that the routine *format* modifies the locations that are modified by the procedure *proc*. Depending on the routine used to invoke *format*, the function *modifies* will yield a different set of locations.

Following, we describe the encoding of framing for agents with open arguments; framing for closed arguments is presented in our technical report [24].

Modifies Clauses. We have extended Eiffel with *modifies clauses*. Each routine contains a modifies clause which is defined as a comma separated list of locations. To express what locations are modified by an agent, we introduce the function *modifies*. The definition of *modifies clauses* and routine declarations is the following:

> *Mclause* ::= *Mclause*, *Mclause*
> | *VarId*
> | *modifies*(*VarId*, *VarId*, *VarId*)
> *Routine* ::= *RoutineId* (*VarId* : *Type*) : *Type*
>   require
>   *BoolExp*
>   modify
>   *Mclause*
>   do
>   *Instr*
>   ensure
>   *BoolExp*
>   end

where *boolExp* are boolean expressions, *RoutineId* routine identifiers, *VarId* variable identifiers, and *Instr* instructions.

Encoding of Modifies Clauses. To encode the routine *modifies*, we introduce an uninterpreted function $modifies which takes an agent a, its target and argument values, the current heap, an object value o, and a field name f, and yields *true* if the agent a with its target and argument modifies the field f of the object o. The signature of this function is the following:

$$\$modifies : Value \times Value \times Value \times Heap \times Value \times FieldId \rightharpoonup Bool$$

Modifies clauses are encoded in a similar way to Spec#, but cosidering the mapping of the Eiffel function *modifies*. Modifies clauses are a list of applications of the function *modifies* and variable identifiers. Given the modifies clause in the source language:

$$modifies(a_1, t_1, p_1), ..., modifies(a_n, t_n, p_n), v_1, ..., v_m$$

this clause is encoded in Boogie2 as:

ensures $\forall o : ObjectId$; $fId : FieldId$:
$$\left(\begin{array}{l} not\ \$modifies(a_1, t_1, p_1, Heap, o, fId) \wedge ...\wedge \\ not\ \$modifies(a_n, t_n, p_n, Heap, o, fId) \\ \wedge\ o \neq v_1\ \wedge ...\ \wedge\ o \neq v_m \end{array} \right) \Rightarrow\ Heap[o, fId] = old(Heap)[o, fId]$$

For example, the modifies clause of the routine *format* is encoded as follows:

ensures $\forall o : ObjectId$; $fId : FieldId$:
$$not\ \$modifies(proc, f, Current, Heap, o, fId) \Rightarrow Heap[o, fId] = old(Heap)[o, fId]$$

This property expresses that for all objects o, and all fields fId that are not modified by the agent *proc* with the target f and argument *Current*, the value of the field $o.fId$ in the current heap is equal to the value of $o.fId$ in the old heap. The expression $Heap[o, fId]$ yields the value of the field fId of the object o in the current heap.

Initializing Agents. To address the frame problem for agents, we need to link the uninterpreted function $modifies(proc, t, p)$ with the locations that the routine *proc* modifies. We solve this by applying the same approach used to reason about agent pre- and postconditions. Thus, our methodology connects the uninterpreted function $modifies with the concrete set of locations that the agent modifies.

Given a procedure pr, the agent initialization $a := $ **agent** pr generates the following assumptions:

assume $\forall t, p : ObjectId$; $h_1 : Heap : \$precondition(a, t, p, h_1) = \$pre_{pr}(t, p, h_1)$
assume $\forall t, p : ObjectId$; $h_1, h_2 : Heap :$
$$\$postcondition(a, t, p, h_1, h_2) = \$post_{pr}(t, p, h_1, h_2)$$
assume $\forall t, p, o : ObjectId$; $fId : FieldId$; $h_1 : Heap :$
$$\$modifies(a, t, p, h_1, o, fId) = \$modifies_{pr}(t, p, h_1, o, fId)$$

The assumptions for the functions $precondition and $postcondition are the same assumptions as described in Section 3.2. The third assumption relates the uninterpreted function $\$modifies$ with the modifies clause of pr. The function $\$modifies_{pr}$ yields *true* if the procedure pr modifies the field $o.fId$ for the target t and argument p. The definition of this function is generated from the modifies clause of the procedure pr.

For example, assuming that the routine *align_left* in the class *FORMATTER* (Section 2.1) modifies its argument p, then $modifies_{align\_left}$ is defined as

$$\$modifies_{align\_left}(Current, p, h, o, fId) \triangleq (h[o] = p)$$

Limitations. The current implementation of modifies clauses is not powerful enough to express some non-interference properties. One can express that an agent a modifies a set of locations s, and an agent b modifies another set of locations r, however, we cannot express that these locations are disjoint.

The same problem arises when verifying agents with open targets. An example of the use of open target is the routine *do_all* defined in the class *LIST* of the Eiffel base library. The *do_all* routine takes an agent with open target, and invokes the agent for all elements of the list. To verify the routine *do_all*, one needs to reason about non-interference at an abstract level, because the invocation of the agent for the *ith* element of the list might violate the precondition of the agent for the *jth* element of the list. To address this problem, a mechanism to support non-interference reasoning is required, as discussed in our technical report [24]. Extending our implementation to support this mechanism is part of future work.

5 Applications

In this section we study the applicability of our methodology to a range of examples which illustrate challenging aspects of reasoning about function objects.

5.1 Formatter Example

To verify the routine *format*, the methodology generates the following Boogie2 code[9]:

```
format(proc : PROCEDURE[FORMATTER, PARAGRAPH]; f : FORMATTER)
  1   assume $precondition(proc, f, Current, Heap)
  2   assert $precondition(proc, f, Current, Heap)
  3   h0 := Heap
  4   havoc Heap
  5   assume $postcondition(proc, f, Current, Heap, h0)
  6   assume ∀o : ObjectId; fId : FieldId :
            not $modifies(proc, f, Current, Heap, o, fId) ⇒ Heap[o, fId] = h0[o, fId]
  7   assert $postcondition(proc, f, Current, Heap, h0)
  8   assert ∀o : ObjectId; fId : FieldId :
            not $modifies(proc, f, Current, Heap, o, fId) ⇒ Heap[o, fId] = h0[o, fId]
```

---

[9] To simplify the presentation, we use the signature of the function in Eiffel.

$apply\_align\_left(f : FORMATTER; p : PARAGRAPH)$

1   **assume not** $p.\$left\_aligned$
2   $a := \mathbf{agent}\{FORMATTER\}.align\_left$
3   **assume** $\forall t_1, p_1 : ObjectId; h : Heap :$
         $\$precondition(a, t_1, p_1, h) = \$pre_{align\_left}(t_1, p_1, h)$
4   **assume** $\forall t_1, p_1 : ObjectId; h, h' : Heap :$
         $\$postcondition(a, t_1, p_1, h, h') = \$post_{align\_left}(t_1, p_1, h, h')$
5   **assume** $\forall t_1, p_1, o : ObjectId; \; fId : FieldId; h : Heap :$
         $\$modifies(a, t_1, p_1, h, o, fId) = \$modifies_{align\_left}(t_1, p_1, h_1, o, fId)$
6   **assert** $\$precondition(a, f, p, Heap)$
7   $h_0 := Heap$
8   **havoc** $Heap$
9   **assume** $\$postcondition(a, f, p, Heap, h_0)$
10 **assume** $\forall o : ObjectId; \; fId : FieldId :$
         $\textbf{not } \$modifies(proc, f, p, Heap, o, fId) \Rightarrow Heap[o, fId] = h_0[o, fId]$
11 **assert** $p.\$left\_aligned$
12 **assert** $\forall o : ObjectId; \; fId : FieldId :$
         $o \neq p \Rightarrow Heap[o, fId] = h_0[o, fId]$

Fig. 3. Proof obligations of the routine $apply\_align\_left$

The pre- and postcondition of *format* are translated in the lines 1 and 7, respectively. The modifies clause of *format* is translated in line 8. The agent invocation is translated in the lines 2-6. This translation assumes the postcondition and the modifies clause of *call* in lines 5 and 6. The proof is straightforward since the **assume** and **assert** instructions in lines 1 and 2, lines 5 and 7, and lines 6 and 8 refer to the same heap.

The most interesting case in the verification of function object is the verification of clients that use function objects, such as $apply\_align\_left$. The application of the methodology to this routine generates the Boogie2 code presented in Figure 3.

Similar to the previous example, lines 1 and 11 are generated by the translation of the pre- and postcondition; line 12 is the translation of the modifies clause. The declaration **agent** $\{FORMATTER\}.align\_left$ generates lines 2-5. The precondition and postcondition of the routine $align\_left$ is denoted by $\$pre_{align\_left}$ and $\$post_{align\_left}$ respectively; the modifies clause of $align\_left$ is denoted by $\$modifies_{align\_left}$. The invocation of the routine *format* produces lines 6-10. The current heap is stored in h_0 in line 7 to be able to evaluate the postcondition in line 9.

The key points in the proof are the **assert** instructions at lines 6, 11 and 12. By the definition of $\$pre_{align\_left}$, $\$post_{align\_left}$, and $\$modifies_{align\_left}$ we know:

$$\forall t_1, p_1 : ObjectId; h : Heap : \$pre_{align\_left}(t_1, p_1, h) = \; not \; p_1.\$left\_aligned \quad (1)$$

$$\forall t_1, p_1 : ObjectId; h, h' : Heap : \$post_{align\_left}(t_1, p_1, h, h') = \; p_1.\$left\_aligned \quad (2)$$

$$\$modifies_{align\_left}(Current, p, h, o, fId) \; = h[o] \neq p \quad (3)$$

In particular, $pre_{align\_left}(f, p, Heap) = not\ p.\$left\_aligned$. Then, the assertion at line 6 is proven using the assumptions at lines 1 and 3, and (1). The assertion at line 11 is proven in a similar way using the assumptions at lines 4 and 9, and (2). Finally, the assertion at line 12 is proven in a similar way using the assumptions at lines 5 and 10, and (3).

5.2 Archive Example

In the archive example, the most interesting proof is the proof of the routine *main*. The routine *log* is interesting to show how to specify and prove closed arguments. To prove these routines, we apply the methodology described in Section 3.3 (to simplify the example, we omit the the translation for framing). The proof for the routine *log* is similar to the proof of the *format* routine. The only change is the use of the function $precondtion_1$ which takes only three arguments (the procedure *log_file*, the string s and the heap). The generated proof obligations are the following:

$log(log\_file : PROCEDURE[ANY; TAPE];\ s : STRING)$
  1 **assume** $precondition_1(log\_file, s, Heap)$
  2 **assert** $precondition_1(log\_file, s, Heap)$
  3 $log\_file.call(s)$

The translation of the routine *main* is as follows:

$main(c : CLIENT)$
  1 **create** $t.make$
  2 **assert** $t.\$is\_loaded$
  3 $a := $ **agent** $t.store$
  4 **assume** $\forall p_1 : ObjectId;\ h : Heap :$
          $precondition_1(a, p_1, h) = \$pre_{store}(a, t, p_1, h)$
  5 **assume** $\forall p_1 : ObjectId;\ h, h' : Heap :$
          $postcondition_1(a, p_1, h, h') = \$post_{store}(a, t, p_1, h, h')$
  6 **assert** $precondition_1(a, "Hello World", Heap)$
  7 $c.log(a, "Hello World")$

The proof of routine *main* translates the agent in lines 3-5. The function $precondition_1$ is used to express the precondition of the agent with closed target. Using the assumption at line 4 and the knowledge of line 2, one can prove the **assert** instruction at line 7.

6 Experiments

We have implemented an automatic verifier for agents, called *EVE Proofs*, following the architecture of the Spec# verifier [2]. Given an Eiffel program, the tool generates a Boogie2 [16] file, and uses the Boogie verifier to prove the generated

Table 1. Examples automatically verified by *EVE Proofs*

Name	Classes	Agents	Agent calls	LOC Eiffel	LOC Boogie2	Time [s]
1. Formatter	3	2	2	116	414	1.57
2. Archiver	4	1	1	119	440	1.58
3. Command	3	2	4	120	435	1.61
4. Calculator	3	11	11	243	817	25.14
5. ATM	4	13	20	486	1968	73.72
6. Cell / Recell	3	4	4	151	497	1.71
7. Counter	2	2	4	96	356	1.53
8. Sequence	5	2	4	200	526	1.78
Total	27	37	50	1513	5453	108.64

program. The tool is integrated in *EVE* [10] (the Eiffel Verification Environment), and it can be downloaded from `http://eve.origo.ethz.ch/`. Once the user has specified pre- and post-conditions, and invariants, the verification is completely automatic.

EVE Proofs translates each agent initialization into Boogie2 assumptions as described in Section 3 and Section 4. These assumptions are generated inside the body of the Boogie2 procedure corresponding to the Eiffel routine. Thus, Boogie only considers the agent properties inside the procedure where the agent is used.

Using *EVE Proofs*, we have automatically proven a suite of examples: the examples presented in Section 2, and several more agent-intensive programs to model graphical user interfaces. The examples can be downloaded from `http://se.ethz.ch/people/tschannen/examples.zip`. The experiments were run on a machine with a 2.71 GHz dual core Pentium processors with 2GB of RAM.

Table 1 presents the results of the experiments. For each example, the table shows the number of classes, agents, agent calls, and lines of code in Eiffel, as well as the number of lines of the encoding in Boogie2. The last column shows the running time of Boogie (the dominant factor in the verification).

The formatter and archiver examples have been discussed in the previous sections. The third example is a typical implementation of the command pattern [12]. It defines a command class that uses an agent to store an action, which will be executed when the command's execute function is called. This pattern is also used in the *calculator* and *ATM* examples, which model applications using graphical user interfaces (GUI). The *calculator* example implements the GUI of a simple calculator with buttons for the digits, and basic arithmetic operations such as addition, subtraction, and multiplication. The *ATM* example implements a GUI for an ATM machine, and it also implements client code where a pin number is entered, and money is deposited and withdrawn from an account. These two examples are of particular interest because the GUI libraries in Eiffel typically use agents to react on events.

The ATM and calculator example make extensive use of the command pattern and therefore have more agents. Due to the increased number of agent calls and more difficult contracts, the proof of these examples takes significantly longer than the smaller examples. The ATM example is slower than the Calculator because the ATM example has more agent calls.

The cell/recell example is an extension of an example by Parkinson and Bierman [29] with agents. The *counter* example implements a simple counter class with increase and decrease operations. The last example defines a class hierarchy for integer sequences introducing an arithmetic and Fibonacci sequence.

Graphical user interfaces use agents intensively. We have performed some experiments to check the verification time in such applications. The results have shown that increasing the number of agent initializations in a routine slighlty increases the overall verification time of that routine. This time increase is due to the additional assumptions that are generated for each agent. The new assumptions are then used by Boogie, and thus slow down the verification. Since the verification methodology is modular, the assumptions are local to a specific routine. The increase of agent initializations in one routine does not affect the verification time of other routines.

7   Related Work

Jacobs [14] as well as Müller and Ruskiewicz [23] extend the Boogie verification methodology to handle C# delegates. They associate pre- and postconditions with each delegate type. When the delegate type is instantiated, they prove that the specification of the method refines the specification of the delegate type. At the call site, one has to prove the precondition and may assume the postcondition of the delegate. By contrast, the methodology presented here "hides" the specification behind abstract predicates. Callers will in general require the predicates to hold that they need in order to call an agent. The approach taken by Jacobs, Müller, and Ruskiewicz splits proof obligations into two parts, the refinement proof when the delegate is instantiated and the proof of the precondition when the delegate is called. This split makes it difficult to handle closed parameters, in particular, the closed receiver of C# delegates. Both previous works use some form of ownership [21] to ensure that the receiver of a delegate instance has the properties required by the method underlying the delegate. Our methodology requires only one proof obligation when the agent is called and can be generalized to several closed parameters more easily.

Parkinson and Bierman [28,29] introduce abstract predicates to verify object-oriented programs in separation logic. Abstract predicates are a powerful means to abstract from implementation details and to support information hiding and inheritance. Distefano and Parkinson [9] show the applicability of abstract predicates by implementing a tool to verify Java programs. The tool handles several design patterns such as the visitor pattern, the factory pattern, and the observer pattern. The predicates we use for the preconditions and postconditions of agents are inspired by abstract predicates. Even though Parkinson and Bierman's work and Distefano and Parkinson's work do not handle function objects, we believe that the ideas presented in this paper also apply to their setting.

Birkedal et al. [4] present higher-order separation logic, a logic for a second-order programming language, and use it to verify an implementation of the Observer pattern [19]. In contrast to separation logic, the methodology presented in this paper is designed to work with standard first-order theorem provers.

Contracts have been integrated into higher-order functions. Findler et al. [11] integrate contracts using a typed lambda calculus with assertions for higher-order functions. Honda et al. [13,3] introduce a sound compositional program logic for higher-order functions. Régis-Gianas and Pottier [30] develop a Hoare logic for a call-by-value programming language equipped with higher-order functions. Kanig and Filiatre [17] present a tool to verifier higher-order functions. The tool uses an intermediate language; the tool is intended to be used for verification tools targeting ML-like programming languages. Function objects in object-oriented languages are more complex than higher-order functions in functional languages because of the heap and side-effects. Although the pre- and postconditions of agents are side-effect free, agent calls are not: agent calls can access the heap, and can modify any attribute. This makes the verification of function objects harder compared to functional programming languages.

Börger et al. [5] present an operational semantics of C# including delegates. The semantics is given using abstract state machines. However, this work does not describe how to apply this model to specify and verify C# programs.

Schoeller [32] has developed an automatic verifier for a subset of Eiffel. The tool generates Boogie code, and uses the Boogie verifier to prove the generated Boogie program. However, Schoeller's tool does not handle agents. Paige and Ostroff [27], and Nordio et al. [25] have formalized semantics for a subset of Eiffel, but these works do not include agents. Our encoding of the routines *precondition* and *postcondition* is based on previous work on pure routines by Darvas and Leino [8,7], and Leino and Müller [22].

8   Conclusions and Future Work

We have introduced a verification methodology to verify higher-order functions, and we have implemented an automatic verifier for function objects. The verifier takes an Eiffel program, translates it to Boogie2, and uses the Boogie verifier to prove the generated code. Our experiments with automatic proofs indicate that the methodology is able to specify and verify function objects by introducing side-effect free routines which model abstractly the pre- and postcondition of the function objects. The experience so far suggests that a complete verification chain leading to fully automatic verification of object-oriented programs with function objects is possible.

Although presented in Eiffel, the verification methodology is not dependent on a specific programming language; we see no major obstacles in applying it to other languages supporting function objects.

As future work we plan to extend the framing methodology to handle non-interference. In particular, we plan to extend the implementation to be able to prove library classes such as *linked lists*. Furthermore, we plan to investigate how to apply a similar methodology to generics (in particular *constrained generics*).

Acknowledgements

We thank Stephan van Staden and Manuel Oriol for their insightful comments on drafts of this paper. Calcagno was supported by EPSRC.

References

1. Banerjee, A., Naumann, D., Rosenberg, S.: Regional Logic for Local Reasoning about Global Invariants. In: Vitek, J. (ed.) ECOOP 2008. LNCS, vol. 5142, pp. 387–411. Springer, Heidelberg (2008)
2. Barnett, M., Leino, R., Schulte, W.: The Spec# Programming System: An Overview. In: Barthe, G., Burdy, L., Huisman, M., Lanet, J.-L., Muntean, T. (eds.) CASSIS 2004. LNCS, vol. 3362, pp. 49–69. Springer, Heidelberg (2005)
3. Berger, M., Honda, K., Yoshida, N.: A logical analysis of aliasing in imperative higher-order functions. In: ICFP '05: Proceedings of the tenth ACM SIGPLAN international conference on Functional programming, pp. 280–293. ACM, New York (2005)
4. Biering, B., Birkedal, L., Torp-Smith, N.: BI-hyperdoctrines, higher-order separation logic, and abstraction. In: ToPLAS (2008)
5. Börger, E., Fruja, N.G., Gervasi, V., Stärk, R.F.: A high-level modular definition of the semantics of C#. Theor. Comput. Sci. 336(2-3), 235–284 (2005)
6. Clarke, D., Drossopoulou, S.: Ownership, encapsulation and the disjointness of type and effect. In: OOPSLA '02, vol. 37, pp. 292–310. ACM Press, New York (2002)
7. Darvas, Á.: Reasoning About Data Abstraction in Contract Languages. PhD thesis, ETH Zurich, Switzerland (to appear, 2009)
8. Darvas, A., Leino, K.R.M.: Practical reasoning about invocations and implementations of pure methods. In: Dwyer, M.B., Lopes, A. (eds.) FASE 2007. LNCS, vol. 4422, pp. 336–351. Springer, Heidelberg (2007)
9. Distefano, D., Parkinson, M.J.: jStar: Towards Practical Verification for Java. In: OOPSLA '08: Proceedings of the 23rd ACM SIGPLAN conference on Object oriented programming systems languages and applications, pp. 213–226 (2008)
10. EVE: Eiffel Verification Environment, http://eve.origo.ethz.ch
11. Findler, R.B., Felleisen, M.: Contracts for higher-order functions. SIGPLAN Not. 37(9), 48–59 (2002)
12. Gamma, E., Helm, R., Johnson, R., Vlissides, J.: Design Patterns: Elements of Reusable Object-Oriented Software. Addison Wesley, Reading (1994)
13. Honda, K., Yoshida, N., Berger, M.: An observationally complete program logic for imperative higher-order frame rules. In: LICS '05: Proceedings of the Symposium on Logic in Computer Science, USA, pp. 260–279. IEEE Computer Society, Los Alamitos (2005)
14. Jacobs, B.: A Statically Verifiable Programming Model for Concurrent Object-Oriented Programs. PhD thesis, Katholieke Universiteit Leuven (2007)
15. Rustan, K., Leino, M.: Specification and verification of object-oriented software. Marktoberdorf International Summer School 2008, lecture notes (2008)
16. Rustan, K., Leino, M.: This is boogie 2. Technical Report Manuscript KRML 178, Microsoft Research (2008)
17. Kanig, J., Filliâtre, J.-C.: Who: A Verifier for Effectful Higher-order Programs. In: ACM SIGPLAN Workshop on ML, Edinburgh, Scotland, UK (2009)

18. Kassios, I.T.: Dynamic Frames: Support for Framing, Dependencies and Sharing Without Restrictions. In: Misra, J., Nipkow, T., Sekerinski, E. (eds.) FM 2006. LNCS, vol. 4085, pp. 268–283. Springer, Heidelberg (2006)
19. Krishnaswami, N., Aldrich, J., Birkedal, L.: Modular verification of the subject-observer pattern via higher-order separation logic. In: FTJP (2007)
20. Leavens, G.T., Leino, K.R.M., Müller, P.: Specification and verification challenges for sequential object-oriented programs. Formal Aspects of Computing 19(2), 159–189 (2007)
21. Leino, K.R.M., Müller, P.: Object invariants in dynamic contexts. In: Odersky, M. (ed.) ECOOP 2004. LNCS, vol. 3086, pp. 491–516. Springer, Heidelberg (2004)
22. Leino, K.R.M., Müller, P.: Verification of equivalent-results methods. In: Drossopoulou, S. (ed.) ESOP 2008. LNCS, vol. 4960, pp. 307–321. Springer, Heidelberg (2008)
23. Müller, P., Ruskiewicz, J.N.: A modular verification methodology for C# delegates. In: Abrial, J.-R., Glässer, U. (eds.) Rigorous Methods for Software Construction and Analysis. LNCS, vol. 5115, pp. 187–203. Springer, Heidelberg (to appear, 2009)
24. Nordio, M., Calcagno, C., Meyer, B., Müller, P.: Reasoning about Function Objects. Technical Report 615, ETH Zurich (2008)
25. Nordio, M., Calcagno, C., Müller, P., Meyer, B.: A Sound and Complete Program Logic for Eiffel. In: Oriol, M. (ed.) TOOLS-EUROPE 2009. Lecture Notes in Business and Information Processing, vol. 33, pp. 195–214 (2009)
26. O'Hearn, P.W., Yang, H., Reynolds, J.C.: Separation and information hiding. In: POPL '04, pp. 268–280 (2004)
27. Paige, R., Ostroff, J.: ERC: an Object-Oriented Refinement Calculus for Eiffel. Formal Aspects of Computing 16, 51–79 (2004)
28. Parkinson, M., Bierman, G.: Separation logic and abstraction. In: POPL '05, vol. 40, pp. 247–258. ACM, New York (2005)
29. Parkinson, M.J., Bierman, G.M.: Separation logic, abstraction and inheritance. In: POPL '08, pp. 75–86. ACM, New York (2008)
30. Régis-Gianas, Y., Pottier, F.: A hoare logic for call-by-value functional programs. In: Audebaud, P., Paulin-Mohring, C. (eds.) MPC 2008. LNCS, vol. 5133, pp. 305–335. Springer, Heidelberg (2008)
31. Reynolds, J.C.: Separation logic: A logic for shared mutable data structures. In: LICS (2002)
32. Schoeller, B.: Making classes provable through contracts, models and frames. PhD thesis, ETH Zurich (2007)

Welterweight Java

Johan Östlund and Tobias Wrigstad

Uppsala University

Abstract. This paper presents Welterweight Java (WJ), a new minimal core Java calculus intended to be a suitable starting point for investigations in the semantics of Java-like programs. To this end, WJ adds a few extra pounds to Featherweight Java. WJ is imperative and stateful, which is a frequent extension of Featherweight Java. To account for the importance of concurrency, WJ models Java's thread-based concurrency and lock-based synchronisation. The design of WJ is distilled from recent work on concurrent Java-like systems. We believe that the calculus is a good starting point for extensions. We illustrate the potential of the calculus by showing two extensions. The first is a version of WJ extended with deep ownership. This serves two purposes—it is a minimal formalisation of ownership, interesting in its own right, and shows how easily WJ can be extended. The second is a simple non-null types system.

1   Introduction

Standard formalisms for Java-like languages greatly simplify formal investigations of novel programming constructs. Not only do they allow reuse of sound boilerplate definitions, but they greatly enhance readability and comparisons and combinations of different proposals. Just to name one example, Malayeri and Aldrich show how useful and easy to follow extensions of a standard system can be in [14]. All changes and extensions to the core formalism used are nicely marked. This makes understanding the new system a lot less of a hurdle when the reader is familiar with the core formalism. Building on well-understood blocks, facilitates communicating future research that focus on specific parts of a language, or specific constructs, in a clear and concise way.

Featherweight Java (FJ) [13] is the currently most popular Java "base formalism" and is both simple and concise due to careful selection of features and enables formulation of a simple type soundness proof which is extensible to generics. An interesting omission is mutable state, which is at the heart of most Java programs. In FJ objects are immutable and field updates result in new objects.

While in many cases sufficient, it makes FJ a less suitable basis for formalising language constructs that interplay with aliasing. Moreover, FJ does not model threads and synchronisation.

This paper presents Welterweight Java (WJ) as an alternative core calculus to FJ when capturing Java's imperative features is important. WJ models Java-style threads and Java-style concurrency control, supports aliasing and thread-local stack frames. To simplify proofs and reduce proof size, but without loss

J. Vitek (Ed.): TOOLS 2010, LNCS 6141, pp. 97–116, 2010.

of expressiveness, WJ is based on statements rather than expressions and uses explicit casts in favour of implicit subsumption. The resulting calculus is small and manageable and fits comfortably on a small number of pages. WJ is distilled and inspired from recent Java-like formalisms by the authors [23,24], and collaborators [21] where imperative features and thread support was needed. As a result, the formalism is malleable and easily extensible, as illustrated in this paper by two extensions of WJ with ownership and non-null types. Since the number of extensions of FJ greatly surpass those extending GFJ, we have chosen to omit generics. Adding it should be straightforward.

This paper represents the current state of WJ. It is based on internal needs and our understanding of what most researchers want in a core formalism. To this end, we do not model access modifiers, final fields or generics. To facilitate widespread adoption, we are making WJ's LATEX sources available on-line [15]. In the future, these will be accompanied by Ott [19] sources and mechanised proofs. However, having a *spatially* minimal formalism is important. In our experience, Ott often falls short in this respect.

This paper makes the following contributions:

1. It presents a simple, easy-to-extend Java formalism that is closer to Java than FJ. In particular it
   - is imperative and models aliasing and stack-frames
   - models thread-based concurrency and synchronisation
   - was built for simple extensions—it is a "pluggable types type system"
2. It contains the standard meta-theoretic results of progress and preservation of the aforementioned system
3. It shows how to extend WJ to support ownership types and non-null types

Outline. Section 2 introduces WJ, Section 3 extends WJ with a simple ownership types system. Section 4 extends WJ with non-null types. Section 5 discusses related work. Section 6 concludes.

2   Introducing Welterweight Java

WJ's syntax is shown in Fig. 1. To simplify matters, WJ only has statements and every statement, except sequencing, `lock` and `unlock`, assigns to a variable or field, all or which are mutable. Local variables must be declared at the beginning of a method before any statements are executed. Fields and variables are initialised with `null` and there is no `null` literal in the syntax. The class `Object` is at the root of every class hierarchy and is defined implicitly for every program P as `class Object { }`. For simplicity, it is omitted from the static syntax and there is no explicit syntax for method returns. Instead a value assigned to the special variable `ret` is returned when the method exits, similar to Pascal and friends. Synchronisation blocks are modelled through `lock` and `unlock` statements. Removing locks from the formalism is as simple as removing `lock` and `unlock` from the syntax and remove the (LOCK)/(UNLOCK) rules from the semantics. We assume that classes, fields and local variables have unique names.

$$
\begin{array}{llr}
P ::= \overline{C} & & program \\
C ::= \texttt{class } c \texttt{ extends } d \texttt{ \{ } \overline{F} \; \overline{M} \texttt{ \}} & & class \\
F ::= t \, f & & field \\
M ::= t \, m \, (\overline{t} \; \overline{x}) \texttt{ \{ } \overline{t} \; \overline{x} \; s \texttt{ \}} & & method \\
s ::= s; s \mid x = y.f \mid x = z \mid y.f = z \mid x = \texttt{new } t\,() & & statement \\
\quad \mid \; x = (t) \; z \mid x = y.m(\overline{z}) \mid x = \texttt{start } t\,() \mid \texttt{lock } z \mid \texttt{unlock } z & & \\
t ::= c, d & &
\end{array}
$$

Fig. 1. WJ's syntax. c,d are class names, f,m are field and method names, and x, y, z are names of variables or parameters where $x \neq \texttt{this}$. By convention, y is always used in receiver position and z in argument position. For simplicity, we assume that names of classes and fields are unique. The special variable $\texttt{ret}$ is used to return values from a method. We use prime notation in the standard fashion. In the spirit of FJ [13] we write $\overline{x}$ for a possibly empty sequence $x_1 \ldots x_n$. We write $\overline{t} \; \overline{x}$ as a shorthand for the possibly empty sequence $t_1 \, x_1 \ldots t_n \, x_n$. $\overline{F}$ is shorthand for the possibly empty sequence $t_1 \, f_1 \ldots t_n \, f_n$. Further we write $\overline{z} : \overline{t}$ for a sequence $z_1 : t_1 \ldots z_n : t_n$. $\overline{T}$ is short for the *set* $T_1 \ldots T_n$. Other uses of the overbar notation should be obvious.

2.1 Class-Table

For functions and relations g, g', we define $g \bullet g' \; (x)$ as: $g(x)$ if $g(x)$ is defined, otherwise $g'(x)$. For tuples, $(f, g) \bullet (f', g') = (f \bullet f', g \bullet g')$. For a program P we define the class table $\mathcal{CT}$ as: $\mathcal{CT}(c) = (\{\overline{f} : \overline{t}\}, \{\overline{m} \mapsto \overline{M}\}) \bullet \mathcal{CT}(d)$ when $\texttt{class } c \texttt{ extends } d \texttt{ \{ } \overline{F} \; \overline{M} \texttt{ \}} \in P$, $\overline{F} = \overline{t \, f}$ and each m is the name of the method it maps to. For $\texttt{Object}$, we define $\mathcal{CT}(\texttt{Object}) = (\epsilon, \epsilon)$ and $\epsilon(x) = \bot$. Notably, $\bullet$-composition models lookup in inheritance hierarchies and lookups of non-existing elements return $\bot$ and $\bot(x) = \bot$. As we do not model overloading, method names are unique in a class body (but may occur in other class bodies).

Using our class table, we can define helper predicates in a simple and straightforward way in Fig. 2.

2.2 Static Semantics

WJ's static semantics is shown in Fig. 3. A program is a number of class declarations rooted in $\texttt{Object}$. A program is well-formed if its classes are well-formed. A class is well-formed if its fields and methods are well-formed and overriding methods preserve types. A method is well-formed if its body is well-formed under the type environment $E ::= [\,] \mid E[y : t] \mid E[f : t]$ (see Fig. 4) constructed from the current $\texttt{this}$, the method's formal parameters, local variable declarations, or fields and the special variable $\texttt{ret}$, used for returning a value from the method. Well-formed statements can be sequenced in the standard fashion into a well-formed compound statement. Without loss of expressiveness, subsumption is replaced by explicit casts. Assignment to a field or variable is well-formed if the type of the right-hand side is the same as the declared type of the left-hand side. The type of a field is the field's declared type in the receiver. A method call is well-formed if the types of the actual arguments are the same as the types of the formal parameters. The type of the method is obtained by looking it up

Static Lookup Functions.   Given a well-formed class table CT, we define:

$\mathsf{fields}(c) = \mathit{fst}(CT(c))$ Lookup all fields for class c

$\mathsf{ftype}(c.f) = \mathsf{fields}(c)(f)$ Lookup type of field f in class c

$\mathsf{methods}(c) = \mathit{snd}(CT(c))$ Lookup all methods for class c

$\mathsf{mtype}(c.m) = \bar{t} \to t$ when $\mathsf{methods}(c)(m) = t\ m(\bar{t}\ \bar{x})\{\ \bar{t'}\ \bar{x'}\ s\ \}$, otherwise $\bot$
    Lookup signature of method m in class c

$\mathsf{mbody}(c.m) = (\bar{x}, \bar{x'}\,\mathtt{ret}, s)$ Lookup variables and body of method m in class c

Fig. 2. Lookup functions. Notably, since we do not model field overriding, $\bullet$-composition for fields is equivalent to set union.

(WF-PROGRAM)
$$\frac{\vdash C \text{ for all } C \in P}{\vdash P}$$

(WF-CLASS)
$$\frac{\vdash d <: \mathtt{Object} \qquad \vdash \overline{F} \qquad \mathtt{this} : c \vdash \overline{M} \qquad \forall m.\ \mathsf{mtype}(d.m) \neq \bot \Rightarrow \mathsf{mtype}(c.m) = \mathsf{mtype}(d.m)}{\vdash \mathtt{class}\ c\ \mathtt{extends}\ d\ \{\ \overline{F}\ \overline{M}\ \}}$$

(WF-ROOT-CLASS)
$$\frac{}{\vdash \mathtt{class}\ \mathtt{Object}\ \{\}}$$

(WF-FIELD)
$$\frac{\vdash t}{\vdash t\ f}$$

(WF-METHOD)
$$\frac{\mathtt{this} : c, \bar{x} : \bar{t}, \bar{x'} : \bar{t'}, \mathtt{ret} : t \vdash s}{\mathtt{this} : c \vdash t\ m(\bar{t}\ \bar{x})\{\ \bar{t'}\ \bar{x'}\ s\ \}}$$

(S-SEQUENCE)
$$\frac{E \vdash s \qquad E \vdash s'}{E \vdash s; s'}$$

(S-ASSIGN)
$$\frac{E \vdash x : t \qquad E \vdash z : t}{E \vdash x = z}$$

(S-NEW)
$$\frac{E \vdash x : t}{E \vdash x = \mathbf{new}\ t()}$$

(S-SELECT)
$$\frac{E \vdash y : t \qquad E \vdash x : \mathsf{ftype}(t.f)}{E \vdash x = y.f}$$

(S-UPDATE)
$$\frac{E \vdash y : t \qquad E \vdash z : \mathsf{ftype}(t.f)}{E \vdash y.f = z}$$

(S-FORK)
$$\frac{\mathsf{mtype}(t.\mathtt{run}) = \epsilon \to \_ \qquad E \vdash x : t}{E \vdash x = \mathbf{start}\ t()}$$

(S-CAST)
$$\frac{E \vdash z : t' \qquad E \vdash x : t}{E \vdash x = (t)\ z}$$

(S-CALL)
$$\frac{E \vdash y : t \qquad \mathsf{mtype}(t.m) = \bar{t} \to t' \qquad E \vdash \bar{z} : \bar{t} \qquad E \vdash x : t'}{E \vdash x = y.m(\bar{z})}$$

(S-LOCK)
$$\frac{\vdash E \qquad z \in \mathit{dom}(E)}{E \vdash \mathbf{lock}\ z}$$

(S-UNLOCK)
$$\frac{\vdash E \qquad z \in \mathit{dom}(E)}{E \vdash \mathbf{unlock}\ z}$$

(VAR)
$$\frac{\vdash E \qquad E(x) = t}{E \vdash x : t}$$

Fig. 3. WJ's static semantics. E is the standard type environment mapping variables to types and $<:$ is subtyping, defined in Fig. 6. Note that the rule (VAR) is not part of the syntax but a helper rule used by many s-rules.

$T ::= \mathsf{S}\ \rho$	Thread	$H ::= [\,]\ \mid\ H[\iota \mapsto (t, \rho, F)]$	Heap
$S ::= \epsilon\ \mid\ S\ \langle L, s \rangle$	Stack	$F ::= [\,]\ \mid\ F[f \mapsto v]$	Fields
$L ::= [\,]\ \mid\ L[y \mapsto v]$	Stack frame	$E ::= [\,]\ \mid\ E[y : t]\ \mid\ E[f : t]$	Local type env
$v ::= \iota\ \mid\ \mathtt{null}$	Value	$\Gamma ::= [\,]\ \mid\ \Gamma[\iota \mapsto t]$	Store-type

Fig. 4. Syntax of type environments, stacks, heaps

Lookup in Stack

$L[x \mapsto v](y) = v$ when $x = y$, else $L(y)$; $[\,](y) = \bot$

Lookup in Object

$F[f \mapsto v](f') = v$ when $f = f'$, else $F(f')$; $[\,](f) = \bot$

Lookup in Heap

$H[\iota \mapsto (t, \rho, F)](\iota') = (t, \rho, F)$ when $\iota = \iota'$, else $H(\iota')$; $[\,](\iota) = \bot$

For convenience, define $H(\iota.f) = F(f)$ when $H(\iota) = (\_, \_, F)$, else $\bot$

Update Object in Heap

$H(\iota.f) := v = H'[\iota \mapsto (t, \rho, F[f \mapsto v])]$ when $H = H'[\iota \mapsto (t, \rho, F)]$; if $H(\iota) = \bot$ or $H(\iota.f) = \bot$, then $\bot$

Fig. 5. Lookup and update of fields and variables

(SUB-DIR)	(SUB-TRANS)	(SUB-REF)	(TYPE)
$P(c) = \mathtt{class}\ c\ \mathtt{extends}\ d\ \cdots$	$\vdash t <: t'' \quad \vdash t'' <: t'$	$\vdash t$	$c \in dom(CT)$
$\vdash c <: d$	$\vdash t <: t'$	$\vdash t <: t$	$\vdash c$

Fig. 6. Types. Following CLASSICJAVA [12], we use $\cdots$ for "unimportant omissions."

in the declared type of the receiver, obtained from E. Any class that defines a zero-arity run method can be used to create and start a new thread. Last, synchronising is only allowed on defined variables. The helper rule (VAR) looks up the type of a variable in a well-formed E.

2.3 Dynamic Semantics

WJ's dynamic semantics is formalised as a small-step reduction semantics. The reduction relation $\xrightarrow{l}$ represents a single step of evaluation. The label l describes the action. Basic thread-scheduling is modelled as a non-deterministic choice from the unordered set $\overline{T}$ in (D-SCHEDULE). Each such, unlabeled, "scheduling step" picks one of the threads for reduction and performs one action. Deadlocks are the only thing that can lead to reduction being stuck.

Threads, stacks, heaps, frames, etc. are defined in Fig. 4. A thread consists of a stack S and a thread id ρ. As a convenience, given $\overline{T} = S_1\ \rho_1 \ldots S_n\ \rho_n$ we define $ids(\overline{T}) = \rho_1 \ldots \rho_n$. A stack is an ordered list of frame and statement tuples denoted $\langle L, s \rangle^m$ where $m ::= t.m$ and identifies the method to which the stack frame "belongs." The tag m is not strictly necessary, but simplifies proving preservation by linking dynamic frames to a correct static type environment.

A configuration consists of a heap H and an unordered collection of threads, $\overline{T}$. A heap is a map from locations ι to objects, which are triples of type, locking thread (possibly none, denoted ϵ) and fields F. Stack frames, L, are defined similar to fields, and map variable names x, y, z to values. Lookup and updates to H, F, and L happen in the standard fashion, *i.e.*, $L[x \mapsto v](y) = v$ if $x = y$, else $L(y)$ and $[\,](y) = \bot$, etc., see Fig. 5.

$$\text{(D-SCHEDULE)} \quad \frac{H \mid T \xrightarrow{\iota} H' \mid \overline{T'}}{H \mid T\overline{T} \longrightarrow H' \mid \overline{T'}\,\overline{T}}$$

$$\text{(D-DEAD)} \quad \frac{H' = \mathsf{unlock}(\rho, H)}{H \mid \mathsf{ERR}\ \rho \xrightarrow{\mathsf{err}} H' \mid \epsilon}$$

$$\text{(D-FINISHED)} \quad \frac{H' = \mathsf{unlock}(\rho, H)}{H \mid \langle L, \epsilon \rangle^{\mathsf{m}}\ \rho \xrightarrow{\mathsf{fin}} H' \mid \epsilon}$$

$$\text{(D-RETURN)} \quad \frac{L'(\mathbf{ret}) = v}{H \mid S\,\langle L, x = \cdots\,;\, s \rangle^{\mathsf{m}}, \langle L', \epsilon \rangle^{\mathsf{m}'}\ \rho \xrightarrow{\mathsf{ret}} H \mid S\,\langle L[x \mapsto v], s \rangle^{\mathsf{m}}\ \rho}$$

$$\text{(D-ASSIGN)} \quad \frac{L(z) = v}{H \mid S\,\langle L, x = z;\, s \rangle^{\mathsf{m}}\ \rho \xrightarrow{\mathsf{asgn}} H \mid S\,\langle L[x \mapsto v], s \rangle^{\mathsf{m}}\ \rho}$$

$$\text{(D-SELECT)} \quad \frac{L(y) = \iota \qquad H(\iota.f) = v}{H \mid S\,\langle L, x = y.f;\, s \rangle^{\mathsf{m}}\ \rho \xrightarrow{\mathsf{sel}} H \mid S\,\langle L[x \mapsto v], s \rangle^{\mathsf{m}}\ \rho}$$

$$\text{(D-UPDATE)} \quad \frac{L(y) = \iota \qquad L(z) = v}{H \mid S\,\langle L, y.f = z;\, s \rangle^{\mathsf{m}}\ \rho \xrightarrow{\mathsf{up}} H(\iota.f := v) \mid S\,\langle L, s \rangle^{\mathsf{m}}\ \rho}$$

$$\text{(D-NEW)} \quad \frac{F = [f \mapsto \mathbf{null} \mid f \in dom(\mathsf{fields}(t))] \qquad H' = H[\iota \mapsto (t, \epsilon, F)] \qquad \iota \text{ is fresh}}{H \mid S\,\langle L, x = \mathbf{new}\ t();\, s \rangle^{\mathsf{m}}\ \rho \xrightarrow{\mathsf{new}} H' \mid S\,\langle L[x \mapsto \iota], s \rangle^{\mathsf{m}}\ \rho}$$

$$\text{(D-CALL)} \quad \frac{\begin{array}{c} L(y) = \iota \qquad H(\iota) = (t, \cdots) \qquad \mathsf{mbody}(t.m) = (\overline{x'}, \overline{x''}, s') \\ L(\overline{z}) = \overline{v} \qquad L' = [\mathbf{this} \mapsto \iota][\overline{x'} \mapsto \overline{v}][\overline{x''} \mapsto \overline{\mathbf{null}}] \end{array}}{H \mid S\,\langle L, x = y.m(\overline{z});\, s \rangle^{\mathsf{m}}\ \rho \xrightarrow{\mathsf{call}} H \mid S\,\langle L, x = y.m(\overline{z}); s \rangle^{\mathsf{m}}\ \langle L', s' \rangle^{t.m}\ \rho}$$

$$\text{(D-CAST)} \quad \frac{L(z) = \mathbf{null} \qquad \bigvee \qquad \left(L(z) = \iota \qquad H(\iota) = (t', \cdots) \qquad \vdash t' <: t\right)}{H \mid S\,\langle L, x = (t)\ z;\, s \rangle^{\mathsf{m}}\ \rho \xrightarrow{\mathsf{cast}} H \mid S\,\langle L[x \mapsto L(z)], s \rangle^{\mathsf{m}}\ \rho}$$

$$\text{(D-FORK)} \quad \frac{\begin{array}{c} F = [f \mapsto \mathbf{null} \mid f \in dom(\mathsf{fields}(t))] \qquad H' = H[\iota \mapsto (t, \epsilon, F)] \\ T = \langle [\mathbf{this} \mapsto \iota][\overline{x} \mapsto \overline{\mathbf{null}}], s' \rangle^{t.\mathbf{run}}, \rho' \\ \mathsf{mbody}(t.\mathbf{run}) = (\epsilon, \overline{x}, s') \qquad \iota \text{ and } \rho' \text{ are fresh} \end{array}}{H \mid S\,\langle L, x' = \mathbf{start}\ t();\, s \rangle^{\mathsf{m}}\ \rho \xrightarrow{\mathsf{fork}} H' \mid (S\,\langle L[x \mapsto \iota], s \rangle^{\mathsf{m}}\ \rho)\ T}$$

$$\text{(D-LOCK)} \quad \frac{L(z) = \iota \qquad H = H'[\iota \mapsto (t, \rho', F)] \qquad \rho' \in \{\epsilon, \rho\}}{H \mid S\,\langle L, \mathbf{lock}\ z;\, s \rangle^{\mathsf{m}}\ \rho \xrightarrow{\mathsf{lock}} H'[\iota \mapsto (t, \rho, F)] \mid S\,\langle L, s \rangle^{\mathsf{m}}\ \rho}$$

$$\text{(D-UNLOCK)} \quad \frac{L(z) = \iota \qquad H = H'[\iota \mapsto (t, \rho, F)]}{H \mid S\,\langle L, \mathbf{unlock}\ z;\, s \rangle^{\mathsf{m}}\ \rho \xrightarrow{\mathsf{unlock}} H'[\iota \mapsto (t, \epsilon, F)] \mid S\,\langle L, s \rangle^{\mathsf{m}}\ \rho}$$

$$\mathsf{unlock}(\rho, [\,]) = [\,] \qquad \mathsf{unlock}(\rho, H[\iota \mapsto (t, \rho', F)]) = \mathsf{unlock}(\rho, H)[\iota \mapsto (t, \rho'[\epsilon/\rho], F)]$$

Fig. 7. WJ's dynamic semantics

$$\text{(D-SELECT-ERR)} \quad \frac{}{H \mid S \langle L[y \mapsto \text{null}], x = y.f; s\rangle^m \, \rho \xrightarrow{\text{sel.err}} H \mid \text{ERR} \, \rho}$$

$$\text{(D-UPDATE-ERR)} \quad \frac{}{H \mid S \langle L[y \mapsto \text{null}], y.f = z; s\rangle^m \, \rho \xrightarrow{\text{up.err}} H \mid \text{ERR} \, \rho}$$

$$\text{(D-CALL-ERR)} \quad \frac{}{H \mid S \langle L[y \mapsto \text{null}], x = y.m\,(\overline{z}); s\rangle^m \, \rho \xrightarrow{\text{call.err}} H \mid \text{ERR} \, \rho}$$

$$\text{(D-CAST-ERR)} \quad \frac{F(z) = \iota \qquad H(\iota) = (t', \cdots) \qquad \vdash t' \nleqslant : t}{H \mid S \langle L, x = (t)\, z; s\rangle^m \, \rho \xrightarrow{\text{cast.err}} H \mid \text{ERR} \, \rho}$$

$$\text{(D-LOCK-ERR)} \quad \frac{}{H \mid S \langle L[z \mapsto \text{null}], \text{lock } z; s\rangle^m \, \rho \xrightarrow{\text{lock.err}} H \mid \text{ERR} \, \rho}$$

$$\text{(D-UNLOCK-ERR)} \quad \frac{F(z) = \text{null} \qquad \bigvee \qquad \left(F(z) = \iota \qquad H(\iota) = (t, \rho', F') \qquad \rho' \neq \rho\right)}{H \mid S \langle L, \text{unlock } z; s\rangle^m \, \rho \xrightarrow{\text{unlock.err}} H \mid \text{ERR} \, \rho}$$

Fig. 8. WJ's dynamic semantics part II

The reductions are mostly standard. Method calls push a new stack frame and eventually result in an assignment from the special variable ret to the LHS of the method call statement. Reductions for null-pointer dereferencing and erroneous casts reduce to ERR and can be found in Fig. 8. Reduction *on* an error is modelled in (D-DEAD) and notably removes the thread's lock on all objects in the heap before the thread itself is descheduled and removed from the list of live threads. This corresponds to Java's semantics.

It is not possible to take a lock on an object that is already locked: such a statement cannot be reduced. If all threads in the system are in this state, the system is deadlocked and the reduction is stuck, see second clause of Theorem 1 (Progress).

Initial Configuration. Rather than having free-standing expressions in a program, we pick some class c with a zero-arity run method and create a new thread from it. When $\text{methods}(c)(\text{run}) = t \text{ run}()\{ \, \overline{t} \, \overline{x} \, s \, \}$ the initial configuration is:

$$[\iota \mapsto (c, \epsilon, [\,])] \mid \langle [\text{this} \mapsto \iota][\overline{x} \mapsto \overline{\text{null}}], s \rangle \, \rho$$

where ρ is a fresh id for the new thread.

2.4 Meta-theory

A configuration is well-formed under a standard store-type Γ, defined in Fig. 4. A thread is well-formed if each frame of its stack is well-formed under Γ and a local type environment E, derived from the corresponding method. A frame is well-formed if its local variables are well-formed and the method body s is well-formed. Finally, a heap H is well-formed under Γ if the types of all objects in H correspond to those in Γ, all locks are held by live threads and values in fields respect the declared field types modulo subtyping.

$$
\begin{array}{cc}
(\epsilon\text{-E}) & \dfrac{}{\vdash []}
\end{array}
\qquad
(\text{WF-E})\ \dfrac{\vdash E \quad \vdash t \quad y \notin dom(E)}{\vdash E[y:t]}
\qquad
(\epsilon\text{-}\varGamma)\ \dfrac{}{\vdash_g []}
\qquad
(\text{WF-}\varGamma)\ \dfrac{\vdash_g \varGamma \quad \vdash t \quad \iota \notin dom(\varGamma)}{\vdash_g \varGamma[\iota:t]}
$$

$$
(\text{WF-CONFIG})\ \dfrac{\mathsf{ids}(\overline{T}) = \varPsi \quad \varGamma;\varPsi \vdash_t \overline{T} \quad \varGamma;\varPsi \vdash_h H}{\varGamma \vdash H \,|\, \overline{T}}
\qquad
(\epsilon\text{-THREAD})\ \dfrac{\vdash_g \varGamma \quad \rho \in \varPsi}{\varGamma;\varPsi \vdash_t \epsilon\,\rho}
\qquad
(\text{WF-THREAD})\ \dfrac{\mathsf{MC}(t.m)=E \quad \varGamma;\varPsi \vdash_t S\,\rho \quad \varGamma;E \vdash_l L \quad E \vdash s}{\varGamma;\varPsi \vdash_t S\,\langle L,s\rangle^{t.m}\,\rho}
$$

$$
(\epsilon\text{-FRAME})\ \dfrac{\vdash_g \varGamma}{\varGamma;[] \vdash_l []}
\qquad
(\text{WF-FRAME})\ \dfrac{\varGamma;E \vdash_l L \quad \varGamma \vdash v:t}{\varGamma;E[x:t] \vdash_l L[x \mapsto v]}
\qquad
(\epsilon\text{-HEAP})\ \dfrac{\vdash_g \varGamma}{\varGamma;\varPsi \vdash_h []}
\qquad
(\text{WF-HEAP})\ \dfrac{\varGamma;\varPsi \vdash_h H \quad \varGamma(\iota)=t \quad \varGamma;\mathsf{fields}(t) \vdash_f F \quad \rho \in \varPsi \cup \{\epsilon\}}{\varGamma;\varPsi \vdash_h H[\iota \mapsto (t,\rho,F)]}
$$

$$
(\text{WF-NULL})\ \dfrac{\vdash_g \varGamma \quad \vdash t}{\varGamma \vdash \mathbf{null}:t}
\qquad
(\text{WF-PTR})\ \dfrac{\varGamma(\iota)=t' \quad t' <: t \quad \vdash_g \varGamma}{\varGamma \vdash \iota:t}
\qquad
(\epsilon\text{-FIELDS})\ \dfrac{\vdash_g \varGamma}{\varGamma;[] \vdash_f []}
\qquad
(\text{WF-FIELDS})\ \dfrac{\varGamma;E \vdash_f F \quad \varGamma \vdash v:t \quad f \notin dom(E)}{\varGamma;E[f:t] \vdash_f F[f \mapsto v]}
$$

Fig. 9. Well-Formedness Rules. For clarity, we subscript judgements relating to threads with t, frames with l, heaps with h, fields with f, and store-typing with g. The rule (WF-THREAD) makes use of a helper predicate MC for extracting the type environment for a certain method. MC is defined thus: $\mathsf{MC}(t.m) = \mathtt{this}:t, \overline{x}:\overline{t}, \overline{x'}:\overline{t'}, \mathtt{ret}:t'$ when $\mathsf{methods}(t)(m) = t'\ m(\overline{t}\ \overline{x})\{\ \overline{t'}\ \overline{x'}\ s\ \}$, otherwise $\perp$.

We formulate the usual progress and preservation theorems. We omit the "scheduling reduction" in (D-SCHEDULE) as it follows trivially from the rest. The proofs make use of lemmata defined on Page 106.

Theorem 1 (Progress). *If* $\varGamma \vdash H \,|\, \overline{T}$, *then either*

1. $\overline{T} = T\,\overline{T'}$ *and* $\exists l$ *s.t.* $H \,|\, T \xrightarrow{l} H' \,|\, \overline{T''}$; *or*
2. $\forall T \in \overline{T},\ T = S\,\langle L[z \mapsto \iota], \mathtt{lock}\ z\,;\,s'\rangle, \rho$ *and* $H(\iota) = (\_,\rho',\_)$ *s.t.* $\rho' \notin \{\rho,\epsilon\}$.

A reduction that does not acquire a lock is always possible and a reduction that does is possible if the subject is not locked, or is already locked by the current thread. The second case above captures the situation where all threads require unavailable locks to proceed, *i.e.*, the entire program is deadlocked (notably, we model system-wide deadlock by getting stuck).

Proof. The proof is straightforward by structural induction on the shape of $\overline{T}$, where most cases are trivial. Reductions which may "err" at run-time, *i.e.*, (D-SELECT), (D-UPDATE), (D-CALL), (D-CAST), (D-LOCK) and (D-UNLOCK), are all guarded by error versions (see Fig. 8) of the rule dealing with null-dereferencing, invalid casts and attempts at releasing a lock that one does not own. By (WF-HEAP) and (WF-FIELDS), a well-formed object (t,ρ,F) has all expected fields in F. □

Theorem 2 (Preservation). *If $\Gamma \vdash H \,|\, \overline{T}$ and $H \,|\, \overline{T} \overset{l}{\longrightarrow} H' \,|\, \overline{T'}$, then there exists a $\Gamma' \supseteq \Gamma$ s.t. $\Gamma' \vdash H' \,|\, \overline{T'}$*

Since there are no expressions in WJ, preservation concerns showing that assignments and initialisations obey declared types in variables and fields, and that method returns must correspond to the declared return type of the method.

Proof. The proof is by structural induction on the shape of $\overline{T}$.

(D-SCHEDULE) follows immediately from the induction hypothesis. It is easy to see that (D-DEAD) results in a heap H' well-formed under Γ.

The remaining cases all take the form $\overline{T} = S\,\rho$, i.e., we are taking a single step in a scheduled thread. We go through them in the order of Fig. 7. We state only the shape of the top-most stack frame, with the exception of returning from a method. We also omit the cases of the error reductions, noting that error reductions never modify values of fields or variables.

The four interesting cases are method call (the new frame is well-typed), method returning (the assignment to a variable in the underlying frame is well-typed), instantiation (fields are well-typed) and forking a new thread (similar to method call and instantiation).

$\langle L, x = z\,;\, s \rangle^{\mathsf{m}}$ Follows immediately from (S-ASSIGN) and Lemma 1 (Lookup).

$\langle L, x = y.f\,;\, s \rangle^{\mathsf{m}}$ Follows immediately from (S-SELECT) and Lemma 1 (Lookup).

$\langle L, y.f = z\,;\, s \rangle^{\mathsf{m}}$ Follows immediately from (S-UPDATE) and Lemma 1 (Lookup).

$\langle L, s\,;\, s' \rangle^{\mathsf{m}}$ Follows from induction hypothesis.

$\langle L, x = y.m(\overline{z})\,;\, s \rangle^{\mathsf{m}}$ From (D-CALL), we are pushing a new frame $\langle L', s' \rangle^{t.m}$ onto the stack s.t. $dom(L') = \{\mathtt{this}, \overline{x}, \overline{x'}\}$. Consequently, we must show that its local variables are well-typed at the start of the execution.

By (S-CALL), we see that $\overline{z}$ correspond to the parameters $\overline{t}\ \overline{x}$ of the method (remember, overriding preserves types), and similar for the type of $y/\mathtt{this}$. Remaining stack variables are all initialised to $\mathtt{null}$. It is easy to see that the type environment E in (WF-METHOD) is identical to that of $\mathsf{MC}(t.m)$ and $E = \mathtt{this} : t, \overline{x} : \overline{t}, E'$ where E' holds local variables and furthermore $E \vdash s'$.

By induction hypothesis, values in $\overline{z}$ and $\mathtt{this}$ have the expected type, so it is easy to see that $\Gamma; \mathtt{this} : t, \overline{x} : \overline{t} \vdash_! [\mathtt{this} \mapsto L(y)][\overline{x} \mapsto L(\overline{z})]$. Since $\mathtt{null}$ can have any well-formed type, and all types in E are well-formed (by construction), $\Gamma; E \vdash_! L'$. The rest follows by (WF-THREAD).

$\overline{T} = S\,\langle L, \epsilon \rangle^{t.m}\rho$ In this case, we can proceed in different ways depending on the shape of S. If S is empty, the thread is simply removed from the list of threads (by (D-FINISHED)), and all objects locked by ρ are unlocked. As with (D-DEAD), it is easy to see that the resulting heap is well-formed (by applying Lemma 2).

If S is non-empty, it has the shape $S = S'\,\langle L', s \rangle^{\mathsf{m}}$, and reasoning becomes a bit more involved. The key is proving that updating a variable in the underlying stack-frame respects its typing.

By (WF-THREAD), $\mathsf{MC}(t.m) = E$ s.t., $\Gamma; E \vdash_{\bar{t}} L$. By (WF-METHOD), $\mathsf{mtype}(t.m) = \_ \to t'$ for some t', so by definition of MC, $\mathtt{ret} : t' \in E$. By (WF-FRAME), $L(\mathtt{ret}) = v$ s.t. $\Gamma \vdash v : t'$.

Now, consider the underlying stack frame $\langle L', s \rangle^m$. Since non-top stack frames are only created in (D-CALL), s must be some $x = y.m(\_)$; s', and the type of y's value is t. By (WF-METHOD), and the static semantics, $E' \vdash x = y.m(\_)$ for some E'. From the induction hypothesis, the type of y corresponds to its run-time value (modulo subsumption). Thus, by (S-CALL), the type of x in E' is t' (since $\mathsf{mtype}(t.m) = \_ \to t'$ and overriding must preserve types).

Since $\Gamma; E' \vdash_l L'$ by well-formed construction, and $E' \vdash x : t'$, clearly $\Gamma; E' \vdash_{\bar{t}} L'[x \mapsto v]$.

$\langle L, x = \mathtt{new}\ t(); s \rangle^m$ By well-formed construction, $\Gamma; \Psi \vdash_{\bar{h}} H$. It is easy to verify that the new object's fields are well-typed since they are initialised with $\mathtt{null}$. By (WF-HEAP), $\Gamma'; \Psi \vdash_{\bar{h}} H[\iota \mapsto (t, \epsilon, [f \mapsto \mathtt{null} \mid f \in dom(\mathsf{fields}(t))])]$ when $\Gamma' = \Gamma[\iota : t]$ and the well-typedness of the entire resulting configuration is trivial and uses Lemma 3 (Extension).

$\langle L, x = \mathtt{start}\ t(); s \rangle^m$ This case is very similar to (D-NEW) (for the object creation) and (D-CALL) (for the thread creation). It is easy to see that adding a well-formed thread with a fresh id to a well-formed configuration, produces another well-formed configuration.

$\langle L, x = (t)\, z; s \rangle^m$ Follows immediately from (S-CAST), (D-CAST) and Lemma 1. In the event of an illegal cast, (D-CAST-ERR) applies.

$\langle L, \mathtt{lock}\ z; s \rangle^m$ Follows from immediately from Lemma 2 (Lock Substitution).

$\langle L, \mathtt{unlock}\ z; s \rangle^m$ Follows from immediately from Lemma 2 (Lock Substitution).
                                                                          $\square$

Theorem 3 (Live Locks). *If $\Gamma \vdash H \mid \overline{T}$, then $\forall \iota \in dom(H). H(\iota) = (\_, \rho, \_)$ s.t. $\rho \in \mathsf{ids}(\overline{T}) \cup \{\epsilon\}$*

All locks in the system belong to existing threads. This means that the system cannot deadlock due to locks held by a thread that has died (or spurious locks), which follows Java's semantics.

Proof. By (D-NEW) and (D-FORK), objects are unlocked when created. It is easy to see that an object can only be locked by a live thread (this happens in (D-LOCK)). Further, by (WF-CONFIG), $\mathsf{ids}(\overline{T})$ is precisely the set of all live thread ids. All other reductions that manipulate locks set the lock to ϵ. $\square$

Lemma 1 (Lookup)

1. *If $\Gamma; \Psi \vdash_{\bar{h}} H$, $\Gamma(\iota) = c$ and $\mathsf{ftype}(c.f) = t$, then $H(\iota.f) = v$ s.t., $\Gamma \vdash v : t$.*
2. *If $\Gamma; E \vdash_{\bar{t}} L$ and $E(y) = t$, then $L(y) = v$ s.t., $\Gamma \vdash v : t$.*

Reading a variable or field in a well-formed stack or heap yields a value of the expected type.

Proof. Follows by straightforward induction on the definition of (WF-FRAME) and (WF-HEAP) respectively.   □

Lemma 2 (Lock Substitution). *If* $\Gamma; \Psi \vdash_{h} H[\iota \rightarrow (t, \rho, F)]$, *then* $\forall \rho' \in \Psi \cup \{\epsilon\}. \Gamma; \Psi \vdash_{h} H[\iota \rightarrow (t, \rho', F)]$ (Substituting the locking thread of an object in a well-formed heap for a live thread id or ϵ yields a well-formed heap.)

Proof. Follows immediately from the definition of (WF-HEAP).   □

Lemma 3 (Extension)

1. *If* $E \vdash s$, $\vdash E'$, *and* $E \subseteq E'$, *then* $E' \vdash s$
2. *If* $\Gamma; \Psi \vdash_{h} H$, $\vdash_{g} \Gamma'$, *and* $\Gamma \subseteq \Gamma'$, *then* $\Gamma'; \Psi \vdash_{h} H$.
3. *If* $\Gamma; E \vdash_{t} T$, $\vdash_{g} \Gamma'$, *and* $\Gamma \subseteq \Gamma'$, *then* $\Gamma'; E \vdash_{t} T$.

Proof The proof is straightforward and follows from structural induction on E, (WF-HEAP) and (WF-FRAME) for the respective cases.

3 Introducing Welterweight Ownership Java

To demonstrate how easily WJ can be extended, we define "Welterweight Ownership Java," WOJ, a minimal deep ownership system [4] similar to [5]. There are several diffrent flavors of ownership types. A reader familiar with ownership types might note that our system follows the Clarkean tradition, as in *e.g.*, [4,5].

Ownership Types The aim of ownership types is to manage aliasing by constraining from where a particular object may be referenced. The result is a strong notion of encapsulation. Every object is *owned* by some other object and can be the owner of other objects, called its representation. Ownership forms a tree rooted in "world," which represents objects that are not part of the representation of any object. Objects are given permissions to reference the representation of other objects, and this is captured in the type system by parameterising types over such permissions. A WOJ program where all objects are owned by world is equivalent to the WJ program obtained by stripping away all ownership annotations and extensions.

A consequence of *deep* ownership is the ability to reason about nesting of objects and distinguish its *inside* (it's transitive representation) from its *outside*. An object's owner is always outside the object itself, and world is the outermost owner. To preserve encapsulation, an object can only be given permission to reference outside objects, in addition to its representation.

Deep ownership systems enjoy the so-called owners-as-dominators property [4], which states that any access to an object in the system must go via its owner (except accesses from inside the object's representation.) This is enforced as each path from the root of the system (world) to an object contains the object's owner. For example, if the links of a linked list belong to the list's representation, it is not possible to manipulate the links directly from outside the list (as no such references may exist). Consequently, all manipulations of the links are mediated by the list itself.

3.1   Extending Welterweight Java with Ownership

The syntactic differences to WJ are minimal:

$$C ::= \text{class } c\langle\text{owner},\overline{p}\rangle \text{ extends } d\langle\overline{\alpha}\rangle \;\{\; \overline{F}\;\overline{M}\;\} \qquad t ::= c\langle\overline{\alpha}\rangle$$

where $\overline{p}$ are owner parameters (*i.e.*, stem from declarations) and $\overline{\alpha}$ are actual owners (*i.e.*, instantiated parameters). Parameters p and q are unique names and actual owners are defined $\alpha ::= p\,|\,\text{owner}\,|\,\text{world}\,|\,\text{this}$ where the latter three keywords denote owners that are always accessible in an object. owner denotes the owner of the current instance, world the outermost owner, and this is used to denote representation objects.

In contrast to more complicated ownership systems (*e.g.*, [3,16]) we do not allow fine-grained control over owner nesting, instead all owner parameters are implicitly nested outside owner.

We often write types thus, $c\langle\sigma\rangle$ where sigma is a map, from owner *parameters* declared in class headers (including owner) to *actual* owners α where the first p is always the special parameter owner. For example, for a type Foo<a,b,c> instantiated from a class class Foo<owner,p,q> we would write Foo<σ> where $\sigma = \{\text{owner} \mapsto \text{a}, p \mapsto \text{b}, q \mapsto \text{c}\}$. The σ is used frequently for "viewpoint adaptation," [8,23] (originally called owner substitution [3,22]), which is defined as straightforward substitution. As an example, let a field in the class Foo have the type Bar<this,p>. Accessing this field via a variable with type Foo<a,b,c>, the field's type is Bar<this,b>, *i.e.*, σ(Bar<this,p>), equivalent to Bar<σ(this),σ(p)>. Note that since this is not in the syntactic category of p, this is never in $dom(\sigma)$. Similar substitutions are applied in method calls to translate declared types in parameters and returns to the owner names visible at the call site. We define the substitution thus:

$$\sigma(c\langle\overline{\alpha}\rangle) = c\langle\sigma(\overline{\alpha})\rangle$$
$$\sigma(E[y:t]) = \sigma(E)[y:\sigma(t)]$$
$$\sigma(E[f:t]) = \sigma(E)[f:\sigma(t)]$$
$$\sigma((\{\overline{f}:\overline{t}\},\{\overline{m}\mapsto\overline{M}\})) = (\{\overline{f}:\sigma(\overline{t})\},\{\overline{m}\mapsto\sigma(\overline{M})\})$$
$$\sigma(t\;m(\overline{t}\;\overline{x})\{\;\overline{t'}\;\overline{x'}\cdots\}) = \sigma(t)\;m(\sigma(\overline{t})\;\overline{x})\{\;\sigma(\overline{t'})\;\overline{x'}\cdots\})$$
$$\sigma(\overline{t}\to t) = \sigma(\overline{t})\to\sigma(t)$$
$$\sigma(\epsilon) = \epsilon$$

Notably, the empty substitution changes nothing and is equivalent to the identity function.

Class tables see a small change due to viewpoint adaptation. $\mathcal{CT}(c)$ when $P(c) = \text{class } c\langle\overline{p}\rangle \text{ extends } d\langle\sigma\rangle \;\{\; \overline{F}\;\overline{M}\;\}$ is defined as $(\{\overline{f}:\overline{t}\},\{\overline{m}\mapsto\overline{M}\}) \bullet \sigma(\mathcal{CT}(d))$, i.e,. the substitution is only applied to the right-hand side operand of the $\bullet$. Here, σ is the map from the owner parameters in d's class header to the actual owners "passed to d" in the declaration of c.

Fig. 10 shows the extended static semantics. Rules changed in the extension bear similar names to those in the original system but adding a prefix (O-). These rules replace the original rules. Rule (O-WF-CLASS) sees a new premise

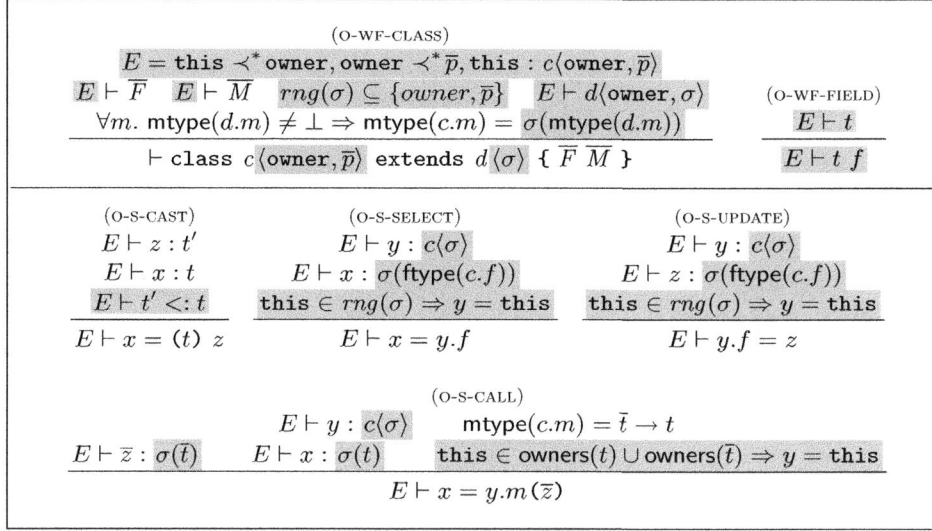

Fig. 10. The differing type rules in WOJ. We define $\mathsf{owners}(c\langle\sigma\rangle) = rng(\sigma)$. For traceability we ▮highlight▮ the changes to the original rules.

$E \vdash d\langle\mathtt{owner}, \overline{\alpha}\rangle$ to make sure valid owner parameters are passed to the super class. For simplicity, we restrict casts to up-casts. Dealing with down-casts in ownership systems is tricky (see, *e.g.*, [22]) and generally ignored.

Rules (O-S-SELECT), (O-S-UPDATE), and (O-S-CALL) use viewpoint adaptation. The containment invariant (last premise in (O-S-SELECT), (O-S-UPDATE) and (O-S-CALL)) makes sure representation is not accessed or leaked outside the object by restricting the target of such field accesses and method calls to be `this`. No changes to the dynamic semantics are necessary, as the type compartment of an object automatically is extended with owner parameters from the redefinition of t.

As seen in Fig. 11, ownership types requires more complex type rules. A type is well-formed if all its owner parameters are well-formed and ordered outside the first owner parameter. As usual [4], `this` is nested inside all visible owners (O-WF-CLASS) and `world` is the global outermost owner (IN-WORLD-O).

3.2   Meta-theory

The changes to the well-formedness rules are minimal. The store type now maps locations to types with owner parameters and (O-WF-HEAP) applies viewpoint adaptation to translate owner names in declared field types to actual owners. As the rules for well-formed type, owner and owner nestings under Γ are identical (modulo minor syntactic differences) to those under E, we omit the former version. Run-time owners are locations ι or `world`, *i.e.*, ι and `world` are in the syntactic category α in the dynamic semantics.

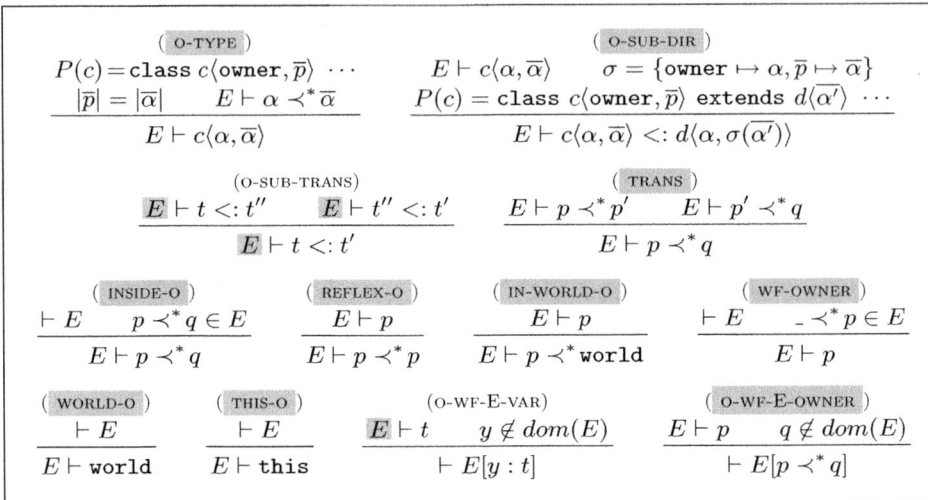

Fig. 11. WOJ Types, owners and extended local type environment E. For completely new rules we highlight the rule name. (O-TYPE) and (O-SUB-DIR) are not new rules, but the syntactic differences are overwhelmingly large. We write $|\overline{p}| = |\overline{\alpha}|$ to denote that $\overline{p}$ and $\overline{\alpha}$ have the same arity. Note that $q \in dom(E)$ and $x \in dom(E)$ only hold when q and x is an owner respective variable—since q and x belong to these syntactic categories.

The progress and preservation theorems are notably unchanged. Additionally, we formulate the standard owners-as-dominators theorem [4] thus:

Theorem 4 (Owners-as-Dominators). *If $\Gamma; \Psi \vdash_h H$, then $\forall \iota, \iota'$ s.t. $H(\iota) = (c, \_, F[f \mapsto \iota'])$ and $\Gamma(\iota') = d\langle \alpha, \_\rangle$ then $\Gamma \vdash \iota \prec^* \alpha$.*

In plain English, an object ι that references another object ι' in one of its fields, must be inside the owner of ι'. As the inside relation is reflexive, this holds even when ι' is in the rep of ι.

Proof. (Sketch) The proof is reminiscent of [4]. Without loss of generality, let c have this, world, owner and a single owner parameter p in its scope. A run-time instance of c pointed to by ι will have a type $c\langle\sigma\rangle$ s.t. $\sigma = \{\texttt{owner} \mapsto \iota', p \mapsto \iota''\}$ for some ι' and ι''. From (O-Γ-INSIDE), $\iota \prec^* \iota'$ and $\iota \prec^* \iota''$ follows immediately (*).

Assume $\Gamma; \Psi \vdash_h H$ s.t. $H(\iota) = (c\langle\sigma\rangle, \_, F)$ and $F(f) = \iota'''$. By (O-WF-HEAP), there exists an $E = \sigma'(\text{fields}(c))$ s.t. $\Gamma; E \vdash_f F$ where $\sigma' = \sigma \cup \{\texttt{this} \mapsto \iota\}$.

By (WF-FIELDS) (indirectly by construction of Γ or (O-WF-NULL)) $\Gamma \vdash t$ holds for any t in E, *i.e.*, for any type $d\langle\alpha\rangle$ of a field in c, either (a) $\alpha \in rng(\sigma')$ or (b) $\alpha = \texttt{world}$. In all other cases, α would be some uninstantiated name, valid only in the static semantics and $\Gamma \vdash t$ would not hold.

If case (a), $\iota \prec^* \alpha$ follows from the observation (*) above, and (O-Γ-REFLEX). In case (b), $\Gamma \vdash \iota \prec^* \alpha$ follows immediately from (IN-WORLD-O).

$$\frac{(\text{O-}\varGamma\text{-INSIDE})\quad \varGamma(\iota)=c\langle\overline{\iota}\rangle \quad \iota'\in\overline{\iota}}{\varGamma\vdash\iota\prec^*\iota'}\qquad \frac{(\text{O-}\varGamma\text{-TRANS})\quad \varGamma\vdash\iota\prec^*\iota''\quad \varGamma\vdash\iota''\prec^*\iota'}{\varGamma\vdash\iota\prec^*\iota'}\qquad \frac{(\text{O-WF-}\varGamma)\quad \varGamma\vdash t\quad \iota\notin dom(\varGamma)}{\vdash_g \varGamma[\iota:t]}$$

$$\frac{(\text{O-WF-NULL})\quad \varGamma\vdash t}{\varGamma\vdash \texttt{null}:t}\quad \frac{(\text{O-}\varGamma\text{-REFLEX})\quad \varGamma\vdash\iota}{\varGamma\vdash\iota\prec^*\iota}\quad \frac{(\text{O-}\varGamma\text{-IN-WORLD})\quad \varGamma\vdash\iota}{\varGamma\vdash\iota\prec^*\texttt{world}}\quad \frac{(\text{O-}\varGamma\text{-WORLD})\quad \vdash_g \varGamma}{\varGamma\vdash\texttt{world}}\quad \frac{(\text{O-}\varGamma\text{-OWNER})\quad \vdash_g \varGamma\quad \iota\in dom(\varGamma)}{\varGamma\vdash\iota}$$

$$\frac{(\text{O-WF-HEAP})\quad \rho\in\Psi\cup\{\epsilon\}\quad \varGamma;\Psi\vdash_h H\quad \varGamma(\iota)=c\langle\sigma\rangle\quad \varGamma\vdash c\langle\sigma\rangle}{\sigma=\{\texttt{owner}\mapsto\alpha,\overline{p}\mapsto\overline{\alpha}\}\quad \sigma'=\sigma\cup\{\texttt{this}\mapsto\iota\}\quad E=\sigma'(\text{fields}(c))\quad \varGamma;E\vdash_f F}{\varGamma;\Psi\vdash_h H[\iota\mapsto(c\langle\sigma\rangle,\rho,F)]}$$

Fig. 12. Updated WF rules for WOJ. For brevity, we omit the definitions of $\varGamma\vdash t$, $\varGamma\vdash p$ and some of the $\prec^*$-rules, as they are copy-and-patch from the equivalent rules under E. While E contains nesting information, we derive dynamic owner nesting from the run-time types in $\varGamma$, see (O-$\varGamma$-INSIDE).

4 Non-null WJ

To further show how WJ can be extended we formalise a simple non-null type system (see *e.g.*, [10,18] for similar but more powerful systems). Variables and fields with a non-null type never contain `null`. Assigning from a non-null type to a "(possibly) null type" is trivially sound, but not the converse. We require a cast from non-null to null type and the cast rule is changed accordingly.

The syntactic changes to WJ are as follows:

$$t ::= \texttt{n}\,c \qquad s ::= \ldots \mid x = \texttt{new}\,c(\overline{z}) \mid x = \texttt{start}\,c(\overline{z}) \qquad \texttt{n} ::= \,!\mid ?$$

All types are decorated with an $\texttt{n}\in\{!,?\}$ annotation for non-null or possibly null, respectively. Non-null fields of an object are initialised in a constructor-like fashion by values passed in at creation time. Fig. 13 shows the extensions to the type system. Notably, we alter the mbody predicate to return a 4-tuple, where the 3rd compartment is local non-null variables in a straightforward fashion. For previously defined helper predicates operating on types, we trivially define $\text{fields}(\texttt{n}\,c) = \text{fields}(c)$ etc., *i.e.*, the type decorator is ignored.

WJ imposes no order on the initialisation of local variables. Clearly, this does not work well with non-null types: initialising them with `null` is not an option and furthermore, a lax ordering of initialisation could lead to cyclic dependencies, *e.g.*, $x = y; y = x$. A possible solution would be to extend WJ with Delayed types [11] à la Fähndrich and Xia. Instead, we choose a simpler approach. We define a helper predicate okinit s.t. $\text{okinit}(x,s)$ holds if x is assigned before it is first read in s. Let $\text{read}(y,s)$ be true if y is ever used as a right-hand side or in a receiver position in s, *i.e.*, $\ldots = y$, $x = y.m(\overline{z})$, $x = y.f$, $y.f = z$, $x = y'.m(\overline{z})$, $\texttt{lock}\,y$, $\texttt{unlock}\,y$, $x = \texttt{start}\,c(\overline{z})$ or $x = \texttt{new}\,c(\overline{z})$, when $y\in\overline{z}$ is in s.

$$\begin{array}{cc}
\text{(NN-SUB)} & \text{(NN-TYPE)} \\
\dfrac{\vdash c <: c' \quad \underline{n' = \;! \Rightarrow n = \;!}}{\vdash \mathbf{n}\, c <: \mathbf{n'}\, c'} & \dfrac{\underline{n \in \{!, ?\}} \quad c \in dom(\mathcal{CT})}{\vdash \mathbf{n}\, c}
\end{array}$$

Fig. 13. Extensions of the type system to support non-null types

Similarly, let $\mathsf{write}(y, s)$ be true if y is ever assigned in s. Then, we can define okinit thus:

$$\mathsf{okinit}(y, s) \iff \forall s_1 \,;\, s_2 \equiv s. \, \mathsf{read}(y, s_2) \Rightarrow \mathsf{write}(y, s_1)$$

where $\equiv$ denotes a possible division of s into sub-statements (this is trivial since our syntax is so simple). An alternative approach would be to make variable declaration a statement and track extensions to E in the static semantics, as we have done in previous work (*e.g.,* [23]).

okinit is used in (NN-WF-METHOD) in Fig. 14. The price for this simplification is an additional value in the dynamic semantics, ∘, used as the initial value for non-null variables. The new well-formedness rule for threads (NN-WF-THREAD) requires okinit to hold for any uninitialised variable. As a side-effect, for proving that non-null typed variables are never be read before assigned a reference value, we extend the dynamic semantics with error rules, similar to dereferencing of null-pointers. These rules are trivial and therefore omitted.

4.1   Extended Semantics and Well-Formedness

The extension to WJ's static semantics to support non-null types is very small. In (NN-WF-CLASS), we make this a non-null variable, and (NN-WF-METHOD) uses the okinit predicate to make sure that local non-null variables are assigned before they are read. Extensions to (NN-S-NEW) and (NN-S-FORK) require that the types of the arguments used for field initialising must be the same as the types of the fields, including (non-)nullity. We extend the dynamic semantics with passing of initialising values for object creation (in (NN-D-NEW) and (NN-D-FORK)) and add initialisation of non-null variables to the dummy ∘ value in (NN-D-CALL).

One additional and one changed well-formedness rule in Fig. 16 are required to deal with uninitialised non-null variables. Notably, they allow non-null variables to contain the special value ∘. For (WF-THREAD), we additionally require that such variables are assigned before they are read.

4.2   Meta-theory

The dynamic semantics of non-null WJ is very similar to WJ and we refrain from stating the progress proof here, since it's very similar to WJ's.

For preservation there is only one interesting change from WJ. We need to show that when constructing a new stack-frame, there is no way that the special value ∘ can ever be read during execution.

$$\frac{\text{(NN-WF-CLASS)}}{d \in dom(\mathcal{CT}) \qquad \vdash \overline{F} \qquad \text{this} : !\, c \vdash \overline{M}}{\vdash \text{class } c \text{ extends } d \ \{ \ \overline{F} \ \overline{M} \ \}}$$

$$\frac{\text{(NN-WF-METHOD)}}{E' = E, \overline{x} : \overline{t}, \overline{x'} : \overline{t'}, \text{ret} : t \qquad E' \vdash s \qquad \forall y : !\, c \in E'. \text{okinit}(y, s)}{E \vdash t \ m(\overline{t} \ \overline{x})\{ \ \overline{t'} \ \overline{x'} \ s \ \}}$$

$$\frac{\text{(NN-S-NEW)}}{\text{fields}(c) = \{\_ : \overline{t}\}}{E \vdash x : !\, c \qquad E \vdash \overline{z} : \overline{t}} \qquad \frac{\text{(NN-S-FORK)}}{\text{mtype}(c.\text{run}) = \epsilon \to \_ \qquad E \vdash x : !\, c}{\text{fields}(c) = \{\_ : \overline{t}\} \qquad E \vdash \overline{z} : \overline{t}} \qquad \frac{\text{(NN-S-CAST)}}{E \vdash z : t'}{E \vdash x : t \qquad \vdash t' <: t}$$

$$\frac{}{E \vdash x = \text{new } c\,(\overline{z})} \qquad \frac{}{E \vdash x = \text{start } c\,(\overline{z})} \qquad \frac{}{E \vdash x = (t) \ z}$$

Fig. 14. Non-null WJ's static semantics

$$\text{(NN-D-NEW)} \ \frac{dom(\text{fields}(c)) = \overline{f} \quad L(\overline{z}) = \overline{v} \quad H' = H[\iota \mapsto (c, \epsilon, [\overline{f} \mapsto \overline{v}])] \quad \iota \text{ is fresh}}{H \mid S \langle L, x = \text{new } c\,(\overline{z}) ; s \rangle^m \rho \xrightarrow{\text{new}} H' \mid S \langle L[x \mapsto \iota], s \rangle^m \rho}$$

$$\text{(NN-D-FORK)} \ \frac{\begin{array}{c} dom(\text{fields}(c)) = \overline{f} \quad L(\overline{z}) = \overline{v} \quad H' = H[\iota \mapsto (c, \epsilon, [\overline{f} \mapsto \overline{v}]] \\ T = \langle [\text{this} \mapsto \iota][\overline{x} \mapsto \text{null}][\overline{y} \mapsto \overline{o}], s' \rangle^{c.\text{run}}, \rho' \\ \text{mbody}(c.\text{run}) = (\epsilon, \overline{x}, \overline{y}, s') \quad \iota \text{ and } \rho' \text{ are fresh} \end{array}}{H \mid S \langle L, x' = \text{start } c\,(\overline{z}) ; s \rangle^m \rho \xrightarrow{\text{fork}} H' \mid (S \langle L[x' \mapsto \iota], s \rangle^m \rho) \ T}$$

$$\text{(NN-D-CALL)} \ \frac{\begin{array}{c} L(y) = \iota \quad H(\iota) = (c, \cdots) \quad \text{mbody}(c.m) = (\overline{x'}, \overline{x''}, \overline{y}, s') \\ L(\overline{z}) = \overline{v} \quad L' = [\text{this} \mapsto \iota][\overline{x'} \mapsto \overline{v}][\overline{x''} \mapsto \text{null}][\overline{y} \mapsto \overline{o}] \end{array}}{H \mid S \langle L, x = y.m\,(\overline{z}) ; s \rangle^m \rho \xrightarrow{\text{call}} H \mid S \langle L, x = y.m\,(\overline{z}) ; s \rangle^m \langle L', s' \rangle^{t.m} \rho}$$

Fig. 15. Non-null WJ's dynamic semantics

Lemma 4 (Non-Nullity). *If* $\Gamma \vdash H \mid T \overline{T}$ *and* $H \mid T \xrightarrow{l} H' \mid \overline{T'}$ *when* $T = S \langle L, s \rangle^{c.m} \rho$ *and* $\text{MC}(c.m) = E$, *then*

1. $s \equiv s' ; s''$, $E \vdash y : !\, c'$, $\text{read}(y, s'')$ *and* $\neg\text{write}(y, s')$ *implies* $L(y) = \iota$;
2. $s \equiv x = y.f ; s'$ *and* $E \vdash y.f : !\, c'$ *implies* $H(L(y).f) = \iota$

for some ι. (Variables of non-null type never observably contain null or $\circ$.)

Proof. The proof is by mutual induction assuming the lemma holds and using negation-as-failure.

For y to contain null, it must have been previously assigned, since it is initialised with $\circ$. By the rules for assignment, the source of this assignment, must have been a non-null type. Since (NEW) and (START) always return references, the source must have been (1) a variable (possibly via a cast), (2) a field access or (3) a method call. (1) and (2) are not possible from the assumption, and (3) reduces to (1) since ret must have been a non-null variable.

$$\frac{\substack{(\text{NN-WF-THREAD}) \\ \mathsf{MC}(c.m) = E \quad \Gamma;\Psi \vdash_{\overline{t}} S\,\rho \\ \Gamma;E \vdash_{\overline{t}} L \quad E \vdash s \quad \forall y \mapsto \circ \in L.\,\mathsf{okinit}(y,s)}}{\Gamma;\Psi \vdash_{\overline{t}} S\,\langle L,s \rangle^{c.m}\,\rho}
\qquad
\frac{\substack{(\text{ NN-WF-FRAME }) \\ \Gamma;E \vdash_{\overline{t}} L}}{\Gamma;E[x\,:\,!\,c] \vdash_{\overline{t}} L[x \mapsto \circ]}$$

Fig. 16. Extended/modified well-formedness rules for frames and threads

The proof that y cannot contain $\circ$ is similar, but relies on the use of okinit in (NN-WF-METHOD) to require that y must have been previously assigned.

The argument for fields is similar. □

5　Related Work

In addition to Featherweight Java [13] which has been discussed in the introduction, several core formalisms have been proposed over the years.

Flatt, Krishnamurthi and Felleisen's CLASSICJAVA [12] is imperative and supports aliasing and mutable objects. Originally constructed to bootstrap a proposal for adding Mixins to Java, the clean and concise formalism has been extended several times (*e.g.*, [6,20]). While relatively simple, CLASSICJAVA defines no less than 27 different predicates and relations for its static semantics alone. WJ removes interfaces from the formalism, which simplifies type rules and well-formedness rules. WJ also adds stack frames, local variables, threads and locks.

Bierman, Parkinson and Pitts model Java's imperative features in MJ, Middleweight Java, [2]. WJ is similar to MJ, but the MJ formalism is much too detailed to be used as a core formalism. For example, MJ distinguishes between statements, expressions, and expressions that can be promoted to statements. While closely and accurately reflecting the way Java works, we believe that this level of detail is unnecessarily complex for many formalisms. MJ also does not model threads and synchronisation.

Parkinson and Strniša's LJ [17] is an extensible minimal imperative fragment of Java and the closest one to WJ. It's Ott definition and relatively accessible Isabelle/HOL proofs are available on-line and thus LJ serves a good starting point where mechanised proofs are desired. WJ and LJ are similar in that they both only have statements. LJ uses implicit subsumption instead of explicit casts and does not have stack frames nor threads and synchronisation.

Apart from these extensible core formalisms a plethora of other one-off purpose-specific formalisms that model state and concurrency have been published. We name only a few of these, as we find them to be less suitable candidates for extension.

Ahern and Yoshida [1] formalise a Java-like core language to capture the semantics of Java RMI. This work extends FJ and MJ and adds, among other things, concurrency and synchronisation. Ahern and Yoshida also add other common and interesting concurrency features such as wait/notify. However, adding such constructs to our system should not be too difficult.

Cunningham, Drossopoulou and Eisenbach [7] formalise a version of the Universes ownership types system [9] with the property that well-typed programs are race free. The system models stacks, synchronisation and concurrency by spawning single expressions. This system is a simplified version of the original Universes proposal and does not enforce the owners-as-modifiers property.

6   Conclusion

We have presented WJ, a minimal imperative Java formalism. We argue that WJ is a suitable core Java formalism for extensions to Java-like languages that need imperative features and threads. The core formalism has been extracted from recent work on Loci [23], a system for simple thread-locality in Java, and AtomicJava [21], adding type-based data-centric synchronisation to Java. Subsets of WJ has also been used in Mini-Thorn [24], adding a novel form of gradual typing to a Java-like language. The WJ formalism is very concise and easy to fit into even a short paper, as demonstrated here. Dealing with statements only and avoiding implicit subsumption simplifies proofs and reduces proof sizes. The full proofs for WJ will be made available on the WJ web site [15] along with the LATEX sources for easy inclusion into a paper.

Acknowledgements. We thank Sylvain Lebresne for comments on the presentation and Jan Vitek for insightful comments and explanations of AtomicJava.

References

1. Ahern, A., Yoshida, N.: Formalising Java RMI with Explicit Code Mobility. In: Proceedings of OOPSLA, pp. 403–422 (2005)
2. Bierman, G.M., Parkinson, M.J., Pitts, A.M.: MJ: An imperative core calculus for Java and Java with effects. Technical report, University of Cambridge (2003)
3. Clarke, D., Wrigstad, T.: External Uniqueness is Unique Enough. In: Cardelli, L. (ed.) ECOOP 2003. LNCS, vol. 2743, pp. 59–67. Springer, Heidelberg (2003)
4. Clarke, D.: Object Ownership and Containment. PhD thesis, School of Computer Science and Engineering, University of New South Wales, Sydney, Australia (2001)
5. Clarke, D., Drossopolou, S.: Ownership, encapsulation and the disjointness of type and effect. In: Proceedings of OOPSLA (November 2002)
6. Clifton, C., Leavens, G.T.: MiniMAO₁: Investigating the semantics of proceed. Science of Computer Programming 63(3), 321–374 (2006)
7. Cunningham, D., Drossopoulou, S., Eisenbach, S.: Universes for race safety. In: VAMP '07, September 2007, pp. 20–51 (2007)
8. Dietl, W., Drossopoulou, S., Müller, P.: Generic universe types. In: Ernst, E. (ed.) ECOOP 2007. LNCS, vol. 4609, pp. 28–53. Springer, Heidelberg (2007)
9. Dietl, W., Müller, P.: Universes: Lightweight Ownership for JML. Journal of Object Technology 4(8), 5–32 (2002)
10. Fähndrich, M., Rustan, K., Leino, M.: Declaring and checking non-null types in an object-oriented language. In: Proceedings of OOPSLA, pp. 302–312. ACM, New York (2003)
11. Fähndrich, M., Xia, S.: Establishing object invariants with delayed types. SIGPLAN Not. 42(10), 337–350 (2007)

12. Flatt, M., Krishnamurthi, S., Felleisen, M.: A programmer's reduction semantics for classes and mixins. In: Alves-Foss, J. (ed.) Formal Syntax and Semantics of Java. LNCS, vol. 1523, p. 241. Springer, Heidelberg (1999)

13. Igarashi, A., Pierce, B.C., Wadler, P.: Featherweight Java: a minimal core calculus for Java and GJ. ACM TOPLAS 23(3), 396–450 (2001)

14. Malayeri, D., Aldrich, J.: Cz: multiple inheritance without diamonds. In: Proceedings of OOPSLA, pp. 21–40. ACM, New York (2009)

15. Östlund, J., Wrigstad, T.: Welterweight Java website (2009), http://user.it.uu.se/~johos902

16. Östlund, J., Wrigstad, T., Clarke, D., Åkerblom, B.: Ownership, Uniqueness, and Immutability. In: Objects, Components, Models and Patterns (Proceedings of 46th International Conference on Objects, Models, Components, Patterns). Lecture Notes in Business Information Processing, vol. 11, pp. 178–197. Springer, Heidelberg (2008)

17. Parkinson, M., Strniša, R.: Lightweight Java web pages (2008–2009), http://www.cl.cam.ac.uk/research/pls/javasem/lj/

18. Qi, X., Myers, A.C.: Masked types for sound object initialization. SIGPLAN Not. 44(1), 53–65 (2009)

19. Sewell, P., Nardelli, F.Z.: Ott Website (2010), http://www.cl.cam.ac.uk/~pes20/ott/

20. van Dooren, M., Joosen, W.: A modular type system for first-class composition inheritance. Technical Report Report CW 534, Department of Computer Science, K.U.Leuven (January 2009)

21. Vaziri, M., Tip, F., Dolby, J., Hammer, C., Vitek, J.: A type system for data-centric synchronization. To appear at ECOOP 2010 (2010)

22. Wrigstad, T., Clarke, D.: Existential owners for ownership types. Journal of Object Technology 6(4) (May/June 2007)

23. Wrigstad, T., Pizlo, F., Meawad, F., Zhao, L., Vitek, J.: Loci: Simple thread-locality for java. In: Drossopoulou, S. (ed.) ECOOP 2009 – Object-Oriented Programming. LNCS, vol. 5653, pp. 445–469. Springer, Heidelberg (2009)

24. Wrigstad, T., Nardelli, F.Z., Lebresne, S., Östlund, J., Vitek, J.: Integrating typed and untyped code in a scripting language. In: POPL '10, pp. 377–388. ACM, New York (2010)

Read-Only Execution for Dynamic Languages

Jean-Baptiste Arnaud[1], Marcus Denker[1], Stéphane Ducasse[1], Damien Pollet[1],
Alexandre Bergel[2], and Mathieu Suen

[1] INRIA Lille Nord Europe - CNRS UMR 8022 - University of Lille (USTL)
[2] PLEIAD Lab, Department of Computer Science (DCC), University of Chile, Santiago, Chile

Abstract. Supporting read-only and side effect free execution has been the focus of a large body of work in the area of statically typed programming languages. Read-onlyness in dynamically typed languages is difficult to achieve because of the absence of a type checking phase and the support of an open-world assumption in which code can be constantly added and modified. To address this issue, we propose Dynamic Read-Only references (DRO) that provide a view on an object where this object and its object graph are protected from modification. The read-only view dynamically propagates to aggregated objects, without changing the object graph itself; it acts as a read-only view of complex data structures, without making them read-only globally. We implement dynamic read-only references by using smart object proxies that lazily propagate the read-only view, following the object graph and driven by control flow and applied them to realize side-effect free assertions.

1 Introduction

During the execution of a program, an object is aliased each time it is passed as a message argument or referenced by a variable. While imperative (and in particular object-oriented) programs rely on aliasing and side effects to produce computation, unwanted side effects occurring through different aliases to a shared object are a source of many bugs.

For instance, contracts, as provided by Eiffel [1], use pre- and post-conditions placed before and after a method body. Contracts should not influence the program behavior; in fact they can be ignored once the program is stable, for performance reasons. However, nothing besides convention actually prevents pre- or postconditions from having side effects, which may lead to insidious bugs. Ensuring functional purity of contracts would be too strong: a pre-condition could perfectly rely on internal side-effects, as long as it does not change the state of the rest of the program. It is also difficult to ensure side-effect free assertions in the presence of both late binding and imperative code [2].

Note that in statically typed languages, visibility qualifiers (such as private and protected for methods) have little effect to prevent malicious side effects and other non-local modifications. Indeed, an alias may leak critical objects to untrusted parties, as illustrated in the following code snippet of a browser-side script [3]:

```
class DocumentProxy {
  // public API goes here
  private var docServerSocket = new ServerSocket(...);
  public hole() { return docServerSocket }}
```

J. Vitek (Ed.): TOOLS 2010, LNCS 6141, pp. 117–136, 2010.

In this example, the *public* method hole() returns the object referenced by the *private* variable docServerSocket. While we cannot affirm whether this code is poorly designed (it essentially depends on how hole() is used), the encapsulation DocumentProxy defined for itself is definitely broken since docServerSocket can be modified at will once obtained from hole(). A number of mechanisms have flourished to address this situation. They may be classified as either (i) enforcing that a reference cannot escape based on *aliasing control*, or (ii) allowing only non-modifiable methods to be invoked using a *limited interface*.

Alias Control. There have been a number of proposals to detect aliasing problems and control them in statically typed languages [4–7]. Ownership types [6, 8] allow objects to participate in more than one container while Balloon types [5], Islands [4] don't. In the latter case they forbid objects inside the aggregate to refer to objects outside it, making it impossible to share an object between two containers. Ownership types [6] provide full alias encapsulation. They statically restrict programs so that no aliases may *escape* an aggregate object's encapsulation boundary.

Dynamic object ownership [3, 9] is one of the rare answers to this problem in the context of dynamically typed languages. Dynamic ownership protects aliases and enforces encapsulation by maintaining a dynamic notion of object ownership and restricting messages based on their ownership. It classifies aggregated objects into purely internal ones (the representation) and the ones which may be accessible in read-only mode from the outside (the arguments).

Limited Interface. In this family of solutions, references can leak and objects can be freely accessed, but their interfaces are restricted. Several approaches have been proposed, such as capabilities which control the interface of an object [10–13]. In these approaches, an object offers a limited interface when it wants to limit access. Birka *et al* add a readonly type qualifier, which makes all state transitively reachable from a read-only reference immutable [14]. Encapsulation policies also propose different per-reference encapsulation interfaces [15, 16].

Our solution: Dynamic read-only references. Objects do not exist in isolation but are connected to other objects, thus forming a graph. In this case, there is a need to control when side effects can occur and how the immutability propagates to aggregated objects. In particular, the same object may need to offer full access from a reference, but be read-only from another reference. This situation occurs, for example, when one implements side-effect free assertions or Design by Contract precondition checks. The objects involved in the assertions should not be modifiable from the assertion itself, but they can be referenced and changed from other parts of the program. Another example is when an aggregate object should be able to mutate its elements and at the same time give read-only references of such elements to its clients [3, 9].

Instead of relying on static types (which we simply cannot in a dynamic language) or restricted interfaces, we opt for an approach based on dynamic immutability propagation over an overlay of references starting from an object. Our solution to support dynamic read-only references (DRO) in dynamically typed languages is the following: A read-only reference is a transparent proxy where methods attempting side effects raise an exception instead. By transparent, we mean that, from a programmer perspective, it is not possible to tell the object apart from its proxy.

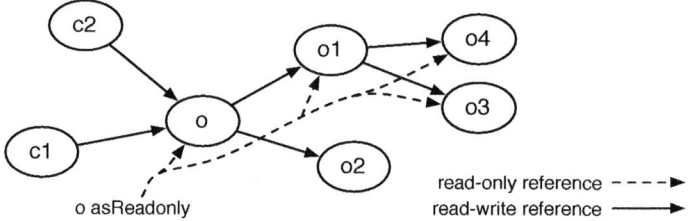

Fig. 1. A control flow lazy propagation of readonly

Finally, our approach is dynamic in the sense that object immutability is lazily propagated *following the execution flow and without modifying* the object graph itself. Figure 1 shows that two objects c1 and c2 refer to o which in turn refers to o1 and o2 and so on. A readonly reference to o is a dynamic layer following the control flow of the execution (here object o2 was not involved in the execution while o3 and o4 were). From the perspective of the readonly reference on o it is not possible to modify the state of the reached objects (o, o1, o3, o4). However via the objects c1 and c2 the object o can be modified.

Contributions. In this paper:

- We identify the problems with immutability and the need for dynamic read-only views and its propagation in an object graph (Section 2);
- We propose a flexible model of dynamic read-only execution adapted to dynamically typed languages based on the lazy propagation of object immutability without object modification, and illustrate it (Sections 3 and 4);
- Section 5 formally describe key properties of Dynamic Read-Only references using the operational semantics of SmalltalkR, an extension of SmalltalkLite [17];
- We describe a generic implementation and its performance, and finally we discuss key design points and their consequences for a generalization of our approach to security concerns (Section 6).

2 The Challenges of Dynamic Read-Only Execution

Read-only execution is appealing for a number of reasons, ranging from easier synchronization to lowering the number of potential bugs due to side effects, aliasing and encapsulation violation [2, 3, 5]. Mechanisms prohibiting variable mutation are now common in programming languages (*e.g.*, Java has the final keyword, C++ and C# have const). This prevents the reference and not the referee to be modified.

In dynamically typed languages, few attempts have been made to provide immutable objects. VisualWorks Smalltalk[1] and Ruby support immutable objects using a per object flag that tells whether the fields of the object may be modified. Since immutability is a property embedded in the object itself, once created, immutable objects cannot be modified via any alias. In this section, we discuss the challenges of realizing read-only execution in dynamically typed languages.

---

[1] http://www.cincomsmalltalk.com

Different Views for Multiple Usages. Read-only execution is often needed in cases where objects taking part in the read-only execution are at the same time (*e.g.,* from another thread of execution) referenced normally with the ability to do side-effects. A clear illustration of this need is assertion execution: within the scope of an assert method invocation, objects should not be modified, else this could lead to subtle bugs depending on the evaluation of assertions.

What we want to stress here is not only the need for immutability but also the fact that such a property can be dynamic and that the same object can be simultaneously referenced read-only from one object, and write-enabled from another object.

The Case of Object Creation. One interesting question appears when thinking about objects that are created locally and used in a method but never stored in an object. As far as the rest of the system is concerned, these objects are disconnected: changing them does not change the overall state of the system. It is natural to think that newly created objects are not read-only even when referenced from a read-only execution context. Storing a newly created object within a read-only view should raise an error.

Flexibility to Support Experiments. Having read-only object references is one solution of a larger problem space. Several possible reference semantics and variants have been proposed in the literature such as Lent, Shared, Unique or Read-only. In addition, read-only is just one element in the larger spectrum of capability-based security model [13]. Therefore the current model should be flexible to be able to explore multiple different semantics. Just providing one fixed model for how the read-only property works is not enough (see Section 7). The model and its implementation should be flexible enough to be able to grow beyond pure read-only behavior.

Challenges for Read-Only Execution in Dynamically Typed languages. The key challenge is then:

> How do we provide flexible read-only execution on a per reference-basis in the context of complex object graph with shared state without static type analysis support?

Some work such as encapsulation policies [15, 16] offer the possibility to restrict an object's interface on a per reference basis, but they do not address the problem of propagating the read-only property to aggregate references. Encapsulation policies are static from this point of view. ConstrainedJava offers dynamic ownership checking [3] but the focus is different in the sense that ConstrainedJava makes sure that object references do not leak while we are concerned about offering a read-only view.

3   Dynamic Read-Only References

Our approach to introduce immutability in a dynamically typed language is based on dynamic read-only references. Dynamic read-only references can offer different behavior for immutability to *different* clients. Such references are based on the introduction of a special object, called handle, by which clients interact with the target object. A handle is a *per reference* transparent proxy, *i.e.,* identity is the same as the object they represent. The handle therefore forms a reification [18] of the concept of an object reference: a reference is now modeled by an object. Similar reifications have been realized

Fig. 2. A reference to an object can be turned into a read-only reference

in other contexts, one example is *Object Flow Analysis*, which models aliases as objects [19]. Another example is *delMDSOC*, an execution model for Aspect Oriented languages [20].

3.1 Handle: A Transparent Per Reference Proxy

Conceptually, a handle is an object that represents its target; it has the same identity as its target, but redefines its behavior to be read-only.

At the implementation level, handles are special objects. When a message is sent to a handle, the message is actually applied to the target object, but with the handle's behavior —*i.e.*, the receiver is the target object, but the method is *resolved in the handle*. In essence, a handle never executes messages on itself, rather it replaces the behavior of messages that are received by its target.

Handler creation example. Figure 2 illustrates the creation of a read-only reference. First, we get an object and we assign it into the variables a and b. Second, via the variable b, the object is asked to become read-only. This has as effect to create a handle.

Identity of Handle and Object. Contrary to traditional proxies [21] and similarly to Encapsulators [22], a handle and its target have the same identity — the handle is transparent. Not having transparency could lead to subtle bugs because most of the code is not (and does not have to be) aware of the existence of handles: for example, without transparency, adding a target and its handle to a set would break the illusion that the handle is the same object as the target since both would be added to the set.

3.2 Enabling Read-Only Behavior

As explained above, a handle can have a different behavior than its target for the same set of messages. Specifically, we redefine all the methods to offer the expected read-only behavior. To install a handle on a target, we rewrite the target's methods and install them into a *Shadow class* that the handle references:

1. Store accesses in globals and in instance variables signal an exception;
2. Read accesses to globals, instance variables and to the self pseudo-variable are dynamically wrapped in read-only references.

Figure 3 illustrates this behavioral transformation. The class OrderedCollection defines an instance variable array, and three methods: the method grow which modifies the state of the collection by modifying the contents of the instance variable array, the method add: which conditionally invokes other methods and the method array which returns a reference to this object. The Shadow class of the handle for this object contains three

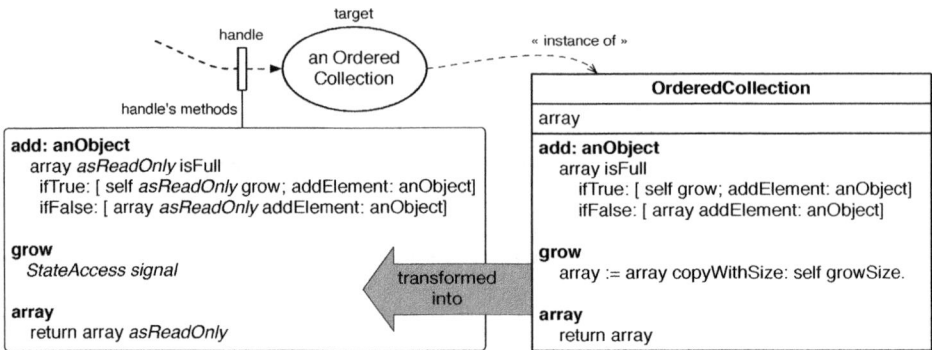

Fig. 3. The handle holds the read-only version of the target's code, with instance variable accesses and affectations rewritten

methods. The method grow which raises an exception. The method array which returns a read-only reference to the internal array. The method add: is transformed according to the transformation we described above: self/this, instance variables and globals are asked to be read-only and modification raise an error.

Objects referenced by temporary variables are not transformed into read-only references because they do not change the state of the object. Objects referenced by arguments may be read-only references, but only because of an earlier transformation.

Note that this transformation is recursive and dynamic. It happens at run-time and is driven by the control-flow. This recursive propagation is explained in the next section.

3.3   Step by Step Propagation

The read-only property dynamically propagates to an object's state when it is accessed. Figure 4 illustrates how immutability is propagated to the state of a list of students. When the graduation: message is sent to a read-only Promotion instance, first the message do: is sent to the read-only students instance variable. This invokes the read-only version of the Array»do: method, and in turn the read-only version of Student»hasGoodGrades. Since hasGoodGrades does not modify its receiver (here the Student instance), the execution continues this way until it reaches a student with grades good enough to pass. At that point, we are still in the read-only version of the Promotion»graduation method, so we execute the read-only version of graduate, which throws an exception, since in its original version it modifies the student's diploma instance variable.

This example shows that immutability is propagated to the references of instance variables and global variables recursively and on demand, based on the execution flow of the application. Note that execution fails only when it reaches an assignment to an instance variable or a global variable.

Global Variables and Classes. Access to global variables is controlled the same way as access to instance variables: write access is forbidden (it raises an exception), any read is wrapped in a creation of a read-only handle. As classes are objects in Smalltalk, accesses to classes leads to the creation of a read-only handle for that class. Any change of

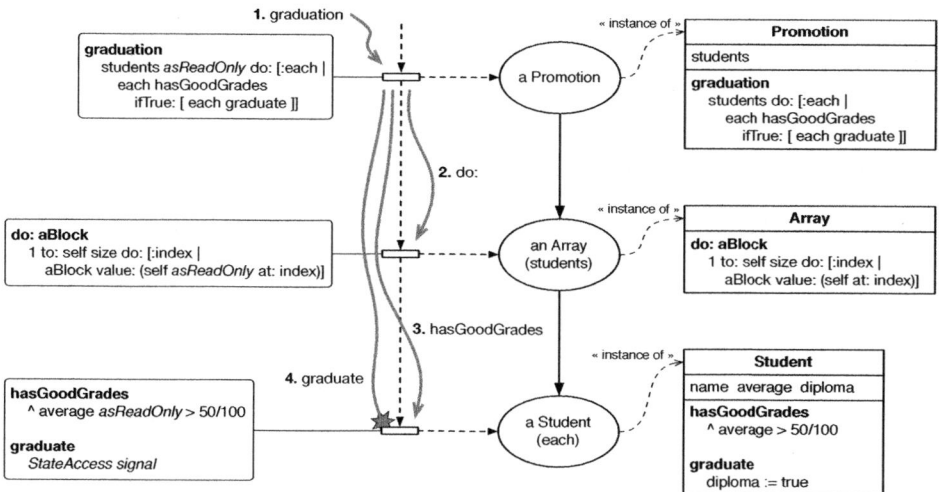

Fig. 4. When we send the graduation message via a read-only reference to the Promotion instance, execution proceeds via read-only handles, until the graduate method attempts a side-effect

the structure of the class, *e.g.,* adding or removing methods or changing the inheritance hierarchy is therefore forbidden.

Newly Created Objects. Even though referencing a class will result in a read-only handle, using the class to create a new Object will not result on this object being wrapped in a read-only handle. A new object has only one reference, therefore changing this object will not lead to a side effect: all other objects of the program remain unchanged. We can therefore just have new objects be created normally, allowing modification. Any try to store the newly created object will result in an error, making sure that the object never has any influence on the rest of the system.

Temporary Variables. Temporary variables only live for the extend of the execution of one method. They are not stored in an object if not done explicitly. Therefore, we can safely keep temporary variables with read-write semantics: reading does not wrap the reference in a handle, writing is allowed.

Arguments. We do not wrap arguments or return values. If a value is used as an argument, it has to come from somewhere: it is either read from an instance variable, and therefore already read-only. Or it was created locally in a method and is not connected to any other object in the system. We can therefore hand over arguments without any special wrapping: either the reference passed is already read-only or it is read-write, it is handed over unchanged.

Block Closures. For closures, there are two cases to distinguish: executing a block read-only and passing a block to a method of a read-only data-structure as an argument. For read-only execution, the objects representing closures need to support a read-only execution mode. For this, all instance and global variable reads are wrapped in a handler. In addition, we need to wrap all variable reads defined outside of the closure and the arguments.

4   Examples

We now present how DRO is applied to solve two critical problems: side effect-free assertions and read-only collections.

4.1   Example Revisited: Side Effect Free Assertions

An assertion is a boolean expression that should hold at some point in a program. Assertions are usually used to define pre- and post-conditions: in a service contract, if the precondition is fulfilled, then the postcondition is guaranteed. Assertions are supported by a number of languages, including Eiffel, Java, Smalltalk, and C#. It is reasonable to expect a program to behave to the same bit when assertions are removed to gain performance. However, none of the languages supporting assertion can enforce behavior preservation when removing assertions, because the assertion code could perform any method call or side effect.

Writing an assertion for *e.g.*, a ServerSocket object requires that the object is not changed during the execution of the assertion (which can be repeated multiple times), while it can be modified outside the contract. To illustrate our point, consider the following method definition extracted from the trait implementation of Pharo:

```
Behavior>>flattenDown: aTrait
  | selectors |
  self assert: [self hasTraitComposition and:
    [self traitComposition allTraits includes: aTrait]].
  selectors := (self traitComposition transformationOfTrait: aTrait) selectors.
  self basicLocalSelectors: self basicLocalSelectors , selectors.
  self removeFromComposition: aTrait.
```

The assertion is highlighted in **bold**. It contains five message sends (hasTraitComposition, and:, traitComposition, allTraits, and includes:). If one of these message leads to a side effect, then the assertion will be not easily removable and may lead to subtle bugs.

Using dynamic read-only object references, we define a safe alternative for the assertion mechanism as follows:

```
Object>>safeAssert: aBlock
  self assert: aBlock asReadOnly
```

Like assert:, the method safeAssert: is defined in the class Object, the common superclass of all classes in Pharo. All classes will therefore be able to call this method. The parameter aBlock is a closure that will be evaluated by the original assert: with aBlock value. However, before delegating to the original implementation, we make the block read-only by rewriting all accesses the block does to variables defined outside itself. This includes all instance variable accesses, accesses to temporary variables from an outer block or method, as well as the special variables self and thisContext. Temporary variables are not wrapped in read-only handlers. The new assertion in our example thus becomes:

```
self safeAssert: [self hasTraitComposition and:
    [self traitComposition allTraits includes: aTrait]].
```

The preservation of object identity is important in our case: an object has the same identity as its read-only counterpart. When defining assertions, the self reference within the block provided to safeAssert: is the same identity than outside the block.

With DRO, the contract code can be executed guaranteeing that no side-effect occurs. Therefore, no bugs concerning unwanted state changes can happen.

4.2   Read-Only Data Structures

In general, read-only references provide the programmer with the possibility to hand out safe references to internal data-structures. As soon as the reference that is handed to a client as a read-only handle, it is guaranteed that no modification may happen through this reference. For example, we can use read-only structures to make sure that the programmer gets notified if (s)he attempts to modify a collection while iterating on it. This is indeed a subtle way to shot oneself in the foot; bugs introduced this way are difficult to track because they may rely on the order and identity of the elements. To be safe, the idiomatic way is to iterate on a copy of the collection and modify the original.

Java provides support for requesting an *unmodifiable collection* for any collection. This is a wrapper object that protects the collection from modification, while allowing the programmer to access or enumerate the content like a standard collection object. In Smalltalk, it is common to hand out a copy of a collection if the collection itself is used internally.

With dynamic read-only references, one solution is to offer a safeDo: method that propagates read-only status to the collection. Attempts to change the collection will then lead to an error.

```
Collection>>fullSafeDo: aBlock
    ^ self asReadOnly do: aBlock
```

Note here that the read-only status gets propagated to the block arguments, as we can easily see in the implementation of do:. The parameter passed to the block is read via the instance variable array, which is automatically wrapped in a read-only handler. This read-only reference provides read-only versions of all methods of class Array, including at:, resulting in a read-only reference passed to the block.

```
OrderedCollection>>do: aBlock
    "Override the superclass for performance reasons."
    | index |
    index := firstIndex.
    [ index <= lastIndex]
        whileTrue:
            [ aBlock value: (array at: index).
            index := index + 1 ]
```

All other variables referenced in the block, *i.e.,* globals, temporary variables of the enclosing methods or instance variables of the class are not read-only. The execution of the block itself is not done in a read-only context, just accesses to the collection (and all objects contained) are read-only.

Our solution with DRO provides a way to protect accesses to the entire object graph, starting at the read-only reference to the collection. In Section 7, we discuss that a better way of controlling the propagation is needed.

5   SMALLTALK/R: **DRO Operational Semantics**

We now formalize the model described in Section 3 by providing an operational semantics for Dynamic Read-Only execution using the formalism of ClassicJava [23]. The goal of this formalization is to provide the necessary technical description when implementing DRO in one's favorite language. It should be noted that this formalism models the read-only behavior. To keep it simple, it does not follow the implementation. This means that we do not model references. The time when the read-only behavior is propagated therefore is different: it happens at the time of message send, not handle creation. We decided to provide this simplified formalism as a first step, we plan to extend it as future work when we go beyond pure read-only behavior.

For this purpose we extend SMALLTALKLITE whose description is given in appendix. SMALLTALKLITE has been presented in our previous work [17], it should therefore not be considered as a contribution. SMALLTALKLITE is a Smalltalk-like dynamic language featuring single inheritance, message-passing, field access and update, and **self** and **super** sends. It is similar to CLASSICJAVA, but removes interfaces and static types, and fields are private, so only local or inherited fields may be accessed. SMALLTALKLITE is generic enough to be considered as a formal foundation targeting languages other than Smalltalk (e.g., Ruby).

We provide the necessary extension of SMALLTALKLITE to capture the semantics of Dynamic Read-Only execution. We call SMALLTALK/R the resulting extended language (Figure 5).

First, we augment the set of expressions and evaluating contexts with a new keyword, readonly. This keyword takes an expression as parameter and, at execution time, evaluates the expression and makes the result as read-only. Read-onlyness is expressed with $\lfloor ... \rfloor$. A value enclosed into these half square brackets cannot be mutated. A read-only value is written $\lfloor v \rfloor$ and can only result from evaluating a readonly expression. The readonly keyword belongs to the surface syntax, whereas $\lfloor ... \rfloor$ designates a read-only reference. The expression readonly e evaluates to a $\lfloor o \rfloor$ reference.

The immutability property is propagated through instance variable and global access such as class references (Section 3.2). In SMALLTALKLITE, the only global accesses permitted are class references in new expressions.

A new rule for the readonly keyword has to be added. The expression readonly o is simply reduced into $\lfloor o \rfloor$.

Subsequently, reduction rules must be adjusted to take the immutability property into account: field assignment leads to an error; calling a method propagates the read-only object reference into the method body; the read-only object reference is also propagated with super calls.

Message lookup is achieved through the notation $\langle c, m, x^*, e \rangle \in_P^* c'$: we look for a method called m, with the arguments x^*, and a method body e. The lookup begins

$$e = ... \mid \textbf{readonly } e$$
$$E = ... \mid \textbf{readonly } E \mid \lfloor E \rfloor$$
$$v, o = ... \mid \lfloor oid \rfloor$$

$P \vdash \langle E[\textbf{readonly } o], \mathcal{S} \rangle \hookrightarrow \langle E[\lfloor o \rfloor], \mathcal{S} \rangle$ [read-only]

$P \vdash \langle E[\lfloor o \rfloor .f], \mathcal{S} \rangle \hookrightarrow \langle E[\lfloor v \rfloor], \mathcal{S} \rangle$ [get]
     where $\mathcal{S}(o) = \langle c, \mathcal{F} \rangle$ and $\mathcal{F}(f) = v$

$P \vdash \langle E[\lfloor o \rfloor .f{=}v], \mathcal{S} \rangle \hookrightarrow \langle E[\textbf{error}], \mathcal{S}] \rangle$ [set]

$P \vdash \langle E[\lfloor o \rfloor .m(v^*)], \mathcal{S} \rangle \hookrightarrow \langle E[\lfloor o \rfloor \, [\![e[v^*/x^*]]\!]_{c'}], \mathcal{S} \rangle$ [send]
     where $\mathcal{S}(o) = \langle c, \mathcal{F} \rangle$ and $\langle c, m, x^*, e \rangle \in_P^* c'$

$P \vdash \langle E[\textbf{super}\langle \lfloor o \rfloor , c \rangle .m(v^*)], \mathcal{S} \rangle \hookrightarrow \langle E[\lfloor o \rfloor \, [\![e[v^*/x^*]]\!]_{c''}], \mathcal{S} \rangle$ [super]
     where $c \prec_P c'$ and $\langle c', m, x^*, e \rangle \in_P^* c''$ and $c' \leq_P c''$

Fig. 5. Extensions made on SMALLTALKLITE resulting in SMALLTALK/R

in the class c and c' is the first class among superclasses of c that defines this method. $\langle m, x^*, e \rangle$ is a method definition, $\langle c, m, x^*, e \rangle \in c'$ is a different notation that says $\langle m, x^*, e \rangle$ is looked up starting in c.

No special treatment is needed for super calls. If the receiver is readonly (as in **super**$\langle \lfloor o \rfloor , c \rangle$), then the method lookup starts in the super class of c, that we call c'. Following the notation of CLASSICJAVA, direct subclass is designed using $c \prec_P c'$. The method to lookup is $\langle m, x^*, e \rangle$ and it is searched starting in c'. It is found in c'', using the operator $\in_P^*$. Naturally, we have the relation $c' \leq_P c''$. The formulation illustrates the simplicity of readonly feature of the DRO model.

6 Implementation

We implemented DRO in Pharo by (1) extending the virtual machine and (2) using a byte-code rewriting engine [24].

VM changes. The Squeak/Pharo Virtual machine was modified to support transparent proxies. Our implementation is more general than required for strict read-only execution. It offers a per reference handle as presented in Section 3, while for DRO we only need a per class method dictionary containing the rewritten methods. We did that because we see dynamic read-only references as just one case of a more general scheme for security alternatives in the realm of object capability model [13].

Virtual machine modifications were required because in Smalltalk reflection would allow one to easily change handles. Thus the user of a handle could corrupt the handle integrity and send forbidden messages. By implementing handles at the VM level we ensure that handles are tamperproof. In addition, handles have a different method lookup than normal objects: when a handle receives a message, the VM looks the method up in the handle's shadow class, but applies it on its target object. Also, the current implementation does not wrap integer, boolean and nil objects, since those are naturally immutable. We changed the virtual machine to treat a handle and the object pointed to as identical. Technically this is realized by a special check in the byte-code implementing identity.

Runtime infrastructure. In addition to the VM changes, Figure 6 presents the principles of our implementation at the runtime level. When an object should offer a read-only behavior, a handle is created. The creation of the handle leads to the definition of a shadow class and its inheritance chain - in the style of Encapsulators [22, 25] A shadow class is an anonymous class which in the context of DRO will be used by the modified handle method lookup. In such shadow classes, methods are rewritten to implement the semantics described before.

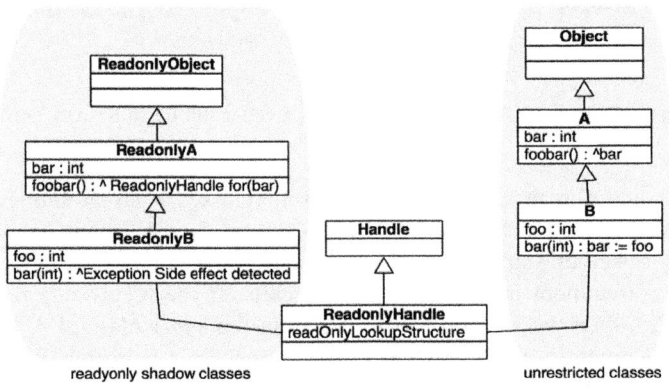

Fig. 6. Shadow classes as an implementation of DRO

We use the ByteSurgeon byte-code transformation framework [24] to dynamically rewrite methods and install them in the shadow classes.

Shortcomings of the Current Implementation The current implementation does not support primitive virtual machine calls and weak references (*i.e.,* referenced ignored by the garbage collector). Both limitations will be resolved in a future version.

Benchmarks. We present preliminary benchmarks to asses the cost of implementing DRO on a real system [2]. We compare the performance of a DRO VM, a virtual machine where the DRO is enabled, and a standard VM, for both the case of using standard references and using read-only references. We take a method returning a simple literal and execute it one million times using the MessageTally profiler to measure the slowdown of executing a message send. In addition, we measure the slowdown of object creation by executing one hundred thousand iterations. As we can see in the table, message sends are slowed down by 8%. In the case of read-only references, the overhead is maximal 16%.

Very time-consuming is the creation of a handle in the case when the shadow class needs to be created. In this case, all methods of the class of the object and all super-classes are copied and modified. This naturally takes time but needs to be done only once for each class.

---

[2] The benchmarks were done on a MacBook Pro Core2Duo 2.4Ghz.

	Standard VM	DRO VM	Slowdown	DRO VM (to handle)	Slowdown
send	1109.3 ms	1200.5 ms	8.22 %	1290.1 ms	16.30 %
creating instance	595.9 ms	780.4 ms	30.96 %	NA	NA

7 Discussion

Scoping Propagation. In our approach, we cannot control the scope of immutability propagation: for the whole subgraph of objects reached during execution we construct the read-only overlay. Therefore a collection accessed as read-only cannot have elements with a different access behavior: in the following example, accessing the elements of the collection will propagate the immutability to the elements:

(aCol asReadOnly at: 1) changeStateOfElement

Our approach supports argument exposure [7] in the sense that when the collection is accessed as read-only, its elements are read-only too. A related problem is the question of how to allow harmless side-effects. For example, often programs need to cache calculated values. With a strict read-only execution model, this is not possible.

The problem is that it is not clear how a scoping mechanism for limiting read-only propagation should look like. Care needs to be taken to not break the read-only model completely. This is part of our future work: we imagine both a static scoping mechanism based on program annotations and one based on dynamically scoped variables.

Implementation Alternatives. The implementation approach chosen uses rewriting byte-codes to change behavior of methods combined with hidden (per reference) object proxies that are realized by changing the virtual machine. Alternatively, we could have generalized the idea of a per-object immutability bit and encoded immutability in the object pointer. Dynamic languages already encode small integers directly in the pointer using a tag bit. Extending tagging to multiple bits has been done and is especially feasible in systems with 64bit pointers.

We decided against this implementation strategy as it would constrain the model to just be about immutability, with no way of controlling the propagation. As we discussed before, scoping the propagation of read-only behavior is essential. Besides propagation, with having handles be special objects (hidden by the virtual machine), but in the end fairly normal nevertheless, we can start to experiment with other mechanism besides pure read-only behavior. All these experiments would not be possible in a system that encodes behavioral modification in a single bit.

An interesting question is how much of the implementation of the transparent handles can be realized without virtual machine changes. The reason for the VM change is the need to hide the proxy completely: the proxy is indistinguishable from the object and there is no way (not even using reflection) to reference the object directly. Purely reflective approaches (*i.e.,* rewriting bytecode for identity) are always visible to introspection and therefore not easy to realize in a completely transparent way.

Threads. Threads are interesting to look at in the context of our read-only model. We do not construct globally immutable object graphs, the object graph is only read-only when accessed through a read-only reference. In general, it is of course not guaranteed that objects are only referenced by read-only references. Therefore, DRO can not guarantee any immutability properties for shared resources. The non-atomic step-by-step propagation of read-only itself is thread-safe. Read-only execution does not change the state of any existing object, reads happen the same as in normal execution (non-atomic) and of course are impacted by other threads changing the same data-structure just as any normal execution.

In the past, work on context-orientation often encoded context as a per-thread property. [26, 27]. But it is not clear that the concepts of *context* and *thread* should be that closely related. In our model, read-only is orthogonal to threads. Propagation happens along the flow of references lazily driven by the control flow. This property will be especially interesting as soon as the ideas are used for other properties than read-only behavior.

Towards more Secure Systems. Dynamic Read-Only references offer a good infrastructure but not the complete solution to build more secure systems. First, the kind of access rights they offer is limited, it is either full access or read-only, while we expect a large range of different rights [7]. Second, a dedicated security model is missing. Still this is interesting to discuss the limits of DRO in this specific scenario.

Let's illustrate this point. In Smalltalk, the reflective structure, *i.e.,* the hierarchy of all classes and methods, is represented by normal objects and can therefore be changed at runtime. Although this is the basis for reflection, it may lead to problematic situations. If we consider method addition to a class, we can either use the official API by sending the message #addSelector:withMethod: to the class, or directly modify the internal structure of the class, as any object. A class keeps its methods in a dictionary, which can be easily accessed through the accessor methodDict. Therefore, it is tempting to directly modify the method dictionary: aClass methodDict at: aSelector put: aMethod.

But manipulating the method dictionary directly will lead to errors [3], for example internal data-structures are not updated and the cache of the VM are not reset.To solve this problem, we can offer a read-only interface to the class internal representation: the user will not be able to modify the internal class structure. However, we then have to grant access accordingly to the public API. If we offer a read-only version of the object class, then even using the public API method #addSelector:withMethod: is useless, since the complete object graph is read-only. Otherwise, we can provide a dedicated read-only interface, but without an additional model to grant access, a malicious developer can still obtain references to the unprotected class. Generalizing DRO to solve this problem is clearly a future research direction.

8   Related Work

The work presented in this paper takes place in a large spectrum of other works ranging from ownership control to capabilities, via controlling interfaces and context-oriented programming. We present here the most significant work with a stress on dynamically typed solutions, but the list is not exhaustive.

Immutability. VisualWorks Smalltalk supports immutable objects: a per-object flag that tells whether the fields of the object may be modified. Once created, immutable objects cannot be modified via any reference, and the flag does not propagate to the object subgraph.

In School [28], the *old* qualifier prevents the modification of the fields of old objects. On old objects, the type checker only allows invoking side-effect free methods, and treats the return values from these invocations as old. This ensures that the only non-old (and thus mutable) objects that a method can use are the ones it creates itself.

Hakonen *et al* [10] propose the concept of *deeply immutable references*; they only discuss possible implementation strategies without presenting a working implementation. In Javari, Birka *et al* [14] extend Java with a static type system of transitively read-only references. These works are the most similar to our dynamic read-only references; the main difference is that they are proposed for statically typed languages. In particular, Javari methods have to be declared read-only *à priori*; unmodified Java code is conservatively considered to have side-effects. In contrast, our approach does not require any modification besides the initial creation of a read-only reference. Javari's read-only references can still authorize side effects on some fields that are not part of the object's abstract state; for instance, this allows caching or immutable collections of mutable elements. Currently, our implementation propagates immutability to all fields. Finally, since Javari programs runs on the unmodified JVM, it is possible that object wrappers break identity, while our handles are transparent.

Joe-E is a subset of Java based on an object-capability model supporting purely functional methods and type checking [2, 13]. In Joe-E, a purely functional method does not have side-effects and its behavior only depends on its arguments. In our example of contracts, ensuring functional purity would be too strong: a pre-condition could perfectly rely on internal side-effects, as long as it does not change the state of the rest of the program. Functional purity is also difficult to ensure in the presence of both late binding and imperative code, without resorting to an entirely different programming style.

Alias Control and Dynamic Object Ownership. Dynamic object ownership [3, 9] is one of the rare propositions to control alias in the context of dynamically typed languages. Dynamic object ownership implements Flexible Alias Ownership [8]: every object which is part of the representation of an aggregate object is owned by that object and should not be visible outside the aggregate. The ownership of every object is stored into a dedicated field and it is used to verify the validity of every message send. Dynamic ownership enforces *representation encapsulation*, which states that an encapsulated object (representation object in Noble's jargon) can only be accessed via its encapsulating object, and *external independence*, which states that an object should not depend on the mutable state of an object that is external to it. Using ownership, a visibility rule is defined: an object is visible to another one if they are both encapsulated inside the same object (if they belong to the same ownership tree). Messages are then only sent if the receiving object is visible to the sending object.

The problem that DRO solves is different but related to the one of dynamic ownership. The goal of dynamic read-only references is not to enforce encapsulation per se, but to offer different interfaces of the same object, dynamically and to different clients. We do not distinguish object ownership or containment, nor do we enforce that components should be accessed through their owner.

Limiting interface approaches. Encapsulation policies [15, 16] belong to the family of work that restrict interfaces. Like DRO, encapsulation policies have per-reference semantics. An object can expose different interfaces based on its different references. However, the approaches have two differences. First, there is no propagation of propriety in encapsulation policies. Second, DRO do not change the original object interface, and the cancellation occurs inside method body depending on the execution path, while with encapsulation policies forbid whole methods *à priori*.

In Erights [13], capabilities are used to enforce security by not giving the possibility of a client to access the object interface. While the focus of DRO is different from capabilities (restricting interface), we plan to generalize it in the future to support capability-based security propagation [7].

Context-Oriented Programming. ContextL [29] provides a notion of *layers*, which define context-dependent behavioral variations. Layers are dynamically enabled or disabled based on the current execution context. To some extent, the work presented in this paper is related to context-oriented programming: the behavior of an object is modified depending on a context [26]. But other than prior work on context oriented programming, our read-only context is not purely defined by the thread of execution. With DRO, the propagation of changed behavior is dynamic and lazily following the flow of data in the application. Scoping side-effects has been the focus of two recents works. Worlds [30] provide a way to control and scope side-effects in Javascript. Tanter proposed a more flexible scheme: contextual values [31] are scoped by a very general context function.

Aspect-Oriented Programming. The idea to dynamically on the fly change code based on control flow has been used for realizing *continuous weaving* [32]. Here join-point shadows are introduced in the code on the fly (and lazily) at runtime based on actual control flow. Contrary to our work the change of code does not happen per reference. delMDSOC [20, 33] is a delegation based machine model for AOP. Hidden proxies are introduced to model join points as *loci of late binding*. Similar to the implementation described in this paper, transparent proxies override the methods of an object to introduce calls to advice code. Proxies can be scoped towards the current thread. Continuous weaving is used to model control flow pointcuts. One basic difference to our work is that the goal of delMDSOC is to define a general execution substrate for AOP systems. As future work, we plan to explore how to map our read-only model to delMDSOC.

9 Conclusion

Being able to assert that during a given scope an object cannot be modified is a valuable property, for example for assertions and design-by-contract. While most existing prior work focused on type systems to support the confinement and controlled accesses to aliases, there is a need to offer a solution for latently typed languages where a static approach is not possible. In this paper, we present Dynamic Read-Only references. Our solution to the propagation of immutability is based on the dynamic propagation of the property following the object graph, lazily driven by the control flow of the program.

Our future work is to understand what abstractions should be proposed to the programmer to control the scope of the propagation. In addition, following [7], we would like to see if the same mechanism can be applied to various alias semantics: immutable, borrowed, unique, shared. Finally one question we want to investigate is how the concepts presented here can be applied to offer a basis for security abstractions in dynamically typed languages.

Acknowledgments. We warmly thank James Noble for his excellent feedback on early versions of the paper and discussions about *ConstraintedJava*. We gratefully acknowledge the financial support of the DGA of the French government for the grant of M. Suen. M. Denker gratefully acknowledges the financial support of the Swiss NSF for the project "Biologically inspired Languages for Eternal Systems" (SNF Project No. PBBEP2-125605, Apr. 2009 - Mar. 2010). We gratefully acknowledge the financial support of ESUG (the European Smalltalk User Group)[3]. This work has been partially sponsored by the STICAmSud CoRea Project.

References

1. Meyer, B.: Applying design by contract. IEEE Computer (Special Issue on Inheritance & Classification) 25(10), 40–52 (1992)
2. Finifter, M., Mettler, A., Sastry, N., Wagner, D.: Verifiable functional purity in java. In: Proceedings of CCS'08, pp. 27–31 (2008)
3. Donald, G., James, N.: Dynamic ownership in a dynamic language. In: Costanza, P., Hirschfeld, R. (eds.) Proceedings of the 2007 Symposium on Dynamic Languages, DLS 2007, pp. 41–52. ACM, New York (2007)
4. Hogg, J.: Islands: aliasing protection in object-oriented languages. In: Proceedings of the 6th Annual Conference on Object-Oriented Programming Systems, Languages and Applications (OOPSLA'91), pp. 271–285 (1991)
5. Almeida, P.S.: Balloon types: Controlling sharing of state in data types. In: Aksit, M., Matsuoka, S. (eds.) ECOOP 1997. LNCS, vol. 1241, pp. 32–59. Springer, Heidelberg (1997)
6. Clarke, D.G., Potter, J.M., Noble, J.: Ownership types for flexible alias protection. In: Proceedings OOPSLA '98, pp. 48–64. ACM Press, New York (1998)
7. Boyland, J., Noble, J., Retert, W.: Capabilities for sharing, a generalisation of uniqueness and read-only. In: Knudsen, J.L. (ed.) ECOOP 2001. LNCS, vol. 2072, p. 2. Springer, Heidelberg (2001)
8. Noble, J., Vitek, J., Potter, J.: Flexible alias protection. In: Jul, E. (ed.) ECOOP 1998. LNCS, vol. 1445, pp. 158–185. Springer, Heidelberg (1998)
9. Noble, J., Clarke, D., Potter, J.: Object ownership for dynamic alias protection. In: Proceedings TOOLS '99, November 1999, pp. 176–187 (1999)
10. Hakonen, H., Leppänen, V., Raita, T., Salakoski, T., Teuhola, J.: Improving object integrity and preventing side effects via deeply immutable references. In: Fenno-Ugric Symposium on Software Technology, pp. 139–150 (1999)
11. Miller, M.S., Shapiro, J.S.: Paradigm regained: Abstraction mechanisms for access control. In: Proceedings of the Eigth Asian Computing Science Conference, pp. 224–242 (2003)
12. Fong, P.W.L., Zhang, C.: Capabilities as alias control: Secure cooperation in dynamically extensible systems. Technical report, Department of Computer Science, University of Regina (2004)

---

[3] http://www.esug.org/

13. Miller, M.S.: Robust Composition: Towards a Unified Approach to Access Control and Concurrency Control. PhD thesis, Johns Hopkins University, Baltimore, Maryland, USA (May 2006)
14. Birka, A., Ernst, M.D.: A practical type system and language for reference immutability. In: Proceedings of OOPSLA'2004, pp. 35–49 (2004)
15. Schärli, N., Ducasse, S., Nierstrasz, O., Wuyts, R.: Composable encapsulation policies. In: Odersky, M. (ed.) ECOOP 2004. LNCS, vol. 3086, pp. 26–50. Springer, Heidelberg (2004)
16. Schärli, N., Black, A.P., Ducasse, S.: Object-oriented encapsulation for dynamically typed languages. In: Proceedings of 18th International Conference on Object-Oriented Programming Systems, Languages and Applications (OOPSLA'04), October 2004, pp. 130–149 (2004)
17. Bergel, A., Ducasse, S., Nierstrasz, O., Wuyts, R.: Stateful traits and their formalization. Journal of Computer Languages, Systems and Structures 34(2-3), 83–108 (2008)
18. Friedman, D.P., Wand, M.: Reification: Reflection without metaphysics. In: LFP '84: Proceedings of the 1984 ACM Symposium on LISP and functional programming, pp. 348–355. ACM, New York (1984)
19. Lienhard, A.: Dynamic Object Flow Analysis. Phd thesis, University of Bern (2008)
20. Haupt, M., Schippers, H.: A machine model for aspect-oriented programming. In: Ernst, E. (ed.) ECOOP 2007. LNCS, vol. 4609, pp. 501–524. Springer, Heidelberg (2007)
21. Gamma, E., Helm, R., Johnson, R., Vlissides, J.: Design Patterns: Elements of Reusable Object-Oriented Software. Addison Wesley, Reading (1995)
22. Pascoe, G.A.: Encapsulators: A new software paradigm in Smalltalk-80. In: Proceedings OOPSLA '86, ACM SIGPLAN Notices, November 1986, vol. 21, pp. 341–346 (1986)
23. Flatt, M., Krishnamurthi, S., Felleisen, M.: A programmer's reduction semantics for classes and mixins. Technical Report TR 97-293, Rice University (1999)
24. Denker, M., Ducasse, S., Tanter, É.: Runtime bytecode transformation for Smalltalk. Journal of Computer Languages, Systems and Structures 32(2-3), 125–139 (2006)
25. Ducasse, S.: Evaluating message passing control techniques in Smalltalk. Journal of Object-Oriented Programming (JOOP) 12(6), 39–44 (1999)
26. Hirschfeld, R., Costanza, P., Nierstrasz, O.: Context-oriented programming. Journal of Object Technology 7(3) (March 2008)
27. Denker, M., Suen, M., Ducasse, S.: The meta in meta-object architectures. In: Proceedings of TOOLS EUROPE 2008. LNBIP, vol. 11, pp. 218–237. Springer, Heidelberg (2008)
28. Ierusalimschy, R., de la Rocque Rodriguez, N.: Side-effect free functions in object-oriented languages. Computer Languages 3/4(21), 129–146 (1995)
29. Costanza, P., Hirschfeld, R.: Language constructs for context-oriented programming: An overview of ContextL. In: Proceedings of the Dynamic Languages Symposium (DLS) '05, co-organized with OOPSLA'05, October 2005, pp. 1–10. ACM, New York (2005)
30. Warth, A., Kay, A.: Worlds: Controlling the scope of side effects. Technical Report RN-2008-001, Viewpoints Research (2008)
31. Tanter, É.: Contextual values. In: Proceedings of the 4th ACM Dynamic Languages Symposium (DLS 2008), Paphos, Cyprus, July 2008. ACM Press, New York (to appear, 2008)
32. Hanenberg, S., Hirschfeld, R., Unland, R.: Morphing aspects: incompletely woven aspects and continuous weaving. In: AOSD '04: Proceedings of the 3rd international conference on Aspect-oriented software development, pp. 46–55. ACM, New York (2004)
33. Schippers, H., Janssens, D., Haupt, M., Hirschfeld, R.: Delegation-based semantics for modularizing crosscutting concerns. In: OOPSLA '08: Proceedings of the 23rd ACM SIGPLAN conference on Object oriented programming systems languages and applications, pp. 525–542. ACM, New York (2008)

34. Flatt, M., Krishnamurthi, S., Felleisen, M.: Classes and mixins. In: Proceedings of the 25th ACM SIGPLAN-SIGACT Symposium on Principles of Programming Languages, pp. 171–183. ACM Press, New York (1998)
35. Felleisen, M., Hieb, R.: The revised report on the syntactic theories of sequential control and state. Theor. Comput. Sci. 103(2), 235–271 (1992)

Appendix: SMALLTALKLITE

The syntax of SMALLTALKLITE is shown in Figure 7. SMALLTALKLITE is similar to CLASSICJAVA, but eliding the features related to static typing.

To simplify the reduction semantics of SMALLTALKLITE, we adopt an approach similar to that used by Flatt *et al* [34], we annotate field accesses and **super** sends with additional static information that is needed at "run-time". This annotated syntax is shown in Figure 8. The figure also specifies the evaluation contexts for the annotated syntax in Felleisen and Hieb's notation [35].

$P \vdash \langle \epsilon, S \rangle \hookrightarrow \langle \epsilon', S' \rangle$ means that we reduce an annotated expression ϵ in the context of a (static) program P and a (dynamic) store of objects S to a new expression ϵ' and (possibly) updated store S'. An annotated expression ϵ is essentially an expression e in which field names are decorated with their object contexts, *i.e.*, f is translated to $o.f$, and **super** calls are decorated with their object and class contexts. Annotated expressions and their subexpressions reduce to a value, which is either an object identifier or nil. Subexpressions may be evaluated within an expression context E.

The store consists of a set of mappings from object identifiers $oid \in \text{dom}(S)$ to tuples $\langle c, \{f \mapsto v\} \rangle$ representing the class c of an object and the set of its field values. The initial value of the store is $S = \{\}$.

Translation from the main expression to an initial annotated expression is specified out by the $o[\![e]\!]_c$ function (see Figure 9). This binds fields to their enclosing object context and binds **self** to the *oid* of the receiver. The initial object context for a program is nil. (*i.e.*, there are no global fields accessible to the main expression). So if e is the main expression associated to a program P, then $\text{nil}[\![e]\!]_{\text{Object}}$ is the initial annotated element. The reductions are summarized in Figure 10.

$$
\begin{array}{ll}
P = defn^* e & meth = m(x^*)\ \{\ e\ \} \\
defn = \textbf{class}\ c\ \textbf{extends}\ c\ \{\ f^* meth^*\ \} & c = \text{a class name}\ |\ \text{Object} \\
e = \textbf{new}\ c\ \ |\ x\ |\ \textbf{self}\ |\ \text{nil} & f = \text{a field name} \\
\quad |\ f\ |\ f{=}e\ |\ e.m(e^*) & m = \text{a method name} \\
\quad |\ \textbf{super}.m(e^*)\ |\ \textbf{let}\ x{=}e\ \textbf{in}\ e & x = \text{a variable name}
\end{array}
$$

Fig. 7. SMALLTALKLITE syntax

$$
\begin{array}{l}
\epsilon = v\ |\ \textbf{new}\ c\ \ |\ x\ |\ \textbf{self}\ |\ \epsilon.f\ |\ \epsilon.f{=}\epsilon\ |\ \epsilon.m(\epsilon^*)\ |\ \textbf{super}\langle o, c\rangle.m(\epsilon^*)\ |\ \textbf{let}\ x{=}\epsilon\ \textbf{in}\ \epsilon \\
E = [\,]\ |\ o.f{=}E\ |\ E.m(\epsilon^*)\ |\ o.m(v^*\ E\ \epsilon^*) \\
\quad |\ \textbf{super}\langle o, c\rangle.m(v^*\ E\ \epsilon^*)\ |\ \textbf{let}\ x{=}E\ \textbf{in}\ \epsilon \\
v, o = \text{nil}\ |\ oid
\end{array}
$$

Fig. 8. SMALLTALKLITE annotated syntax

$$o[\![\textbf{new } c]\!]_c = \textbf{new } c \qquad\qquad o[\![f]\!]_c = o.f$$
$$o[\![x]\!]_c = x \qquad\qquad o[\![f{=}e]\!]_c = o.f{=}o[\![e]\!]_c$$
$$o[\![\textbf{self}]\!]_c = o \qquad\qquad o[\![e.m(e_i^*)]\!]_c = o[\![e]\!]_c.m(o[\![e_i]\!]_c^*)$$
$$o[\![\textsf{nil}]\!]_c = \textsf{nil} \qquad\qquad o[\![\textbf{super}.m(e_i^*)]\!]_c = \textbf{super}\langle o,c\rangle.m(o[\![e_i]\!]_c^*)$$
$$o[\![\textbf{let } x{=}e \textbf{ in } e']\!]_c = \textbf{let } x{=}o[\![e]\!]_c \textbf{ in } o[\![e']\!]_c$$

Fig. 9. Annotating expressions

$P \vdash \langle E[\textbf{new } c], \mathcal{S}\rangle \hookrightarrow \langle E[oid], \mathcal{S}[oid \mapsto \langle c, \{f \mapsto \textsf{nil} \mid \forall f, f \in_P^* c\}\rangle]\rangle$ [*new*]
    where $oid \notin \mathrm{dom}(\mathcal{S})$

$P \vdash \langle E[o.f], \mathcal{S}\rangle \hookrightarrow \langle E[v], \mathcal{S}\rangle$ [*get*]
    where $\mathcal{S}(o) = \langle c, \mathcal{F}\rangle$ and $\mathcal{F}(f) = v$

$P \vdash \langle E[o.f{=}v], \mathcal{S}\rangle \hookrightarrow \langle E[v], \mathcal{S}[o \mapsto \langle c, \mathcal{F}[f \mapsto v]\rangle]\rangle$ [*set*]
    where $\mathcal{S}(o) = \langle c, \mathcal{F}\rangle$

$P \vdash \langle E[o.m(v^*)], \mathcal{S}\rangle \hookrightarrow \langle E[o[\![e[v^*/x^*]]\!]_{c'}], \mathcal{S}\rangle$ [*send*]
    where $\mathcal{S}[o] = \langle c, \mathcal{F}\rangle$ and $\langle c, m, x^*, e\rangle \in_P^* c'$

$P \vdash \langle E[\textbf{super}\langle o, c\rangle.m(v^*)], \mathcal{S}\rangle \hookrightarrow \langle E[o[\![e[v^*/x^*]]\!]_{c''}], \mathcal{S}\rangle$ [*super*]
    where $c \prec_P c'$ and $\langle c', m, x^*, e\rangle \in_P^* c''$ and $c' \leq_P c''$

$P \vdash \langle E[\textbf{let } x{=}v \textbf{ in } \epsilon], \mathcal{S}\rangle \hookrightarrow \langle E[\epsilon[v/x]], \mathcal{S}\rangle$ [*let*]

Fig. 10. Reductions for SMALLTALKLITE

new c [*new*] reduces to a fresh *oid*, bound in the store to an object whose class is c and whose fields are all nil. A (local) field access [*get*] reduces to the value of the field. Note that it is syntactically impossible to access a field of another object. The annotated expression notation $o.f$ is only generated in the context of the object o. Field update [*set*] simply updates the corresponding binding of the field in the store. When we send a message [*send*], we must look up the corresponding method body e, starting from the class c of the receiver o. The method body is then evaluated in the context of the receiver o, binding **self** to the receiver's *oid*. Formal parameters to the method are substituted by the actual arguments. We also pass in the actual class in which the method is found, so that **super** sends have the right context to start their method lookup.

super sends [*super*] are similar to regular message sends, except that the method lookup must start in the superclass of class of the method in which the **super** send was declared. When we reduce the **super** send, we must take care to pass on the class c'' of the method in which the **super** method was found, since that method may make further **super** sends. **let in** expressions [*let*] simply represent local variable bindings.

Errors occur if an expression gets "stuck" and does not reduce to an *oid* or to nil. This may occur if a non-existent variable, field or method is referenced (for example, when sending any message to nil). For the purpose of this paper we are not concerned with errors, so we do not introduce any special rules to generate an error value in these cases.

Optimizing Aspect-Oriented Mechanisms for Embedded Applications

Christine Hundt, Daniel Stöhr, and Sabine Glesner

Berlin Institute of Technology (TU Berlin),
Berlin, Germany
{resix,dstoehr,glesner}@cs.tu-berlin.de
http://www.pes.tu-berlin.de/

Abstract. As applications for small embedded mobile devices are getting larger and more complex, it becomes inevitable to adopt more advanced software engineering methods from the field of desktop application development. Aspect-oriented programming (AOP) is a promising approach due to its advanced modularization capabilities. However, existing AOP languages tend to add a substantial overhead in both execution time and code size which restricts their practicality for small devices with limited resources. In this paper, we present optimizations for aspect-oriented mechanisms at the level of the virtual machine. Our experiments show that these optimizations yield a considerable performance gain along with a reduction of the code size. Thus, our optimizations establish the base for using advanced aspect-oriented modularization techniques for developing Java applications on small embedded devices.

Keywords: aspect-orientation, embedded systems, mobile devices, Java virtual machine, optimization.

1 Introduction

Mobile devices like smart phones and other hand held devices are becoming more widely-used. At the same time, more complex applications for such devices are developed and used. To provide a short time to market, these applications have to be *reusable*, *adaptable*, *extensible*, and easily *portable* to a wide variety of hardware devices. Low-level languages like C or even assembler are no longer sufficient for that aim. With the steadily increasing demands, it becomes inevitable to adopt more advanced software engineering methods from the field of desktop application development. Aspect-oriented programming (AOP) is a promising approach, which could meet these requirements due to its advanced modularization capabilities.

Moreover, in the context of embedded devices, we have to cope with an increased *variability* among the various static and dynamic versions of an application. Static variability arises when the same application is running on similar, yet different platforms of a product line. Dynamic variability emerges when the

J. Vitek (Ed.): TOOLS 2010, LNCS 6141, pp. 137–153, 2010.

device changes its context and the application running on it needs to adapt to new boundary conditions. With AOP, variable parts of an application can be properly modularized and dynamically combined.

On the other hand, mobile devices will always have limited resources (CPU, memory) compared to desktop computers. This is a problem because advanced programming languages in general and especially existing AOP languages tend to add a substantial overhead in execution time and code size. If we want to use their advanced modularization capability for small devices, we have to optimize the execution of aspect-oriented programs.

In this paper, we propose optimizations for relevant parts of the execution of aspect-oriented programming languages.

Our optimizations are mainly designed and implemented on the level of the Java virtual machine (VM). Opposed to the implementation in Java byte code, this has the advantage that everything realized inside the VM itself does not need to be interpreted but is executed natively. At the same time, the application code size can be reduced if AOP features are implemented only once in the VM. Implementing these features in byte code causes a lot of reoccurring code fragments in different methods and classes. However, this will lead to a specialized virtual machine, which may appear as a drawback at first sight. On the other hand, in the context of embedded systems a large amount of different virtual machines for every single hardware configuration is necessary anyway.

We implement our optimizations for the AOP language ObjectTeams [13]. Our experimental results show that our approach is able to significantly reduce the execution time, and to furthermore reduce the code size of adapted classes.

This paper is structured as follows: Section 2 gives an overview of aspect-oriented programming and virtual machines. In Section 3, we present our optimizations of aspect activation and aspect execution. In Section 4, we explain our implementation of these optimizations in the existing execution environment of ObjectTeams together with experimental results. In Section 5, we discuss related work and in Section 6, we conclude and outline future work.

2 Background

2.1 Aspect-Oriented Programming

Aspect-oriented programming (AOP) [15] facilitates the modularization of *cross-cutting concerns*, which are *scattered* across the module structure in purely object-oriented designs. At the same time, it prevents the *tangling* of independent concerns in the same module. Thus, AOP provides for enhanced *separation of concerns*. The crosscutting concerns are implemented in separate *aspect* modules. They expand a base program at defined points in the execution (*join points*), which are specified by *aspect bindings*.

AOP Mechanisms. There is no closed definition of aspect-orientation, resulting in a large variety of aspect-oriented programing languages. Most of these languages are extensions to existing object-oriented programming languages. A common mechanism is the adaptation of base methods by aspect methods. This adaptation can be specified in different ways. The exact execution point can be stated as *before*, *after*, or *instead* of the base method. Moreover, the adaptation can be constrained by further conditions like the execution context, the active thread, or the dynamic activation state of an aspect.

We selected the programming language *ObjectTeams* (OT/J) [12,13,2] to implement our optimizations. In addition to common aspect-oriented mechanisms, OT/J supports advanced collaboration-based modularization mechanisms. In OT/J, aspect functionality is defined in *role* classes, which adapt individual base classes. *Role methods* can be bound to corresponding *base methods* with *callin* bindings. Such binding causes the execution of the role method after, before or instead of the base method. Roles are contained in *team* classes, which define a collaboration context for them. Teams can be dynamically activated and deactivated. This activation can be *global* or *thread-local*. Although a team in OT/J means more, than just a collection of aspects, the term "team" is used synonymously with "aspect" in the context of this paper.

The mechanisms in OT/J, that are touched by our optimizations, concern aspect *activation* and aspect *execution*. *Aspect activation* occurs whenever a team gets activated, and thereby all callin bindings of its contained roles get activated. Therefore the team has to be registered with all base classes it contains roles for. The reverse applys for team *deactivation*. During *aspect execution*, for all base method calls the involved aspects have to be looked up, checked for activity, and get executed. The optimization potential of these AOP mechanisms is discussed in section 3.

Aspect Weaving. While aspect bindings specify the points at which an aspect should be effective, we need a mechanism, which actually forces the execution of the corresponding aspect methods. This *aspect weaving* mechanism inserts calls to aspect methods as well as various infrastructural elements. It can operate at different levels. The aspects can be woven *statically* into the base program at compile-time. *Run-time weaving* can be performed at class loading time before the base classes are executed by the JVM or even later during the execution of the program. Static weaving keeps the run-time overhead low, but limits the flexibility of the adaptation and increases the code size. More dynamic weaving allows more flexible context-aware adaption of the executed applications, but also suffers from more effort at run-time.

Currently, OT/J performs load-time bytecode transformation to weave the aspects into the bytecode of the base classes. The resulting bytecode is subsequently executed by a standard JVM. Typically, the Sun JVM is used, which is not suitable for small devices because it is too large.

2.2   Virtual Machines

Virtual machines [17] execute architecture-independent code by interpretation or just-in-time (JIT) compilation. While the execution is generally faster using JIT-compilation, [5] discusses a number of advantages of interpreters which especially apply to embedded systems. So, Bytecode uses less memory than the corresponding machine code. Also, interpreters are more portable to different architectures and significantly smaller and simpler to maintain than JIT-compilers.

We have selected the JamVM [1] for implementing our optimizations. It supports the full JVM specification version 2 [16], although it is extremely small and applicable for embedded devices. It has been ported to different architectures, like ARM and MIPS. The JamVM is implemented in C, with a small amount of platform-dependent assembler code. It does not contain a JIT, but its interpreter is highly optimized, implementing many state-of-the-art techniques such as *direct-threading*, *quick instructions* [7], *stack-caching* [6] and *superinstructions* [5]. A comparison of Java VMs on ARM based systems [4] shows that the JamVM is a good choice for embedded Java development.

The JamVM provides an efficient mechanism to access internal data and functions like class loading and reflection. At the Java-side, a class with native method declarations serves as an interface. Calls to these internal native methods are directly forwarded to implementations in the VM code. This is comparable to JNI (Java Native Interface), with a little less overhead and without dynamic libraries. We can exploit this mechanism to make new aspect-specific functionality available to the Java code, thus integrating it with the existing aspect execution mechanism.

3   Optimizing AOP Mechanisms

Adding aspect-oriented mechanisms on top of an existing programming language generally introduces a certain amount of overhead. This overhead can be critical with respect to space or time. Both kinds of overhead are critical for embedded devices with limited memory and computation power and have to be addressed by our effort to optimize aspect-oriented program execution. Hence, we aim at reducing the size of additional code as well as at its optimized execution.

The overhead of aspect-oriented program execution is caused by additional control flow using additional data structures. Our approach is to successively shift the weaving mechanism to the JVM-level. On one hand, this is a precondition for our long-term goal, namely the dynamic weaving of aspects at run-time. On the other hand, inside the VM, we expect a rich potential for the optimization of aspect-oriented execution mechanisms because at this level, we have direct access to the data structures necessary to support method execution.

Shifting functionality from the bytecode to the VM-level has the general advantage that the VM code will be natively executed instead of being interpreted. To further optimize the aspect-oriented execution we use additional data structures to store additional information that is useful for the execution of aspectual code (e.g., aspect registration, activation, role caching). Furthermore, we introduce additional *bytecode instructions* that make use of the newly introduced data structures and which are significantly faster than the corresponding Java bytecode.

3.1   Aspect Activation

During weaving, aspects have to be *registered* with the base classes they adapt. When executing an adapted base method, the aspects are looked up in order to execute the bound aspect methods. The registration mechanism is usually realized as a list data structure which is associated to the bound base class. In aspect languages supporting dynamic *activation* and *deactivation* of aspects, these data structures have to be dynamically updatable during run-time.

Commonly, the necessary data structures and methods are added at the level of Java bytecode to the involved classes. This increases the code size, and the activation methods have to be interpreted just as normal application methods. Furthermore, OT/J supports sophisticated activation policies. Aspects can be activated explicitly/implicitly and globally/thread-locally (see [13], §5). These policies cannot be implemented efficiently at the level of Java bytecode. Thread-local activation, for example, makes the execution of an aspect dependent on the current thread context. In Java, this is only inefficiently distinguishable using the Java class `ThreadLocal`.

Hence, adding the aspect registration and activation mechanism to the VM-level can reduce the code size and enhances the run-time performance by making the corresponding methods native. Residing in the VM, these methods have access to internal data structures and mechanisms, which is another performance advantage.

Activation Infrastructure. In the original OT/J implementation, the infrastructure that is necessary to register a team (aspect) is added to the byte-code of every adapted base class. It consists of arrays for storing team instances as well as methods to access these data structures (`addTeam(Team)` and `removeTeam(Team)`). These methods are called when activating or deactivating a team instance.

Similar to the *advice instance tables* of [10], we propose to move the aspect registration mechanism to the JVM-level, allowing various optimizations. First, we can move the data structures to the VM-internal data structures that represent classes. To allow access to these data during aspect activation, we need to extend the interface of the VM. In a second step, we introduce a *global cache* as optimization for consecutive activation and deactivation of the same aspect instance. This is a common pattern for implicit team activation. Note that implicit team activation guarantees a coherent aspectual control flow if a public method of a team or a role is called, cf. [13], §5.3.

Activation Mechanism. The activation of a team instance includes more than just registering it with the corresponding base classes. For the support of thread-local and global team activation, as well as for (nested) implicit team activation, more complex mechanisms are required. For example, it is necessary to keep track of individual threads and the nesting depth of implicit activation. So far, the team activation mechanism has been implemented in the super class of all team classes `org.objectteams.Team` in Java. This requires several fields, such as hash maps, locks, counters and booleans.

While explicit de-/activation may occur rather infrequently, implicit activation and calls to the method isActive, which states whether a team is active for a given thread, constitute a relevant part during the execution of an OT/J program. To optimize the execution time of the activation mechanism, we decided to implement the team activation as native VM methods. We moved the necessary team fields to the VM-internal representation of team objects. The methods we made native cover explicit and implicit team activation and deactivation as well as the isActive method. Since the method signatures did not change from the original to the native implementation, there is no difference for the programmer in using the old or the new OT/J implementation. With these adaptations, we not only decrease the execution time for the activation methods but also reduce the size of instantiated team objects.

3.2   Aspect Execution

The execution of aspectual behavior is typically realized by additional calls to aspect instances. In OT/J, this includes looking up the next adapting team instance, determining the corresponding role object (*lifting*), and calling the bound role method. The team lookup depends on dynamic aspect activation. The method execution requires dynamic method lookup.

We propose a specialized aspect dispatch mechanism working on VM-internal activation infrastructures. To make this available to the Java code, we introduce new bytecode instructions. Aspect execution is subject to special conditions that do not apply to method dispatch in general. Optimizations can exploit these conditions and, for example, explicitly cache frequently used objects, like role objects.

Aspect Lookup. In the original OT/J implementation, the base class' array that contains all activated teams (see Section 3.1) had been iterated whenever an adapted base method was executed. This was necessary to call the corresponding aspect methods. Therefore, every base class contained specific *wrapper* methods for each adapted base method. This procedure caused significant overhead because the wrapper methods had to browse the base class' team array using Java structures and methods. Furthermore, during the search, each contained team had to be checked for thread-local activity before an aspect could be executed.

Based on the optimization moving the team activation infrastructure into the VM, we can additionally improve base method execution by shifting this lookup procedure to the VM level, too. The VM-internal information can now be accessed through a new bytecode instruction, which can be called repetitively during base method execution. With each call, this instruction returns the next active aspect to be executed. Thus, we can avoid the overhead in execution time, produced by the afore used Java structures, and we can decrease the bytecode size for each base method as well.

Role Dispatch. Aspect execution in ObjectTeams implies the call of a role method that implements the aspect functionality. Before the role method can be called the appropriate role object has to be determined. This dispatch includes *lifting* the base object to a role object in the context of a given team. Here, the management of the resulting role object is to be optimized. Theoretically, a base object can be lifted to n role objects, but in practice, it is very often the same role object to which a base is lifted. A special case of repeated usage of the same role object occurs if a role defines multiple aspect bindings to the same base method. Every single role method call includes lifting the base object to the same role object. So caching of the role objects is a potential optimization.

Using a cache usually includes a check whether the cache is (still) valid. To decide whether the role cache has become invalid, the semantics of the lifting mechanism has to be considered. The ObjectTeams language definition ([13], §2.3(a)) states "Lifting is guaranteed to yield the same role object for subsequent calls regarding the same base object, the same team instance and the same role class". This means that the role cache of a given base object can be invalidated if the aspect execution concerns another team instance or another role class (of the same team). Furthermore, the role object could have been explicitly removed by the programmer.

The simplest form of a role object cache just caches the last role object for every base object. Such a cache will be most profitable if many calls to the same role object succeed. In the worst case, every role method call goes to another role object, and the cache is invalid every time. Multiple callins from different roles to the same base method cause such a scenario. Hence, the cache validation check has to be very efficient to minimize the overhead in case of cache misses. If a base method has callins from different roles, these will mostly belong to different team classes. Thus, we first have to check whether the cached role belongs to the expected role and team class. Only if this is true, we have to check the team instance.

To decide whether this optimization is profitable, we did a simulation to estimate how expensive regular lifting is compared to a cache access. Therefore, we directly called the lifting method and a variant using a simple Java implementation of the cache. In the best case, that is if the cache is *always valid*, the execution time improves by a factor of 14.8. If the cache contains the right role every *second* time, the improvement is still 10%. In the worst case, that is if the cache is *always invalid*, the performance degrades by 10%. These results indicate that a role cache is a worthwhile optimization to be implemented within the VM.

4   Implementation and Benchmarks

We have implemented the optimizations introduced in Section 3 in the JamVM [1] version 1.5.4 and measured their benefit with several suitable micro benchmarks. As our goal is to reduce the AO-specific overhead, each of these benchmarks measures a separate part of the AOP mechanisms, affected by one of our optimizations. To isolate the effect of the respective optimization, the involved aspect methods and base methods have empty bodies. The improvement for real-world applications depends on the fraction of the use of the optimized AOP mechanisms. For every optimization, we have incrementally adapted the weaving component of OT/J to use the new VM-internal mechanisms. With this approach, we were able to sustain the full functional range of the OT/J language at any time.

To differentiate the effects of the individual optimizations, we measured them separately. We performed each benchmark multiple times and took the arithmetic mean as result for our charts. Finally, we benchmarked all optimizations together in Section 4.3. We executed the benchmarks on an Intel Pentium processor with 3.4 GHz.

In addition to execution time, we also analyzed the effect on code size. In general, the size of runtime structures of classes and objects is more relevant than the woven base bytecode because the latter is only hold in memory during class-loading. So, if data fields (e.g. the lists of activated team instances) are shifted from the bytecode to the runtime structures, this only reduces the bytecode size. Reducing method code, on the other hand, also leads to smaller runtime structures. Therefore, we focus on method implementation when describing the effect of our optimizations on code size.

4.1   Aspect Activation

To optimize the execution time of aspect activation, we developed a VM-internal mechanism for aspect registration and implemented a native team activation mechanism.

VM-internal Activation Infrastructure. To move the team registration mechanism to the VM-level, we extended the data structure representing a class inside the JamVM by a reference to the newly introduced registration data structure. In contrast to the previous weaving strategy of OT/J, now *every* class has this structure. Initially, this causes a very small overhead (20 bytes on x86 architecture). Only if a class is actually adapted by an aspect (team), advanced initialization and memory allocation take place.

To integrate the new data structures with the remaining aspect execution mechanism of OT/J at bytecode-level, we provide an interface for adding, removing and retrieving team instances to a base class. We implemented this interface analogously to the native interfaces provided by the JamVM (see 2.2).

Next, we implemented a global cache for team activation. This cache stores the previous state of the activation structure when a new team instance is added to a base class. If the same team instance is removed instantly, the cache is written back to the corresponding activation structure before any other 'add' or 'remove' operation is performed. Thus, no team instances have to be moved in memory.

We have measured the benefit of this optimization with the following benchmark, cf. Figure 1. A team-level method was executed 3000 times, causing 3000 implicit team activations and subsequent deactivations. The corresponding team class contained one role class bound to a base class. Thus, activating an instance of this team led to registration with one base class. We have varied the number of previously activated team instances from 0 to 1000.

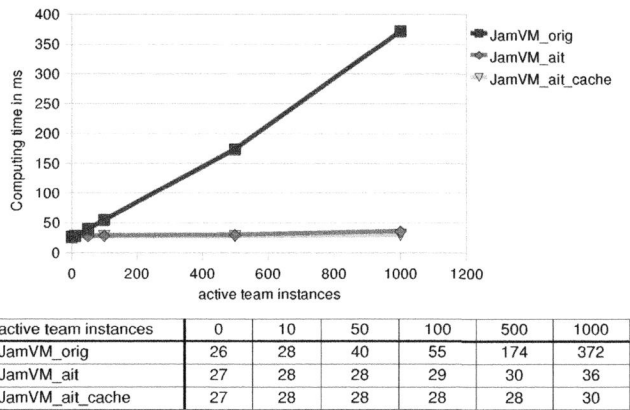

active team instances	0	10	50	100	500	1000
JamVM_orig	26	28	40	55	174	372
JamVM_ait	27	28	28	29	30	36
JamVM_ait_cache	27	28	28	28	28	30

Fig. 1. Benchmark results for the native activation infrastructure

We compared the performance of the original JamVM (JamVM_orig) with the optimization that moves the activation infrastructure to the VM (JamVM_ait) and with the version with an additional global cache (JamVM_ait_cache).

Our experimental results showed that JamVM_ait yields a considerable performance gain compared to JamVM_orig. The execution time was reduced by a factor of almost 2 for 100 instances and improves, the more team instances are activated. Compared to that, the gain of JamVM_ait_cache is minimal for this benchmark. It becomes more significant when even more team instances are active. This can be explained by the fact that array copying is implemented very efficient inside the VM and leads to notable overhead only for many entries.

In addition to the runtime improvement, by this optimization we significantly reduced the bytecode size of adapted base classes. Now, the methods for adding and removing teams are omitted and only once implemented in the VM code. Including code blocks and constant pool entries, this implies a code reduction by about 800 bytes per adapted base class. Moreover, the wrapper code for every adapted base method could be reduced by about 90 bytes.

Native Activation Mechanism. To integrate the team class fields into the teams' VM-internal representation, we created a *teamdata* structure holding the required hash maps, booleans and object locks. Now, every team object structure contains a reference to its teamdata, which can only be accessed from inside the VM. Likewise, a VM-global array for global activated teams had to be added. Also, we had to intervene in the VM's thread handling to deactivate teams for ended threads and to activate global active teams for all newly started threads. After that, we could implement the team activation methods analogously to the way it was done in the original Java Team class. A significant optimization we made affected the handling of the base class' map for activated threads. If a team gets deactivated for a single thread, now the hash map gets rearranged in case that the thread was involved in a collision before. Thus, we gain speed whenever the map is checked for an activated thread, which affects all native activation methods.

To assess the native method's effect, we implemented a benchmark that creates a variable number of threads and that measures the computation time for activating or deactivating a team for every single thread. It also measures the time for the `isActive` method while all teams are activated or deactivated. The left chart in figure 2 shows the results of the native and original implementation for an `activate` and a following `isActive` call, while the right chart shows the same for a `deactivate` call. The benchmark revealed an improvement of the execution time for all native activation methods. As seen, computing time for team activation has been reduced by 75% in the average case, and checking an active team for activation costs 90% less time than before. Deactivating the team for all threads and to call the `isActive` method afterwards takes both about 80% less computing time. Corresponding benchmarks for global and implicit team activation showed that their execution time improved similarly.

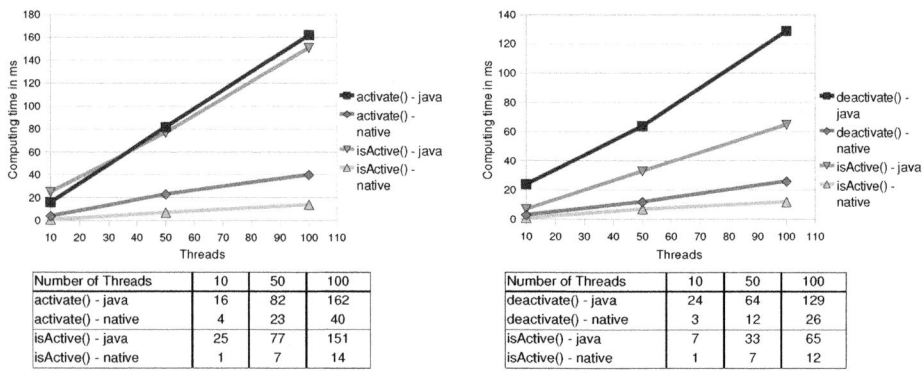

Fig. 2. Benchmark results for native team activation

Since this benchmark only measured the performance for single team activation methods, we must still clarify, how strong the effect would be in a real-world application. But even if the `activate` and `deactivate` methods are rarely used, an improvement should be present in an overall program, because the `isActive` method is executed once per activated team instance whenever a base method is called.

4.2   Aspect Execution

To improve aspect execution, we optimized the team lookup and the dynamic role dispatch. We introduced special bytecode instructions and implemented a cache for the recently used role object.

Aspect specific Byte Code Instructions. We created two new opcodes, which are `getaspects` and `nextaspect`, to replace the original Java method calls, used to work on the base class' team list. They work on a new VM-internal data structure, the *aspect iterator*, which keeps track of the aspects to be executed. A base class can have several active aspect iterators at a time, one for each concurrent base method call. That is why every aspect iterator has to be accessed via the current operand stack and is not directly connected to the base class itself.

The data flow between the new opcodes and the aspect iterator is demonstrated in a simplified example for the execution of a base method with *before callins* (see figure 3).

When a base class checks for any active aspects, `getaspects` is executed first. In step 1.1, the opcode takes a base class reference from the actual operand stack in order to initialize an aspect iterator. The iterator contains an array with all teams that are active for some thread and relevant for the base class. As shown in step 1.2, this array is taken from the VM-internal base class structure, which was extended by this array in the previous optimizations, mentioned above. It is copied to ensure that the activated roles of the base class do not change during the base method call. Furthermore, the aspect iterator holds an index counter, used to traverse the team array. After initialization, the aspect iterator is put on top of the stack (see 1.3).

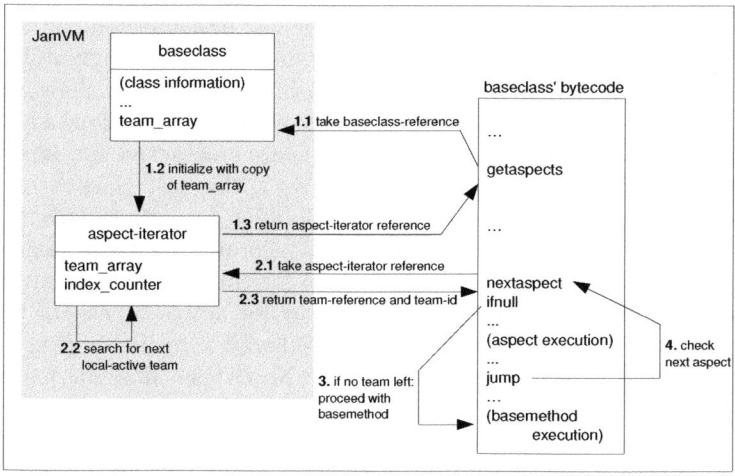

Fig. 3. Simplified example for execution of the new opcodes

The teams, stored in the aspect iterator, can be accessed through the `nextaspect` opcode. When the VM executes `nextaspect`, it takes an aspect iterator reference from the stack (see step 2.1). Afterwards, in step 2.2, it traverses the aspect iterator's teamarray and checks each team for thread-local activity by using the native methods, discussed in the previous section. If a local-active team is found, a reference to it and its team id is put atop of the stack (see step 2.3). Also, the index of the following team is stored in the aspect iterator's index counter to state where the lookup has to begin for the next `nextaspect` call. After the execution of the `nextaspect` opcode has finished, the returned team can be handled.

This procedure can be repeated by following step 4 to cover all teams adapting the base method call. If the end of the team array is reached during a `nextaspect` call, a null reference is put on the stack and the aspect iterator gets destroyed (see step 3). However, the real integration of the new opcodes into the base class' bytecode is more sophisticated than our example, e.g., by using a recursive structure instead of a simple loop. By doing this, a more efficient coverage for all kinds of callins at once is achieved.

An additional optimization, which is not fully implemented yet, provides lazy copying for the aspect iterator's team array. Thus, the aspect iterator works on a reference to the original array until the activation status of a team, which is related to the base class, changes. This optimization requires an extension of the VM-internal base class structure with a list of its current treated aspect iterators.

To measure the optimization gain of execution time, we implemented a small benchmark. It consists of a base class, holding a base method with empty body, and of a team class, adding an empty aspect method as callin to the base method. Thus, most of the base method's computation time is used to perform the newly implemented bytecode. Initially, 100 team class instances are created and globally activated. After that, the base method is called a variable number of times and the computation time from the first to the last base method call is measured. The chart shown in figure 4 compares the results from the original implementation with the results from the new one. As shown in the left chart, about 25% of computing time has been saved using the new implementation. The difference gets more significant if the instantiated teams are only active for another thread than the one calling the base method. This way, the base class' array of active teams is filled will all 100 teams, but when looking for active aspects, all teams have to be skipped. In this case, about 85% computing time has been saved (see right chart). The high performance gain for thread-local deactivated teams is explained by the new handling of the array for active teams. In the original implementation, the array had to be traversed with a recursion over many Java method calls until an active team was found. Now this is done in one step at the VM-level.

With this optimization we could reduce the bytecode size of adapted base classes by about 290 bytes. Additionally, the wrapper code for every adapted base method could be reduced by about 100 bytes.

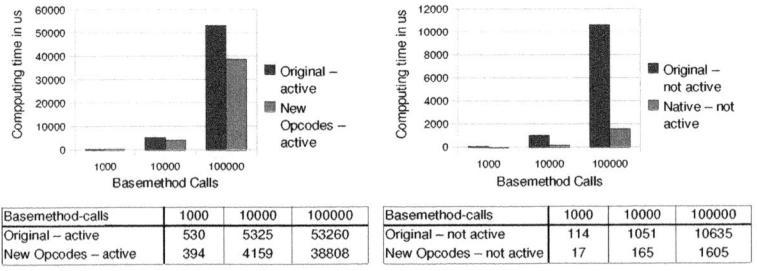

Fig. 4. Benchmark results for the new opcodes

Caching lifted Roles. To optimize the runtime for base object lifting, we implemented a single role cache per base object. This cache had to be integrated into the existing lifting process of OT/J.

When an object is allocated, we do not want to make any assumptions whether it will eventually be adapted and thus becomes a base object. This also facilitates dynamic aspect weaving (see 2.1). Hence, we integrated the cache into the general object layout of the VM. Initially, we do not allocate any memory, but set the field to NULL. The allocation takes place when the cache is used the first time. So, the overhead for normal objects is minimal (size of a pointer).

In addition to the cached role object, the cache data structure stores the qualified role class name (including team class name) and the associated team instance. This information is necessary for cache validation, which first checks the role class name and afterwards compares the team instances. The reference to the cached role has to be immutable for a particular role object. Otherwise it would be invalidated when the garbage collector *compacts* the heap.

To grant the lifting process access to the role cache, we introduced native interface methods for storing and retrieving the cached role. To integrate the role cache with the lifting process, it has to be used at every lifting site. The role cache could be checked before every call of the lifting method, but in this case, the many places where this can happen have to be located (lifting call targets/parameters at callin, lifting objects at assignment). A simpler way of integration is to adjust the lifting method itself. The generation of the lifting method is done when a team class is compiled. So, to insert the usage of our role cache, the code generation of the OT/J compiler had to be changed. Before a role is created or looked up in the team-internal data structures, our role cache is consulted. If the cache contains a valid role object, it is instantly returned. Otherwise, the original functionality of the lifting method is executed. In this case, the calculated role object is stored in the role cache before it is returned.

If a role has been removed from a team instance by calling the API method unregisterRole(Object aRole), a subsequent lifting request causes the creation of a new role object. In this case, the cached role object must be removed. In our current implementation, the unregistration method had been adapted to set the cached role of the affected base object to NULL. This is an overapproximation because the actual cached role may have been another one.

Solely measuring the effects of the role cache on the lifting mechanism resembles the results of the simulation described in 3.2. To evaluate the effect on real aspect execution runtime we also benchmarked the effect of the cached lifting during a callin. A base method was adapted by an after callin. It was repetitively called, causing a lifting of the corresponding base object to the involved role object. To provoke cache misses, another base method adapted by another role class was called in between. The base method was called 1000 times and the presented results are the arithmetic means of 100 runs. As shown in figure 5, we get an improvement of 15.4% if the cache is *always valid*. In the worst case, that is if the cache is *always invalid*, the performance only decreased by 4.4%.

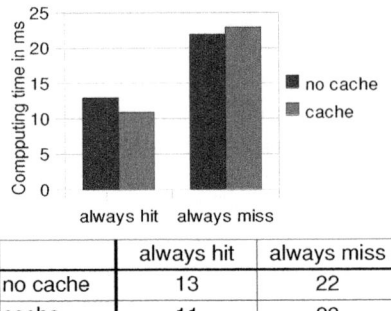

	always hit	always miss
no cache	13	22
cache	11	23

Fig. 5. Benchmark results for the role cache

Due to the additional cache access code, this optimization increased the byte-code size by about 55 bytes for every lifting method.

4.3   Combining All Optimizations

To evaluate the overall performance gain of our optimizations, we combined the optimizations presented in this paper. We constructed a benchmark comprising the *activation* and *execution* mechanisms considered by our approach. A team level method was executed 1000 times, causing implicit activations. Furthermore, the method calls a base method, which is adapted by an *after* callin of the afore activated team. Thus, also aspect execution including lifting is considered. The results are the arithmetic means of 10 benchmark runs. Executed by the original JamVM the benchmark took 22 ms. With all optimizations enabled, we could reduce the execution time to 6 ms. This means that with our optimizations, this benchmark could be executed more than three times faster.

In this paper, we improved the aspect *activation* of OT/J by developing a VM-internal activation infrastructure as well as a native team activation mechanism. The VM-internal activation infrastructure significantly reduces the runtime over-head of team activation, especially for larger numbers of active teams. Based on this adaptation, we have achieved a high performance gain by implementing a native team activation mechanism. Of particular importance is the 80 to 90% faster team activation check because this functionality is also involved in aspect execution.

We further optimized the aspect *execution* of OT/J by additional bytecode instructions and a role cache. Our newly introduced bytecode instructions pro-vide an optimized usage of the VM-internal activation infrastructure. This op-timization guarantees an efficient team lookup, especially for thread-local team activation. By the introduction of a role cache, we could improve the pure lifting mechanism by up to 93%. This leads to an improvement of the general aspect execution by up to 15.4 %.

Although we only executed micro benchmarks so far, our results demonstrate that our optimizations are very promising. Of course, we need to perform more experiments to finally estimate the benefit for real-world applications.

5   Related Work

Optimizations for the execution of aspect-oriented programming languages have been proposed by many approaches.

Some of them improve the run-time performance by restraining the dynamic capabilities of a language. For example, the aspect dispatch can be optimized by replacing dynamic aspect method lookup by static method calls [8]. This is not applicable to our problem because we appraise the dynamic method lookup of aspect methods important for an adequate modularization of software. As our approach, Aspect C++ [18] is also intended for the generation of small and efficient code for constrained environments. However, it does not focus on reusability of the aspects and uses a purely static weaving mechanism only.

Other approaches integrate optimizations into the execution environment of aspect-oriented languages. For example, [9], [10] extend the Jikes Research Virtual Machine to directly support general AOP language mechanisms. The introduced Advice Instance Tables (AIT) have inspired our team activation infrastructure. However, this work does not target embedded small applications because the Jikes VM is not suitable for embedded systems.

In [3], well-known virtual machine optimization techniques are adapted to improve aspect-oriented run-time performance. These optimizations are based on a JIT compiler and primarily aim at eliminating overhead caused by previous optimizations of the compile-time. As motivated in 2.2, we chose a virtual machine without a JIT compiler, by contrast. Furthermore, compilation-time reduction, although desirable, is not our focus because usually applications for embedded systems are compiled at more powerful host systems.

Various optimizations ([7], [6], [5]) have been developed to optimize the interpretation of Java bytecode in general. Our optimizations have to be integrated into these existing optimizations. At the same time, they can be enhanced for the specific needs of aspect-oriented program execution.

In [14], we analyzed the main sources of overhead and proposed preliminary optimizations. In this paper, we develop additional optimizations to further improve aspect activation and aspect execution. In contrast to the existing approaches, we are targeting embedded devices, while providing full dynamic language capabilities. For that purpose, we implemented our optimizations in a suitable virtual machine and concentrate on the runtime performance and memory consumption.

6   Conclusion and Future Work

Advanced modularization mechanisms like aspect-oriented programming are qualified to meet the increasing demands to applications for embedded mobile devices, such as *reusability, adaptability, extensibility,* and *portability*. However, without adequate optimizations their practicality to small devices with limited resources is restricted by overheads in execution time and code size. In this paper, we have presented optimizations for aspect activation and aspect execution at the level of the virtual machine, aiming for an applicability of AOP for small embedded device Java applications.

Our experiments show that these optimizations yield a considerable performance gain of up to 90% for common used aspect-oriented mechanisms. At the same time, we were able to reduce the code size of the adapted classes, which is also important for small devices.

In future work, we plan a deeper integration of the aspect execution mechanism into the virtual machine. Therefore, we investigate how *delegation-based AOP* [11] can be adapted to further shift the execution mechanism for OT/J into the virtual machine. Delegation-based AOP proposes an object-based machine model for aspect-oriented languages based on object-oriented ones. Objects are referenced indirectly by proxies. The activation of an aspect results in the insertion of an additional element in the delegation chain. Our plan is to develop a specialized *invoke* instruction that is also responsible for calling adapting aspect methods.

Furthermore, it could be valuable to investigate the benefit of more sophisticated role caching strategies. Multiple role objects could be cached for one base object, e.g., one for every participating team class. To determine the benefit of a role cache, we could *statically* analyse, whether a base object is often *lifted* to the same role object.

Next, we want to further validate our results on a real embedded device, the Linux-based open source smart phone Freerunner. Finally, we plan to accomplish a case study based on an existing OT/J implementation of a game product line.

References

1. JamVM homepage, http://jamvm.sourceforge.net
2. Object Teams homepage, http://www.eclipse.org/objectteams/
3. Bockisch, C., Arnold, M., Dinkelaker, T., Mezini, M.: Adapting Virtual Machine Techniques for Seamless Aspect Support. In: OOPSLA '06: Proceedings of the 21st annual ACM SIGPLAN conference on Object-oriented programming systems, languages, and applications, pp. 109–124. ACM, New York (2006)
4. buglabs.net. Java VMs Compared (2008), http://bugblogger.com/java-vms-compared-160/
5. Casey, K., Gregg, D., Anton Ertl, M., Nisbet, A.: Towards Superinstructions for Java Interpreters. In: Krall, A. (ed.) SCOPES 2003. LNCS, vol. 2826, pp. 329–343. Springer, Heidelberg (2003)
6. Ertl, M.A., Gregg, D.: Combining Stack Caching with Dynamic Superinstructions. In: IVME '04: Proceedings of the 2004 workshop on Interpreters, virtual machines and emulators, pp. 7–14. ACM, New York (2004)
7. Ertl, M.A., Thalinger, C., Krall, A.: Superinstructions and Replication in the Cacao JVM interpreter. Journal of.NET Technologies 4, 25–32 (2006)
8. Golbeck, R.M., Kiczales, G.: A Machine Code Model for Efficient Advice Dispatch. In: VMIL '07: Proceedings of the 1st workshop on Virtual machines and intermediate languages for emerging modularization mechanisms, p. 2. ACM, New York (2007)

9. Haupt, M.: Virtual Machine Support for Aspect-Oriented Programming Languages. PhD thesis, Software Technology Group, Darmstadt University of Technology (2006)
10. Haupt, M., Mezini, M.: Virtual Machine Support for Aspects with Advice Instance Tables. L'Objet 11(3), 9–30 (2005)
11. Haupt, M., Schippers, H.: A Machine Model for Aspect-Oriented Programming. In: Ernst, E. (ed.) ECOOP 2007. LNCS, vol. 4609, pp. 501–524. Springer, Heidelberg (2007)
12. Herrmann, S.: Object Teams: Improving Modularity for Crosscutting Collaborations. In: Proceedings of Net. Object Days, pp. 248–264. Springer, Heidelberg (2002)
13. Herrmann, S., Hundt, C., Mosconi, M.: ObjectTeams/Java Language Definition — version 1.0. Technical Report 2007/03, Fak. IV, Technical University Berlin (2007)
14. Hundt, C., Glesner, S.: Optimizing Aspectual Execution Mechanisms for Embedded Applications. In: Proceedings of the First Workshop on Generative Technologies (WGT) 2008. Electronic Notes in Theoretical Computer Science, vol. 238, pp. 35–45 (2009)
15. Kiczales, G., Lamping, J., Mendhekar, A., Maeda, C., Lopes, C., Loingtier, J.-M., Irwin, J.: Aspect-Oriented Programming. In: Aksit, M., Matsuoka, S. (eds.) ECOOP 1997. LNCS, vol. 1241, pp. 220–243. Springer, Heidelberg (1997)
16. Lindholm, T., Yellin, F.: Java Virtual Machine Specification. Addison-Wesley Longman Publishing Co., Inc., Amsterdam (1999)
17. Smith, J., Nair, R.: Virtual Machines: Versatile Platforms for Systems and Processes. Morgan Kaufmann, San Francisco (June 2005)
18. Spinczyk, O., Lohmann, D., Urban, M.: Advances in AOP with AspectC++. In: New Trends in Software Methodologies Tools and Techniques. Frontiers in Artificial Intelligence and Applications, pp. 33–53 (2005)

Contract-Driven Testing of JavaScript Code

Phillip Heidegger and Peter Thiemann

Albert-Ludwigs-Universität Freiburg, Germany
{heidegger,thiemann}@informatik.uni-freiburg.de

Abstract. JSConTest is a tool that enhances JavaScript with simple, type-like contracts and provides a framework for monitoring and guided random testing of programs against these contracts at the same time. Function contracts in JSConTest serve a dual role as specifications of the input/output behavior and as test case generators. Generation of test data for a contract is generally random, but it can be guided by annotations on the contract to achieve higher coverage. Annotations may indicate dependencies among parameters and the result or they may select lightweight program analyses, the results of which influence the choice of test data. A case study substantiates that JSConTest finds type-related errors with high probability.

1   Introduction

High quality software systems should be correct, reliable, and maintainable. Developers try to achieve these qualities for their product by applying well-known software development processes, like the V-model, RAD, RUP, AUP, XP, Scrum, just to name a few. A commonality of all these processes is that they prescribe a substantial amount of testing [28]. On top of that, the processes that emphasize correctness usually include some variant of Meyer's Design by Contract [27].

Nowadays, an increasing number of systems is being developed using scripting languages like Perl, PHP, Ruby, and JavaScript. These languages greatly speed up the development process because of the flexibility gained by their dynamic language features (dynamic typing, weak typing, meta programming, etc). However, this flexibility makes it harder to specify the intended behavior of a system and to demonstrate that the system adheres to a specification. Thus, it is much harder to establish correctness, reliability, and maintainability of such a system.

A promising avenue of related measures to increase the assurance in code in dynamic languages is the introduction of gradual typing [32], of contracts that are monitored at run time [17, 34, 33, 20], and of languages that enable the interoperation and the gradual migration of functionality between statically typed and untyped parts of a program [35, 26, 4]. A common theme of these works is that the statically typed part of the code is shielded from the untyped (or dynamically typed) parts by type or contract annotations. The run-time monitoring of these annotations guarantees that badly composed data from the untyped parts does not corrupt the statically typed parts of the program.

J. Vitek (Ed.): TOOLS 2010, LNCS 6141, pp. 154–172, 2010.

Our work is inspired by the aforementioned ideas to make scripting languages safer but takes a different path influenced by work on testing. We strive to help programmers improve the quality of *existing programs now*, so that designing a new language is not an option. We believe that quality software should document and specify its definitions with contracts, hence we developed a typing-inspired contract facility that can be gradually introduced into existing programs. As a software verification is not feasible for an incompletely specified system, we aim for contract monitoring and for automatic contract validation via guided random testing. Furthermore, a failed verification attempt rarely produces a counterexample, whereas testing provides one immediately. Programmers find this outcome of a validation more appealing than abstract error messages as extensive testing is a common approach for finding programming errors in scripts.

Our target language is JavaScript [12], a language that is widely used for web-based applications. Originally, JavaScript was conceived for writing small scripts that animate web pages (Dynamic HTML) or transfer data to and from Java applets that do the heavy lifting for the application. It is an interpreted language with a weak, dynamic type system. Nevertheless, Web 2.0 applications contain a substantial part of JavaScript code and there are substantial libraries[1] that support the creation of such applications.

Contributions

We have developed the tool JSConTest that defines a contract language for JavaScript. The contract language enables the programmer to attach software contracts to arbitrary top-level definitions. Contracts can be as simple as type signatures and as complex as the programmer desires. JSConTest creates a test suite from the thus annotated program that addresses the validation of the contracts in two ways: It implements run-time contract monitoring and it performs random testing with input data derived from the contracts. JSConTest minimizes test cases that exhibit program errors using the ideas of delta debugging [36], which is a systematic approach to shrinking a test case. The programmer can choose the desired degree of assurance by selectively specifying contracts and by adjusting the precision of the contracts used.

To improve the coverage of random testing, JSConTest can perform guided random testing, which includes results from program analyses in the selection of test data. In many cases, guided random testing achieves coverage similar to concolic testing, but without requiring symbolic evaluation or solving of equations. In addition, JSConTest facilitates the inclusion of user-specified tests as well as user-specified contracts.

The current version of the tool can be downloaded from the web[2].

---

[1] Wikipedia lists 23 JavaScript libraries.
[2] http://proglang.informatik.uni-freiburg.de/jscontest/

```
1  /** int → int */
2  function f(x) { return 2 * x; };
3
4  /** (int,int) → bool */
5  function p(x,y) {
6    if (x != y) {
7      if (f(x) == x + 10) return "true"; // contract violation
8    };
9    return false;
10 };
```

Fig. 1. JavaScript code with contracts

2   A Tour of JSConTest

Suppose a programmer writes a function p in JavaScript which is intended to serve as a predicate on two integer values. Such a function has type signature (int,int) → bool. JSConTest lets the programmer specify a signature for a function by writing it in a special comment above the function as shown in Fig. 1. Unfortunately, the function may violate its contract because it contains a **return** statement that returns a string instead of a boolean value. A static type system would reject the definition of p with this contract, but JSConTest needs to produce a concrete counterexample, first.

To do so, JSConTest generates a test suite from the program that contains code for the contracts of functions f and p. The test suite contains a registry that keeps track of which contract belongs to which function. Running the test suite amounts to visiting each contract in the registry, generating and executing random test cases for it, and collecting test cases for which the contract failed.

For the particular example code, it is highly unlikely that random testing actually detects the problem with the code. Spotting this defect requires the test case generator to guess a value for x such that $x * 2 == x + 10$ holds, but a random integer solves this equation only with very low probability (2^{-32}). (The value of y is uncritical with very high probability.) For example, a failing test case would set x to 10 and y to 1208, so that both conditions in the code are true and p returns the string value "true". For this return value, the check against the contract bool fails and JSConTest reports a counterexample.

However, it is to be expected that a large number of random tests can be applied to p without finding a counterexample.[3] So, the question is: How can we increase the probability that JSConTest finds a counterexample that exposes the defect in the code?

One possibility is to write down an additional, more specific contract for the function as in /** (int,int) → bool | (10,int) → bool */. This contract is an example

---

[3] To run these tests in a browser near you use
http://proglang.informatik.uni-freiburg.de/jscontest/ex1.html
To view the static results of such a test run see:
http://proglang.informatik.uni-freiburg.de/jscontest/s_ex1.html

for a combined contract, where the function has to obey each of the contracts separated by "|". The second contract uses the singleton contract 10 to force the examination of x=10. With this contract, JSConTest finds a counterexample almost certainly (with probability $1 - 2^{-32}$), but proceeding in this way leads to unnatural and unreadable contracts, which get close to manually specified test cases. In fact, using combinations of singleton contracts exclusively corresponds to specifying single test cases. For instance, the test case contract /** (10,1208) → true */ also spots the problem.

2.1 Guided Random Testing

To address the problem without requiring the tester to manually inspect the code, JSConTest offers *guided* random tests that rely on the results of program analysis. Annotations on the contracts tell the system which analysis to perform and how to use the result of the analysis. For example, applying the annotation @numbers to the integer contract instructs the system to statically collect all constant numbers from the code and to build its arguments by evaluating expressions randomly constructed from these numbers and the primitive arithmetic operations.

In the example, the contract (int@numbers,int) → bool would be suitable for p. Thus instructed, the analysis collects the list of constants [0,1,10] and passes it to the generator of the contract int together with the four default operations [+,−,*,/]. Instead of generating a completely random integer value, the generator of the contract generates a random expression tree, where the leaves are values from the list of constants (with probability 0.5) or random integers (with probability 0.5), and uses the value of that expression tree as the input value. The nodes of the tree are picked from the operation set to yield expression trees like $(0 - 10 * 1 + 1289)$. The probabilities for creating a leaf or an internal node are chosen such that the probability of generating small trees is high. Thus, the probability to generate a tree with value 10 for x is high[4].

The web page http://proglang.informatik.uni-freiburg.de/jscontest/ ex1a.html illustrates that usually less that ten test cases need to be generated to find a counterexample for the contract.

Another example (see Fig. 2) demonstrates that the success of the expression tree approach is not accidental, even though finding a counterexample in this case amounts to finding a solution to a Diophantine equation. The code in Fig. 2 has a similar defect as p but hides it under more complicated conditions. JSConTest usually finds the counterexample x=18, y=11, z=4 in a few seconds.

The example code in Fig. 3 demonstrates another use of collected information. The function h is a predicate for an object and should return only boolean values. But the return statement in line 4 returns the string value "true". To find this defect, JSConTest has to randomly generate an object with at least two properties, p and quest, the values of which must convert to true. As in the previous examples, the probability of randomly generating an object with these

---

[4] The probability is greater than 12^{-1}, but we skip the details as they are not important.

```
1  /** (int@numbers,int@numbers,int@numbers) → bool */
2  function fut_1(x,y,z) {
3    if ((x*3+5 == y*5+4) && (x*2−1 == z*9 − 1))
4      return "true";
5    return false;
6  };
```

Fig. 2. Complicated conditions

```
1  /** (object) → bool */
2  function h(x) {
3    if (x && x.p && x.quest)
4      return "true";
5    return false;
6  };
```

Fig. 3. Object access

two labels is virtually zero. For this reasons, there is an analysis @labels that collects the labels (i.e., field and method names) that occur textually inside the function. For the example code in Fig. 3, the analysis @labels returns the set {q,quest}, because the function body of h contains these two labels in line 3. Changing the object contract to object@labels leads to the quick discovery of a counterexample (usually in five tests or less).

2.2 Monitoring

Another aspect of JSConTest is run-time monitoring of contracts. To this end, JSConTest inserts assertions into the bodies of functions that have a contract (as specified by Findler and Felleisen [15]). Every time a function with a combination of contracts is called, the test library checks which contracts have argument parts that accept the passed parameters. If no such contract exists, then the arguments are not valid and the function call is rejected (because the caller does not respect the contract). This rejection is signaled as an event, which can be picked up by a registered event handler. A handler may ignore the event, print a warning, stop program execution, or it may invoke a debugger at that point. If the arguments are valid, then the result value of the function is checked against the result parts of the contracts that accepted the arguments. Failure of any of these checks is again signaled as an event.

As an example, consider the function g in Fig. 4, which calls function f from Fig. 1. The code contains an error in a literal: The programmer mixed up the digit zero and the letter O, writing "3O" instead of "30". This error causes NaN to be passed to f, where it is caught by the argument part of its contract (int) → int. Such an error would be very hard to spot without contracts and monitoring because of JavaScript's liberal type conversions.

```
1  /** (int,int) → bool */
2  function g(x,y) {
3    return (f(x * "3O") == 60); // error
4  }
```

Fig. 4. Catching an error in a string literal

$$i \in \text{int}, f \in \text{float}, s \in \text{string}, b \in \text{bool}$$

Primitive contracts

$p ::=$	$\text{undf} \mid \top$	undefined, any value
	$\mid \quad \text{bool} \mid b$	boolean values
	$\mid \quad \text{string} \mid s$	string values
	$\mid \quad \text{int} \mid i \mid [i; i]$	integers, integer intervals
	$\mid \quad \text{number} \mid f \mid [f; f]$	floats, float intervals
	$\mid \quad \text{object}$	object
	$\mid \quad \text{js:ident}$	defined in JavaScript

Composite contracts

$c ::=$	p	
	$\mid \quad c@\text{numbers} \mid c@\text{strings} \mid c@\text{labels}$	analysis information
	$\mid \quad (d, \ldots, d) \; \text{->} \; d$	functions
	$\mid \quad \{p_1 : c_1, p_2 : c_2, \ldots, p_n : c_n(, \ldots)^?\}$	objects
	$\mid \quad [c]$	arrays

Annotations

$$a ::= \text{~noAsserts} \mid \text{~noTests} \mid \text{\#Tests:} i$$

Dependent contracts

$$d ::= c \mid c(\$i, \ldots, \$i) \mid \text{id}(\$i)$$

Top-level contracts (embedded in JavaScript comments)

$$t ::= \text{/**} \; c \, a^* \; (\mid c \, a^*)^* \; \text{*/}$$

Fig. 5. Syntax of contracts

3 Contracts

Fig. 5 summarizes the syntax of JSConTest's contract language. Its main design goal is to let programmers specify interfaces easily. Compared to the design by contract methodology, these contracts play a dual role as checkable assertions that can be attached to JavaScript values (contract monitoring) and as test case generators for such values and functions.

The primitive contracts are analogous to types used in languages with a static type system (e.g., Java, C, C++). They correspond roughly to the types available in JavaScript. Their interpretation is strict, that is, it does *not* include the application of JavaScript's type conversions. For example, the contract bool accepts only the values true and false, the contract int accepts any integral value, and the contract number accepts any number except NaN. For the primitive datatypes there are also singleton contracts, which only accept a single value. Singleton contracts for floats, integers, strings, and booleans are specified by simply writing the corresponding literal value. There is also support for intervals

```
1  /** (int,int) → bool */
2  function comp(x,y) {
3      if ((x == y) && (x < 10) && (x > 1)) return "true";
4      return false;
5  }
```

Fig. 6. A comparison operator

of integers and floats with the syntax [i;i] or [f;f]. For instance, [0;1.0] is the float interval between zero and one, inclusively.

In some cases, a contract may be desired that checks a result *after* applying type conversions. For example, as JavaScript can convert any value to a boolean, a predicate might as well return a value of arbitrary type as long as it converts correctly according to the intention of the predicate. In this case, it would be overly restrictive to check the result against the singleton contract true. Alas, the syntax does not provide singleton contracts that test after conversion, but they may be defined manually as explained in the next paragraph.

The primitive contract form js:ident allows programmers to roll their own contracts by writing an appropriate definition directly in JavaScript. This contract form enables having concise specifications of function interfaces which encapsulate complex test code. JSConTest supports the construction of such handwritten contracts by providing various utility functions.

Composite contracts are built from primitive contracts by combining them in different ways. An enriched contract adds specific guidance (in the form of a static analysis) to the test case generation for a contract, it does not change its interpretation as an assertion. Our current implementation supports three analyses. The analysis @numbers collects all numeric constants from the function body, the analysis @strings collects string constants, and the @labels analysis static property names. A function contract specifies contracts for the arguments (and their number) and the result. An object contract specifies contracts for the listed properties of an object. An acceptable object may have further properties, which are not checked. Writing "..." at the end of the field specifications of the object contract forces the generator to randomly add further properties to the object. Otherwise, only the properties specified for the object are generated. Arrays are considered homogeneous, so an array contract specifies a single contract for all elements of the array.

Function contracts may contain various kinds of dependencies. For example, the parameters of a function may depend on each other as illustrated by the example code in Fig. 6. The contract /** (int@numbers,int@numbers) → bool */ can find a counterexample, but only with probability on the order of 10^{-3} although @numbers = [0,1,10] has just three elements. The problem is that a test case serving as a counterexample needs to set x and y to the same value between one and ten.

Adding a second contract (int@numbers,id($1)) → bool to comp significantly raises the probability to find a counterexample. This contract expresses that passing a copy of the first argument as the second argument is a case, which should receive special treatment. If p is supposed to be a comparison, then the additional contract (top,id($1)) $\rightarrow$ true expresses this kind of information.

The dependencies must be acyclic. The compiler detects and rejects any cyclic definitions of dependent contracts.

As JavaScript is a higher-order language, JSConTest must be able to deal with functions that accept function-typed arguments and return function-typed results (recursively). Hence, our framework cannot content itself with contract checkers at function type, but generators at function type are also needed. At this point, the dual role of our contracts pays off because both roles are needed, because in general:

> Implementing $(A \rightarrow B)$.check   requires A.generate and B.check
> Implementing $(A \rightarrow B)$.generate requires A.check and B.generate

In particular, the generator for $(A \rightarrow B)$ produces a function that first invokes A.check on its argument x and signals failure if the check fails. Then it uses B.generate (potentially exploiting dependencies as already explained) to create an output value y for the function. Depending on the programmer's choice between pure or impure functions, this value can be memoized.

At the top-level, each function may have a list of contracts attached to it. A function must fulfill all of them, thus JSConTest generates tests as well as assertions for all contracts. A number of annotations can be attached to each contract to modify the behavior of the contract compiler. If ~noTests is present in the annotations, the contract is not added to the test suite. The annotation ~noAsserts avoids the generation of assertions for the contract. The annotation #Tests:i changes the number of tests that the generated test suite executes for the contract. These annotations are only needed in special situations. Our case study in Sec. 5 runs into some of them and provides a detailed explanation.

4 Implementation

The contract compiler is implemented in roughly 6000 lines of OCaml (including about 2000 lines devoted to parsing JavaScript). It parses the JavaScript file, creates an abstract syntax tree of the source code, and parses the contracts from the comments of the JavaScript code. Next, the compiler analyzes the dependencies between the contracts to ensure that they are acyclic. Finally, it generates code for the contracts as well as code to connect them to the test framework. Depending on the chosen options and annotations, it additionally transforms the functions under contract by adding monitoring assertions.

The test library consists of about 1900 lines of browser-independent JavaScript. It comprises three parts. The first part manages test cases and assertions. The second part provides utility function for handwritten contracts. The third part deals with event handlers, which provide a user-configurable way of reacting to contract violations and assertions.

4.1   Test Cases and Assertions

Besides using the syntax introduced in Fig. 5, the library may also be used to construct contracts manually. For that reason (and also to simplify compilation), the library contains many predefined contracts, for example Top, Null, Undefined, Boolean, True, False, String, Number, Function, Object, PObject, AInteger. Most of them are self explanatory, but PObject and AInteger deserve further explanation. PObject is a contract that takes an array of property names as argument. It implements object contracts that rely on information generated by the label analysis of the contract compiler. The behavior of AInteger is similar. It takes two parameters, the list of constants found in the function body and a list of binary functions for combining two integer values. By default, the second parameter is initialized to the basic arithmetic operations.

As a concession to the dual role of contracts, any object implementing a primitive contract provides two methods, one to check if a value adheres to the contract and another to randomly generate a value that is guaranteed to adhere to the contract.

4.2   Custom Contracts

The library contains a number of operations on contracts, for example, a union and an intersection operation. There is also a number of contracts for objects, which facilitate the specification of a set of properties, each with its own contract, or which restrict property names to those composed of only characters and digits, but no special characters, etc. It is also possible to specify recursive contracts for objects by using names as follows:

```
1 Let ("o", EObject[{name: "m",
2                    contract: Function ([Name ("o")], Boolean)}])
```

Let binds a contract to a name and this contract can be retrieved with the Name function. EObject constructs an object contract from an association list of property names to contracts. The resulting contract describes an object with an m method the argument of which must be an object of the same kind.

Currently, this facility is not reflected in the surface contract language, because the main purpose of the contract language is to easily specify the interface of a function and we did not encounter an example where it was needed, yet.

The library contains further functions that aid in writing contracts from scratch. For example, the constructor newSContract: (check, generate, description) → Contract creates a fully general contract. The function check: Top → bool is called by the test library to check if a value fulfills a contract. The procedure generate: void → value creates a valid value for the contract, viz., every value returned by the generate function must pass the check function. The third parameter is a string that identifies the contract if an event handler asks it for a string representation. To support the implementation of custom contracts, a set of check functions, viz. isNull, isTrue, isInt, isUInt, isArray, isObject, and a set of generators is available, viz. genNull, genBoolean, genInt, genUInt, genNumber, genLength, genString,

```
1 function check(x,y) {
2    return x === y;
3 };
4 function generate(v) {
5    return v;
6 };
7 Id = new newSContract(check,generate,"Id");
```

Fig. 7. Implementation of the dependent contract Id

genObject. Some of the generators take parameters, which can be used to modify their default behavior, but they all work without parameters, too. In such a case, all aspects of the value are chosen randomly.

4.3   Dependent Contracts

For dependent contracts, the methods check and generate have additional arguments. For example, consider the dependent function contract (bool,int) → Id($2). In this case, the check method of the Id contract is eventually invoked with two parameters (see Fig. 7 for its definition). The first parameter is the value that is to be checked and the second one is the value that is referred to by the $2 part of the contract, viz. the integer value of the second argument of the checked function.

The test for such a contract first generates argument values according to bool and int. Then it computes the result of the function call on these arguments and invokes the check method for Id with the result and the generated int value. In this particular case, Id.check tests its arguments for equality so that the contract describes a function that ignores its first argument (which must be boolean) and returns its second, integer argument.

In general, the check method for a dependent contract has the signature check: (Top, ...) → bool, where Top stands for the value against which the contract is to be checked and the (arbitrary many) remaining arguments are the ($i,...,$j) additional parameters passed to the contract.

In principle, there could even be a contract with a variable number of arguments such as Dep in this contract: (int,Dep($1),Dep($1,$2)) → bool. A test for this contract calls the generate methods for int, then for Dep with one extra parameter, and finally for Dep with two extra parameters. The order of these contract invocations is determined by the preceding dependency analysis, that is, it would be the same for the contract (Dep($3),Dep($3,$1),int) → bool.

Analogous to the case of the check method, the signature of the generate method changes for a dependent contract. The new signature is generate: (...) → value, which means that the generate method can use the information from the values on which the contract depends to generate its result.

```
1  var f =
2    (function () {
3      function f_own (x) {
4        var p_1 = TESTS.assertParams(["p_0"], arguments, f_own);
5        return p_1.assertReturn((2. * x));
6      };
7      (function () {
8        function f (x) {
9          return (2. * x);
10       };
11       f_own.toString = function() {return f.toString();};
12     })();
13     return f_own;
14   })();
15 /* compiled code for p and g is omitted */
16 (function () {
17   var c_0 = TESTS.Function([TESTS.Integer], TESTS.Integer);
18   TESTS.add("f", f, c_0, 1000. );
19   TESTS.setVar("p_0", c_0);
20 })();
21 /* test cases for p and g are omitted */
```

Fig. 8. Compiled code for function f

4.4   Event Handler

The library communicates its results through an event handler framework. Generated tests and assertions always invoke the event handler framework to publish their results as events.[5] Using the function registerEventHandler, any number of event handler objects can be registered with the library. Allowing the user of the test framework to execute arbitrary JavaScript code for each event is the most flexible way of configuring the framework.

A logger is a special kind of event handler as shown for the createEnumLogger in Fig. 9. A logger can be provided to create a nice browser output, another one to create a log file, publish the results to a web service (createWebLogger), and so on.

An event handler object can also provide an interface to a debugger. Such an event handler may stop execution and invoke the debugger at each failing assertion. Unfortunately, the JavaScript specification does not prescribe a standard interface for such tools, so the library cannot supply a generic solution for this purpose.

4.5   Transformation

We illustrate the transformation of contracts into JavaScript code with an example. Fig. 8 shows the result of compiling the contract for function f from Fig. 1.

---

[5] There are many further events fired during test case evaluation, which allows good customization of the testing framework.

```
1  <!DOCTYPE html PUBLIC "−//W3C//DTD XHTML 1.0 Strict//EN"
2          "http://www.w3.org/TR/xhtml1/DTD/xhtml1−strict.dtd">
3  <html xmlns="http://www.w3.org/1999/xhtml" xml:lang="en" lang="en">
4    <head>
5      <title>Test Framework</title>
6      <meta http−equiv="Content−Script−Type" content="text/javascript"/>
7      <link href="style.css" rel="stylesheet" type="text/css" />
8      <script type="text/javascript" src="testsrandom.js"></script>
9      <script type="text/javascript" src="ex1.test.js"></script>
10     <script type="text/javascript">
11       var dl = TESTS.createEnumLogger('logger',"ul");
12       TESTS.registerEventHandler(dl);
13     </script>
14   </head>
15   <body onload="TESTS.run()">
16     <h1>Test Framework</h1>
17     <div id="logger"></div>
18   </body>
19 </html>
```

Fig. 9. HTML page generated to drive a test suite

The compiled code consists of three parts. The first part is the function enriched with assertions (line 2-6). The second part overrides the toString method of the function object (line 7-13). The override ensures that the toString method returns the original source code rather than the compiled code after the transformation. The goal is to facilitate interaction with a debugger and also to have the test framework produce readable output. The last part is code that creates the contracts and adds test cases to the test framework (line 16-21).

The code makes frequent use of the JavaScript idiom (**function**() {...}) () to create a new nested scope in which to execute the body .... Nested scopes avoid the pollution of the (single) JavaScript namespace with auxiliary definitions.

Similarly, the compiled code employs a single, configurable global object (default: TESTS) to interact with the framework. No further global variables are used. This strategy is required because JavaScript has no namespace management and also because static scoping is not guaranteed[6]. To avoid global variables, the library provides an attribution mechanism to read and write values (getVar, setVar). The real implementation chooses names that are highly unlikely to clash with user defined ones.

4.6 Driver

Fig. 9 shows the HTML page generated as a driver for the test suite for the program `ex1.test.js`. It loads the library (line 8) and the compiled contracts

---

[6] For example, source code may be loaded dynamically by an HTTP-Request and then executed by an eval expression, which may place bindings in an arbitrary scope.

(line 9). The script from line 10 to line 13 registers a logger. In line 15 the run method is registered as the onload handler to execute the tests after the page has been loaded. The content of the page is empty except for the title and a div element, in which the logger inserts the results of the tests.

5   Case Study: Huffman Decoding

In this case study we implement a Huffman decoder in JavaScript and specify its interface with the contract system. Writing this decoder is not difficult, but nevertheless JSConTest uncovered errors during its development. Usually, the test framework found counterexamples after just one or two test runs. In each case, the counterexample simplified the debugging of the code significantly.

After some iterations of fixing small errors in the functions under test, we found an error in the specification. The contract js:ht is a custom contract for Huffman trees. A Huffman tree is either a node or a leaf. A node then contains two Huffman trees as children. Leaves and nodes both contain additional information, which we ignore for now. The problem is that a valid Huffman tree has to have a depth greater than zero. If the tree consists of only one leaf, no bits are consumed by the decoder to generate an output string and the decoder enters an infinite loop. We discovered this bug when our framework generated a Huffman tree of the form HuffmanLeaf {s: '', w: ...}. This input results in a stack overflow which is reported by our framework as a failing test.

The fix for this problem was to adjust the generator for Huffman trees. We use the function restrictTo from our library to filter the result of the generator, such that trees containing only one leaf are rejected.

The contract constructor newSContract suffices to create ht. Fig. 10 contains the definition of the check function. The generate function makes use of the library function genTree for generating random trees (also presented in Fig. 10). One contract of genTree is: (Top → bool, [void → value], [op], [0;1.0], true) → value. The first parameter is a predicate, the second one an array (serving as a list) of functions that generate the leaves of the tree. The second array [op] contains a list of objects that contain functions that generate a new value from a list of values. The arity of these objects specifies how many subtrees the individual function takes. The fourth parameter is a probability to choose an operation during the generation. The last parameter specifies whether the first array is a list of functions that generate values. If this parameter is set to false, then the method assumes that the array itself contains values. As the functions isHuffmanLeaf, isHuffmanNode, and isHuffmanTree already exist in the original code, the custom contract ht requires just 13 lines of code and three lines of contract specification (line 15,18,21).

Using the custom contract ht, it is easy to write the contracts for the other operations on Huffman trees. The function huffmandecode has as contract (js:ht, [[0;1]]) → string, a function returning a string, where the first parameter is a Huffman tree and the second one an array of bits, which are integers from the interval [0;1].

```
1  function generate() {
2    function genRandomLeaf() {
3      return makeHuffmanLeaf(TESTS.genStringL(1), TESTS.genNInt(0,1));
4    };
5    function genRandomNode(l,r) {
6      return makeHuffmanNode([],TESTS.genNInt(0,1),l,r);
7    };
8    function cdes() { return "makeHuffmanNode"; };
9    var gN = { getcdes: cdes, arity: 2, f: genRandomNode};
10   return TESTS.genTree(isHuffmanTree,[genRandomLeaf],[gN],0.5,true);
11  };
12  var gen = TESTS.restrictTo(isHuffmanNode,generate);
13  var ht = new TESTS.newSContract(isHuffmanTree,gen,"HuffmanTree");
14
15  /** Top → bool */
16  function isHuffmanLeaf(v) { /* function body here */ };
17
18  /** Top → bool */
19  function isHuffmanNode(v) { /* function body here */ };
20
21  /** Top → bool | js:ht → true ~noAsserts */
22  function isHuffmanTree(v) { /* function body here */ };
```

Fig. 10. Custom contract ht — check for a Huffman tree

For this contract, the dual role of isHuffmanTree as the type test to be used by the programmer as well as for defining the ht contract leads to a circularity. Its contract specifies that isHuffmanTree is applicable to any value and returns a boolean. The second half says that if the argument is a Huffman tree, then it should return true. The circularity arises when doing contract monitoring for this function. In that case, an invocation of isHuffmanTree asserts the contract ht on its argument, which in turn uses isHuffmanTree for checking it, which gives rise to an infinite loop. Hence, the `~noAsserts` annotation is needed to avoid generating assertions for this contract.

To obtain some intuition of the quality of guided random testing, we applied mutation testing [2,1] to the Huffman decoder. The mutator swaps makeHuffman-Leaf and makeHuffmanNode, [left,right], [true,false], [0,1], and [===,==,!=,!==], [-,+]. The mutator randomly determines the number of modifications to apply and repeatedly applies a modification at a random place in the program.

Our test run generated 716 mutations of the original huffman.js, which were all submitted to the contract compiler and then the resulting test runs were analyzed. There were 88 files (about 12% of all files) for which all contracts passed successfully. All other files were rejected outright by our test suite. The average run time of each file in the browser is 5 seconds.

It is not surprising that there are modified versions for which all tests pass, because some of the randomly chosen modifications (e.g., swapping left and right) create files, in which nothing is wrong from a typing perspective. For these 88 files, we verified manually that the modifications of these files are not observable at the type level, e.g. if a contract states Top → bool and inside the function body **return** true; is changed to **return** false;, the contract is fulfilled by the original and the modified version. Finding such bugs is either the job of a hand-written test suite or of a more detailed specification. There were also modifications that affected the contracts themselves. For example, a modification that swaps 0 and 1 increased the number of tests from 50 to 51 because it took place in a ... #Tests:50 annotation. Such a modification does not affect the semantics of the program.

As the generated tests rejected 88% of the mutations, we argue that our testing framework detects a type error with very high probability.

6   Related Work

Purely manual testing per se does not guarantee any kind of coverage criterion and its effectiveness depends highly on the experience of the tester and on the system of the chosen approach to testing. Hence, manual testing should be backed up by further kinds of testing. Random testing [3,21] is one promising candidate, which is surprisingly effective [18], but which does not give guarantees with respect to coverage [29, 10]. However, there are a number of approaches and tools that support random testing and that employ various means for improving coverage.

JCrasher [9] is a black-box random testing tool for the Java programming language. It analyzes a set of classes with the goal to find a crashing program fragment involving methods of these classes. It constructs fragments by applying methods with random parameters to randomly constructed objects and then using these objects as a basis for randomly generating further method calls. There is no further specification of contract needed for JCrasher as the failure criterion is a program crash.

In contrast, JSConTest can test against user-specified contracts and can also do run-time monitoring. Moreover, JSConTest improves coverage by performing a limited amount of glass-box testing by collecting constants from the code to performed guided testing.

The QuickCheck library [8] for Haskell, a purely functional programming language, enables the statement of properties of program constructs, which are then automatically tested. Test cases are randomly generated from the types of the variables in properties. Additionally, programmers can specify their own generators. In contrast, JSConTest derives its test cases from contracts, which can be more expressive than types, and it is only geared to test contracts (although it could be extended to test properties as well). JSConTest handles test case generation for imperative JavaScript objects, which goes beyond functions and primitive data. Another difference is that QuickCheck performs pure black-box testing whereas JSConTest's inclusion of program analysis information places it on the brink to glass-box testing.

DoubleCheck [11] is an adaptation of QuickCheck to the ACL2 language implemented in the PLT programming environment [16][7]. It is used as a verification aid to generate counterexamples for properties of programs that ACL2 cannot prove right away. The idea is to restate these properties guided by the counterexamples. PLT-Redex also comes with a random testing facility that has detected errors in semantics specifications [24].

RUTE-J [2] is a framework that enables writing unit tests for Java that make use of some portion of randomness. It can randomize a list of method calls as well as input data and it performs minimization of failing test cases.

Randoop [30] is a tool for directed random testing of Java classes. It generates test cases in a similar way as JCrasher, but additionally uses the test outcomes as feedback to avoid creating useless or outright erroneous tests.

Similarly, the ARTOO system [7] performs adaptive random testing for Eiffel. It adapts previous ideas from the ART approach [6] to an object-oriented setting. Its underlying idea is that tests are more effective if they evenly cover the parameter space of the method under test. Its execution requires a distance metric on the input values.

A highly effective approach to randomized testing is the DART system [19]. It performs what has been coined concolic testing: it combines running concrete test cases with symbolic execution of the underlying code. Guided by the outcome of concrete test cases it generates symbolic predicates for the branches taken in the computation. It employs theorem proving to systematically falsify these predicates and thus attempts to cover all branch alternatives, which is often successful. JSConTest is inspired by this system, but relies on a much more lightweight approach (collecting constants), which requires a larger number of test cases, for increasing the coverage.

A different approach to generating test cases is bounded exhaustive testing, which systematically enumerates all inputs below a certain size threshold. This approach is implemented, for example, in the Smallcheck system for Haskell [31] and also in the Korat system for Java [5]. The idea here is that counterexamples are usually small and that the exhaustive tests give some guarantees, at least for finite structures like functions over finite domains. This approach is complementary to the random testing approach presently chosen by JSConTest.

There are also JavaScript testing frameworks, for example, JSUnit[8], JsTester[9], FireUnit[10], JSCoverage[11], JSMock[12], and rhinounit[13]. However, these frameworks are in the tradition of unit testing frameworks like JUnit[14]. Their focus is on automating the execution of unit tests, but not on the creation of these

---

[7] The DrScheme teaching languages also provide QuickCheck-style testing of contracts.

[8] http://www.jsunit.net/

[9] http://jstester.sourceforge.net/

[10] http://fireunit.org/

[11] http://siliconforks.com/jscoverage/

[12] http://jsmock.sourceforge.net/

[13] http://code.google.com/p/rhinounit/

[14] http://junit.org/

tests, which is left to the human developer. In contrast, JSConTest only requires the manual construction of interface specifications, which is a good idea anyway. Also, JSConTest is currently restricted to functional testing of the JavaScript code, it does not test the interactive behavior (GUI testing), nor the interface to web services via XmlHTTPRequest. These extensions are left to future work.

JSConTest is inspired by, but complementary to work on type analysis for JavaScript [23, 22]. The focus of these works is to determine the type safety of JavaScript programs by static analysis (abstract interpretation and constraint-based analysis, respectively). Neither work supports type specifications, nor test case generation.

7   Conclusion

JSConTest is the first testing tool for JavaScript that supports the specification of type contracts. These type contracts are validated in two ways, by contract monitoring and by guided random testing. The latter is a new approach to improve the coverage of random testing, which is very effective and easy to implement. Contract violations are usually discovered within a few test runs. Mutation testing shows that JSConTest verifies type contracts with a high probability.

In future work, we plan to extend the generators in the style of JCrasher and Randoop. We also plan to incorporate specifications for side effects. As the current generation procedure for objects constructs only trees, we plan to lift this restriction by incorporating a generation algorithm as in Shekoosh [13].

We also want to explore the approach of Leitner and coworkers [25] for test case minimization, because it is reported to yield better performance results than delta debugging, which is currently used in JSConTest.

Finally, the static analysis component could be extended with a control flow analysis. This additional analysis would enable us to collect constants not just from the body of the function under test, but also from the functions reachable from the functions under test.

Acknowledgment. Shriram Krishnamurthi, Arjun Guha, Stephane Ducasse, and the anonymous referees of TOOLS suggested many improvements to an early version of the paper.

References

1. Andrews, J.H., Briand, L.C., Labiche, Y.: Is mutation an appropriate tool for testing experiments? In: ICSE '05: Proc. 27th International Conference on Software Engineering, pp. 402–411. ACM, New York (2005)
2. Andrews, J.H., Haldar, S., Lei, Y., Li, F.C.H.: Tool support for randomized unit testing. In: RT '06: Proceedings of the 1st International Workshop on Random Testing, Portland, Maine, pp. 36–45. ACM, New York (2006)
3. Bird, D.L., Munoz, C.U.: Automatic generation of random self-checking test cases. IBM Syst. J. 22(3), 229–245 (1983)

4. Bloom, B., Field, J., Nystrom, N., Östlund, J., Richards, G., Strniša, R., Vitek, J., Wrigstad, T.: Thorn: Robust, concurrent, extensible scripting on the JVM. In: Arora, S., Leavens, G.T. (eds.) Proc. 24th ACM Conf. OOPSLA, Orlando, Florida, USA, pp. 117–136. ACM, New York (2009)
5. Boyapati, C., Khurshid, S., Marinov, D.: Korat: Automated testing based on Java predicates. In: ISSTA '02: Proc. 2002 ACM SIGSOFT International Symposium on Software Testing and Analysis, Roma, Italy, pp. 123–133. ACM, New York (2002)
6. Chen, T.Y., Kuo, F.-C., Merkel, R.G., Tse, T.H.: Adaptive random testing: The ART of test case diversity. J. Systems and Software 83(1), 60–66 (2010)
7. Ciupa, I., Leitner, A., Oriol, M., Meyer, B.: ARTOO: Adaptive random testing for object-oriented software. In: Schäfer, W., Dwyer, M.B., Gruhn, V. (eds.) ICSE 2008, pp. 71–80. ACM, New York (2008)
8. Claessen, K., Hughes, J.: QuickCheck: A lightweight tool for random testing of Haskell programs. In: Wadler, P. (ed.) Proc. ICFP 2000, Montreal, Canada, September 2000, pp. 268–279. ACM Press, New York (2000)
9. Csallner, C., Smaragdakis, Y.: JCrasher: An automatic robustness tester for Java. Software—Practice & Experience 34(11), 1025–1050 (2004)
10. Duran, J., Ntafos, S.: An evaluation of random testing. Transactions on Software Engineering 10(4), 438–444 (1984)
11. Eastlund, C.: DoubleCheck your theorems. In: ACL2 2009, Boston, MA (2009)
12. ECMAScript Language Specification, ECMA International, ECMA-262, 5th edn. (December 2009),
    http://www.ecma-international.org/publications/files/ECMA-ST/Ecma-262.pdf
13. Elkarablieh, B., Zayour, Y., Khurshid, S.: Efficiently generating structurally complex inputs with thousands of objects. In: Ernst [14], pp. 248–272
14. Ernst, E. (ed.): ECOOP 2007. LNCS, vol. 4609. Springer, Heidelberg (2007)
15. Findler, R.B., Felleisen, M.: Contracts for higher-order functions. In: Peyton-Jones, S. (ed.) Proc. ICFP 2002, Pittsburgh, PA, USA, October 2002, pp. 48–59. ACM Press, New York (2002)
16. Findler, R.B., Flanagan, C., Flatt, M., Krishnamurthi, S., Felleisen, M.: DrScheme: A pedagogic programming environment for Scheme. In: Hartel, P.H., Kuchen, H. (eds.) PLILP 1997. LNCS, vol. 1292, pp. 369–388. Springer, Heidelberg (1997)
17. Findler, R.B., Flatt, M., Felleisen, M.: Semantic casts: Contracts and structural subtyping in a nominal world. In: Odersky, M. (ed.) ECOOP 2004. LNCS, vol. 3086, pp. 364–388. Springer, Heidelberg (2004)
18. Forrester, J.E., Miller, B.P.: An empirical study of the robustness of Windows NT applications using random testing. In: 4th USENIX Windows System Symposium, Seattle (August 2000)
19. Godefroid, P., Klarlund, N., Sen, K.: Dart: Directed automated random testing. In: Proc. 2005 ACM Conf. PLDI, Chicago, IL, USA, June 2005, pp. 213–223. ACM Press, New York (2005)
20. Gray, K.E., Findler, R.B., Flatt, M.: Fine-grained interoperability through mirrors and contracts. In: Proc. 20th ACM Conf. OOPSLA, San Diego, CA, USA, pp. 231–245. ACM Press, New York (2005)
21. Hamlet, R.G.: Random testing. In: Marciniak, J. (ed.) Encyclopedia of Software Engineering, pp. 970–978. Wiley, Chichester (1994)
22. Heidegger, P., Thiemann, P.: Recency types for dynamically-typed object-based languages. In: 2009 International Workshop on Foundations of Object-Oriented Languages (FOOL'09), Savannah, Georgia, USA (January 2009),
    http://www.cs.cmu.edu/~aldrich/FOOL09/heidegger.pdf

23. Jensen, S.H., Møller, A., Thiemann, P.: Type analysis for JavaScript. In: Palsberg, J., Su, Z. (eds.) SAS 2009. LNCS, vol. 5673, pp. 238–255. Springer, Heidelberg (2009)

24. Klein, C., Findler, R.B.: Randomized testing in PLT Redex. In: Workshop on Scheme and Functional Programming 2009, Boston, MA, USA (2009)

25. Leitner, A., Oriol, M., Zeller, A., Ciupa, I., Meyer, B.: Efficient unit test case minimization. In: Proceedings of the twenty-second IEEE/ACM international conference on Automated software engineering, Atlanta, Georgia, USA, November 2007, pp. 417–420 (2007)

26. Matthews, J., Findler, R.B.: Operational semantics for multi-language programs. ACM TOPLAS 31, 12:1–12:44 (2009)

27. Meyer, B.: Object-Oriented Software Construction, 2nd edn. Prentice-Hall, Englewood Cliffs (1997)

28. Myers, G.J., Sandler, C.: The Art of Software Testing. John Wiley & Sons, Chichester (2004)

29. Offutt, A.J., Hayes, J.H.: A semantic model of program faults. In: 1996 ACM SIGSOFT International Symposium on Software Testing and Analysis, San Diego, CA, USA, January 1996, pp. 195–200 (1996)

30. Pacheco, C.: Directed Random Testing. Ph.D., MIT Department of Electrical Engineering and Computer Science, Cambridge, MA, USA (June 2009)

31. Runciman, C., Naylor, M., Lindblad, F.: Smallcheck and Lazy Smallcheck: Automatic exhaustive testing for small values. In: Haskell '08: Proc. of the first ACM SIGPLAN Symposium on Haskell, Victoria, BC, Canada, pp. 37–48. ACM, New York (2008)

32. Siek, J., Taha, W.: Gradual typing for objects. In: Ernst [14], pp. 2–27

33. Tobin-Hochstadt, S., Felleisen, M.: Interlanguage migration: From scripts to programs. In: Dynamic Languages Symposium, DLS 2006, Portland, Oregon, USA, pp. 964–974. ACM, New York (2006)

34. Tobin-Hochstadt, S., Felleisen, M.: The design and implementation of typed scheme. In: Wadler, P. (ed.) Proc. 35th ACM Symp. POPL, San Francisco, CA, USA, January 2008, pp. 395–406. ACM Press, New York (2008)

35. Wadler, P., Findler, R.B.: Well-typed programs can't be blamed. In: Castagna, G. (ed.) ESOP 2009. LNCS, vol. 5502, pp. 1–16. Springer, Heidelberg (2009)

36. Zeller, A., Hildebrandt, R.: Simplifying and isolating failure-inducing input. IEEE Trans. Softw. Eng. 28(2), 183–200 (2002)

Late Binding of AspectJ Advice

Ryan M. Golbeck, Peter Selby, and Gregor Kiczales

University of British Columbia
{rmgolbec,pselby,gregor}@cs.ubc.ca

Abstract. The non-local nature of advice applicability in AspectJ means that in many implementations small changes to aspects can require much of the program code to be scanned and possibly rewritten. This can slow down application startup, including the edit-compile-debug development cycle.

Late binding of advice has been suggested to improve the situation, at the potential cost of runtime performance. We propose and evaluate two virtual machine (VM) internal late binding approaches, that operate at whole-class and whole-method granularity.

Our evaluation shows that in VMs that allow bytecode mutation the preferred approach is to scan and rewrite methods the first time they are executed. In other VMs, whole-class scanning and rewriting at load time performs better. A separate interpreter based approach has startup performance similar to that of the whole-class approach; but micro-benchmarks suggest the latter out-performs the former over time.

1   Introduction

Many aspect-oriented programing (AOP) languages [1–5] include a dynamic join point model using pointcuts and advice. Implementation of this type of join point model is affected by the typical implementation trade-off concerning early or late binding: early binding improves performance by avoiding runtime advice dispatch overhead, but it is slow to update when the code or system configuration changes. The non-local with respect to lexical program structure semantics of pointcuts and advice exacerbates this problem because a small change to a pointcut can require rescanning the entire program.

Late binding improves update performance by paying a higher runtime cost. Deferring binding to load time can be done using a modified external class loader and available virtual machine (VM) interfaces; however, all loaded parts of the program must still be scanned. Simple measurements shows that common programs execute only about 50% of loaded methods; this means that complete scanning of loaded code may lead to needless work and impair application startup performance.

We focus on VM startup performance in this work, because it is a major concern in the developer community. VM teams devote significant resources to improving it [6]. We present two approaches to in-VM advice binding using bytecode rewriting. We implemented each of these approaches in the Jikes RVM [7],

J. Vitek (Ed.): TOOLS 2010, LNCS 6141, pp. 173–191, 2010.

and have performed a thorough performance analysis and comparison to other approaches. This benchmark analysis quantifies the startup improvement of AspectJ programs using VM-internal late binding over VM-external approaches, and shows that the primary consideration when choosing between in-VM implementation techniques are VM-imposed design constraints.

The contributions of this paper are:

- implementation of two late binding, in-VM AspectJ implementations;
- integration of both implementations with previously known steady state optimizations;
- performance evaluation of the two implementations with comparison to other implementation approaches;
- an analysis of all measured implementations, quantifying the performance limitations of VM-external approaches, and showing that the choice between the two in-VM approaches is driven by VM-imposed design constraints rather than their performance characteristics.

This paper is organized as follows. Section 2 summarizes the properties of AspectJ and VMs that impact our implementation. Sections 3 and 4 describe our two approaches and their respective implementation in the Jikes RVM. Section 5 discusses our benchmarking methodology, implementation, collected results and analysis. We conclude the paper with related work, future work, and conclusions in Sects. 6, 7, and 8 respectively.

2   Background

2.1   AspectJ

AspectJ has a dynamic *join point model* (JPM) in which a *dynamic join point* is a well-defined point in the execution of the program.[1] In this paper we use the term *join points* to refer to the dynamic join points of AspectJ's dynamic JPM.

The role of advice *weaving* in AspectJ is to coordinate advice body execution with the execution of the join points at which that advice applies. So, advice weaving is a dispatch-style operation with both lookup and invocation phases, where lookup determines the set of advice that applies at a particular join point, and invocation runs the applicable advice.

Traditionally, advice weaving is done statically by processing Java bytecode, either during or after compilation, but before runtime [8, 9]. Since AspectJ's join points are points in the execution of the program, they are runtime-only constructs. So, to perform static weaving, an implementation must identify the program's *join point shadows*. These are the points in the program text which give rise to join points at runtime. Weavers which process bytecode must identify these shadows in the bytecode of the program, referred to as *matching*, and then rewrite those sections of the program to effect advice dispatch, refered to as

---

[1] AspectJ also has a static JPM, where a static join point is a member in the program. However, we limit our focus to the dynamic JPM in this paper.

munging [8] (we use the terms rewriting and munging interchangeably). Munging includes adding not only calls to synthetic methods containing applicable advice bodies, but also various guards to implement the dynamic parts of the matching semantics. When weaving is done statically, all program classes must be scanned and potentially rewritten before execution. For large programs, this can cause onerous edit-run-test cycle times for even simple program changes.

VM supported approaches to late binding of advice include dynamic advice dispatch via integration with the VM's interpreter [10, 11], load-time bytecode rewriting via integration with the class loader [12], code generation via integration with the just-in-time (JIT) compiler [13] and also runtime bytecode rewriting [14].

Load-time bytecode rewriting functions the same as the traditional static approach, except rewriting is performed as a class is loaded by the VM, and hence it incurs a cost. Load-time rewriting can be done external to the VM using available Java VM APIs, or it can be done internal to the VM by coupling it with the VM's internal class loading infrastructure.

Code generation based advice binding operates on static program text like bytecode rewriting. It also identifies join point shadows in the program; but, instead of rewriting the program code, it generates instructions to execute advice if required during compilation.

Interpreter-based advice dispatch, however, operates on join points directly. As join points are executed by the interpreter, they are used to check for applicable advice. If any advice applies to the currently executing join point, the advice bodies are executed directly by the interpreter, as appropriate. Because each join point shadow can give rise to any number of join points at runtime, an interpreter-based advice dispatch implementation may perform more, less, or even about the same amount of advice dispatch work as a rewriting implementation depending on how much and what parts of the program are executed.

In this paper we look specifically at the trade-offs among four different approaches that allow late binding of advice: load-time VM-external rewriting, load-time VM-internal whole class rewriting, prior to first execution VM-internal whole method rewriting and an interpreter-based approach.

2.2   VMs and Startup

The startup performance of a VM is more difficult to describe than the steady state performance. A typical steady state performance evaluation of a VM will be measured by running a program repeatedly until the execution time of each run stabilizes. At this point, most costs associated with loading and any JIT compiling of the program are eliminated from additional runs. By contrast, measuring the startup performance of a VM has to take these costs into consideration.

In addition, there is no obvious point during execution of a program where we can say that startup is complete. Put differently, there is no easy way to say how much loading, optimizing compilation, and early garbage collection (GC) activity should be considered part of a program starting up.

Table 1. Summary of startup runs of Eclipse 3.5.0, Tomcat 6.0.20 and the average over the DaCapo 9.10-beta0 benchmark suite. The columns show the number of methods loaded, executed, and compiled along with the ratio of executed to loaded methods, and compiled to executed methods for each benchmark. These numbers were obtained using JVMTI on IBM J9 VM.

Benchmark	# loaded methods	# executed methods (exec/loaded)	# JIT compiled methods (compiled/exec)
Eclipse	81663	35445 (43.4%)	3386 (9.5%)
Tomcat	13797	6380 (46.2%)	584 (9.2%)
DaCapo Average	7903	3891 (49%)	783 (20%)

Speed of program execution, GC, class loading, and the cost of optimizing code all have an effect on startup performance. However, conversations with IBM engineers [6] guided us to focusing on minimizing the cost of class loading because of its large influence on overall startup performance.

The typical way to measure startup performance is to run real-world programs to some predefined point at which the execution time measurement is taken. Two key programs used are Eclipse and Tomcat [6]. In Eclipse, the startup time can be taken to be the time from execution until the workbench has been initialized, and in Tomcat the time it takes until applications can be served. Available Java benchmark suites simulate program startup by running each benchmark only once per VM invocation [15, 16].

We present the results of a simple measurement of methods loaded, called, and JIT compiled for a startup run of Eclipse and Tomcat (as defined above), and for each of the benchmarks in the DaCapo [15] benchmark suite in Table 1. The table shows that all these programs exhibit method execution/load ratios roughly in the range of 45-55%. Eclipse and Tomcat have a method JIT compiled to executed ratio of around 9%; DaCapo is higher at 20%. This suggests the the smaller DaCapo benchmarks may execute too large a fraction of the loaded code to accurately represent the startup characteristics of larger and more complex programs.

As a final element of important background information, we note that adding in-VM weaving support is constrained by design invariants in the VM. For example, many VMs use read-only space to store data that can be shared across multiple instances of the VM on the same machine. In particular, some VMs store bytecode in these spaces, so bytecode cannot be modified after it is loaded. Many other design decisions are constrained by the VM architecture, including memory layout, object allocation, etc.

3   Architecture

In previous work [12] we developed a VM-integrated AspectJ architecture. That architecture has four main parts: a front end AspectJ compiler, a VM-internal load time weaver, VM-internal aspect representation, and AspectJ-specific optimization capabilities in the optimizing JIT compiler. The present work builds on the previous architecture by significantly redesigning the load-time weaver to better take advantage of being within the VM boundary and enabling it to operate in two different modes.

We first summarize the previous architecture and then discuss the new load-time weaver architecture.

As the front end compiler we use ajc [8, 17] (the defacto standard AspectJ compiler) which produces standard Java class files. AspectJ-specific data, such as pointcut, advice and aspect declarations are stored as Java attributes in these files so that the VM can extract this information at load time. ajc has the ability to do no, partial or full weaving of the aspects in the program, which allows programmers to weave aspects they are certain will deploy with the program early. Information about which aspects the front end compiler does weave is stored as part of the AspectJ-specific data. The on-disk format of these attributes is standardized by the ajc compiler, and using this format allows our architecture to be both forward and backward compatible with existing AspectJ programs and VMs.

The load time weaver serves three main purposes: it arranges loading of the aspects required by the program; it reads the AspectJ attributes and annotates the VM's internal representation of the program appropriately to identify aspects, advice and pointcuts; and it does any weaving that was not done by the front end compiler.

Finally, the JIT compiler has access to the AspectJ-specific data imported by the load time weaver. This information allows the JIT compiler to improve the generated code quality for some AspectJ constructs. Further details are in [12].

Our previous work focused on the overall design and steady state performance of programs running under this architecture. With that focus in mind we used a naive implementation of the load time weaver. In this work, we expand upon this area of the architecture by redesigning the load time weaver to operate in two modes and take advantage of its access to VM-internal representations. The two modes are distinguished by the granularity at which weaving is performed: class-level or method-level. Both modes delay weaving as long as possible, but in each case all advice weaving on a unit of the given granularity must be performed before any part of that unit can be executed by the VM.

When operating at *class-level granularity* the weaver waits until a class is loaded before performing weaving on that class. This level of granularity naturally weaves all classes as they are loaded into the VM by the VM's dynamic class loader. Since only classes that end up being used during a particular run of the VM are loaded, only those classes are woven.

When operating at *method-level granularity* the weaver waits until a method in a class must be executed before weaving that method. This method hooks into the VM's interpreter (or baseline compiler in the case of Jikes RVM) to weave applicable advice before first execution. The effect of using this level of granularity is that only those methods that are actually executed are woven.

Because both modes use bytecode rewriting techniques, efficient bytecode based matching and munging is important for both approaches. It is conceivable that pointcut matching could be optimized differently for the two granularities, to take advantage of the fact that at class-level granularity a presumably larger amount of code is woven, all of which has static shadows in the same class. We have not pursued this yet. Instead we use the same matching mechanism for both granularities.

In summary, the execution of an AspectJ program follows these steps: (1) VM initialization; (2) parse AspectJ aspects definition file; (3) load specified aspects one at a time and store their meta-data; (4) load the main class of the program to be run; and (5) proceed with execution. As execution proceeds, the VM will weave dynamically loaded classes as they are loaded if using the class-level approach, or weave methods just prior to their first execution if using the method-level approach.

4   Implementation

As discussed in the previous section, our current focus is on a redesign of the VM-integrated load time weaver (LTW) component of our previous architecture [12]. Given this, we reuse the previous front end compiler (ajc) and integrate our new LTW implementation with our previous implementation of AspectJ-specific JIT optimizations. We build on the Jikes Research Virtual Machine (RVM) 3.1.0 [7].

Since the two weaving granularities share much of their code and infrastructure, we discuss the parts common to both before looking at the differences.

The first job of the LTW is to ensure that aspects required by the program are loaded before the program begins execution. This is accomplished by reading an XML file that describes the aspects required by the program to be executed (the location of this file is standardized by ajc). Aspects are loaded through the standard class loading infrastructure of the VM, and this loading happens after VM initialization, but before the VM begins executing the main method of the program.

The second role of the LTW is to read the AspectJ-specific data stored in some of the loaded classes and aspects. This occurs while a class or aspect is being loaded by the VM, but again, before any initialization occurs. This process translates on-disk pointcuts into an internal representation that maps type references in pointcuts directly to VM-internal types where possible (wildcard type patterns cannot be so mapped). This type of mapping is unavailable to VM-external implementations, which must therefore duplicate the type hierarchy and consume more time and space to load the aspects.

Finally, the most time-intensive work done by the LTW is advice weaving. As discussed in Sect. 2, advice weaving is naturally broken down into advice lookup and advice invocation phases. In a bytecode rewriting based implementation these two phases correspond concretely to pointcut matching and bytecode munging.

Our pointcut matcher is based closely on the ajc implementation of pointcut matching: pointcuts are stored in an abstract syntax tree (AST) style form and matching consists of exploring this pointcut AST based on the the bytecode shadow in question. Each bytecode shadow has a number of static properties (such as target type, target name, arguments, etc) which guide the exploration of the tree representation of the pointcut. We do not explore any heuristic re-ordering of the pointcut in this work.

Our bytecode munger avoids the use of the convenient but expensive bytecode manipulation toolkits (such as asm [18] or bcel [19]) used by ajc and other bytecode weaving implementations. It processes one complete method at a time, using five passes over the method's bytecode:

1. The method's bytecode is converted to a list representation from an array.
2. All branches and exception table pointers are resolved in the list representation.
3. For each join point shadow in the method, we attempt a match against every registered pointcut. Each match attempt can produce one of three answers: static match, static fail, or match with dynamic residual. Static match and fail occur when there is enough static information available at the join point shadow to definitively match or fail the pointcut. In the residual case some dynamic information is required to complete the matching, such as checking the dynamic type of an object.

   In the case of static fail, no munging is done at the shadow, otherwise the bytecode instructions are added around the shadow to invoke advice execution, possibly with dynamic checks as required. As discussed below, we do this munging in a way that does not require modifying the class' constant pool.
4. The offsets of all bytecodes in the list are recomputed to reflect the addition of bytecodes during munging.
5. The bytecode list is converted back to an array of correct size to replace the original bytecode of the method.

Actual advice execution is done by inserting bytecode instructions that use the VM's method invocation infrastructure. When using this approach external to a VM, we would have to use an `invokevirtual` instruction and would have to modify the constant pool of the containing class to contain string references to the appropriate methods of the aspect. We avoid this overhead by extending the internal bytecodes understood by the VM in a straightforward manner. For each of several bytecodes that take as their parameter an index into the constant pool (including, `invokevirtual`, `invokestatic`, and `instanceof`), we create a new VM-internal bytecode (called `internalinvokevirtual`, etc). Each of these works like its original, except that its argument is an index into the global method (or type) table.[2] Otherwise the implementation of these bytecodes is the same as their original namesakes except for where the method or type reference is retrieved.

---

[2] Each method and type in the JikesRVM has a unique integer ID which we can use to refer to it.

This change allows us to add new references to existing classes—new instructions to call advice methods or do residual testing—without having to modify the class's constant pool, a potentially expensive operation. Note that this does not change the external Java bytecode interface of the VM.

The two modes of weaving granularity differ in the point in time at which the weaving occurs for each method. As discussed in the previous section, class-level granularity weaves every method in a class just before the class is initialized, whereas method-level granularity weaves a method just before it is executed. In the Jikes RVM, these two points translate into class-level weaving occurring just before a class is initialized, and method-level weaving occuring just before the baseline compiler compiles a method for the first time.

Our current implementation supports a subset of AspectJ's constructs, including `call` and `execution` shadows, `before`, and `after returning` advice, and reference, kinded, `within`, `this`, `target`, `args`, `if`, and `cflow` pointcuts. We support only the singleton aspect instantiation model.

5   Evaluation

Because we are focusing on startup performance considerations, our benchmark suite is designed to measure different facets of program startup. We use four groups of benchmarks to compare our class- and method-level in-VM weavers against the ajc compile-time weaver (ajc), the ajc VM-external load-time weaver (ajc ltw), and Naseer's interpreter dispatch implementation [11].

For data collection, we use the statistically rigorous data collection methodology described by Georges et al. [20] and report the average running time of various benchmarks over multiple invocations of the complete benchmark being measured. We compute 95% confidence intervals for each of the reported averages. For all of the benchmarks except the DaCapo suite, we compute running times for an increasing number of iterations to show how the performance of the VM unfolds. We do not do this for the DaCapo benchmarks because of their longer running time: it takes a prohibitively long time to obtain enough measurements to reduce the confidence interval sufficiently.

We note that neither our in-VM weavers nor the interpreter dispatch implementation implement the complete AspectJ language with respect to dynamic join points. But the missing features primarily affect the code generated by a weaver, and that code must be generated by any implementation. So we believe that our analysis captures the critical startup performance characteristics even if the implementations were expanded to cover the full language.

5.1   Benchmarks

The first group of benchmarks, the *macro benchmarks*, are intended to measure overall application startup performance. Ideally we would use the same kind of real world programs used by VM development teams to measure Java application startup performance. Unfortunately, neither Tomcat nor Eclipse with the GUI enabled, will run on Jikes RVM 3.1.0. So, we use all those DaCapo benchmarks (dacapo-9.10-beta0) that do run on Jikes RVM 3.1.0 as our macro benchmarks.[3] This substitution could potentially jeopardize our results, but the analysis reported in Table 1 suggests the DaCapo benchmarks have class loading characteristics sufficiently similar to that of the ideal benchmarks to make this an appropriate strategy.

We run the macro benchmarks in two different ways: the first is a plain execution to establish a baseline; the second includes an aspect with a single `call` pointcut that does not match any benchmark code. This is intended to measure the additional cost a weaver pays when there are pointcut and advice pairs that must be woven.

The next three groups of benchmarks are micro benchmarks designed to measure different startup characteristics of the implementations.

The *basic startup cost benchmarks* group consists of four benchmarks. The first, "staticLoad", measures how long it takes the VM to startup and shutdown (the benchmark does no appreciable amount of other work). "staticLoadWith-Infr", measures the cost of loading the basic infrastructure code used by the weaver implementations by measuring the time required for the VM to startup and shutdown when an empty aspect definition file is present. "1000Methodsloaded" is focused on class loading. It instantiates 100 identical classes containing 10 methods, each of which contains 100 method calls. Only one method of one class is executed for each iteration of the benchmark loop. "500MethodsExec" is focused on executing half of loaded code. It is nearly the same as 1000Methods Loaded, except that 50% of the loaded methods are executed during each iteration of the benchmark (each iteration executes the same methods). The choice to execute 50% of loaded methods is justified by the results in Table 1; it is roughly the percentage of loaded methods that are executed in a typical startup run of Eclipse, Tomcat and DaCapo.

The *advice execution benchmarks* measure the execution of several combinations of pointcuts and advice involving both statically matched and residually tested advice. These benchmarks are a subset of those used in our previous work [11, 12].

The *special advice execution benchmarks* are intended to support comparisons to Naseer's interpreter dispatch implementation [11]. They measure the cost of unadvised method execution, as well as statically matched and residually guarded advice. These special benchmarks are run with the JIT compiler disabled because Naseer's implementation does not support the JIT compiler.

Further details of the benchmarks, including version and machine details, are discussed in appendix A.

5.2   Results

Figure 1 shows the graphs of the results of the macro benchmarks. It shows four implementations: ajc, ajc ltw, and both of our in-VM weaving implementations,

---

[3] The DaCapo suite does contain an Eclipse benchmark, but because it does not use the GUI, this benchmark is supported by Jikes RVM 3.1.0.

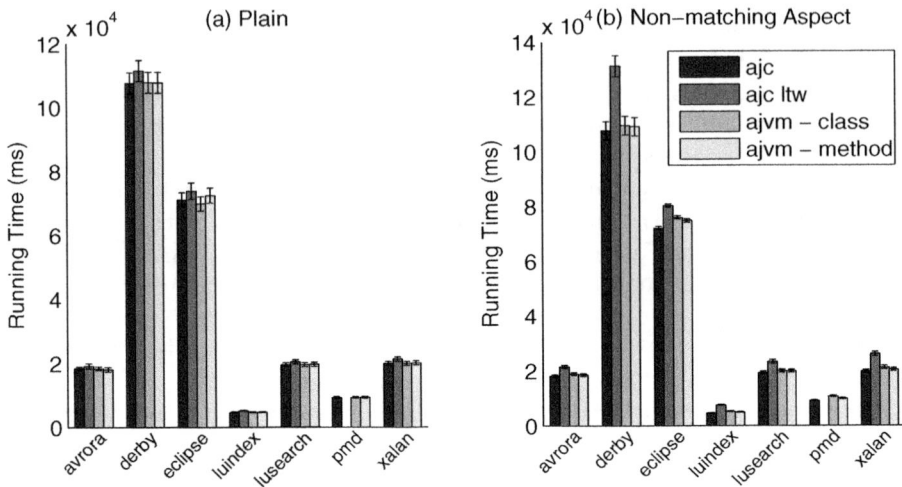

Fig. 1. Macro Benchmarks. a) shows a normal run of the suite; b) shows the suite run with the inclusion of a single advice that does not match any benchmark code.

labeled as "ajvm - class level" and "ajvm - method level." Error bars show the 95% confidence interval computed for that set of results. The y-axis shows the wall clock running time of the benchmark, and the x-axis groups results by benchmark. Figure 1a) shows that in most cases, simply having a late binding advice implementation available does not slow down the startup performance of pure Java because the results show no statistically significant differences.

Figure 1b) shows the run containing an aspect with one non-applicable advice. The ajc load time weaver could not run the "pmd" benchmark, so that result is omitted. The results here more clearly show the costs paid by each weaving implementation based on the amount of code each must scan to prove that the advice does not apply. This run is more representative of what happens in a program containing advice, and the results show a 1.07x (eclipse) to 1.5x (luindex) cost paid by ajc ltw over the method level approach. Also, the results show a significant but smaller cost when using class level over method level weaving. Recall, however, that the DaCapo benchmarks have a higher percentage of their executed methods optimized than Eclipse or Tomcat during startup, suggesting that these benchmarks have a higher workload which can amortize the differences in startup speed over longer executions.

We show just one graph of all of the iterations from one benchmark in Fig. 2. This shows the result of running the "1000MethodsLoaded" benchmark from the basic startup benchmark group. This benchmark includes all four late binding implementations and static ajc, and it is run with the JIT compiler disabled because we include Naseer's interpreter-based advice dispatch implementation. The x-axis is the number of iterations of the benchmark loop that are executed, and the y-axis is the wall clock running time from VM startup to benchmark completion. Since we do not measure every single iteration individually, actual

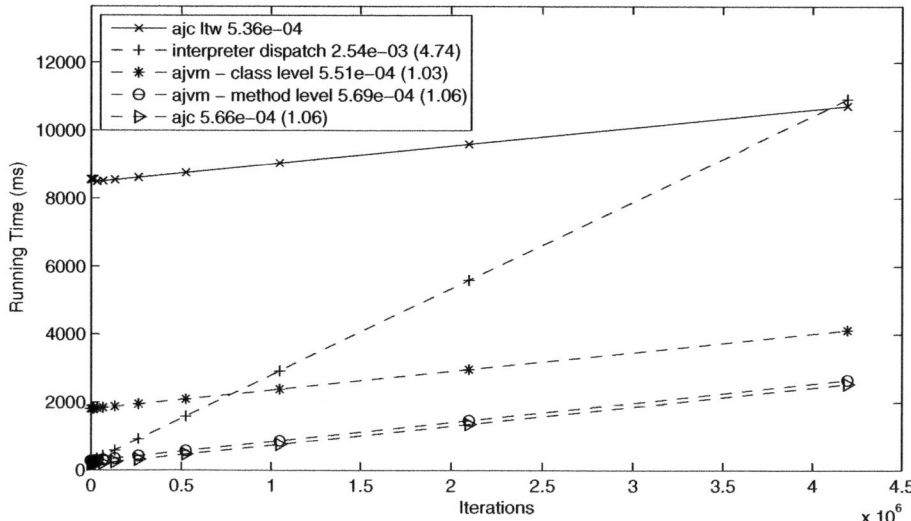

Fig. 2. 1000MethodsLoaded w/ JIT compiler disabled. The legend is annotated with the actual slope value, and slope relative to ajc ltw in parenthesis.

measured values are marked on the graph with either $x, +, *, o$ or $\triangleright$, depending on the implementation. Values between measured points are linearly interpolated.

From this graph we can see not only the startup performance difference between the implementations when the iteration count is 1, but we can also see the performance of each of the implementations over time compared to one another. The results of these benchmark are unsurprising in that ajc ltw takes ~8s (32x) longer to startup than method level, and class level takes ~1.5s (6.8x) longer to startup than method level. The interpreter dispatch and method level weaver are the quickest to startup. Furthermore, the slopes of the curves, representing performance over time, is relatively the same for all bytecode based weavers because all of them have the opportunity to generate much the same woven bytecode; the interpreter dispatch implementation has a much steeper slope because each join point execution is much more expensive due to pointcut matching and dynamic dispatch.

The majority of the micro benchmark runs follow the same pattern as in Fig. 2: the final slope of the curves for each implementation measured is the same (with noted exceptions), even though the overall shape and slope of the curves differ between benchmarks. For that reason, instead of graphing each, we summarize the results.

The first is a series of bar graphs for each of the benchmark groups like the bar graph shown for the DaCapo results in Fig. 1. These bar graphs are shown in Figs. 3 through 5. We can use these types of graphs as a summary since, as shown above, the variability for most of the benchmarks are captured in the first iteration. Note that since nearly all loaded code is executed in these benchmarks, we do not see a difference in the performance of class and method level in-VM weaving.

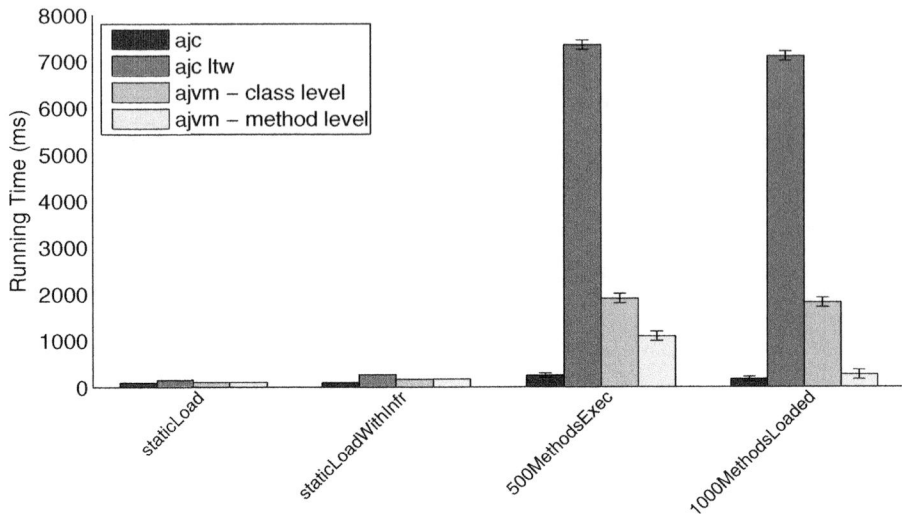

Fig. 3. Basic Startup Cost Benchmarks

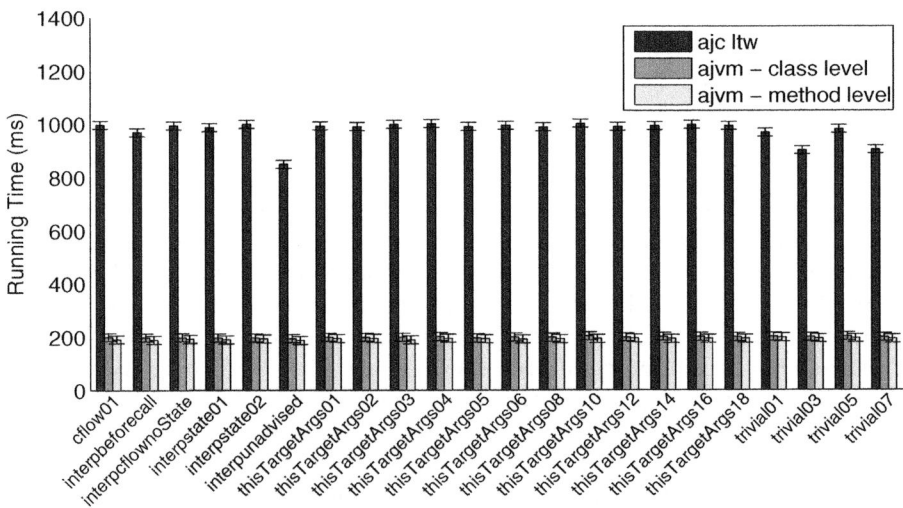

Fig. 4. Advice Execution Benchmarks

All benchmarks but two showed statistically indistinguishable slopes because of the similarity of their steady state performance. The exceptions are the cflow benchmarks and, more subtly, some of the state capture benchmarks in which our two in-VM approaches out-perform ajc ltw. These improvements can be accounted for by the differences in the bytecode generated between implementations in the case of state capture, and the steady state optimizations available to in-VM implementations in the case of cflow [12, 21].

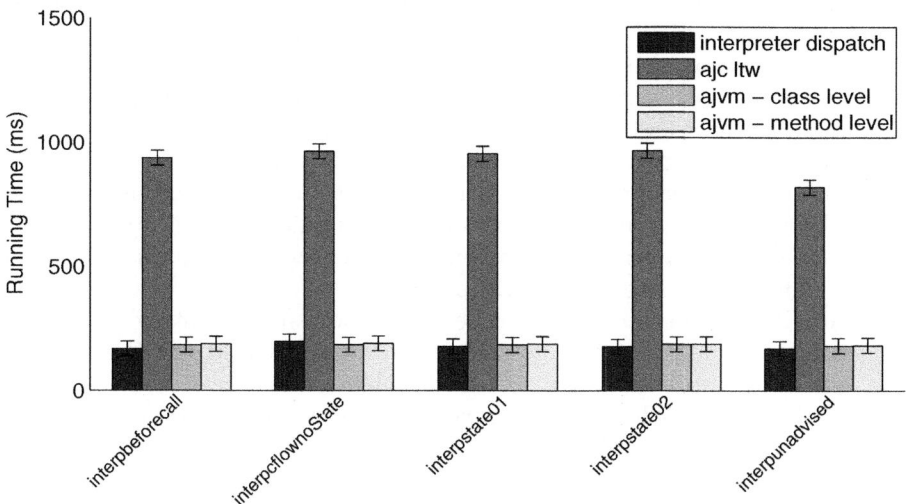

Fig. 5. Special Advice Execution Benchmarks

5.3   Analysis

The plain static startup benchmarks shown in Fig. 3 and the macro benchmarks in Fig. 1a) show that simply having a late binding advice weaving implementation available does not slow down pure Java programs. This is because when no aspects are present, much of the weaving infrastructure can be short-circuited.

The macro benchmarks that contain a single non-matching advice shown in 1b) show that when there is advice in a program that may apply to any bytecode, the speed of class loading is impacted when the bytecode needs to be scanned. Specifically, ajc ltw is impacted more than the others.

Figure 3's "500MethodsExec" and "1000MethodsLoaded" show the relative performance costs when we micromeasure class loading. These results show the improvement of in-VM weaving over ajc ltw (~6.8s or 4.7x), and the significant, but relatively smaller improvement of method level weaving over class level weaving (~0.8-1.5s or 1.7x-6.7x).

Figure 5 shows the results of the special advice execution benchmarks. These results show that there is no statistically significant difference in startup between the interpreter weaver and in-VM bytecode weavers. However, Fig. 2 shows that interpreter dispatch has a significantly higher slope, and hence higher cost, when repeatedly executing each benchmark. In a full hybrid implementation, however, this overhead is likely to be minimal as a method which is frequently executed will be recompiled by the JIT compiler, relaxing the slope significantly.

These results taken together suggest that VM-external implementations, although necessary in some cases, have inherent performance limitations when performing weaving for late binding of advice. These limitations stem from the fact that a VM-external weaver must duplicate structures it is unable to access in the VM, and that it is limited to class-level granularity of weaving.

Comparing our implementation of in-VM class level weaving to the ajc load time weaver quantifies the cost that ajc ltw pays duplicating in-VM structures and using a convenient but expensive bytecode manipulation toolkit. However, our class-level implementation still shows performance degradation over our method level weaver and over interpreter dispatch.

Although the interpreter dispatch implementation does not support the JIT compiler, preventing us from making a more robust comparison, our micro benchmarks show that first run benchmarks startup as quickly using interpreter dispatch as method level weaving. However, interpreter dispatch pays a significant price in runtime code execution performance.

Finally, it is important to remember that these implementations were developed in the context of a large VM which already constrains the design of feature additions such as a weaver. So, although method level weaving and interpreter dispatch may have similar performance characteristics, some VMs contain read-only areas of memory where method bytecode is loaded and hence not modifiable. Therefore, an implementation of method level weaving in this VM will either become more expensive because class-copying is required, or it will be unimplementable. This suggests that the choice between using method level bytecode weaving and interpreter dispatch is driven by such design constraints, rather than their respective startup performance characteristics, which turn out to be quite similar.

6   Related Work

The most commonly used AspectJ implementation is ajc [8, 17, 22], which is an implementation based on bytecode rewriting. It has modes that allow it to perform weaving on a class at any stage before being loaded into the VM: compile time, post-compile time, and load-time. However, because of its VM-external implementation, it is inherently prevented from having a more efficient integration with VM-internal data structures. We use many of the same techniques as in ajc, and some of the code from ajc in implementing out approach; but our approach allows a closer integration with the VM, and hence allows us to reduce code size, and improve performance.

The AspectWerkz [23] and ajc projects merged circa January 2005. Prior to this merge, AspectWerkz operated in much the same way as ajc except it used a separate XML file and embedded annotations to specify pointcuts and advice rather than new language syntax. However, AspectWerkz supported dynamic weaving by hooking into VMs that support the Java Hotswap architecture.

abc[9, 24, 25] is also a bytecode rewriting approach outside the VM. abc implements the AspectJ language, with a focus on generating optimized code. It uses an open, extensible compiler framework which allows it to be easily extended for research purposes. abc's non-local optimizations in the frontend compiler are orthogonal to our load time weaving implementation because our implementation meets the load time architectural requirements described by Golbeck [12].

JAsCo [4, 26] is an AOP implementation that is also based on bytecode rewriting, but it primarily uses a hook-based approach in which generic hooks are inserted into the bytecode which call into JAsCo's advice dispatcher to handle the advice weaving. For optimization purposes, JAsCo also supports the ability to inline the advice dispatch code, as ajc and abc would, using Java VM compliant interfaces.

PROSE [27] was one of the first implementations which integrated AOP functionality into the VM; its implementation is based on the Jikes RVM. It implements an AspectJ-like language which supports much of the functionality of AspectJ, but which also includes the ability to dynamically deploy aspects. Early versions of PROSE used the Java VM debugging interface to add hooks into the running program to effect advice dispatch, whereas more recent versions of PROSE integrated directly into the VM execution layers with two types of weaving: hook based weaving and runtime JBC weaving. Hook based weaving works on principles similar to those discussed above in that the code is rewritten with hooks at runtime to call into PROSE's runtime architecture to dispatch advice, and runtime JBC weaving works by weaving the VM's internal JBC representation directly at runtime.

Steamloom [14, 28], like PROSE, integrates advice weaving into the VM, and is based on the Jikes RVM. Steamloom implements a fully dynamic AspectJ-like AOP language by integrating a runtime rewriting based weaver which rewrites the VM's internal representation of the JBC. This weaver can weave and unweave advice execution logic to deploy and undeploy aspects at runtime. Steamloom's load time and weaving architecture has not been optimized for efficient load time or first run performance; it currently uses a memory intensive representation for access to the internal representation of the bytecode for easy manipulation and rewriting. It has been optimized for steady state performance, whereas our implementation has been optimized for startup performance.

The Nu [10, 29] VM augments the interpreter in the Sun Hotspot VM to effect advice weaving; the optimizing compiler is not yet supported. It extends the VM with two additional bytecodes which control a VM interval weaver. It uses the *point-in-time* join point model [5] with a dynamic language semantics and method execution and return dynamic join points.

Previous work on interpreter-based dispatch implementation [11] is used as a point of comparison in this paper. This work supports the majority of the AspectJ language, including all of the join point shadows, and is also designed to provide efficient startup performance.

AJVM is past work on VM-aware AspectJ implementations discussed in [12, 13]. This work presented a completed architecture including an aspect-aware VM, and evaluated an implementation of that architecture from a perspective of steady-state performance. This paper completes some of the future work of AJVM, specifically addressing the load time weaving portion of the architecture, and evaluated different options compatible with the AJVM architecture from a startup performance perspective.

ALIA [30] is an interface designed to more completely separate frontend compilers and VM internal weaving mechanisms to support runtime weaving and dynamic deployment of aspects. It makes AOP language constructs into first class entities inside the VM to allow user programs to have a consistent interface to the VM for controlling the runtime weaver. Our work and ALIA are largely orthogonal: although we only support ajc's load time weaving interface for advice weaving inside the VM, our architecture should be largely applicable to alternate VM interfaces including ALIA.

7 Future Work

The most immediate future work is to complete our implementation to support all of the AspectJ pointcuts and advice, as well as inter-type declarations. However, none of the features missing from our implementation appear to present difficulties for our architectures or experiment.

As an initial implementation, we used a relatively naive data structure and algorithm for doing bytecode munging on methods. Although our experiments show that this approach is relatively efficient, it should be possible to optimize this implementation to reduce the number of passes over the bytecode required.

We also used pre-existing code from ajc for much of our pointcut matching logic. This code could potentially be further optimized by pre-populating tabular data structures, such as in [11], when aspects are loaded. These, or similar, data structures could be used to improve the performance of the matching stage of advice weaving.

8 Conclusion

We presented two approaches for implementing late binding of advice in AspectJ using an aspect-aware VM. Both of these approaches were extensions of, and hence compatible with, previous AspectJ architecture work which demonstrated efficient steady-state performance of AspectJ programs.

We evaluate an implementation of each of the proposed approaches, together with comparisons to the ajc load time weaver and an interpreter based dispatch implementation. Our evaluation quantifies the inherent costs paid by VM-external approaches. Furthermore, our evaluation and design constraint analysis show that the startup performance between the interpreter dispatch and method level rewriting options for VM-integrated implementations is largely the same. Given this, we can conclude that the choice between these two implementation strategies depends on the design constraints imposed by the VM.

Acknowledgments

This research was partially supported by the IBM Centers for Advanced Studies and the Natural Sciences and Engineering Research Council of Canada (NSERC).

References

1. Kiczales, G., Lamping, J., Menhdhekar, A., Maeda, C., Lopes, C., Loingtier, J.M., Irwin, J.: Aspect-oriented programming. In: Aksit, M., Matsuoka, S. (eds.) ECOOP 1997. LNCS, vol. 1241, pp. 220–242. Springer, Heidelberg (1997)
2. Mezini, M., Ostermann, K.: Conquering aspects with Caesar. In: AOSD '03: Proceedings of the 2nd international conference on Aspect-oriented software development, pp. 90–99. ACM Press, New York (2003)
3. Rajan, H., Sullivan, K.: Eos: instance-level aspects for integrated system design. In: ESEC/FSE-11: Proceedings of the 9th European software engineering conference held jointly with 11th ACM SIGSOFT international symposium on Foundations of Software Engineering, pp. 297–306. ACM Press, New York (2003)
4. Suvée, D., Vanderperren, W., Jonckers, V.: JAsCo: An Aspect-oriented Approach Tailored for Component Based Software Development. In: AOSD '03: Proceedings of the 2nd international conference on Aspect-oriented software development, pp. 21–29. ACM, New York (2003)
5. Masuhara, H., Endoh, Y., Yonezawa, A.: A Fine-Grained Join Point Model for More Reusable Aspects. In: Kobayashi, N. (ed.) APLAS 2006. LNCS, vol. 4279, pp. 131–147. Springer, Heidelberg (2006)
6. IBM J9 Team Members. Personal Communication (2009)
7. Alpern, B., Attanasio, C.R., Cocchi, A., Lieber, D., Smith, S., Ngo, T., Barton, J.J., Hummel, S.F., Sheperd, J.C., Mergen, M.: Implementing Jalapeño in Java. In: OOPSLA '99: Proceedings of the 14th ACM SIGPLAN conference on Object-oriented programming, systems, languages, and applications, pp. 314–324. ACM Press, New York (1999)
8. Hilsdale, E., Hugunin, J.: Advice weaving in AspectJ. In: AOSD '04: Proceedings of the 3rd international conference on Aspect-oriented software development, pp. 26–35. ACM Press, New York (2004)
9. ABC Group: abc (AspectBench Compiler) http://aspectbench.org
10. Dyer, R., Setty, R.B., Rajan, H.: Nu: Toward a Flexible and Dynamic Aspect-Oriented Intermediate Language Model. Technical report, Iowa State University (June 2007)
11. Naseer, I., Golbeck, R.M., Selby, P., Kiczales, G.: Interpreter Implementation of Advice Weaving. Technical Report TR-2010-01, University of British Columbia (January 2010)
12. Golbeck, R.M., Davis, S., Naseer, I., Ostrovsky, I., Kiczales, G.: Lightweight Virtual Machine Support for AspectJ. In: AOSD '08: Proceedings of the 7th international conference on Aspect-oriented software development, pp. 180–190. ACM, New York (2008)
13. Golbeck, R.M., Kiczales, G.: A Machine Code Model for Efficient Advice Dispatch. In: VMIL '07: Proceedings of the 1st workshop on Virtual machines and intermediate languages for emerging modularization mechanisms, p. 2. ACM Press, New York (2007)
14. Haupt, M., Mezini, M., Bockisch, C., Dinkelaker, T., Eichberg, M., Krebs, M.: An Execution Layer for Aspect-Oriented Programming Languages. In: Vitek, J. (ed.) Proceedings of the First International Conference on Virtual Execution Environments (VEE'05), Chicago, USA, June 2005, pp. 142–152. ACM Press, New York (2005)

15. Blackburn, S.M., Garner, R., Hoffmann, C., Khang, A.M., McKinley, K.S., Bentzur, R., Diwan, A., Feinberg, D., Frampton, D., Guyer, S.Z., Hirzel, M., Hosking, A., Jump, M., Lee, H., Moss, J.E.B., Moss, B., Phansalkar, A., Stefanović, D., VanDrunen, T., von Dincklage, D., Wiedermann, B.: The DaCapo Benchmarks: Java Benchmarking Development and Analysis. In: OOPSLA '06: Proceedings of the 21st annual ACM SIGPLAN conference on Object-oriented programming systems, languages, and applications, pp. 169–190. ACM Press, New York (2006)
16. Standard Performance Evaluation Corporation: SPECjvm2008, http://www.spec.org/jvm2008/
17. AspectJ Team: AspectJ Project, http://www.eclipse.org/aspectj/
18. OW2 Consortium: ASM, http://asm.ow2.org/
19. Apache Software Foundation: Apache BCEL, http://jakarta.apache.org/bcel/
20. Georges, A., Buytaert, D., Eeckhout, L.: Statistically Rigorous Java Performance Evaluation. In: OOPSLA '07: Proceedings of the 22nd annual ACM SIGPLAN conference on Object-oriented programming systems, languages and applications (2007)
21. Bockisch, C., Kanthak, S., Haupt, M., Arnold, M., Mezini, M.: Efficient Control Flow Quantification. SIGPLAN Not. 41(10), 125–138 (2006)
22. Kiczales, G., Hilsdale, E., Hugunin, J., Kersten, M., Palm, J., Griswold, W.G.: An Overview of AspectJ. In: Knudsen, J.L. (ed.) ECOOP 2001. LNCS, vol. 2072, pp. 327–355. Springer, Heidelberg (2001)
23. Bonér, J., Vasseur, A.: AspectWerkz, http://aspectwerkz.codehaus.org/index.html
24. Avgustinov, P., Christensen, A.S., Hendren, L., Kuzins, S., Lhohák, J., Lhoták, O., de Moor, O., Sereni, D., Sittampalam, G., Tibble, J.: abc: an extensible AspectJ compiler. In: AOSD '05: Proceedings of the 4th international conference on Aspect-oriented software development, pp. 87–98. ACM Press, New York (2005)
25. Avgustinov, P., Christensen, A.S., Hendren, L., Kuzins, S., Lhoták, J., Lhoták, O., de Moor, O., Sereni, D., Sittampalam, G., Tibble, J.: Optimising AspectJ. In: PLDI '05: Proceedings of the 2005 ACM SIGPLAN conference on Programming language design and implementation, pp. 117–128. ACM Press, New York (2005)
26. Vanderperren, W., Suvée, D., Verheecke, B., Cibrán, M.A., Jonckers, V.: Adaptive Programming in JAsCo. In: AOSD '05: Proceedings of the 4th international conference on Aspect-oriented software development, pp. 75–86. ACM, New York (2005)
27. Popovici, A., Alonso, G., Gross, T.: Just-in-time Aspects: Efficient Dynamic Weaving for Java. In: AOSD '03: Proceedings of the 2nd international conference on Aspect-oriented software development, pp. 100–109. ACM Press, New York (2003)
28. Bockisch, C., Haupt, M., Mezini, M., Ostermann, K.: Virtual Machine Support for Dynamic Join Points. In: AOSD '04: Proceedings of the 3rd International Conference on Aspect-oriented Software Development, pp. 83–92. ACM Press, New York (2004)
29. Dyer, R., Rajan, H.: Nu: A dynamic aspect-oriented intermediate language model and virtual machine for flexible runtime adaptation. In: AOSD '08: Proceedings of the 7th international conference on Aspect-oriented software development, pp. 191–202. ACM, New York (2008)
30. Bockisch, C., Mezini, M.: A Flexible Architecture for pointcut-advice Language Implementations. In: VMIL '07: Proceedings of the 1st workshop on Virtual Machines and Intermediate Languages for Emerging Modularization Mechanisms, p. 1. ACM, New York (2007)

A   Benchmark Details

We compare our implementation against ajc ltw version 1.5.2 running on Jikes RVM 3.1.0[4]. We also compare against the interpreter weaver from [11], which is based upon Jikes RVM 2.9.2, where possible.

All of our Jikes RVM builds use the "production" build configuration, and use the default value of 1 CPU. The benchmarks were run on a 3Ghz dual core Intel Pentium 4 machine with 1GB memory running Ubuntu Linux 9.10 with kernel 2.6.31.

All of the benchmarks are run with the same harness, and only the DaCapo benchmarks differ in the main benchmark loop. Our main benchmark harness is configured to run each benchmark an increasing number of iterations. We run each iteration of the given benchmark and implementation pair a sufficient number of times to get a mean result in the confidence interval we require for that benchmark.

For all benchmarks other than those in the DaCapo suite, the benchmark has a basic structure of two classes and an aspect. Each consists of a SuperClass which contains a method with 20 identical DJP shadows in a loop. It is this loop that is iterated a configurable number of times. Each of these shadows is a call to an alternate method in the class which increments and tests a counter. This class is extended by a SubClass, which is the class instantiated by the benchmark harness. This class hierarchy allows the testing of both static and dynamic pointcut matching.

The advice body in the aspect of the benchmark also increments and tests a counter. The exact counter being incremented varies depending on the benchmark (it may increment a counter in a class capture as a dynamic value). The aspect pointcut and advice type is the primary variant between different benchmarks.

Note that these benchmarks are part of a larger suite we have constructed and used to also measure the steady-state performance of JIT optimized AspectJ code. The counter increment and test in the method and advice bodies are designed to prevent the optimizing compiler from optimizing away the bodies, calls, and possibly the advice entirely.

Finally, some of the Dacapo benchmarks actually execute $n + 1$ times because they have a built-in "warm up" phase where they executed the whole benchmark once, which is not configurable. So, 1 iteration actually runs the benchmark twice.

---

[4] Note that our implementation is also based on Jikes RVM 3.1.0.

EriLex: An Embedded Domain Specific Language Generator

Hao Xu

University of North Carolina at Chapel Hill
Chapel Hill, NC 27599, USA
xuh@cs.unc.edu

Abstract. EriLex is a software tool for generating support code for embedded domain specific languages (EDSLs). It supports specifying syntax, static semantics, and dynamic semantics of an EDSL, mixing the method chaining style and the functional nesting style in the EDSL embedding, and using native types and values in the EDSL. The EriLex approach to EDSL embedding assumes only basic object-oriented features and generics in the host language and does not require any particular technology in the definition or implementation of host languages and tools. The generated support code allows the EDSLs to reuse not only host language compilers but also host language semantic editors.

1   Introduction

Research on domain specific languages (DSLs) involves many aspects of programming languages, such as design of meta languages, composition of language specifications, and guarantee of static properties. The research on embedded domain specific languages (EDSLs) [12] focuses on reusing the infrastructure of a general purpose programming language and providing abstraction for software libraries in the form of DSLs. In particular, the approach in which DSL constructs are embedded in an existing general purpose programming language by defining new abstract data types and operators is called the "embedding" pattern [16].

The main advantage of the "embedding" pattern is that it requires minimum coupling with the host language: it does not require meta language constructs in the host language; it does not require that the host language be defined in a particular flavor of grammar; and it does not require that the host language compiler be extensible. The EDSLs rely on the syntax and semantics of the host language, but not how the syntax and semantics are defined or implemented. As a result, the "embedding" pattern is applicable to a wide range of host languages and allows the host languages to evolve as general purpose programming languages without breaking the EDSLs as long as the host languages are backward compatible in syntax and semantics. Another advantage of this pattern is that no external tools or preprocessors are needed when EDSL code is compiled, as EDSL code is host language code, which can be compiled using the host language compiler.

J. Vitek (Ed.): TOOLS 2010, LNCS 6141, pp. 192–212, 2010.

Typed vs Untyped. Untyped encoding of EDSLs can be easily done using abstract data types, but has several problems when an EDSL has more than one types. First, the values of the EDSL need to be tagged with their types that are checked at run time [6], which reduces performance of EDSLs. Second, even the simplest type errors are not checked statically and can cause runtime exceptions. For example, suppose that we have an EDSL that supports both integral and boolean values. In untyped encoding, errors in EDSL code such as adding an integral value to a boolean value are discovered only at runtime, which could be problematic if the code is running on a server. Typed embedding of EDSLs into statically typed host languages such that only well-typed EDSL terms are well-typed in the host languages solves this problem. Not only can we rule out type errors statically using the host language compiler, but also provide typing information which may help host language compiler optimize EDSL code without even knowing that the code is written in an EDSL. However, typed embedding of EDSLs is more complex as it can not be implemented directly by writing or extending the host language parser and type checker, but requires encoding EDSL terms as host language terms.

Functional vs Object-oriented (OO). In functional programming languages, the encoding of EDSL terms are usually nested calls to functions or constructors, which we call the functional nesting style (FNS) of embedding. It has been shown that functional programming languages are capable of typed encoding of EDSLs [6].

Few research has been done in nonfunctional OO programming languages. Method chaining style (MCS) programming is a unique idea in OO programming that is less known in the research community compared to ideas such as generalized algebraic data types (GADTs) [18,24]. In practice, MCS programming is supported by software libraries such as jMock [1] and Hibernate Criteria Query [14] to group logically related method calls into one compact piece of code and enforce rules how the methods should be used, as illustrated by the following example in Java.

Example 1. An example of Hibernate Criteria Query EDSL program [14].

```
1 List cats = sess.createCriteria(Cat.class)
2     .add( Restrictions.like("name", "Fritz%") )
3     .setFetchMode("mate", FetchMode.EAGER)
4     .setFetchMode("kittens", FetchMode.EAGER)
5     .list();
```

In this example, the method types are designed so that programmers can not make a query without specifying the collection to select from.

Manual Coding vs Automatic Code Generation. Manually coded MCS EDSLs in software libraries usually do not have a systematic way of encoding typed EDSLs. Also, when the rules for combining methods into method chains is complex, manual coding can be very tedious. As will be discussed in Sect. 4.2, MCS embedding essentially encodes an automaton that simulates a parser (and a type checker) of an EDSL on the type level of the host language, where classes represent states and methods represent transitions. Even in untyped EDSLs, encoding a complex automaton for an EDSL grammar that has many productions requires many classes and methods and any change to the grammar can result in changes of the classes and methods. Manually encoding EDSLs exposes this complexity to EDSL designers, while using a tool to generate EDSL embeddings encapsulates the complexity and allows EDSL designers to focus on the EDSL logic. However, there are few tools that support generating EDSL embeddings.

The Challenges. The main challenges in creating a general tool that supports automatic generation of encoding for a wide range of EDSLs are:

1. How to support both typed and untyped EDSLs;
2. How to support declarative specification of static semantics;
3. How to support mixing the FNS and the MCS;
4. How to support interoperability of EDSLs with host languages;
5. How to support nonfunctional OO host languages;
6. Can we reuse existing tools such as semantic editors without modification?

The EriLex Approach. The EriLex[1] approach is based on a generalized version of the MCS encoding which encodes statically both syntax and static semantics of EDSLs and supports mixing the MCS and the FNS in the encoding. EriLex generates support code for EDSLs from specifications written in the EriLex Specification Language (ESL). The type of the EDSLs are checked statically, based on the assumption that users do not modify, replace, or override the generated code. The MCS encoding is natural in OO programming languages as it models state transition systems which are coalgebraic structures that naturally fit into the OO programming paradigm. MCS encoding also allows EDSLs to reuse host language tools such as semantic editors.

This paper is organized as follows: Section 2 briefly overviews the tool; Section 3 presents features of the EriLex Specification Language using examples; Section 4 informally describes how the EriLex Code Generator (ECG) works; Section 5 discusses tool reuse, usability of EDSLs, and ESL as an EDSL; Section 6 discusses related work; Section 7 concludes the paper.

2   EriLex Overview

EriLex is composed of two main components, the EriLex Specification Language (ESL) and the EriLex Code Generator (ECG).

The high-level workflow of EriLex is illustrated in Fig. 1. The EDSL designer specifies the syntax and semantics of an EDSL in a specification written in the ESL. Then, the EDSL designer runs the ECG which generates from the specification the source code for the EDSL library, called the support code,

---

[1] EriLex, its source code, and examples can be downloaded from
http://www.cs.unc.edu/~xuh/erilex

that implements the syntax and semantics of the EDSL in the host language, so that an EDSL user can write EDSL programs (as method chains of the host language) according to the specification. To run an EDSL program that an EDSL user writes, the EDSL user compiles the EDSL program and the support code using the host language compiler and run the compiled program using the host language runtime.

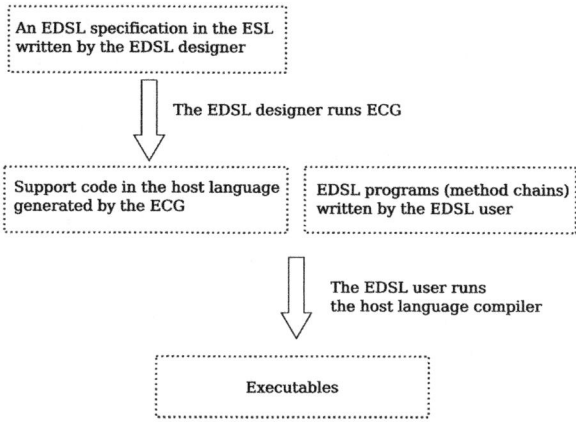

Fig. 1. EriLex workflow

EriLex embeds EDSL tokens as host language methods, and EDSL terms as host language method chains. For every EDSL specification, the ECG generates two methods: `prog` and `run`, which are used, respectively, to start and end a method chain. When a method chain is executed, the generated support code builds an abstract syntax tree (AST) of the EDSL term and evaluates the AST according to the specification of the EDSL. In the next section, we discuss how to specify the syntax and semantics of an EDSL in the ESL.

3 EriLex Specification Language

3.1 A Basic EDSL Example

Example 2. Natural numbers.

```
1 syntax e
2 e -> zero
3 e -> succ e
4
5 dynamic
6 eval: Integer
```

```
7 e -> zero {
8     return 0;
9 }
10 e -> succ e {
11     return eval(e)+1;
12 }
```

A minimal specification of an EDSL is composed of two sections for syntax and dynamic semantics, respectively.

The syntax section (Line 1 to Line 3) starts with `syntax` and consists of a definition of an LL(1) context-free grammar. The symbol that follows `syntax` is the start symbol. Each line in this section of the form nt -> t s_1 ... s_n defines a production of the grammar, where nt is a nonterminal, t is a terminal, and s_k is either a terminal or a nonterminal for all $k \in \{1, \ldots, n\}$. In the support code, the production defines a method t and the context-free grammar defines how the defined methods can be composed to form valid method chains.

The dynamic semantics section (Line 5 to Line 12) starts with `dynamic` and consists of definitions of evaluators. A definition of an evaluator starts with a line of the form $eval : htype$, where $eval$ is the name of the evaluator and $htype$ is the return type of the evaluator, followed by definitions of the form P { host language code } which defines a component of the evaluator for terms produced by production P. In the host language code, the nonterminals on the right hand side of the production can be used as variables and $eval$ can be used as a method.

Running the ECG on this specification generates several classes, one of which is a `Utils` class which has the `prog` method. For the nonterminal e, a class `Ee` is generated where E is the default prefix for generated classes for nonterminals. The `Ee` class has methods `zero`, `succ`, and `run`. An example of programs in this EDSL is `prog().succ().succ().succ().succ().zero().run()`.

3.2   A Simple Typed EDSL

Example 3. Adding boolean values and conditional expressions to Example 2.

```
1  syntax e
2  e -> zero
3  e -> succ e
4  e -> true
5  e -> false
6  e -> if e then e else e
7
8  dynamic
9  eval: Object
10 e -> zero {
11     return 0;
12 }
13 e -> succ e {
14     return (Integer)eval(e)+1;
15 }
16 e -> true {
17     return true;
18 }
19 e -> false {
20     return false;
21 }
22 e -> if e1 then e2 else e3 {
23     return ((Boolean)eval(e1))?
               eval(e2):eval(e3);
24 }
```

Most of the specification are similar to Example 2 except for the last component of the evaluator, in which different occurrences of the nonterminal e are renamed to avoid ambiguity (Line 22 to Line 24). In general, ESL allows renaming the occurrences of nonterminal on the right hand side of the productions to new names. Also, in the generated code, host language keywords such as if, then, else, etc. are renamed by converting their first letters to uppercase.

The generated EDSL works but may cause a runtime type error at a type cast such as on Line 23 when e1 is a natural number. To solve this problem, ESL allows specifying types and typing rules for the EDSL. We add a static section that defines two types, bool and nat, and typing rules to the specification.

```
 1 static
 2 type
 3 ty -> bool
 4 ty -> nat
 5 ty -> t : var
 6 typing e : t
 7
 8 ----------
 9 e -> zero : nat
10
11 e : nat
12 ----------
13 e -> succ e : nat

14
15 ----------
16 e -> true : bool
17
18 ----------
19 e -> false : bool
20
21 e : bool
22 e : t
23 e : t
24 ----------
25 e -> if e then e else e : t
```

Here we show only the static section where the types and typing rules are defined. The static section starts with static and has two subsections (in this example).

The first subsection (Line 2 to Line 5), which starts with type, specifies the grammar of types in the typing rules in a similar fashion as in the syntax section. Here not only do we need to specify the types of the EDSL, which are bool and nat, but also meta variable t used in the typing rules. A meta variable is not part of the type system of the EDSL, but a placeholder for types of the EDSL in the typing rules; in general, all meta variables used in the typing rules need to be defined. The : var construct following a production defines a meta variable.

The second subsection (Line 6 to Line 25), which starts with typing e : t, consists of typing rules. e : t indicate that an EDSL program can have any type. Alternatively, we may specify that an EDSL program must have the nat type by e : nat. In general, one can write $nt : C$, where nt is a nonterminal defined in the syntax section, and C is a type defined in the type subsection.

A typing rule definition consists of zero or more lines of antecedents, a line of dashes, and one line of postcedent. The line of postcedent has the form $P : C$, where C is defined as before and P is a production from the syntax section. Each line of the antecedent has the form $B : C$, where C is defined as before and B is a nonterminal that occurs in P. Each typing rule is written in the ESL in a similar way to the way they are usually written, as shown in Fig. 2.

ECG generates the support code so that only well-typed EDSL program can be compiled. (cf. Sect. 4.3)

$$\frac{e : nat}{succ\ e : nat}$$

```
e : nat
-----------
e -> succ e : nat
```

Fig. 2. Comparison of a typing rule and its specification

3.3 Native Values and Types

The ESL allows using native types in an EDSL specification.

Example 4. Native values and types.

```
1  syntax e
2  e ->  int(i)
3  e ->  bool(b)
4  e -> if e then e else e
5  i : nat
6  b : nat
7
8  static
9  definition
10  i : Integer
11  b : Boolean
12
13  type
14  ty -> t : var
15  typing e : t
16
17  ----------
18  e ->  int(i) : Integer
19
20  ----------

21  e ->  bool(b) : Boolean
22
23  e : Boolean
24  e : t
25  e : t
26  ----------
27  e -> if e then e else e : t
28
29  dynamic
30  eval: Object
31  e -> int(i) {
32      return i;
33  }
34  e -> bool(b) {
35      return b;
36  }
37  e -> if e1 then e2 else e3 {
38      return ((Boolean)eval(e1))?
            eval(e2):eval(e3);
39  }
```

Recall that each production in the syntax section defines a method. On Line 2 and Line 3, two methods are defined. Unlike in previous examples where the methods do not have any parameter, each one of these two methods has one parameter, which are declared as native on Line 5 and Line 6, respectively. For a nonterminal nt, nt : nat declares that nt is a native value. We also added a section starting with definition (Line 9) which defines the types of native values. A method chain written in this EDSL looks like If().bool(true, BOOLEAN).Then ().Int(1, INTEGER).Else().Int(0, INTEGER), where BOOLEAN and INTEGER are generated constants used to mark EDSL types. A type marker is required for any subterm whose typing rule has a postcedent in which the type is not a meta variable as shown on Line 17 to Line 21. We discuss how the requirement of these type markers may be eliminated in Sect. 5.

For EDSLs that support functions, native function wrappers are generated, as shown in the following example.

Example 5. Native function wrappers.

```
 1 syntax
 2 e -> cons(n)
 3 e -> app e e
 4 n : nat
 5
 6 static
 7 type
 8 ty -> t : var
 9 ty -> v : var
10 ty -> fun ty ty  : fun
11 typing f : t
12
13 n : t
14 -----------
15 e -> cons(n) : t
16
17 e : fun v t
18 e : v
19 -----------
20 e -> app e e : t
21
22 dynamic
23 eval:Object
24 e -> cons(n) {
25      return n;
26 }
27 e -> app e1 e2 {
28      return ((fun)eval(e1)).app
               (eval(e2));
29 }
```

On Line 10, the production is marked using : fun, which makes ECG generate an app method in abstract class fun, and abstract classes fun2 and fun3 for binary and tertiary functions.

For example, we can define the variable max as

```
1 fun2<Double,Double,Double> max=new fun2<Double,Double,Double>()
      {
2    public Double app(Double a,Double b) {
3        return Math.max(a,b);
4    }
5 }
```

which can be used as an EDSL function of type fun Double fun Double Double so that we can write method chains such as <Double>app().cons(max).cons (1.0).

3.4 Typing Environments for Higher Order Functions

In this section, we use the simply typed lambda calculus (STLC) with de Bruijn indices as an example to show how to specify a typed EDSL with higher order functions in the ESL.

Example 6. STLC terms can be written in a nameless form using de Bruijn indices. For example, the STLC term $\lambda x.x$ can be written as $\lambda 0$, and the STLC term $\lambda x \lambda y \lambda z.x(yz)$ can be written as $\lambda \lambda \lambda.2(10)$. Furthermore, de Bruijn indices can be represented by Peano numbers, in which the z constructor represents number 0 and the s constructor represents the function $f(x) = x + 1$, so that the term $\lambda x \lambda y . yx$ can be written as $\lambda \lambda . z\ sz$. Next, we specify a simple MCS EDSL so that we can embed STLC terms as method chains.

```
 1 syntax e                        23
 2 e -> z                          24 E |- i : t
 3 e -> s i                        25 -----------
 4 e -> abs e                      26 push E v |- e -> s i : t
 5 e -> app e e                    27
 6 i -> z                          28 push E v |- e : w
 7 i -> s i                        29 -----------
 8                                 30 E |- e -> abs e : fun v w
 9 static                          31
10 type                           32 E |- e : fun v t
11 ty -> t : var                  33 E |- e : v
12 ty -> v : var                  34 -----------
13 ty -> w : var                  35 E |- e -> app e e : t
14 ty -> fun ty ty                36
15 environment                    37 -----------
16 env -> E : var                 38 push E t |- i -> z : t
17 env -> emp                     39
18 env -> push env ty             40 E |- i : t
19 typing emp |- e : t            41 -----------
20                                42 push E v |- i -> s i : t
21 -----------                    43
22 push E t |- e -> z : t         44 dynamic
                                   45 ...
```

Let us take a closer look at the static section. A new subsection (Line 15 to Line 18) starting with environment is added to specify the grammar for typing environments in the typing rules. In this example, a typing environment is modeled as a stack of types. The typing rules include typing environments. A postcedent has the form $A\ |\text{-}\ P\ :\ C$ and a line of an antecedent has the form $A\ |\text{-}\ B\ :\ C$, where A is a typing environment and C, B, and P are defined in the same manner as in Sect. 3.2.

3.5 Parametrized Grammar

The functional nesting style (FNS) is frequently used in functional programming languages. In the FNS, EDSL programs are embedded into host languages as nested functions or constructors. An example of the FNS is sub(add(cons (1),cons(2)),cons(4)). Example 1 from Sect. 1 also uses FNS on Line 2. EriLex supports specifying EDSLs that mix the MCS and the FNS, by utilizing "parametrized grammars".

Let $z, z_1, \ldots, z_n$ denote nonterminals and a denote terminals.

Definition 1. *A* parametrized grammar *is a context-free grammar in the Greibach Normal Form, equipped with an* arity *function that maps every production* $z \to az_1 \ldots z_n$ *in the grammar to an integer* p *between* 0 *and* n. $z_1, \ldots, z_p$ *are parameters (of* a*).* $z_{p+1}, \ldots, z_n$ *are nonparameters. A parametrized grammar also requires that the group of parameters and the group of nonparameters be disjoint.*

We usually write $z \to a(z_1 \ldots z_p) \ldots z_n$ if $z_1 \ldots z_p$ are parameters. Disjointness means that a nonterminal can not be both a parameter and a nonparameter.

Example 7. For example, $e \to var(i), i \to z, i \to s(i)$ a parametrized grammar.

In the generated support code, parameters are translated to formal arguments of methods, as illustrated in the following example.

Example 8. An EDSL in the FNS.

```
 1 syntax p                      14 p -> expr(e) {
 2 p -> expr(e)                  15     return eval(e);
 3 e -> int(n)                   16 }
 4 e -> add(e e)                 17 e -> int(n) {
 5 e -> sub(e e)                 18     return n;
 6 n : nat                       19 }
 7                               20 e -> add(e1 e2) {
 8 static                        21     return eval(e1) + eval(e2);
 9 definition                    22 }
10 n : Integer                   23 e -> sub(e1 e2) {
11                               24     return eval(e1) + eval(e2);
12 dynamic                       25 }
13 eval:Integer
```

The ESL supports parametrized grammar through a simple form as demonstrated on Line 2 where the nonterminal e is made a parameter. We have seen this form in Example 4 , where the `Int` method has a parameter i which has type `Integer`. As shown on Line 4, the ESL also supports more than one parameters. An example of programs in the EDSL is `prog().expr(sub(add(Int(1),Int(2)), Int(4))).run()`.

3.6   An Example: SQL That Uses Prepared Statements

SQL injection is one of the common risks that web applications are exposed to. A robust way to prevent SQL injection is to use prepared statements. In this example, we show an EDSL defined using the ESL that automatically generates prepared statements to prevent SQL injection.

Example 9. Using this EDSL we can write queries that look like:

```
1 use(con).select("*").from("A").where().column("f").eq().string(in)
```

where in is a variable that contains the user input and con is a variable that holds the connection to the database.

First, to make use of the native database connection type, we define the following:

```
1 syntax
2 e -> use(conn) stmt
3 ...
4 definition
5 conn : java.sql.Connection
```

Second, we define the evaluator of the EDSL as follows. We are showing only the evaluator component for the e production.

```
1 eval: Object vars: java.util.ArrayList<Pair<String,Object>>
2 e -> use(conn) stmt {
3    ...
4    String sql = (String)eval(stmt,vars);
5    java.sql.PreparedStatement pstmt = conn.prepareStatement(sql);
6    for(int i=0;i<vars.size();i++) {
7       Pair<String, Object> var = vars.get(i);
8       if(var.fst.equals("string")) {
9          pstmt.setString(i+1, (String)var.snd);
10      } else if(var.fst.equals("int")) {
11         pstmt.setInt(i+1, (Integer)var.snd);
12      }
13   }
14   ...
15 }
```

The evaluator uses the state variable `vars` to store the types and values of input from the user. Line 4 evaluates `stmt`, generating an SQL string with place holders for input values. Then, a prepared statement is created using this SQL string on Line 5 and the input values are filled in, avoiding SQL injection. Using this EDSL, which is closer to the SQL than the interface of the `PreparedStatement` class, programmers do not need to know about prepared statements at all.

4   EriLex Code Generator

4.1   ECG Overview

The ECG takes in an EDSL specification and generates an in memory data structure that represents the support code from which the actual code of the host language is generated. There are two kinds of classes that are generated by EriLex.

– Utility classes such as `Utils`, which provides utility methods and data structures that are largely the same for all EDSLs.
– EDSL-specific classes consisting of
  • classes that represent syntax and typing rules of the EDSL,
  • classes for ASTs, and
  • evaluators.

The ECG requires that the generation target support basic OO features such as classes and methods and generics to the level of Java. Most mainstream OO programming language would qualify.

In this section, we focus on the classes that represent syntax and typing rules of the EDSL. Other kinds of classes are straightforward to construct.

4.2   Generated Support Code for Untyped EDSLs

The general idea of code generation is that for each grammar of EDSL defined in the ESL, there is a corresponding stateless deterministic realtime pushdown automaton (pda for short) that is equivalent to the grammar, and that for that pda, the ESL generates a set of classes representing its transition rules. By transitivity, methods in the generated classes can only be composed in the way that is specified by the grammar. [26]

The pda can be constructed by taking the nonterminals to be the stack symbols and viewing a production $nt \to t \ nt_1 \ \ldots \ nt_n$ as a transition rule that pops nt, pushes $nt_1, \ldots, nt_n$, and is labeled t, so that there is a one-one mapping from transition rules to productions. To represent transition rules, the ECG generates for each nonterminal a generic class that has one type parameter, which is used to construct types for representing the stacks in pda configurations. The ECG also generates a special class, written $\bot$ (Java name Bot), for representing the empty stack. For example, suppose that for nonterminal z, z_1, and z_2, the generated classes are $e_z<\kappa>$, $e_{z_1}<\kappa>$, and $e_{z_2}<\kappa>$, where κ is the type parameter. The type $e_z<e_{z_1}<e_{z_2}<\bot>>>$ represents the pda configuration with z, z_1, and z_2 on the stack.

Next, we discuss the representation of transition rules. In general, a generated method represents a transition rule of the pda: the method name represents the label; the object type in which the method is defined represents the originating configurations; and the return type of the method represents the target configurations. For example, suppose that $e_z<\kappa>$ has two methods with signatures shown below

```
1    public κ a();
2    public ez1<ez2<κ>> b();
```

Method a represents a transition rule $z \to a$ (that pops z and is labeled a), and method b represents a transition rule $z \to bz_1z_2$ (that pops z, pushes z_1, z_2, and is labeled b). Suppose that the originating configuration of the pda is represented by $e_z<\bot>$. Calling method a (resp. method b) on an object of this type transits the pda to the configuration $\bot$ (resp. $e_{z_1}<e_{z_2}<\bot>>$), as shown in Fig. 3(a) (resp. 3(b)).

A method chain represents a sequence of transitions in the pda. The type of any prefix of the method chain represents the configuration of the pda as a result of the transitions represented by the prefix. Next, we look at a concrete example.

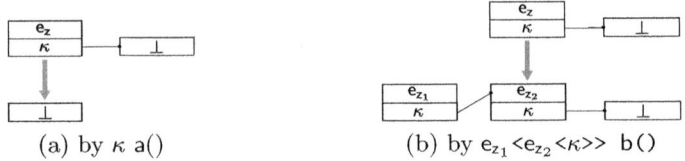

(a) by κ a()   (b) by e_{z_1}<e_{z_2}<κ>> b()

Fig. 3. Transitions from e_z<$\perp$>

Example 10. We look at a generated class for Example 2. Here we show the method signatures only.

```
1 public class Ee<K> {
2     public K zero();
3     public Ee<K> succ();
4 }
```

It is obvious that int val = prog().succ().zero().run(); does not generate error messages, while int val = prog().zero().zero().run(); generates an error message that says that the second zero method is not defined.

4.3 Generated Support Code for Typed EDSLs

Pdas are not expressive enough for representing both syntax and typing rules. Instead, we utilize pdas with storage [9]. A pda with storage is an extension of a pda that allows attaching "storage" to the stack symbols. For example, in a pda with storage where the stack symbols are exactly the nonterminals, we may attach to them "storage" that are typing environments and types of the subterms produced by those nonterminals.

The general idea of code generation is that for each set of typing rules (which subsumes the grammar since they are syntax-directed) of an EDSL defined in the ESL, there is a corresponding pda with storage that is equivalent to the typing rules, and that for that pda with storage, the ESL generates a set of classes representing its transition rules. [26]

Each typing rule can be viewed as a transition rule of the pda with storage, where the postcedent corresponds to originating configurations while the antecedents correspond to target configurations. The production that is subsumed by the typing rule governs the label and the stack while the types and typing environments govern the storage.

Similar to untyped encoding, the ECG generates a method for each transition rule: the method name represents the label; the object type in which the method is defined represents the originating configurations; and the return type of the method represents the target configurations.

Example 11. Now we look at some of the generated classes for a typed EDSL based on Example 6 extended with a cons construct that introduces a native value.

```
1 syntax
2 e -> cons(n)
3 n : nat
4
5 static
```

```
6 typing
7 E |- n : t
8 ----------
9 E |- e -> cons(n) : t
10 ...
```

Here we show the method signatures only.

```
1 public class fun<t1, t2> {}
2 public class push<t1, t2> {}
3 public class emp {}
4 public class Bot {}
5 public class Utils {
6     public static <t> Ee<Bot,t,emp> prog();
7 }
8 public class F<S,T> { ... }
9 public class ID<S> extends F<S,S> { ... }
10 public class Ee<K,t,E> {
11     public t cons(t n);
12     public <w,v> Ee<K,w,push<E,v>> abs(F<fun<v,w>,t> cast);
13     public <v> Ee<Ee<K,v,E>,fun<v,t>,E> app();
14 }
15 public class Ei<K,t,E> {
16     public <E1> K z(F<push<E1,t>,E> cast);
17     public <E1,v> Ei<K,t,E1> s(F<push<E1,v>,E> cast);
18 }
```

For each terminal symbol that appears in the `type` and `environment` section of the specification, a class is generated as shown on Line 1 to Line 3. But no class is generated for meta variables. The `fun`, `push`, and `emp` classes serve as constructors of host language types that represent EDSL types and typing environments. The `Bot` class represents the empty pda stack. The `F<S,T>` utility class and the `ID<S>` utility class which extends `F<S,S>` are used to encode type equality.

The generated class `Ee` has three type parameters. The first type parameter is the same as that in support code generated for an untyped EDSL. The other type parameters represent the "storage", where the second type parameter represents the type of (the subterm produced by) the nonterminal and the third parameter represents the typing environment of (the subterm produced by) the nonterminal.

Figure 4 shows the correspondence between the method signature and the typing rule (transition rule) for production `e -> abs e`, where the corresponding parts of the typing rule and the method signature are connected by connectors. In a pda with storage, the applicability of a transition rule depends on not only the top stack symbol of the originating configuration, but also the "storage" attached to that symbol, which in our application, is the type and typing environment given in the postcedent of the typing rule (recall that the postcedent corresponds to the originating configuration). The encoding of this dependency is a little complex when the type in the postcedent is not a metavariable, as shown in Fig. 4(a) where, when translated to the transition rule, the requirement is that the type in the "storage" attached to the top stack symbol be `fun v w` as specified in the postcedent. Because Java does not support a straightforward way of specifying the structure of a type parameter of the class, the ECG has to generate the `cast` parameter and require EDSL users to pass in an instance of `ID<fun<v,w>>` when `abs` is called, which says, intuitively, that the type parameter t should have the structure `fun<v,w>`. Given the argument, the host language will statically generate the subtyping constraint `ID<fun<v,w>><:F<fun<v,w>,t>`, which enforces the type equality `fun<v,w>=t`.

```
public class Ee<K,t,E>{
    public <w,v> Ee<K,w,push<E,v>> abs(F<fun<v,w>,t> cast);
}
push E v |- e : w
------------
E |- e -> abs e : fun v w
```
(a) Postcedent

```
public class Ee<K,t,E>{
    public <w,v> Ee<K,w,push<E,v>> abs(F<fun<v,w>,t> cast);
}
push E v |- e : w
----------
E |- e -> abs e : fun v w
```
(b) Antecedent

Fig. 4. Encoding of typing rules

As an example showing how this encoding works, suppose that we have a prefix of method chains `<Integer>prog()` with type `Ee<Bot,Integer,emp>` which represents a stack with only one symbol e with attached storage `Integer,emp`, which means that the type of the stack symbol is `Integer`. If we append a method call to `app` to the prefix, the type of the new prefix `<Integer>prog().<Double>app()` becomes `Ee<Ee<Bot,Double,emp>,fun<Double,Integer>,emp>`, as shown in Fig. 5, which represents a stack with two symbols which are both e with attached storage, respectively, `fun<Double,Integer>,emp` and `Double,emp`, which means that the type of the top stack symbol (resp. second stack symbol) is `fun Double Integer` (resp. `Double`). Therefore, the following

```
1 <Integer>prog().<Double>app().cons(1).run();
```

has a type error, while the following does not have any type error.

```
1 ID<fun<Double,Integer>> tyF = new ID<fun<Double,Integer>>();
2 <Integer>prog().<Double>app().abs(tyF).cons(1).cons(2.0).run();
```

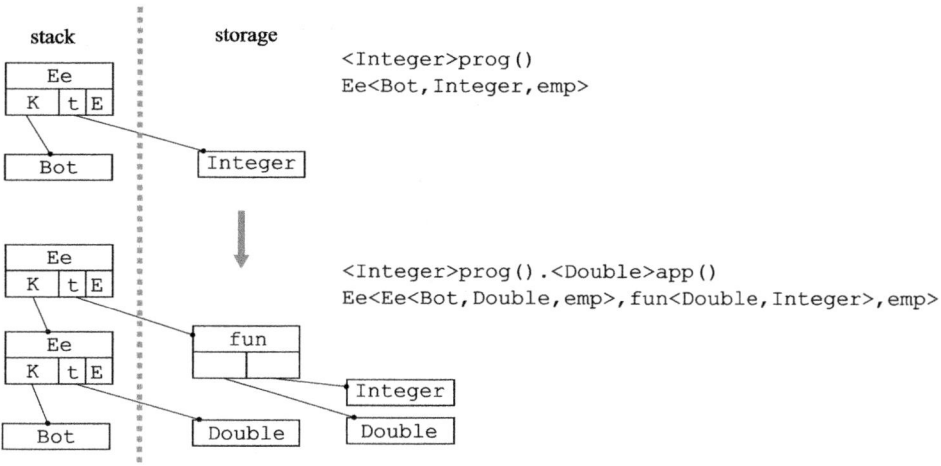

Fig. 5. Encoding pda with storage

5   Discussions

Tool Reuse Reuse is one of the fundamental goals of software design. EriLex takes a first step towards editor reuse. Why is editor reuse important? According to the online report from Netbeans Quality Dashboard [3][2], the Netbeans Integrated Development Environment (IDE) has over 4,000,000 lines of code. While developer tools such as IDEs are an important factor in the popularity of a programing language, the workload for programming a tool for a new programming language can be prohibitively heavy. Therefore, both the expertise and efforts in the existing tools are simply too large a resource to be left un-reused. Three kinds of common tool support – syntax checking during typing, type checking during typing, and auto-completion – are provided in the semantic editor of Netbeans for Java. The MCS effectively establishes the mappings as shown in Table 1, which allows MCS EDSLs to reuse functions provided by the semantic editor without any modification to the IDE.

Table 1. Mappings

Tool Support	auto-completion		checking during typing	
EDSL	parser state	next tokens	syntax	type
host language	class type	methods	syntax/type	type

Improving Usability of EDSLs. The usability of an EDSL is highly dependent on the capabilities of the host language. We use Java as the main host language for EriLex because it has mature developer tools and large user base. However,

---

[2] Data may change as Netbeans is an open source software under active development.

the previous examples also show that we can improve the usability of EDSLs if we can improve the host language in the following aspects:

1. The symbols "(", ")", and "." can not be omitted.
2. Operators can not be use as method names.
3. Without type inference, type arguments need to be written explicitly.
4. Overloaded methods can not have the same parameter type but different return type. This restricts all grammars to LL(1).
5. Error messages are very difficult to parse or translate to those of EDSLs. If an error occurs, it is very difficult to locate the error.

We propose the following improvements to the host language.

1. Make the syntax flexible.
2. Infer type arguments for methods automatically.
3. Support the `where` construct [13] with which the ECG can generate code without `cast`, for example, `public <w,v> Ee<K,w,push<e,v>> abs()where fun<v,w>=t;`
4. Support (nondisjoint) union types so that we can simulate nondeterminism.
5. Provide an interface for writing customized error message generator.

Improvement 1 and 2 are already partially or completely supported by Scala [8]. Improvement 3 has also been shown to be feasible in C♯ [13], but is not implemented in the current C♯ release. Improvement 4 may be difficult to implement because of the interaction with other features in Java. Improvement 5 can be implemented in the following manner. We can write a external tool that reads and parses the output of the Java compiler and output the translated error messages. However, because there lacks a "specification" for compiler output, maintaining the tool would not be very easy.

ESL as an EDSL. Although it is easy to embed the ESL into Java in an untyped manner, typed embedding of the ESL turns out to be more difficult. Type checking an ESL specification is complex. For example, we need to check that terms that appear in the typing rules conform to the syntax of terms. Also, to avoid embedding the host language into the host language, we need to define a host language neutral symbolic transformer language for specifying dynamic semantics of EDSLs. The current experimental solution (under development) consists of the following:

- Make ESL host language neutral, and complement it using host language methods as native functions.
- Divide the language specification into three phases: syntax, typing, and transformers; and divide the specification language into three subsets: syntax, typing, and transformers, accordingly.
- In each phase, specialize the general version of the subset of the specification language used in the current phase with specifications from the previous phases.

In the first phase, the designer specifies the syntax of the EDSL terms, type, and typing environments using a general embedded syntax specification language. In the second phase, the designer run the typing language specializer, which generates a specialized embedded version of the typing language so that only well-formed EDSL terms, types, and typing environments can be written. Using the specialized type language, the designer defines the typing rules. In the third phase, the designer runs the transformer language specializer, which generates a specialized embedded version of the transformer language so that only well-formed and well-typed EDSL terms can be written. Using the specialized transformer language, the designer defines transformers.

6   Related Work

Implementation patterns for executable DSLs can be categorized as follows: interpreter, compiler/application generator, preprocessor, embedding, extensible compiler/interpreter, commercial off-the-shelf, and hybrid. [16]

JTS [4], MontiCore [11], and MetaBorg [5] generate from a language specification preprocessors that translate from the extended host language syntax to the basic host language syntax. Many of these approaches provide specification languages or meta language constructs for defining languages, language extensions, or language compositions. Although these approaches have more flexibility, preprocessors are needed when the DSL code is compiled. The preprocessors and host language grammars used to generate the preprocessors need to be updated whenever the host language syntax changes.

Converge [23] provides language constructs that support delimited DSL blocks which are processed by arbitrary user-defined functions at compile time. The functions can be interpreters, preprocessors, or both. Converge is flexible but may lead to undecidable compilation.

Compiler/application generators such as ASF+SDF [15] and Meta Programming System [2] generate compilers and tools such as editors for DSLs from a language specification.

Extensible compilers/interpreters such as Language Boxes/Helvetia [20], XMF [7], and Katahdin [21] allow extending the host language with new constructs for defining internal DSLs. Language Boxes, which is implemented on top of the extensible compiler framework Helvetia, supports seamless extension to the host language (Smalltalk) by defining extensions to host language grammar defined in PEG and transformation on AST nodes. It supports tool reuse such as syntax highlighting and debugging by extending the tools of the host language. XMF is a language that allows defining DSLs at run time. It provides meta language constructs for defining DSLs and delimiting DSL blocks. Katahdin is also a dynamically typed scripting language that allows seamless extension of the host language at runtime based on PEG. In all of these approaches, extensibility of the host language is required. Also, in dynamically typed languages, which also include Ruby, type errors in EDSLs are captured at runtime.

Typed embedding of EDSLs captures type errors at compile time, which reduces the cost of software defect. Most of the research on typed EDSLs is on type safety and runtime efficiency (such as tagless interpreter) in the functional setting. Proposals for embedding typed languages into typed host languages include those based on GADT [24,18], dependent types (in D-Meta [17], DML [25], and MetaOCaml Concoqtion [10], to name a few), ordinary functions [6] (in ML, Haskell, or MetaOCaml), or higher order abstract syntax [19], which are all in the functional nesting style. Our approach differs from these approaches in that the FNS models an EDSL as an algebra with an additional typing structure attached to it (for example, GADTs can be thought of as ADTs with typing constraints), which naturally fits into functional programming languages, while the MCS models an EDSL as a state transition system which is a coalgebraic data structure, which naturally fits into OO programming languages. As mentioned in Sect. 1, in practice, there are manually coded MCS EDSLs but manually coding EDSLs distracts the EDSL designer with all the complexity of MCS encoding.

Ott [22] is a metalanguage designed for expressing semantics and a tool for compiling language specifications into proof assistant code, LATEX code, and type definitions, but is not designed for generating MCS encoding of EDSLs.

Our approach is also applicable in other OO programming languages such as C++. However, extensive use of type parameters may cause the compiled code to be very large in C++, as it creates a copy of a template for every different type argument. Languages that use erasure such as Scala and Java do not have this overhead.

7   Conclusion

In this paper, we presented EriLex, a software tool for generating support code for both typed and untyped EDSLs based on specifications written in the ESL. The ESL has very few constructs yet is expressive enough for a range of EDSLs. EriLex supports declarative specification of static semantics, mixing the FNS and the MCS, and using native types and values in the EDSL. EriLex only assume the basic object-oriented feature and generics in the host language and does not require any particular technology in the definition or implementation of host languages and tools. The generated code reuses not only the host language compilers but also the semantic editors. Future work includes finding usable way to define the dynamic semantics that is language neutral, and usably defining the typed ESL as an EDSL.

Acknowledgment

Many thanks to Lorenzo Bettini for his assistance and suggestions for improving the paper, anonymous referees and for their suggestions for improving the paper, and Lei Wei and David Plaisted for proofreading a draft of the paper.

References

1. jMock, http://www.jmock.org
2. Meta Programming System, http://www.jetbrains.com/mps/
3. Netbeans quality dashboard (2009),
   http://quality.netbeans.org/sourcelines/summary-teams.html
4. Batory, D., Lofaso, B., Smaragdakis, Y.: JTS: Tools for implementing domain-specific languages. In: ICSR '98, p. 143. IEEE Computer Society, Washington (1998)
5. Bravenboer, M., Visser, E.: Concrete syntax for objects: domain-specific language embedding and assimilation without restrictions. In: OOPSLA '04, pp. 365–383. ACM, New York (2004)
6. Carette, J., Kiselyov, O., Shan, C.c.: Finally tagless, partially evaluated: Tagless staged interpreters for simpler typed languages. J. Funct. Program. 19(5), 509–543 (2009)
7. Clark, T., Sammut, P., Willans, J.: Superlanguages, Developing Languages and Applications with XMF, 1st edn. Ceteva (2008)
8. Cremet, V., Garillot, F., Lenglet, S., Odersky, M.: A core calculus for Scala type checking. In: Královič, R., Urzyczyn, P. (eds.) MFCS 2006. LNCS, vol. 4162, pp. 1–23. Springer, Heidelberg (2006)
9. Engelfriet, J., Vogler, H.: Pushdown machines for the macro tree transducer. Theor. Comput. Sci. 42(3), 251–368 (1986)
10. Fogarty, S., Pasalic, E., Siek, J., Taha, W.: Concoqtion: indexed types now? In: PEPM '07, pp. 112–121. ACM, New York (2007)
11. Grönniger, H., Krahn, H., Rumpe, B., Schindler, M., Völkel, S.: MontiCore: a framework for the development of textual domain specific languages. In: ICSE Companion, pp. 925–926 (2008)
12. Hudak, P.: Building domain-specific embedded languages. ACM Computing Surveys 28 (1996)
13. Kennedy, A., Russo, C.V.: Generalized algebraic data types and object-oriented programming. In: OOPSLA '05, pp. 21–40. ACM, New York (2005)
14. King, G., Bauer, C., Andersen, M.R., Bernard, E., Ebersole, S.: Hibernate reference documentation 3.5.1 (2010), http://www.hibernate.org/docs.html
15. Klint, P.: A meta-environment for generating programming environments. In: Bergstra, J.A., Feijs, L.M.G. (eds.) Algebraic Methods 1989. LNCS, vol. 490, pp. 105–124. Springer, Heidelberg (1991)
16. Mernik, M., Heering, J., Sloane, A.M.: When and how to develop domain-specific languages. ACM Comput. Surv. 37(4), 316–344 (2005)
17. Pasalic, E., Taha, W., Sheard, T.: Tagless staged interpreters for typed languages. SIGPLAN Not. 37(9), 218–229 (2002)
18. Peyton Jones, S., Vytiniotis, D., Weirich, S., Washburn, G.: Simple unification-based type inference for GADTs. SIGPLAN Not. 41(9), 50–61 (2006)
19. Pfenning, F., Elliot, C.: Higher-order abstract syntax. In: PLDI '88, pp. 199–208. ACM, New York (1988)
20. Renggli, L., Denker, M., Nierstrasz, O.: Language Boxes: Bending the host language with modular language changes. In: SLE '09, pp. 274–293 (2009)
21. Seaton, C.: A programming language where the syntax and semantics are mutable at runtime. Tech. Rep. CSTR-07-005, University of Bristol (2007)
22. Sewell, P., Nardelli, F.Z., Owens, S., Peskine, G., Ridge, T., Sarkar, S., Strniša, R.: Ott: effective tool support for the working semanticist. In: ICFP '07, pp. 1–12. ACM, New York (2007)

23. Tratt, L.: The Converge programming language. Tech. Rep. TR-05-01, Department of Computer Science, King's College London (2005)
24. Xi, H., Chen, C., Chen, G.: Guarded recursive datatype constructors. SIGPLAN Not. 38(1), 224–235 (2003)
25. Xi, H., Scott, D.: Dependent types in practical programming. In: POPL '98, pp. 214–227. ACM Press, New York (1998)
26. Xu, H.: A general framework for method chaining style embedding of domain specific languages. UNC Technical Report (2009)

Domain-Specific Program Checking

Lukas Renggli[1], Stéphane Ducasse[2], Tudor Gîrba[3], and Oscar Nierstrasz[1]

[1] Software Composition Group, University of Bern, Switzerland
http://scg.unibe.ch/
[2] RMoD, INRIA-Lille Nord Europe, France
http://rmod.lille.inria.fr
[3] Sw-eng. Software Engineering GmbH, Switzerland
http://www.sw-eng.ch

Abstract. Lint-like program checkers are popular tools that ensure code quality by verifying compliance with best practices for a particular programming language. The proliferation of internal domain-specific languages and models, however, poses new challenges for such tools. Traditional program checkers produce many false positives and fail to accurately check constraints, best practices, common errors, possible optimizations and portability issues *particular to domain-specific languages*. We advocate the use of dedicated rules to check domain-specific practices. We demonstrate the implementation of domain-specific rules, the automatic repair of violations, and their application to two case-studies: (1) Seaside defines several internal DSLs through a creative use of the syntax of the host language; and (2) Magritte adds meta-descriptions to existing code by means of special methods. Our empirical validation demonstrates that domain-specific program checking significantly improves code quality when compared with general purpose program checking.

1   Introduction

The use of automatic program checkers to statically locate possible bugs and other problems in source code has a long history. While the first program checkers were part of the compiler, later on separate tools were written that performed more sophisticated analyses of code to detect possible problem patterns [Joh83]. The refactoring book [Fow99] made code smell detection popular, as an indicator to decide when and what to refactor.

Most modern development environments (IDEs) directly provide lint-like tools as part of their editors to warn developers about emerging problems in their source code. These checkers usually highlight offending code snippets on-the-fly and greatly enhance the quality of the written code. Contrary to a separate tool, IDEs with integrated program checkers encourage developers to write good code right from the beginning. Today's program checkers [HP04] reliably detect issues like possible bugs, portability issues, violations of coding conventions, duplicated, dead, or suboptimal code, *etc.*

Many software projects today use *domain-specific languages* (DSLs) to raise the expressiveness of the host language in a particular problem domain. A common approach is to derive a new pseudo-language from an existing API. This technique

J. Vitek (Ed.): TOOLS 2010, LNCS 6141, pp. 213–232, 2010.

is known as a *Fluent Interface*, a form of an *internal domain-specific language* or *embedded language* [Fow08]. Such languages are syntactically compatible with the host language, and use the same compiler and the same runtime infrastructure.

As such DSLs often make creative use of host language features with atypical use of its syntax. This confuses traditional program checkers and results in many false positives. For example, chains of method invocations are normally considered bad practice as they expose internal implementation details and violate the Law of Demeter [Lie89]. However in internal DSLs, method chaining is a commonly applied technique to invoke a sequence of calls on the same object where each call returns the receiver object for further calls. In other words, the DSL *abstracts* from the traditional use of the host language and introduces new idioms that are meaningful in the particular problem domain.

Traditional program checkers work at the level of source code. Tools like *intensional views* [MKPW06] and *reflexion models* [MNS95, KS03] check for structural irregularities and for conformance at an architectural level. Furthermore tools like *PathFinder* [HP00] have been used to transform source code into a model and apply model checking algorithms.

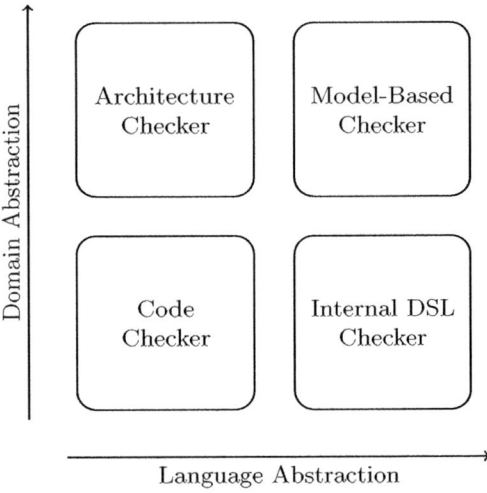

Fig. 1. Dimensions of program checking

Figure 1 depicts the dimensions of program checking. Traditional program checkers tackle the axis of *domain abstraction* at different levels. We argue that a different set of rules is necessary as developers *abstract from the host language*. Our thesis is that standard program checking tools are not effective when it comes to detecting problems in domain-specific code. In this paper we advocate the use of dedicated program checking rules for program that know about and check for the specific use-cases of internal domain-specific languages. As with traditional rules this can happen at the level of the source code or at a higher architectural or modeling level.

We will demonstrate two different rule-sets that each work at a different level of domain abstraction:

1. Seaside is an open-source web application framework written in Smalltalk [DLR07]. Seaside defines various internal DSLs to configure application settings, nest components, define the flow of pages, and generate XHTML. As part of his work as Seaside maintainer and as software consultants on various industrial Seaside projects, the first author developed *Slime*, a Seaside-specific program checker consisting of a set of 30 rules working at the level of the abstract syntax tree (AST). We analyze the impact of these rules on a long term evolution of Seaside itself and of applications built on top of it.

2. Magritte is a recursive metamodel integrated into the reflective metamodel of Smalltalk [RDK07]. The metamodel of an application is specified by implementing annotated methods that are automatically called by Magritte to build a representative metamodel of the system. This metamodel is then used to automate various tasks such as editor construction, data validation, and persistency. As the metamodel is part of the application source code it cannot be automatically verified. We have implemented a set of 5 rules that validate such a Magritte metamodel against its meta-metamodel.

Our approach to program checking is based on AST pattern matching. This technical aspect is not new. However, our approach builds on that and offers a way to specify declaratively domain specific rules with possible automatic transformations. Our approach uses pattern matching on the AST as supported by the refactoring engine of Smalltalk [BFJR98]. Furthermore we use HELVE-TIA [RGN10], a framework to cleanly extend development tools of the standard Smalltalk IDE. It reuses the existing toolchain of editor, parser, compiler and debugger by leveraging the AST of the host environment. While HELVETIA is applicable in a much broader context to implement and transparently embed new languages into a host language, in this paper we focus on the program analysis and transformation part of it.

The contributions of this paper are: (1) the identification of the need for DSL specific rule checking, (2) the empirical validation over a long period that such DSL specific rules offer advantages over non domain-specific ones, and (3) an infrastructure to declaratively specify domain specific rules and the optional automatic transformations of violations.

The paper is structured as follows: Section 2 introduces the different rule-sets we have implemented. We present the internal domain-specific languages addressed by our rules, and we discuss how we implemented and integrated the rules. In Section 3 we report on our experience of applying these rules on various open-source and commercial systems. Furthermore we present a user survey where we asked developers to compare domain-specific rules with traditional ones. Section 4 discusses related work and Section 5 concludes.

2   Examples of Domain-Specific Rules

In this section we demonstrate two sets of rules at different levels of abstraction: while the first set of rules (Section 2.1) works directly on the source code of web applications, the second set of rules (Section 2.2) uses a metamodel and validates it against the system. While in both cases the source code is normal Smalltalk, we focus on the domain-specific use of the language in these two contexts.

2.1   Syntactic Rules for Seaside

The most prominent use of an internal DSL in Seaside is the generation of HTML. This DSL is built around a stream-like object that understands messages to create different XHTML tags. Furthermore the tag objects understand messages to add the HTML attributes to the generated markup. These attributes are specified using a chain of message sends, known in the Smalltalk jargon as a cascade.[1]

```
1 html div
2     class: 'large';
3     with: count.
4 html anchor
5     callback: [ count := count + 1 ];
6     with: 'increment'.
```

The above code creates the following HTML markup:

```
<div class="large">0</div>
<a src="/?_s=28hVYPUhdMM7mU&1">increment</a>
```

Lines 1–3 are responsible for the generation of the `div` tag with the CSS class `large` and the value of the current `count` as the contents of the tag. Lines 4–6 generate the link with the label *increment*. The `src` attribute is provided by Seaside. Clicking the link automatically evaluates the code on line 5 and redisplays the component.

---

[1] Readers unfamiliar with the syntax of Smalltalk might want to read the code examples aloud and interpret them as normal sentences: An invocation to a method named `method:with:`, using two arguments looks like: `receiver method: arg1 with: arg2`. The semicolon separates cascaded messages that are sent to the same receiver. For example, `receiver method1: arg1; method2: arg2` sends the messages `method1:` and `method2:` to `receiver`. Other syntactic elements of Smalltalk are: the dot to separate statements: `statement1. statement2`; square brackets to denote code blocks or anonymous functions: `[ statements ]`; and single quotes to delimit strings: `'a string'`. The caret `^` returns the result of the following expression.

This *little language* [DK97] for HTML generation is the most prominent use of a DSL in Seaside. It lets developers abstract common HTML patterns into convenient methods rather than pasting the same sequence of tags into templates every time.

As developers and users of Seaside we have observed that while the HTML generation is simple, there are a few common problems that repeatedly appear in the source code of contributors. We have collected these problems and categorized them into 4 groups: possible bugs, non-portable code between different Smalltalk platforms/versions, bad style, and suboptimal code. Spotting such problems early in the development cycle can significantly improve the code quality, maintainability and might avoid hard to detect bugs. We offer details for a case from each group.

Possible Bugs. This group of rules detects severe problems that are most certainly serious bugs in the source code:

- The message `with:` is not last in the cascade,
- Instantiates new component while generating HTML,
- Manually invokes `renderContentOn:`,
- Uses the wrong output stream,
- Misses call to super implementation,
- Calls functionality not available while generating output, and
- Calls functionality not available within a framework callback.

As an example of such a rule we take a closer look at "The message `with:` is not last in the cascade". While in most cases it does not matter in which order the attributes of a HTML tag are specified, Seaside requires the contents of a tag be specified last. This allows Seaside to directly stream the tags to the socket, without having to build an intermediate tree of DOM nodes. In the erroneous code below the order is mixed up:

```
html div
    with: count;
    class: 'large'.
```

One might argue that the design of the DSL could avoid this ordering problem in the first place. However, in the case of Seaside we reuse the existing syntax of the host language and we cannot change and add additional validation into the compiler, otherwise this would not be an internal DSL anymore.

Slime uses a declarative internal DSL to specify its rules. Every rule is implemented as a method in the class `SlimeRuleDatabase`. HELVETIA automatically collects the result of evaluating these methods to assemble a set of Slime rules. The following code snippet demonstrates the complete code necessary to implement the rule to check whether `with:` is the last message in the cascade:

```
1  SlimeRuleDatabase>>withHasToBeLastInCascade
2     ^ SlimeRule new
3        label: 'The message with: has to be last in the cascade';
4        search: (ConditionRule new
5           if: [ :context | context isHtmlGeneratingMethod ];
6           then: (TreeRule new
7              search: '`html `message with: ``@arguments';
8              condition: [ :node |
9                 node parent isCascade and: [ node isLastMessage not ] ]));
```

Line 2 instantiates the rule object, line 3 assigns a label that appears in the user interface and lines 4–9 define the actual search pattern.

The precondition on line 5 asserts statically that the code artifact under test is used by Seaside to generate HTML. The ConditionRule object lets developers scope rules to relevant parts of the software using the reflective API of the host language. This precondition reduces the number of false positives and greatly improves the performance of the rule.

Line 6 instantiates a TreeRule that performs a search on the AST for occurrences of statements that follow the pattern `html `message with: ``@arguments. Search patterns are specified using a string with normal Smalltalk expressions annotated with additional meta-characters. The back-tick ` marks meta-nodes that are not required to match literally but that are variable. Table 1 gives a description of the characters following the initial back-tick.

Table 1. Meta-characters for parse-tree pattern matching

Char	Type	Description
#	literal	Match a literal node like a number, boolean, string, etc.
.	statement	Match a statement in a sequence node.
@	list	When applied to a variable, match any expression. When applied to a statement, match a list of statements. When applied to a message, match a list of arguments.
`	recurse	When a match is found recurse into the matched node.

In our example it does not matter how the variable `html, the message `message: and the arguments ``@arguments are exactly named. Furthermore, ``@arguments is an arbitrary expression that is recursively searched. If a match is found, the AST node is passed into the closure on lines 8 and 9 to verify that the matched node is not the last one of the cascade.

When the Slime rules are evaluated by HELVETIA the matching AST nodes are automatically collected. Interested tools can query for these matches and reflect on their type and location in the code. The "Code Browser" depicted in Figure 2 highlights occurrences while editing code. Reporting tools can count, group and sort the issues according to severity. A more detailed description of the HELVETIA rule engine can be found in our related work [RGN10].

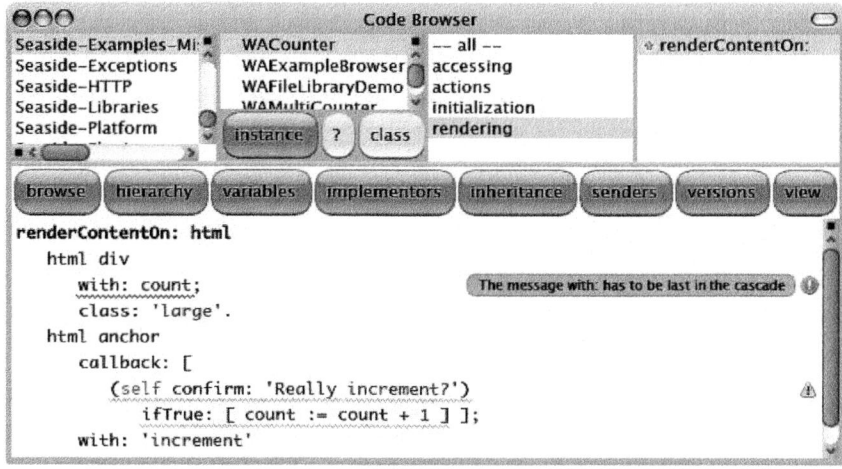

Fig. 2. Integration of domain-specific rules into the "Code Browser"

Many of the detected problems can be automatically fixed. Providing an automatic refactoring for the above rule is a matter of adding a transformation specification:

```
1        replace: [ :node |
2            node cascade
3                remove: node;
4                addLast: node ].
```

Lines 12 and 13 remove the matched node from the cascade and add it back to the end of the sequence. After applying the transformation HELVETIA automatically re-runs the search, to ensure that the transformation actually resolves the problem.

Again the tools from the IDE automatically offer the possibility to trigger such an automatic transformation. For example, when a developer right-clicks on a Slime issue in the "Code Browser" a confirmation dialog with a preview is presented before the transformation is applied. Furthermore it is possible to ignore and mark false positives, so that they do not show up again.

Bad style. These rules detect some less severe problems that might pose maintainability problems in the future but that do not cause immediate bugs. An example of such a rule is "Extract callback code to separate method". In the example below the rule proposes to extract the code within the callback into a separate method. This ensures that code related to controller functionality is kept separate from the view.

```
html anchor
    callback: [
        (self confirm: 'Really increment?')
            ifTrue: [ count := count + 1 ] ];
    with: 'increment'.
```

Other rules in this category include:

- Use of deprecated API, and
- Non-standard object initialization.

The implementation of these rules is similar to the one demonstrated in the previous section on "possible bugs".

Suboptimal Code. This set of rules suggests optimizations that can be applied to code without changing its behavior. For example, the following code triggers the rule "Unnecessary block passed to brush":

```
html div with: [ html text: count ]
```

The code could be rewritten as follows, but this triggers the rule "Unnecessary #with: sent to brush":

```
html div with: count
```

This in turn can be rewritten to the following code which is equivalent to the first version, but much shorter and more efficient as no block closure is activated:

```
html div: count
```

Non-Portable Code. While this set of rules is less important for application code, it is essential for the Seaside code base itself. The framework runs without modification on 7 different platforms (Pharo Smalltalk, Squeak Smalltalk, Cincom Smalltalk, GemStone Smalltalk, VA Smalltalk, GNU Smalltalk and Dolphin Smalltalk), which slightly differ in both the syntax and the libraries they support. To avoid that contributors using a specific platform accidentally submit code that only works on their platform we have added a number of rules that check for compatibility:

- Invalid object initialization,
- Uses curly brace arrays,
- Uses literal byte arrays,
- Uses method annotations,
- Uses non-portable class,
- Uses non-portable message,
- ANSI booleans,
- ANSI collections,
- ANSI conditionals,

- ANSI convertor,
- ANSI exceptions, and
- ANSI streams.

Code like `count asString` might not run on all platforms identically, as the convertor method `asString` is not part of the common protocol. Thus, if the code is run on a platform that does not implement `asString` the code might break or produce unexpected results.

The implementation and the automatic refactoring for this issue is particularly simple:

```
1 SlimeRuleDatabase>>nonPortableMessage
2      ^ SlimeRule new
3          label: 'Uses non-portable message';
4          search: '``@obj asString' replace: '``@obj seasideString';
5          search: '``@obj asInteger' replace: '``@obj seasideInteger'
```

Again the rule is defined in the class `SlimeRuleDatabase`. It consists of two matching patterns (line 4 and 5 respectively) and their associated transformation, so code like `count asString` will be transformed to `count seasideString`.

2.2   Magritte — Code Checking with a Metamodel

Constraint checking is not a new domain. Classic approaches rely on constraints that are specified by the analyst [MKPW06, MNS95, KS03] and that are checked against the actual application code. In this case these rules are external to the execution of the program. Model-driven designs often rely on a metamodel to add more semantics to the code by providing transformations that are either statically (via code generation) or dynamically interpreted. These metamodels come with a set of constraints that can also be used for checking the program.

Magritte is a metamodel that is used to automate various tasks such as editor building, data validation and persistency [RDK07]. In this section we detail its use and the rules that can be derived from the constraints it imposes.

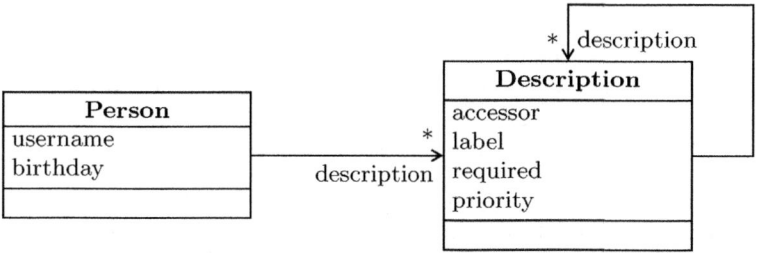

Fig. 3. The domain object `Person` with its Magritte meta-description

On the left side of Figure 3 we see a simple domain class called `Person` with two attributes. To meta-describe a class with Magritte we need corresponding description instances. These description instances are either defined in the source-code or dynamically at run-time. The following code shows an example of how we could describe the attribute `username` in the class `Person`:

```
1 Person class>>usernameDescription
2     <description>
3     ^ StringDescription new
4         accessor: #username;
5         label: 'Username';
6         beRequired;
7         yourself
```

The method returns an attribute description of the type string (line 3), that can be accessed through the method #username (line 4), that has the label 'Username' (line 5), and that is a required property (line 6). The annotation (line 2) lets Magritte know that calling the method returns a description of the receiver. Several such description methods build the metamodel of the `Person` class as visualized with the association from `Person` to `Description` in Figure 3.

Descriptions are interpreted by different services, such as form builders or persistency mappers. For example, a simple renderer that prints the label and the current values would look like this:

```
1 aPerson description do: [ :desc |
2     aStream
3         nextPutAll: (desc label);
4         nextPutAll: ': ';
5         nextPutAll: (desc toString: (desc accessor readFrom: aPerson));
6         cr ]
```

First, given an `aPerson` instance, we ask it for its description and we iterate over its individual attribute descriptions (line 1). Within the loop, we print the label (line 3), we ask the accessor of the description to return the associated attributes from `aPerson` and we transform this value to a string (line 5), so that it can be appended to the output.

We have defined five rules that check for conformance of the source code with the Magritte metamodel. The first two are defined and implemented externally to the Magritte engine:

1. Description Naming. The definitions of the attribute descriptions should relate to the accessor they describe. In our example the accessor is `username` and the method that defines the description is called `usernameDescription`. While this is not a strict requirement, it is considered good style and makes the code easier to read. The implementation points out places where this practice is neglected.

2. Missing Description. Sometimes developers fail to completely describe their classes. This rule checks all described classes of the system and compares them with the metamodel. Instance variables and accessor methods that miss a corresponding description method are reported.

The remaining three rules rely completely on the constraints already imposed by the runtime of Magritte:

3. Description Priorities. In Magritte attribute descriptions can have priorities. This is useful to have a deterministic order when elements are displayed in a user interface. This rule verifies that if a description is used to build user-interfaces then it should have valid priorities assigned to all its attribute descriptions. This rule makes use of the metamodel as well as the reflective system to detect the places where the descriptions are used.

4. Accessor Definition. The Magritte metamodel uses accessor objects to specify how the data in the model can be read and written. This rule iterates over the complete metamodel and checks the accessor object of every description against the code it is supposed to work on. The implementation of the rule is straight forward as it merely delegates to `aDescription` instance the `aClass` under scrutiny:

```
aDescription accessor canReadFromInstancesOf: aClass.
aDescription accessor canWriteToInstancesOf: aClass.
```

5. Description Definition. This rule checks if the specified metamodel can be properly instantiated and, if so, it validates the metamodel against its meta-metamodel. Magritte allows one to check any model against its metamodel, so we can validate `aPerson` against its metamodel:

```
aPerson description validate: aPerson
```

Magritte is described in itself, as depicted in Figure 3. Therefore we can use the meta-metamodel to validate the metamodel in the same way:

```
aDescription description validate: aDescription
```

The above code validates `aDescription` against the description of itself. In case of problems they are recorded by the program checker. In fact this rule is the most powerful of all rules presented here, because it can detect various kinds of different problems in the metamodel, yet it is extremely simple in the implementation as all the functionality is already present in Magritte.

We have developed a similar set of rules for FAME [KV08], a metamodeling library that is independent of the host language and that keeps the metamodels accessible and adaptable at runtime.

3 Case Studies

In this section we present three case studies: In the first two we apply Slime rules to control the code quality. The first one is Seaside itself (Section 3.1). The second one is a commercial application based on Seaside (Section 3.2). We analyze several versions of these systems and we compare the results with the number of issues detected by traditional lint rules. Then we present a survey we ran with Seaside developers concerning their experience with using Slime (Section 3.3). In the third case study we apply the Magritte rules on a large collection of open-source code (Section 3.4) and demonstrate some common issues that remained unnoticed in the code.

3.1 Seaside

Figure 4 depicts the average number of issues over various versions of Seaside. The blue line shows the number of standard smells per class (Lint), while the orange line shows the number of domain-specific smells per class (Slime). To give a feeling how the size of the code base changes in time, we also display the number of lines of code (LOC) below.

In both cases we observe a significant improvement in code quality between versions 2.7 and 2.8. At the time major parts of Seaside were refactored or rewritten to increase portability and extensibility of the code base. No changes

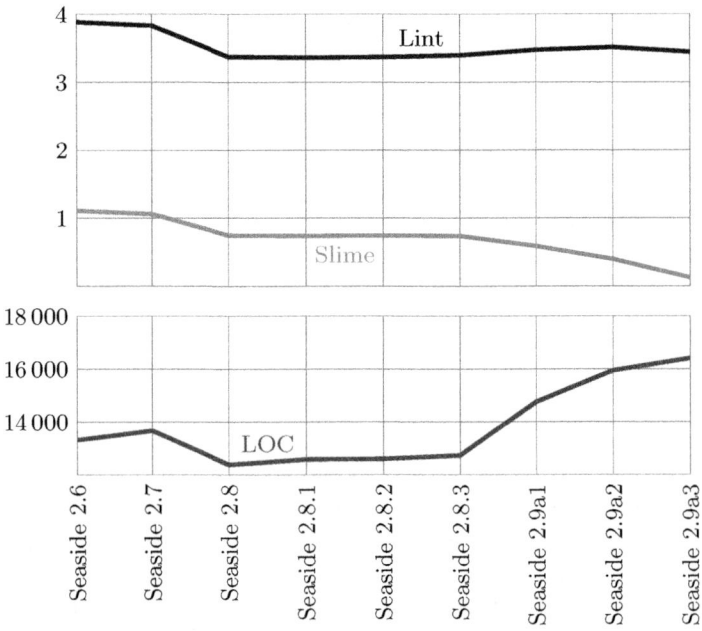

Fig. 4. Average number of Lint and Slime issues per class (above) and lines of code (below) in released Seaside versions

are visible for the various 2.8 releases. Code quality as measured by the program checkers and lines of code remained constant over time.

Starting with Seaside 2.9a1 Slime was introduced in the development process. While the quality as measured by the traditional lint rules remained constant, guiding development by the Slime rules significantly improved the quality of the domain-specific code. This particular period shows the value in domain-specific program checking. While the Seaside code base grew significantly, the number of Slime rules could be reduced to almost zero.

Feedback we got from early adopters of Seaside 2.9 confirms that the quality of the code is notably better. Especially the portability between different Smalltalk dialects has improved. The code typically compiles and passes the tests on all platforms even-though it comes from the shared code repository.

An interesting observation is that even if the Slime smells are reduced and the quality of the code improves, the standard Lint rules continue to report a rather constant proportion of problems. This is due to the fact that the generic Lint rules address the wrong level and produce too many false positives.

We further evaluated the number of *false positives* of the remaining open issues in the last analyzed version of Seaside by manually verifying the reported issues: this is 67% (940 false positives out of 1403 issues reported) in the case of Lint, and 24% (12 false positives out of 51 issues reported) in the case of Slime. This demonstrates, that applying dedicated rules provides a better report on the quality of the software than when using the generic rules.

Due to the dynamic nature of Smalltalk and its lack of static type information it seems to be hard to further improve the quality of Slime rules. We however do see potential in future work to reduce the number of false positives by using static [PMW09] and dynamic [DGN07] type analysis.

3.2 Cmsbox

The Cmsbox[2] is a commercial web content management system written in Seaside. Figure 5 depicts the development of the system over three years. We are external to the development. The company gave us access to their code, but we could not correlate with their internal quality model and bug reports. Still we could deduce some interesting points: We ran the same set of Lint and Slime tests on every fifth version committed, for a total of 220 distinct versions analyzed. The number of lines of code are displayed below, though the absolute numbers have been removed to anonymize the data.

In the beginning we observe a rapid increase of detected issues. This is during the initial development phase of the project where a lot of code was added in a relatively short time. Presumably the violation of standard rules was not a concern for the developers. By contrast the number of Slime issues remained low and showed only gradual increase by comparison. This is a really interesting difference. Since the Slime rules tackle the development of the web interface which was the key part of the development effort, the result shows the benefit of

---

[2] http://www.cmsbox.com/

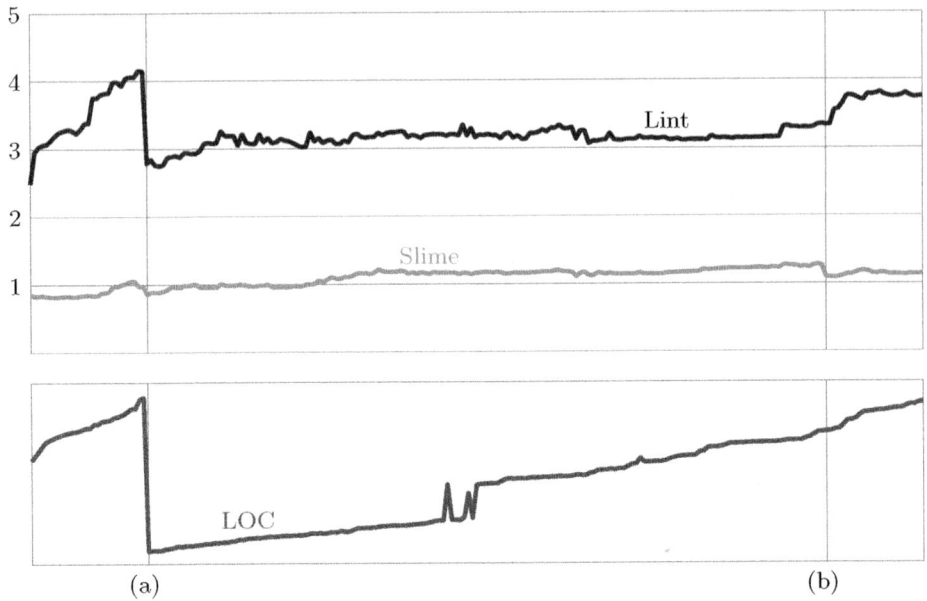

Fig. 5. Average number of Lint and Slime issues per class (above) and lines of code (below) in 220 subsequent development versions of the Cmsbox

using domain-specific code checking: developers focus more on domain-specific issues, rather than the general issues that can typically be resolved much more easily.

The abrupt drop of lint (and to some smaller extent also Slime) issues at point (a) can be explained by the removal of a big chunk of experimental or prototypical code no longer in use. Between versions (a) and (b) the code size grew more slowly, and the code quality remained relatively stable. It is worth noting that the size of the code base grew gradually, but at the same time the proportion of Slime issues stayed constant.

During the complete development of the Cmsbox the standard Lint rules were run as part of the daily builds. This explains why the average number of issues per class is lower than in the case of Seaside. At point (b) Slime rules were added and run with every build process. This accounts for the drop of Slime issues. A new development effort after (b) caused an increasing number of Lint issues. Again it is interesting to see that the better targeted Slime rules remained stable compared to the traditional ones.

Contrary to the case study with Seaside, the Slime issues do not disappear completely. On the one hand this has to do with the fact that the software is not supposed to run on different platforms, thus the rules that check for conformity on that level were not considered by the development team. On the other hand, as this is typical in an industrial setup, the developers were not able to spend a significant amount of time on the issues that were harder to fix and that did not cause immediate problems.

3.3   User Survey

We performed a user study where we asked Seaside developers to complete a survey on their Lint and Slime usage. 23 experienced Seaside developers independent from us answered our questionnaire. First, we asked them to state their use of program checkers:

1. How often do you use Slime on your Seaside code? *4 daily, 4 weekly, 8 monthly, and 7 never.*
2. How often do you use standard code critics on your Seaside code? *3 daily, 5 weekly, 7 monthly, and 8 never.*

On all answers, 16 developers (70%) are using Slime on a regular basis. We asked these developers to give their level of agreement or disagreement on the five-point Likert scale to the following statements:

3. Slime helps me to write better Seaside code: *11 agree, and 5 strongly agree.*
4. Slime is more useful than standard code critics to find problems in Seaside code: *5 neither agree nor disagree, 8 agree, and 3 strongly agree.*
5. Slime does not produce useful results, it mostly points out code that I don't consider bad: *3 strongly disagree, 10 disagree, and 3 neither agree nor disagree.*

To summarize, all developers that use Slime on a regular basis found it useful. 69% of the developers stated that Slime produces more useful results than the standard program checkers, the other 31% could not see a difference. 81% of the developers stated that Slime produces relevant results that help them to detect critical problems in their application.

We see our thesis confirmed in the two case studies and the user survey: While the general purpose Lint rules are definitely useful to be applied to any code base, they are not effective enough when used on domain-specific code. Using dedicated rules decreases the number of false positives and gives more relevant information on how to avoid bugs and improve the source code.

3.4   Magritte

In our third case study we ran the Magritte rules on a large collection of open-source code. This includes Pier[3], an application and content management system; SqueakSource, a source code management system; Conrad, a conference management system; CiteZen, a bibliography toolkit; CouchDB, a database implementation, and a large number of smaller projects that are publicly available.

In total we analyzed 70 768 lines of code in 12 305 methods belonging to 1 198 classes. 307 of these classes had Magritte meta-descriptions attached, where we found a total number of 516 Magritte related issues as listed in Table 2.

The most commonly observed problem is *missing descriptions*. While this is not necessarily a bug, it shows that some authors did not completely describe

---

[3] http://www.piercms.com/

Table 2. Number of issues in meta-described open-source code

Magritte Rule	Issues
Description Naming	37
Description Definition	78
Description Priorities	113
Accessor Definition	120
Missing Description	168

their domain objects. That can either happen intentionally, because they wanted to avoid the use of Magritte in certain parts of their application, or it can happen unintentionally when they forgot to update the metamodel as they added new functionality. This rule is thus helpful when reviewing code, as it identifies code that is not properly integrated with the meta-framework.

We observed also a significant number of errors in the *description definitions*. This happens when the defined metamodel does not validate against the meta-metamodel, which can be considered a serious bug. For example, we found the following description with two problems in the Pier Blog plugin:

```
1  Blog>>descriptionItemCount
2      ^ IntegerDescription new
3          label: 'Item Count';
4          accessor: #itemCount;
5          default: 0;
6          bePositive;
7          yourself
```

The first problem is that the description has no label, a required value in the meta-metamodel. The rule automatically suggests a refactoring (line 3) to add the missing label based on the name of the accessor. The second problem is the default value 0 (line 5), which does not satisfy the condition `bePositive` of the description itself (line 6).

From our positive experience with the Slime rules on the Seaside code-base, we expect a significant improvement of code quality in the realm of Magritte as these rules get adopted by the community. It is important to always keep the model and metamodel in a consistent state, which considerably improves the quality and stability of the code. With a few simple rules we can detect and fix numerous problems in the metamodel definition.

4   Related Work

There is a wide variety of tools available to find bugs and check for style issues. Rutar *et al.* give a good comparison of five bug finding tools for Java [RAF04].

PMD is a program checker that comes with a large collection of different rule-sets. Recent releases also included special rules to check for portability with the

Android platform and common Java technologies such as J2EE, JSP, JUnit, *etc.* As such, PMD provides some domain-specific rule-sets and encourages developers to create new ones. In PMD, rules are expressed either as XPath queries or using Java code. In either case PMD provides a proprietary AST that is problematic to keep in sync with the latest Java releases. Furthermore reflective information that goes beyond a single file is not available. This is important when rules require more information on the context, such as the code defined in sub- and superclasses.

JavaCOP [ANMM06] is a pluggable type system for Java. JavaCop implements a declarative, rule-based language that works on the typed AST of the standard Sun Java compiler. As the rules are performed as part of the compilation process, JavaCOP can only reflect within the active compilation unit, this being a limitation of the Java compiler. While the framework is targeted towards customizable type systems, the authors present various examples where JavaCOP is used for domain-specific program checking. There is currently no integration with Java IDEs and no possibility to automatically refactor code.

Other tools such as *FindBugs* [HP04] perform their analysis on bytecode. This has the advantage of being fast, but it requires that the code compile and it completely fails to take into account the abstractions of the host language. Writing new rules is consequently very difficult (the developer needs to know how language constructs are represented as bytecode), and targeting internal DLSs is hardly possible.

The *Smalltalk Refactoring Browser* [RBJ97] comes with over a hundred lint rules targeting common bugs and code smells in Smalltalk. While these rules perform well on traditional Smalltalk code, there is an increasing number of false positives when applied to domain-specific code. HELVETIA and the domain-specific rules we presented in this paper are built on top of the same infrastructure. This provides us with excellent tools for introspection and intercession of the AST in the host system, and keeps us from needing to build our own proprietary tools to parse, query and transform source code. HELVETIA adds a high-level rule system to declaratively compose the rules, and to scope and integrate them into the existing development tools.

High-level abstractions can be recovered from the structural model of the code. *Intensional Views* document structural regularities in source code and check for conformance against various versions of the system [MKPW06]. *Software reflexion models* [MNS95, KS03] extract high-level models from the source code and compare them with models the developer has specified. *ArchJava* [ACN02] is a language extension to Java that allows developers to encode architectural constraints directly into the source code. The constraints are checked at compile-time. Our approach does not use a special code model or architecture language to define the constraints. Instead our program checkers work with the standard code representation of the host language and make use of existing meta-frameworks such as Magritte or FAME. Furthermore our program checker is directly integrated with the development tools.

5   Conclusion

Our case studies revealed that rules that are targeted at a particular problem domain usually performed better and caused fewer false positives than general purpose lint rules. While more evidence is needed, these initial case studies do point out the benefits of using rules dedicated to domain-specific code over using generic ones.

As we need to accommodate new domain-specific code, the ability to add new dedicated rules is crucial. While we have demonstrated various program checking rules in the context of Seaside and Magritte, we argue that any library that uses domain-specific abstractions should come with a set of dedicated rules. Adding domain-specific rules is straightforward. Using the HELVETIA framework it is possible to declaratively specify new rules and closely integrate them with the host environment. Rules are scoped to certain parts of the system using the reflective API of the host language. The existing infrastructure of the refactoring tools helped us to efficiently perform searches and transformations on the AST nodes of host system. This is the same low-level infrastructure used by the standard lint rules.

Furthermore we have shown that domain-specific rules need to be applied at different levels of abstraction. This can happen at the level of source code, as in the example of Slime; or it can focus more on model checking, where generic rules use a metamodel and the system to validate conformance, as we have shown with Magritte. In both cases the rules were targeted at the particular domain of the respective frameworks only.

We applied the presented techniques only to internal DSLs, that by definition share the same syntax as the host language. As a generalization we envision to extend this approach to any *embedded language* that does not necessarily share the same syntax as the host language. HELVETIA uses the AST of the host environment as the common representation of all executable code, thus it is always possible to run the rules at that level. Since HELVETIA automatically keeps track of the source location it is possible to provide highlighting of lint issues in other languages. The challenge however will be to express the rules in terms of the embedded language. This is not only necessary to be able to offer automatic transformations, but also more convenient for rule developers as they do not need to work on two different abstraction levels.

Acknowledgments

We thank Adrian Lienhard and netstyle.ch for providing the Cmsbox case study. We gratefully acknowledge the financial support of the Swiss National Science Foundation for the project "Bringing Models Closer to Code" (SNF Project No. 200020-121594, Oct. 2008 – Sept. 2010). We also thank ESUG, the European Smalltalk User Group, for its financial contribution to the presentation of this paper.

References

[ACN02]   Aldrich, J., Chambers, C., Notkin, D.: Architectural reasoning in Arch-Java. In: Magnusson, B. (ed.) ECOOP 2002. LNCS, vol. 2374, pp. 334–367. Springer, Heidelberg (2002)

[ANMM06]   Andreae, C., Noble, J., Markstrum, S., Millstein, T.: A framework for implementing pluggable type systems. In: OOPSLA '06: Proceedings of the 21st annual ACM SIGPLAN conference on Object-oriented programming systems, languages, and applications, pp. 57–74. ACM Press, New York (2006)

[BFJR98]   Brant, J., Foote, B., Johnson, R., Roberts, D.: Wrappers to the rescue. In: Jul, E. (ed.) ECOOP 1998. LNCS, vol. 1445, pp. 396–417. Springer, Heidelberg (1998)

[DGN07]   Denker, M., Greevy, O., Nierstrasz, O.: Supporting feature analysis with runtime annotations. In: Proceedings of the 3rd International Workshop on Program Comprehension through Dynamic Analysis (PCODA 2007), pp. 29–33, Technische Universiteit Delft (2007)

[DK97]   van Deursen, A., Klint, P.: Little languages: Little maintenance? In: Kamin, S. (ed.) First ACM-SIGPLAN Workshop on Domain-Specific Languages; DSL'97, January 1997, pp. 109–127 (1997)

[DLR07]   Ducasse, S., Lienhard, A., Renggli, L.: Seaside: A flexible environment for building dynamic web applications. IEEE Software 24(5), 56–63 (2007)

[Fow99]   Fowler, M.: Refactoring: improving the design of existing code. Addison-Wesley Professional, Reading (1999)

[Fow08]   Fowler, M.: Domain specific languages (Work in progress) (June 2008), http://martinfowler.com/dslwip/

[HP00]   Havelund, K., Pressburger, T.: Model checking Java programs using Java PathFinder. International Journal on Software Tools for Technology Transfer (STTT) 2(4), 366–381 (2000)

[HP04]   Hovemeyer, D., Pugh, W.: Finding bugs is easy. ACM SIGPLAN Notices 39(12), 92–106 (2004)

[Joh83]   Johnson, S.C.: Lint, a C program checker. UNIX time-sharing system: UNIX programmer's manual, p. 278 (1983)

[KS03]   Koschke, R., Simon, D.: Hierarchical reflexion models. In: Proceedings of the 10th Working Conference on Reverse Engineering (WCRE 2003), p. 36. IEEE Computer Society, Los Alamitos (2003)

[KV08]   Kuhn, A., Verwaest, T.: FAME, a polyglot library for metamodeling at runtime. In: Workshop on Models at Runtime, pp. 57–66 (2008)

[Lie89]   Lieberherr, K.J.: Formulations and benefits of the Law of Demeter. ACM SIGPLAN Notices 24(3), 67–78 (1989)

[MKPW06]   Mens, K., Kellens, A., Pluquet, F., Wuyts, R.: Co-evolving code and design with intensional views — a case study. Journal of Computer Languages, Systems and Structures 32(2), 140–156 (2006)

[MNS95]   Murphy, G., Notkin, D., Sullivan, K.: Software reflexion models: Bridging the gap between source and high-level models. In: Proceedings of SIGSOFT '95, Third ACM SIGSOFT Symposium on the Foundations of Software Engineering, pp. 18–28. ACM Press, New York (1995)

[PMW09]   Pluquet, F., Marot, A., Wuyts, R.: Fast type reconstruction for dynamically typed programming languages. In: DLS '09: Proceedings of the 5th symposium on Dynamic languages, pp. 69–78. ACM, New York (2009)

[RAF04]   Rutar, N., Almazan, C.B., Foster, J.S.: A comparison of bug finding tools for Java. In: 15th International Symposium on Software Reliability Engineering, ISSRE 2004, pp. 245–256 (2004)

[RBJ97]   Roberts, D., Brant, J., Johnson, R.E.: A refactoring tool for Smalltalk. Theory and Practice of Object Systems (TAPOS) 3(4), 253–263 (1997)

[RDK07]   Renggli, L., Ducasse, S., Kuhn, A.: Magritte — a meta-driven approach to empower developers and end users. In: Engels, G., Opdyke, B., Schmidt, D.C., Weil, F. (eds.) MODELS 2007. LNCS, vol. 4735, pp. 106–120. Springer, Heidelberg (2007)

[RGN10]   Renggli, L., Gîrba, T., Nierstrasz, O.: Embedding languages without breaking tools. In: ECOOP 2010: Proceedings of the 24th European Conference on Object-Oriented Programming, Maribor, Slovenia. LNCS. Springer, Heidelberg (to appear, 2010)

Revisiting Parametric Types and Virtual Classes[*]

Anders Bach Madsen and Erik Ernst

Department of Computer Science, Aarhus University, Denmark
{abachn,eernst}@cs.au.dk

Abstract. This paper presents a conceptually oriented updated view on the relationship between parametric types and virtual classes. The traditional view is that parametric types excel at structurally oriented composition and decomposition, and virtual classes excel at specifying mutually recursive families of classes whose relationships are preserved in derived families. Conversely, while class families can be specified using a large number of F-bounded type parameters, this approach is complex and fragile; and it is difficult to use traditional virtual classes to specify object composition in a structural manner, because virtual classes are closely tied to nominal typing. This paper adds new insight about the dichotomy between these two approaches; it illustrates how virtual constraints and type refinements, as recently introduced in gbeta and SCALA, enable structural treatment of virtual types; finally, it shows how a novel kind of dynamic type check can detect compatibility among entire families of classes.

1   Introduction

In *A statically safe alternative to virtual types* [5], Bruce, Odersky, and Wadler outline the strengths and weaknesses of parametric and virtual types. The description given in that paper has largely defined the common understanding of this relationship. To readers not familiar with *A statically safe alternative to virtual types* by Bruce, Odersky, and Wadler, a summary of the relevant parts can be found in Appendix A. This paper takes an updated view on the situation and argues that the balance has shifted somewhat in favor of virtual types and virtual classes.

Parametric types, which we use interchangeably with *type parameterized classes* in this paper, is a well-known genericity mechanism today because it is supported by a range of programming languages including the Java [13,4], SCALA [26], and C# [16] programming languages. The basic idea is that a class may take named type parameters which may be used like types in the body of the class. Actual type arguments may be passed to such a parameterized class at use sites in order to obtain a class (and type) which works as if the formal type parameters had been replaced by the actuals. The three languages differ somewhat in their approach to type parameterization; in particular, Java has use-site variance by means of wildcards, SCALA has declaration-site variance and higher-order type parameters, and C# has no support for variance but uses a heterogeneous translation scheme which enables very good performance with primitive types. However, these differences do not play an important role in this paper.

---

[*] This work was supported by FTP 274-06-0029.

J. Vitek (Ed.): TOOLS 2010, LNCS 6141, pp. 233–252, 2010.

We will use SCALA in the parametric type examples in this paper. In general, we use SCALA for several things because this language is known in a fairly large community, and it embeds a very nice language design including many features that we discuss.

The strengths that Bruce, Odersky, and Wadler [5] emphasize for parametric types focus on the flexibility of structural composition and decomposition of types. For instance, a `zip` operation on `List` objects should return a `List` of `Pairs`, and the types of each pair should be the element types of each of the `Lists`. Parametric types easily specify this as `List<Pair<A,B>>`, where `A` and `B` are the list element types.

Genericity may also be expressed using class or type valued object members. This kind of language mechanism was introduced decades ago with the notion of virtual patterns in BETA [17]. The *pattern* concept is a generalization of the class and method concepts; we will simplify this and talk about *virtual classes* in this paper. Virtual classes were deeply generalized in gbeta [7,10,11], including generalizations of the type system ensuring provable type soundness [12]. Hence, there is no need to consider that part of the title of [5]. A number of other languages include a similar mechanism. CaesarJ [19,3] provides virtual classes similar to gbeta's and adds several mechanisms for aspect-oriented programming. Object Teams [15,14] provides virtual classes known as members of *team* classes, and extends this with a different set of mechanisms for aspect-oriented programming. Finally, the SCALA programming language [27,2] includes abstract type members, which allow for a similar typing regime as that of virtual classes, but does not include propagating combination [8], later known as deep mixin composition [29]. In this paper we will use gbeta and SCALA in the virtual classes and virtual types examples, respectively. Although gbeta is surely less well-known than SCALA for most readers, it is instructive to consider the gbeta versions because they embody a different set of trade-offs, and sometimes lead to better solutions.

The strengths that Bruce, Odersky, and Wadler [5] emphasize for virtual types focus on the ability to express a mutually recursive family of classes which preserves the intra-family type relationships in derived families. Family polymorphism [9] adds the ability to safely work with multiple class families using dynamic subtype polymorphism, and deep mixin composition adds the ability to compose class families recursively.

The converse of these strengths of the two kinds of genericity follows naturally: Virtual classes in their traditional form are tightly integrated with named types, and they make it hard to conveniently express a type like `List<Pair<A,B>>` for the `zip` method; however, we will show how to overcome this restriction. On the other hand, when F-bounds [6] are used to model a class family with type parameters as described by Bruce, Odersky, and Wadler [5], it is not only verbose and error-prone, it also fails to support family polymorphism and deep mixin composition. Moreover, we show that the typing in such a class family fails to capture the same level of knowledge about the types of certain objects that virtual classes do.

The main contributions of this paper are as follows: We provide new insight into the relationship between the two kinds of genericity, and we introduce a new mechanism similar to dynamic `instanceof` tests for objects to further extend the reach of virtual classes. We have implemented the approach in the language gbeta, and runnable example programs are available for download.[1] The SCALA example programs are available from this site, too.

The rest of this paper is organized as follows. Section 2 describes how type refinements can be used to provide virtual classes and abstract type members with a similar structural flexibility as that of type parameters. Next, Sect. 3 revisits the strengths of parametric types, with updates based on virtual constraints and type refinements; and Sect. 4 revisits the strengths of virtual classes, adding new properties and features that are hard to match using type parameters. Finally, Sect. 5 discusses related work, and Sect. 6 concludes.

2 Adding Expressiveness with Type Refinements

Type refinements are important when considering the flexibility of types involving virtual classes, abstract type members, and the like. This section presents type refinements, and points out some differences between the versions in gbeta and in SCALA.

Type refinements are motivated by the need to create new sets of types. In object-oriented languages like Java and $C^{\#}$, a type can be either an exact class or interface (e.g., for a class used in a new expression), or the *type cone* consisting of all subtypes of a given type (e.g., for a variable). In such languages with nominal type equivalence, it is normally not possible to denote other kinds of sets of types.

Languages with structural type equivalence commonly do not have subtyping, but it is possible to express composite types directly using anonymous type expressions, and the type system is able to judge that two types are identical (or one is a generalization of the other) because they have identical structure (or may be unified). This provides the ability to denote a set of types S which are all structural instantiations of a given type T, but this is different from a type cone because there is no subtype relationship among these types. This kind of type structure is typical for functional languages, but type parameters introduce a similar structurality into an object-oriented context. For instance, the type List<Pair<A,B>> is a typical example of an anonymous type expression which may be used multiple times to create the same type.

With traditional virtual classes or any other approach based on class or type valued object members, a type with a similar meaning as List<Pair<A,B>> would have to be created by subclassing List to some new class ListOfAB, and further-binding a virtual class or type member in ListOfAB to a subclass of Pair which again further-binds its component types to A and B. Apart from the fact that this is verbose, it is also difficult to manage from a software engineering point of view, because all users of this type would have to use this particular ListOfAB class; any other declaration of a similar class, even an exact textual copy with a different name, would be type incompatible with ListOfAB because of the nominal type equivalence criterion. Note that this problem is particularly relevant for collection classes, because they carry no meaning in relation to the application domain. With many classes, it would be dangerous to identify distinct declarations with the same structure, because they represent distinct application domain concepts. Nevertheless, collections and similar domain free entities are common enough to make this a real problem.

---

[1] http://www.cs.au.dk/gbeta/wiki/Tools2010

```
1  abstract class Box {
2     type T
3     val e: T
4  }
5  object Test extends Application {
6     val myBox1 = new Box{ type T = String; val e = "aBox" }
7     val myBox2: Box{ type T <: String } = myBox1
8  }
```

Fig. 1. Type refinements in SCALA

If we add type refinements as in SCALA [26], or the similar mechanism of virtual constraints as in gbeta [11], we obtain the possibility of expressing new kinds of sets of types, including all the subclasses of List whose element type is a subclass of Pair whose component types are A and B. In other words, we can now abstract over a set of nominal types that collectively correspond to the single structural type List<Pair<A,B>>.

To introduce type refinements, we will use a small SCALA example shown in Fig. 1. This defines an abstract class Box, with an abstract type member T and an abstract value e of type T. To create an instance of class Box (line 6), an anonymous subclass is needed in order to specify an actual type T and a concrete value for e. We may omit the type of myBox1 since it can be taken from the new-statement. However, if we use myBox1 in a context where a type must be specified then we must use a type refinement like the one in the definition of myBox2, specifying that type T is at least String. In line 7 it is actually known that type T is exactly String, so we could have used equals (=) instead of subtype (<:) in the type constraint. Both will allow us to use e as a String, but <: is often more flexible because it allows T to be a proper subtype of the declared bound, i.e., it introduces covariance. Finally, contravariance can be expressed using a supertype constraint (>:).

In general, a SCALA type refinement $T\{\bar{C}\}$ denotes the set of objects which are instances of a subtype of the specified type T, such that its type members satisfy the listed constraints $\bar{C}$. Type refinements give the possibility to express use-site type constraints on the type members, and thus on variables and methods that use them. Hence, a type refinement abstracts over all such subtypes whose type members satisfy the constraints, whereas the base type T abstracts over a larger set of types and thereby fails to capture the information about the type members.[2]

In gbeta, a similar mechanism known as *virtual constraints* was introduced in 2003 and documented in a publication in 2006 [11]. Here, constraints on virtual patterns correspond to the type member constraints in SCALA (including covariance, '<=', contravariance, '>=', and invariance '='), but as opposed to SCALA type refinements, it also supports object equality constraints. Note that a full formalization of virtual constraints in gbeta is still under development and to our knowledge there is no

---

[2] In SCALA, type refinement syntax is also used to express structural types, especially in order to provide convenient access to the rows of a relational database, but this is a different language mechanism based on reflection, and it is beyond the scope of this paper.

```
 1   {
 2       GraphTypes: %{ Node:<object; Edge:<object };
 3       Graph: %{ pkg:<@GraphTypes; aNode:^pkg.Node };
 4
 5       action: %( g:^Graph[pkg=ag.pkg] ){
 6         ag:<@Graph
 7       #
 8         ag.aNode | g.aNode
 9       };
10
11       // (1)...
12
13       pkg1,pkg2: @GraphTypes;
14       grA: @Graph %{pkg::@pkg1};
15       grB: @Graph %{pkg::@pkg1};
16       grC: @Graph %{pkg::@pkg2}
17   #
18       grA^ | action %{ag::@grB};
19       //grA^ | action %{ag::@grC};   // Compile-time error
20
21       // (2)...
22   }
```

Fig. 2. Type refinements in gbeta, where we have the ability to check that two package objects are the same and hence compatible. Later on, code for the locations (1) and (2) will be shown.

formalization of SCALA that covers type refinements beside the structural parts. We shall henceforth use the phrase 'type refinement' both for the SCALA and the gbeta mechanism.

A gbeta object may be used as a first class package—because an object provides its members by lookup, including class valued members that may also be used as types—and hence these object constraints are capable of expressing that entire mutually recursive families of classes (and their types) are identical. Consequently, variables and methods using these types are type compatible. We believe that this kind of 'family constraint' is beyond reach in the SCALA type system. We will now illustrate how this feature can be used.

For a language supporting virtual classes and family polymorphism like gbeta, a classical challenge is to share objects between two class families. An example could be a graph family where the virtual classes Node and Edge are declared within a Graph class. Instances of Graph would then be used to build actual graph data structures. When creating two graphs, the types within one family would be incompatible with the types from the other family, and hence nodes and edges could not be moved from graph to graph. Note that this type distinction is per graph object, and hence it allows for an unbounded number of distinct graph class families, or other class families. This is a very useful feature in the cases where such cross-family exchanges are incorrect according to the application domain (e.g., the type system would prevent us from giving a Google.Document to a Microsoft.Employee.read where Google and

```
1    abstract class GraphTypes { type Node }
2
3    abstract class Graph {
4      type pkgT <: GraphTypes
5      val pkg: pkgT
6      var aNode: pkg.Node
7    }
8
9    abstract class Scope {
10     val ag: Graph
11     def action( g: Graph{ type pkgT = ag.pkgT } ) = {
12       g.aNode = ag.aNode   // compile-time error!
13     }
14   }
```

Fig. 3. Using an abstract type member and a value to represent the virtual object pkg from Fig. 2. The constraint in the type refinement creates checks that the types of the package objects are the same. However, this still fails because the check is at the type level and not of the actual objects.

Microsoft are instances of the same class Company), but in the cases where we wish to allow nodes and edges to be exchanged we must change the design slightly.

The modified design uses a 'package class' GraphTypes, which is just a normal class that declares all the types used in the graph family, but no actual graph data structures. To hold graphs, i.e., connected node and edge instances, we create a separate class, Graph, that has access to an instance pkg of GraphTypes. In order to have several graphs with type compatible nodes and edges, we create several instances of Graph whose pkg is bound to the same instance of GraphTypes.

Figure 2 shows a minimal implementation of the graph example in gbeta. An introduction to the gbeta syntax used in the examples can be found in Appendix B. In the example in Fig. 2, we define two classes GraphTypes (line 2) and Graph (line 3). Instances of the class GraphTypes or a subclass are the package objects that can be used to supply the actual classes/types to the Graph class. In the class Graph there is a virtual object pkg, which has initial type GraphTypes (this declaration works essentially like val pkg: GraphTypes in SCALA) and an object reference aNode, which has type pkg.Node (in SCALA: **var** aNode: pkg.Node). In line 13 of Fig. 2 we create two package objects pkg1 and pkg2. Using these package objects we create three Graph instances grA, grB and grC in lines 14–16. The graph instances grA and grB share the same package pkg1 (the meaning of these declarations is corresponds to val pkg = pkg1 in SCALA), whereas grC uses pkg2.

The interesting part is the action method defined in lines 5–9. This method takes one argument g, which is constrained by the type Graph with a type refinement. This type refinement specifies that g.pkg must be the same object as ag.pkg (same type is not sufficient, it must really be the same object). Conceptually, ag is just another argument, but we must declare it in a way that makes it immutable, in order to use it for the dependent type in the type refinement. The object identity constraint is checked statically by the compiler. The method body is then allowed to use the static knowledge that the package objects in g and ag are the same, and therefore their

```
(1)
  discovery: %(ag:^Graph, g:^Graph){
    {
      _ag: @ag;   // In Scala: val _ag = ag
    #
      case _g:g do { // val _g = g, then dynamic typecase on _g
        ? Graph[pkg=_ag.pkg]: _g | action %{ag::@_ag};
      };
    };
  };

(2)
  (grA^,grB^) | discovery;    // Will execute action
  (grA^,grC^) | discovery;    // Will not execute action
```

Fig. 4. In gbeta it is also possible to use the type refinements to dynamically check that two package objects are the same. Note that the immutable reference _ag is needed because _ag is used twice in the **case** and must have the same value both times. The two blocks in this figure should be inserted into Fig. 2 at the marked locations.

internal types are equal. Consequently, the body of the method can assign ag.aNode to g.aNode (SCALA: g.aNode = ag.aNode). The pipe symbol, '|', is used for assignment, method calls and more, with dataflow from left to right, just like operating system shell commands. In line 18 we call the action method with argument grA, and with grB bound to the virtual object ag. The compiler statically determines that this method invocation is type correct because the package object of grA and grB is the same. However, the call in line 19 would fail with a compile-time error, because the package objects of grA and grC are different. Now consider whether we can express the gbeta example from Fig. 2 in SCALA.

The most important parts of Fig. 2 converted to SCALA can be seen in Fig. 3, using a type member and a value to represent the virtual package object pkg from the gbeta example. This modified version is using the type member pkgT in the type refinement in line 11, which gives a constraint at the type level. However, this program cannot be compiled. The problem is in line 12, where the compiler is unable to judge that the types of g.aNode and ag.aNode are compatible, even though they come from the same type of package object. The problem is that our type constraint says nothing about the actual values of pkg, only that they have the same type, and that is not sufficient to ensure that their type member pkgT has the same value. Hence, this version is unsafe and *should* be rejected.

A more direct conversion of the gbeta example in Fig. 2 to SCALA would be to express the type refinement in the action method as shown below.[3]

```
  def action( g: Graph{ val pkg = ag.pkg } )
```

This code may look plausible, but unfortunately it is not valid. The problem is the type refinement where the constraint is that the package objects are the same. However,

---

[3] The complete failing example can be found as Fig3a.scala in the downloads at http://www.cs.au.dk/gbeta/wiki/Tools2010

```
abstract class Pair[Fst, Snd] {
  val fst: Fst
  val snd: Snd
}
class List[A] {
  def zip[B](y1: List[B]): List[Pair[A,B]] = {
    val res = new List[Pair[A,B]]()
    ...
  }
}
object Main extends Application {
  val myl1 = new List[Int]
  val myl2 = new List[String]
  val pairs = myl1.zip(myl2)
}
```

Fig. 5. Traditional zip method implemented in SCALA using parametric types

the SCALA language specification [26], page 21, specifies that all value constraints are for structural comparison and not usable in type constraints. Consequently, this is a compile-time error, and type refinements can only express constraints on type members. Hence, we believe that SCALA is not able to express the example from Fig. 2.

In gbeta, type refinements can be used statically as in Fig. 2, but they can also be used in a dynamic type testing construct, to determine whether two instances of the Graph class have the same package object. This is similar to an instanceof test, and it is a new feature of type refinements in gbeta. The dynamic type constraint test in gbeta is used in Fig. 4, which is an extension of the program in Fig. 2.

The program fragments in Fig. 4 contain two parts, corresponding to the locations (1) and (2) in Fig. 2. The first part is the declaration of the method discovery and the second part is the use of the discovery method. The discovery method takes two arguments of type Graph with no constraints on the package objects. As with the action method, we create an immutable reference to one of the arguments as a field _ag. Using _ag we can refer to its package object in a type refinement. In the case statement we test if the type of (the second argument) g matches any of the listed types (there is only one case, Graph[pkg=_ag.pkg]). If the type of g matches, i.e., if the package object is shared, then the action method is called with _g as argument and _ag bound to ag in the action method. In the second part of the example in Fig. 4, the discovery method is called with the same combination as we used with the action method. Both calls to discovery will compile and run, but only the first invocation of discovery will call the action method, because the package objects are non-identical in the second.

Note that even though SCALA type refinements can define type constraints, they cannot be tested at run-time. This is because the main run-time platform of SCALA is the Java Virtual Machine and the byte code language does not support type argument information. All the type arguments are erased by the compiler before it is passed to the Java Virtual Machine.

```
1    abstract class Pair {
2      type Fst; type Snd; var fst: Fst; var snd: Snd
3    }
4    abstract class List {
5      type elm >: Null
6      var current: elm = null // Dummy one element list
7      abstract class Zipper {
8        val b: List
9        type ElmPair = Pair{ type Fst = List.this.elm;
10                             type Snd = b.elm; }
11       def zip(): List{ type elm = ElmPair } = {
12         val res = new List{ type elm = ElmPair }
13         ...
14         res
15       }
16     }
17     // (1)...
18   }
19   object Main extends Application {
20     val myl1 = new List{ type elm = Integer }
21     val myl2 = new List{ type elm = String }
22     val zipr = new myl1.Zipper{ val b = myl2 }
23     val out: List{ type elm =
24       Pair{ type Fst=Integer; type Snd=String }} = zipr.zip()
25     // (2)...
26   }
```

Fig. 6. Zip implemented in SCALA using type members and type refinements

At this point we have presented type refinements, and illustrated that they are similar but not identical in SCALA and gbeta. Next, they will be used to express types which are similarly convenient as the structural types based on parametric types.

3   Revisiting Strengths of Parametric Types

This section will revisit the examples from section 3 in [5] to determine if type parameterized classes are still the better choice for these kinds of programs. We have chosen to redo the zip method in SCALA, which is shown in Fig. 5. This is a simple conversion from the original Pizza [28] version, which could easily also have been expressed in languages like Java or C#. Note that we do not assume any standard library, so List has nothing to do with the standard SCALA List class. We may now use type refinements to create a type member based version of this example in SCALA, as seen in Fig. 6.

The example is a little bit more complicated in SCALA around line 10, where we create the type constraint Snd = b.elm. Since this constraint is used in the return type of zip, we cannot use the parameter list to declare b. So we create an abstract value b within a wrapper class Zipper that contains our zip method, such that we can refer to

```
1    {
2      Pair: %{
3        Fst:<object; Snd:<object; fst:^Fst; snd:^Snd;
4      };
5      List: %{
6        elm:<object;
7        zip: %(| res:^List[elm=ElmPair]) {
8          b:<@List;
9          ElmPair: Pair%{Fst::elm; Snd::b.elm};
10         #
11         new List %{ elm::ElmPair}^ | res;
12         ...
13       };
14       // (1)...
15     };
16     myl1: @List %{elm::int};
17     myl2: @List %{elm::string};
18     r: ^List[Pair[Fst=int,Snd=string]];
19   #
20     myl1.zip%{ b::@myl2 } | r;
21     // (2)...
22   }
```

Fig. 7. Zip implemented in gbeta using virtual classes and type refinements

b.elm in the type member ElmPair. If we had not declared ElmPair the definition would have to be substituted into the two uses in line 11 and 12. However, this would introduce a name clash in the constraint Fst = List.this.elm, such that we cannot denote the correct elm.

In Fig. 6 on lines 22–24, the use of the zip method is very close to what is proposed in [21,1] and noted in [5], even though this is not a type parameter example. The similarity between the two examples is in the extra allocation of an object. In [21,1] the allocation is used to give the zip method its parametric return type. In the example in Fig. 6 the allocation of the zipr object is used to bind the argument for the zip method to a value, and then used in the type refinement within the type member ElmPair.

Figure 7 is the implementation of the zip method using gbeta's virtual classes and type refinements. To explain the gbeta syntax on line 7, note that the declaration **zip**: %(| res:^T){...} corresponds to the following SCALA declaration (see also Appendix B):

def zip(): T = { **var** res: T; ...; **return** res; }

The gbeta example in Fig. 7 is much simpler than the virtual types version presented by Bruce, Odersky, and Wadler [5]. It is also significantly more concise than the SCALA version, because type refinements work slightly differently, and also because classes and methods are unified in gbeta. This unification makes method activations real objects, which makes the Zipper class from the SCALA example unnecessary.

```
(1)
  scan:%{ current:^elm # ... }; // call inner for each element

(2)
  (myl1.zip%{ b::@myl2 }).scan{ // called at inner
    current.fst@ + current.snd.size | current.fst@
  }
```

Fig. 8. Extension of Fig. 7 with (1) a scan method (implementation elided) in class `List` and (2) an invocation of the scan method from the do-part

Another claim by Bruce, Odersky, and Wadler [5] is that virtual classes are less flexible than parametric types, because all uses of the `zip` method have to be anticipated. This is caused by nominal typing, but due to type refinements this problem does not exist with the implementation in Fig. 7. In general, type refinements would be used everywhere to access such 'repackaged' objects as the list of pairs. The underlying class would be anonymous, not directly denotable by anyone outside the new statement that produces it.

The minimal version of `List` that we have shown so far only supports genericity by means of a type parameter, or a virtual class or type member. At this point we need to consider iteration over the list elements. BETA and gbeta (like Smalltalk) traditionally use *internal iteration*, i.e., an iteration method on the data structure that somehow accepts a piece of code to be executed on each element. In Smalltalk, each iteration method accepts a block as an argument; in BETA and gbeta, the iteration method is *specialized* with the code to execute. This contrasts with the C++ and Java style of iterators which are *external*, i.e., they use an explicit control structure to execute a piece of code repeatedly, while stepping through the data structure by means of an iterator object.

One advantage offered by internal iteration in this context is that we do not need to mention the type of the element being iterated over. In the example in Fig. 8 the gbeta code for extending the example in Fig. 7 is shown. Note that we have omitted the implementation of `scan` for brevity. Here we need not declare the `current` element or its type, because it is inherited from the 'supermethod' `scan`, rather than declared as an argument of a separate block or closure.

The natural choice when implementing iteration in SCALA is to use iterators. However, we wanted to explore the same kind of internal iteration as in gbeta. The SCALA implementation that corresponds to the gbeta version is shown in Fig. 9. The `scan` method takes one argument, which is a function. This function is then applied to all the elements in the list (the implementation in the example is again mostly omitted). When we call the `scan` method we need to pass in an anonymous function that takes one argument with a type matching the element type of the list. Then within the body of the anonymous function we can use the `current` element. Comparing the SCALA version with the gbeta version, we need to create an extra anonymous function in SCALA, and specify the type of the `current` element in this anonymous function.

```
(1)
  def scan(body: elm => Unit) = ... // call body on each element

(2)
  zipr.zip().scan( (current:
    Pair{ type Fst=Integer; type Snd=String }) => {
      current.fst =
          new Integer(current.fst.intValue() +
            current.snd.length());
      ()
    }
  )
```

Fig. 9. Extension of Fig. 6 with (1) a scan method (implementation elided for brevity) for class List and (2) an invocation of the scan method from the main application

3.1 Collections and Subtyping

Collection classes are often a major use case for parametric types, and it is also highlighted in [5] where two different versions using virtual classes are shown. Both versions have severe design implications originating in the virtual class design in BETA. The problem stated in [5], is that using virtual classes will lower the flexibility of the collection hierarchy. As an example Bruce, Odersky, and Wadler show a class Collection with subclass List that are used by creating a subclass StringList of List, and a subclass StringCollection of Collection. Hence, by design StringList is not a subclass of StringCollection, which reduces its reusability.

We show two different versions of this problem that address the flexibility issues using virtual classes. In both examples we create a class Collection with a virtual element elm that will serve as the element type of the collection and create a subclass List of class Collection.

The first solution to the collection problem uses virtual classes and is shown in Fig. 10. Here we create a subclass StringCollection of the class Collection where the element type elm is bound to string. At this point there is no difference between our example and the originally proposed solution [5], so it seems likely that class StringList will not be a subclass of class StringCollection. However, types in gbeta are sets of mixins, which ensures that class StringList is a subclass of class StringCollection. In slightly more detail, gbeta mixin composition is linearization-based [12,22] (and so is SCALA's), and enables multiple inheritance. In gbeta differently ordered lists of the same mixins are considered equivalent as types, but of course instances may have different semantics because of different method overriding relations. The remaining part of the example in Fig. 10 demonstrates that a method takeStringCollection accepts both an instance of StringCollection and an instance of StringList, but not an instance of List.

This design is however not optimal because class StringCollection needs to be used every time a collection of type string is needed—due to the nominal type equivalence. A new class StringCollection2 that also binds its element type elm to string will just make the two collections incompatible.

```
1   {
2       Collection: %{ elm:<object; ... };
3       List: Collection%{ ... };
4       StringCollection: Collection%{ elm:: string; ... };
5       StringList: StringCollection & List;
6
7       takeStringCollection: %(c: ^StringCollection) { ... };
8
9       l: @List; sc: @StringCollection; sl: @StringList;
10  #
11      //l^ | takeStringCollection;      // Compile-time error
12      sc^ | takeStringCollection;
13      sl^ | takeStringCollection;
14  }
```

Fig. 10. Making StringCollection and StringList proper subtypes using virtual classes, mixins and the linearization-based semantics of gbeta

The second solution to the collection problem uses virtual classes and type refinements and is shown in Fig. 11. In this example we do not create any string specific classes of Collection and List, but instead use a type refinement on the type of the argument of the takeColOfString method. The type refinement as seen on line 5 in Fig. 11 creates a constraint so that arguments must be subclasses of Collection and the type of its elements must be string or a subclass of string. We are now able to create two different instances, sc1 and sc2 of class Collection and an instance sl of class List where all of them bind the element type elm to string. All these instances are accepted by the takeColOfString method. This design is simpler and more general than both the first solution and the ones shown in [5]. Comparing the solution shown in Fig. 11 with the original parametric types version, the complexity of the actual collection hierarchy is almost identical. As with parametric types, the complexity has moved to the methods using the collection classes.

In summary, the two difficulties raised in [5] about virtual classes are (1) the sheer length of the programs, and (2) that virtual classes only relate via subtyping. It is still true that virtual classes only relate via subtyping, but adding type refinements on top of virtual classes provides a useful combination as shown in the examples. Furthermore the addition of type refinements makes it possible to write more compact programs with the same expressiveness and generality as using parametric types.

4   Revisiting Strengths of Virtual Classes

Bruce, Odersky, and Wadler [5] illustrate in detail how virtual classes excel at specifying mutually recursive families of classes and preserving the subtype relationships in derived families ('subfamilies'). As described by Bruce, Odersky, and Wadler [5], it is possible in the type parameterized world to create a class family generator using an F-bounded type argument for each member for the family on each member of the family (so we need k^2 type arguments with bounds for a k member family). This

```
1   {
2       Collection:%{ elm:<object; ... };
3       List:Collection%{ ... };
4
5       takeColOfString:%(c:^Collection[elm<=string]) {...};
6
7       1:@List; sc1:@Collection%{ elm::string };
8       sc2:@Collection%{elm::string}; sl:^List%{elm::string};
9   #
10      //1^ | takeColOfString;     // Compile-time error
11      sc1^ | takeColOfString;
12      sc2^ | takeColOfString;
13      new sl^ | takeColOfString;
14  }
```

Fig. 11. Simpler collection hierarchy where the gbeta type refinements are used to detect the different element types of collection

creates a similar typing structure as in the virtual class family, but concrete class families must be created by 'taking the fix-point'. This amounts to creating trivial subclasses of each class family member using the resulting concrete class family members as type arguments. This all adds up to a very verbose solution when using type parameters. However, the amount of typing knowledge also differs between the virtual class family and the F-bound based class family. This has implications for which type safe programs the two approaches are able to express.

To illustrate this new insight, it is not necessary to use a family with many members. A one member family will do, even though such a family may at first glance seem vacuous. However, it enables us to focus on a typing problem with the solution using parametric types and F-bounds; the problem does not arise when using virtual classes. The difference is, in a sense, the tighter association between the types of the members of a virtual family than the corresponding association between the members of an F-bound based family. The example we use is a Chinese box, which is a box that has the ability to wrap itself.

The first implementation of this is done in SCALA using parametric types and F-bounds and is shown in Fig. 12. In line 1 a parametrized class Box[X] is declared to have a variable x of type X. The class Box also has a getter and a setter method that are typed using the parameter type of the class. We then declare a subclass ChineseBox of class Box, which has an F-bounded type parameter as declared in line 6 in Fig. 12. To be able to use the class ChineseBox we have to create a fix-point class Chinese-BoxFix, which will create the class family of one. In the main application we are now able to create an instance of class ChineseBoxFix and call the method selfwrap on it. Without looking at the solution in line 8 in Fig. 12 the straightforward way to implement the method selfwrap would be to call setX with argument this. However, the type of this within class ChineseBox is not a subtype of X, and an explicit dynamic cast (asInstanceof[X]) must be inserted to make the program compile. Note that this is required for type soundness, because the type argument X may be given other values than the intended ones arising in fix-point classes.

```
1    abstract class Box[X] {
2      var x: X
3      def getX(): X = x
4      def setX(x:X): Unit = this.x = x
5    }
6    abstract class ChineseBox[X <: ChineseBox[X]]
7      extends Box[X] {
8        def selfwrap() = setX(this.asInstanceOf[X])
9    }
10   class ChineseBoxFix extends ChineseBox[ChineseBoxFix] {
11     var x = new ChineseBoxFix
12   }
13   object Main extends Application {
14     val x = new ChineseBoxFix
15     x.selfwrap()
16   }
```

Fig. 12. Implementing the ChineseBox example in SCALA using parametric types. The type of this in a ChineseBox is not a subtype of X, so we must add a dynamic cast to the type parameter in method selfwrap.

The second implementation of the Chinese box example is done in gbeta using virtual classes, in Fig. 13. We need to use a first class package in order to establish a definite type for the 'type argument' X; we could also use the block structure, but this is a little bit more flexible. Using the package object Xh in class Box, we can express the type of x as Xh.T (which corresponds to X in the previous example). Besides the fields x and Xh, class Box also has a getX and setX method. The virtual class ChineseBox is initially bound to class Box and is nested within class CB. In class ChineseBox we bind Xh to a new type argument object where the element T is bound to ChineseBox. Now we can use the this reference of ChineseBox as a valid argument to setX. The rest of the example in Fig. 13 just creates an instance of ChineseBox and calls the selfwrap method on that instance. The typing problem is now gone.

Finally, note that virtual classes are not alone in having a nominal nature that often requires the use of a specific, named declaration to avoid spuriously incompatible types. The structurality of parametric types typically removes such name dependencies, but fix-point classes such as the one in Fig. 12 must be used consistently to avoid spurious incompatibilities, e.g., in order to let chinese boxes contain each other.

5   Related Work

Since Bruce, Odersky, and Wadler [5] published their comparison of how parametric and virtual types handled different design problems, a lot of work has happened around virtual types and virtual classes. We have already covered some of the relevant languages like gbeta [7,12,10], SCALA [27,2], CaesarJ [19,3] and Object Teams [15,14]. A recent development with type arguments is that they can be higher-order [20]; essentially, a type argument with a parameter corresponds to a virtual class containing a virtual class, but a detailed treatment of this topic is beyond the scope and space of this paper.

```
1    {
2       TA: %(|this){ T:<object; };      // Type argument
3
4       Box: %{ Xh:<@TA; x: ^Xh.T; getX: %(|x); setX: %(x); };
5
6       CB: %{
7          ChineseBox:<Box %{
8             Xh:: @TA%{ T:: ChineseBox };
9             selfwrap: { this(ChineseBox) | setX };
10         }
11      };
12
13      aCB: @CB; cb: ^aCB.ChineseBox;
14  #
15      new aCB.ChineseBox^ | cb;
16      cb.selfwrap;
17   }
```

Fig. 13. Implementing the ChineseBox example in gbeta using virtual classes. Here the this type of a ChineseBox is a subtype of the required type ChineseBox, so it may safely be used as an argument to setX in selfwrap.

The programming languages Jx [23] and J& [24] support a variant of the concept of families of classes. They are based on the notion of nested inheritance and nested intersection, respectively, and are compiled to Java using the Polyglot compiler framework. Nested inheritance supports the inheritance of packages and classes while allowing classes nested within to be overridden, like virtual classes. J& introduces nested intersection which enables multiple inheritance of two or more packages, combining types and behavior, and resolving conflicts with a relatively small amount of code, and preserving soundness. An alternative to nested intersection is presented with J&$_s$, which supports class sharing [30]. Normally instances from one family can not be used in another family, but if the object is an instance of a shared class in one family is also an instance of the corresponding class in any family that shares the class. Objects can then be viewed from either family. Class sharing supports bidirectional adaptation: not only can objects of a base family be adapted into a derived family, but those of the derived family can be adapted to the base family. All in all, these languages obtain extra flexibility in several ways, but in return they do not support subtype polymorphic access to families as such. Lightweight family polymorphism [32] is an approach to families of classes where the need for path dependent types is removed. Families are represented by classes (not objects) here, and it is always known statically which family is used, when it is accessed from the outside. In return, the language and type system is considerably simpler, and this mechanism is much more compatible with existing mainstream languages and platforms. All these languages could use most of the mechanisms and techniques described in this paper.

The X10 programming language is a modern statically typed object-oriented programming language with constrained types [25]. A constrained type is a form of dependent type, where the types include predicates over the immutable state of objects.

The objects in this calculus do not support class valued features and hence there are no path dependent types, but the static analysis of immutable state including references to other objects involves compiler plugins and the use of automated theorem provers, which would be interesting for us as directions of further research.

Many functional languages in the ML family, like O'Caml and Standard ML, have a distinction between the core language and the module language [33]. The core language is used to define the small scale (implementation) parts, where the module system is used to define the large scale (module) parts of the system. Standard ML offers *sharing specifications* within signatures, which assert that the indicated types or structures are the same. The sharing specifications must be fully known at compile-time. There has been made research to make modules a first-class structure [31] in ML. These first-class structures are similar to objects in a language with virtual classes, but they do not support anything that resembles depth subtyping.

6 Conclusion

The theory about virtual classes and types, and languages implementing them, have evolved in many ways over the past twelve years, since Bruce, Odersky, and Wadler made their comparison of parametric and virtual types. We have shown that type refinements as found in SCALA and gbeta provides some structurality for virtual types and classes. The type refinements in SCALA are restricted to creating constraints at the type level that are checked at compile time. Type refinements in gbeta can constrain both virtual classes and virtual objects, and they are both used in compile time checked types, and inspected in dynamic tests, creating a new mechanism for doing "instanceof tests" at the level of complete families, and even testing whether two dynamically accessed families are compatible. Finally, we have demonstrated that the strengths of virtual classes have more aspects than previously documented; in particular that this in a class family gets a more precise type than it does with parametric types. In summary, the distribution of strengths and weaknesses among parametric types and virtual classes have been redistributed somewhat, with fewer problems and new strengths on the side of virtual types and classes.

Acknowledgments. We would like to thank David Ungar for suggesting that we looked at this topic once more. Without his suggestion, this paper would not have been written. We would also like to thank the anonymous reviewers for valuable feedback and suggestions to improve the paper.

References

1. Agesen, O., Freund, S.N., Mitchell, J.C.: Adding type parameterization to the Java language. In: Proceedings of OOPSLA '97, pp. 49–65 (1997)
2. Altherr, P.: A typed intermediate language and algorithms for compiling scala by successive rewritings. PhD thesis, EPFL (2006),
   http://library.epfl.ch/theses/?nr=3509

3. Aracic, I., Gasiunas, V., Mezini, M., Ostermann, K.: An overview of CaesarJ. In: Rashid, A., Aksit, M. (eds.) Transactions on Aspect-Oriented Software Development I. LNCS, vol. 3880, pp. 135–173. Springer, Heidelberg (2006)
4. Bracha, G., Odersky, M., Stoutamire, D., Wadler, P.: Making the future safe for the past: adding genericity to the Java programming language. In: Proceedings of OOPSLA '98, pp. 183–200 (1998)
5. Bruce, K.B., Odersky, M., Wadler, P.: A statically safe alternative to virtual types. In: Jul, E. (ed.) ECOOP 1998. LNCS, vol. 1445, pp. 523–549. Springer, Heidelberg (1998)
6. Canning, P., Cook, W., Hill, W., Olthoff, W.: F-bounded polymorphism for object-oriented programming. In: Proceedings of the Conference on Functional Programming Languages and Computer Architecture '89, pp. 273–280 (1989)
7. Ernst, E.: gbeta – a Language with Virtual Attributes, Block Structure, and Propagating, Dynamic Inheritance. PhD thesis, Department of Computer Science, Aarhus University, Århus, Denmark (1999)
8. Ernst, E.: Propagating class and method combination. In: Guerraoui, R. (ed.) ECOOP 1999. LNCS, vol. 1628, pp. 67–91. Springer, Heidelberg (1999)
9. Ernst, E.: Family polymorphism. In: Knudsen, J.L. (ed.) ECOOP 2001. LNCS, vol. 2072, pp. 303–326. Springer, Heidelberg (2001)
10. Ernst, E.: Higher-order hierarchies. In: Cardelli, L. (ed.) ECOOP 2003. LNCS, vol. 2743, pp. 303–329. Springer, Heidelberg (2003)
11. Ernst, E.: Reconciling virtual classes with genericity. In: Lightfoot, D.E., Szyperski, C. (eds.) JMLC 2006. LNCS, vol. 4228, pp. 57–72. Springer, Heidelberg (2006)
12. Ernst, E., Ostermann, K., Cook, W.R.: A virtual class calculus. In: Proceedings of POPL '06, pp. 270–282 (2006)
13. Gosling, J., Joy, B., Steele, G., Bracha, G.: The Java Language Specification, 3rd edn. Addison-Wesley, Reading (May 2005)
14. Herrmann, S.: Object teams: Improving modularity for crosscutting collaborations. In: Proceedings of Net. Object days, pp. 248–264 (2002)
15. Herrmann, S., Herrmann, S., Hundt, C., Hundt, C., Mehner, K., Mehner, K.: Translation polymorphism in object teams. Technical report, Technical University Berlin (2004)
16. Kennedy, A., Syme, D.: Design and implementation of generics for the.net common language runtime. SIGPLAN Not. 36(5), 1–12 (2001)
17. Madsen, O.L., Møller-Pedersen, B.: Virtual classes: A powerful mechanism in object-oriented programming. In: Proceedings of OOPSLA '89, pp. 397–406 (1989)
18. Madsen, O.L., Nygaard, K., Møller-Pedersen, B.: Object-Oriented Programming in The Beta Programming Language. Addison-Wesley, Reading (1993)
19. Mezini, M., Ostermann, K.: Conquering aspects with Caesar. In: Proceedings of AOSD '03, pp. 90–99 (2003)
20. Moors, A., Piessens, F., Odersky, M.: Generics of a higher kind. In: Proceedings of OOPSLA '08, pp. 423–438 (2008)
21. Myers, A.C., Bank, J.A., Liskov, B.: Parameterized types for Java. In: Proceedings of POPL '97, pp. 132–145 (1997)
22. Nielsen, A.B., Ernst, E.: Optimizing dynamic class composition in a statically typed language. In: Paige, R.F., Meyer, B. (eds.) TOOLS EUROPE 2008. LNBIP, vol. 11, pp. 161–177. Springer, Heidelberg (1974)
23. Nystrom, N., Chong, S., Myers, A.C.: Scalable extensibility via nested inheritance. In: OOPSLA '04: Proceedings of the 19th annual ACM SIGPLAN conference on Object-oriented programming, systems, languages, and applications, pp. 99–115 (2004)
24. Nystrom, N., Qi, X., Myers, A.C.: J&: nested intersection for scalable software composition. In: Proceedings of OOPSLA '06, pp. 21–36 (2006)

25. Nystrom, N., Saraswat, V., Palsberg, J., Grothoff, C.: Constrained types for object-oriented languages. In: Proceedings of OOPSLA '08, pp. 457–474 (2008)
26. Odersky, M.: The Scala Language Specification. EPFL, Version 2.7 edn. (March 2009)
27. Odersky, M., Cremet, V., Röckl, C., Zenger, M.: A nominal theory of objects with dependent types. In: Cardelli, L. (ed.) ECOOP 2003. LNCS, vol. 2743, pp. 201–224. Springer, Heidelberg (2003)
28. Odersky, M., Wadler, P.: Pizza into Java: translating theory into practice. In: Proceedings of POPL '97, pp. 146–159 (1997)
29. Odersky, M., Zenger, M.: Independently extensible solutions to the expression problem. In: Proc. FOOL 12 (January 2005)
30. Qi, X., Myers, A.C.: Sharing classes between families. In: Proceedings of PLDI '09, pp. 281–292 (2009)
31. Russo, C.V.: First-class structures for Standard ML. In: Smolka, G. (ed.) ESOP 2000. LNCS, vol. 1782, pp. 336–350. Springer, Heidelberg (2000)
32. Saito, C., Igarashi, A., Viroli, M.: Lightweight family polymorphism*. Journal of Functional Programming 18(3), 285–331 (2008)
33. Ullman, J.D.: Elements of ML programming (ML97 ed.). Prentice-Hall, Inc, Upper Saddle River (1998)

A   Summary of *A Statically Safe Alternative to Virtual Types*

This section gives a short summary of *A statically safe alternative to virtual types* [5] by Bruce, Odersky, and Wadler. We only cover sections 1 through 4 (the first twelve pages), because only this part is relevant to the discussion on parametric types and virtual classes in this paper. The contents of these twelve pages is as follows:

Bruce, Odersky, and Wadler introduce the concepts of parametric types as found in Pizza and virtual types as proposed by Kresten Thorup to be included in Java. After introducing both concepts via concrete examples, it is concluded that parametric types offer more compile-time checking, while virtual types offer more flexibility. Parametric types are shown to excel at structurally oriented composition and decomposition, using the zip method on some collection classes like List and Pair. Building the same example using virtual types shows how difficult it is to express object composition in a structural manner, because virtual types are so closely tied to nominal typing. Virtual types are shown to excel at specifying mutually recursive families of classes whose relationships are preserved in derived families. This is shown using 'list with length' and 'alternating lists with length' as a two example families of related classes. Building the same example with parametric types results in a complex and fragile program with explicit fix-point-classes.

B   A Brief Introduction to the gbeta Syntax

In this section we give a small overview of the parts of the gbeta syntax needed to understand the examples in this paper. We use SCALA as a reference and show how gbeta constructs can be approximated in SCALA. Some gbeta constructs cannot be translated, because of the unification of classes and methods, or incompatible semantics.

#	gbeta	SCALA
1	`name:@ type`	`val name : type = new type()`
2	`name:<@ type`	`val name : type`
3	`name::@ object`	`val name = type`
4	`name:^ type`	`var name : type`
5	`name: %{...}`	`class name {...}`
6	`name: %(in|out){1 # E}`	`def (in) = {1;E;out}`
7	`exp1 | exp2`	`exp2 = exp1`

The above table translates from gbeta constructs to very similar SCALA constructs. We have not included all gbeta constructs, only the ones needed to understand the examples in this paper. One important operator is the pipe symbol, '|' (line 7). It is used for assignment (as shown in the table above), for method calls, and more. Dataflow is always from left to right, just like operating system shell commands.

The gbeta language has only one syntactic form declaring classes and methods, because these two concepts are unified into the pattern concept. All patterns can be used as methods, but input and output parameters must be declared in order to pass arguments to and/or get results from a method call. In this paper, we only declare input and output parameters for patterns used as methods. This is shown as lines 5 for class fields and 6 for methods. One important thing to note is that parameters in the input and output lists are in the same scope as the body of the method. This can be illustrated by the following: `%(...x:T...) {...}` is equivalent to `%(...x...) {x:T...}`.

Other fields include object references (4), immutable object references (1) and virtual objects (2 and 3). The first virtual object reference in line 2 is the declaration of a virtual field. The second virtual object reference in line 3 is the binding of the field; the assigned object has to have a subtype of the initially declared type.

Using the above scheme the gbeta examples in this paper can be translated to SCALA. The translation is not complete, but hopefully it is enough to establish an intuition about the examples.

Moles: Tool-Assisted Environment Isolation with Closures

Jonathan de Halleux and Nikolai Tillmann

Microsoft Research
One Microsoft Way, Redmond WA 98052, USA
{jhalleux,nikolait}@microsoft.com

Abstract. Isolating test cases from environment dependencies is often desirable, as it increases test reliability and reduces test execution time. However, code that calls non-virtual methods or consumes sealed classes is often impossible to test in isolation. Moles is a new lightweight framework which addresses this problem. For any .NET method, Moles allows test-code to provide alternative implementations, given as .NET delegates, for which C# provides very concise syntax while capturing local variables in a closure object. Using code instrumentation, the Moles framework will redirect calls to provided delegates instead of the original methods. The Moles framework is designed to work together with the dynamic symbolic execution tool Pex to enable automated test generation. In a case study, testing code programmed against the Microsoft SharePoint Foundation API, we achieved full code coverage while running tests in isolation without an actual SharePoint server. The Moles framework integrates with .NET and Visual Studio.

1 Introduction

In software testing, it is often desirable to test individual components in isolation. It makes testing more robust and scalable. Especially in the context of unit testing, where the intention is to test a single unit of functionality at a time, all irrelevant environment dependencies should be mocked, or simulated, so that the unit tests run quickly and give deterministic results. (This is in contrast to integration testing, where the goal is to test an entire software system, including all environment dependencies, at the same time. Integration tests are usually neither quick, nor entirely reliable.)

However, many programming languages and runtime systems with static type checking and binding have language constructs that enforce the use of particular implementations. For example, in .NET, the code-under-test may call static or non-virtual methods, or it may consume sealed classes. In those cases, the standard .NET runtime does not provide any way to redirect calls for testing purposes. As a result, isolating the code for testing purposes becomes impossible.

In theory, the best solution to the problem is to refactor the code [3], introducing explicit interface boundaries and allowing different interface implementations. However, it is often not possible in practice to refactor existing legacy code, especially when it is provided by a third party.

J. Vitek (Ed.): TOOLS 2010, LNCS 6141, pp. 253–270, 2010.

We have developed a new lightweight framework called Moles to address this problem. The Moles framework allows the test-code to provide alternative implementations for non-abstract methods of any .NET type. Using code instrumentation, the Moles framework will redirect calls to an alternative implementation. An alternative implementation is given as a .NET delegate instance, which consists of a method together with a receiver object. This enables the direct use of closures in languages such as C# 2.0. The Moles framework generates *mole types* which provide explicit type-safe attachment points to register delegates as alternative implementations for every method of the code-under-test. As a welcome side effect of explicit type-safe attachment points, the developer is helped by the Visual Studio editor via automatic code completion when writing delegate attachments for any particular attachment point.

The Moles framework has been designed to work together with the dynamic symbolic execution [4] tool Pex [18,14] to enable automated test generation. Pex relies on tracing control- and dataflow at runtime, analyzing the test-code together with the code-under-test. Pex can only analyze .NET code. When an environment-facing component is invoked that is not implemented in .NET itself, then Pex cannot infer the constraints that reflect the behavior of that component, and as a consequence Pex cannot generate test cases that achieve high code coverage. Moles allow the tester to replace any environment-facing component at test time with .NET code that simulates its behavior, which in turn enables test case generation with Pex. The test cases generated by Pex do not depend on Pex anymore, but they can reproduce their results in isolation, using only Moles.

We have performed a case study, testing code programmed against the SharePoint Foundation [10] API using Moles and Pex, and we were able to achieve full code coverage while running the code in isolation without the need for an actual SharePoint server.

Moles supports .NET 2.0 and higher; Moles integrates with Visual Studio 2008 and higher. Moles is part of Pex, an incubation project for Visual Studio developed at Microsoft Research. Pex is available for academic use and for commercial evaluation.

The main contributions of this paper are:

– The description of a low-level, instrumentation-based detour approach.
– The description of a code generation framework that provides type-safe attachment points for detours in the form of delegates.
– A formalization of the semantics of attaching, detaching, and invoking detours, which enables the analysis of detours, in particular with symbolic execution frameworks.
– An evaluation of the feasibility of our approach in the context of a real-world application.

We will explain the basic idea behind the Moles framework along a simple example in Section 2. Moles leverages several features of .NET and C#, notably delegates, anonymous methods, lambda-expressions, and closures, which we will discuss in Section 3. We will describe in detail the implementation of Moles, and give a formal description of its semantics in Section 4. We describe a case study in which we applied Moles and Pex on a SharePoint application in Section 5. We discuss related work in Section 6, and conclude in Section 7.

2 Motivating Example

Consider a C# method that throws an exception on January 1st of 2000.

```
public static class Y2KChecker {
  public static void Check() {
    if (DateTime.Now == new DateTime(2000,1,1))
      throw new ApplicationException("y2k bug!");
  }
}
```

(Note: Now is a *property* of the DateTime type which is part of the .NET framework. When referencing this property as shown in the code above, a call to a method get_Now is generated by the C# compiler.)

Testing this method is particularly problematic because the program depends on DateTime.Now, a property that in turn depends on the computer clock. In other words, DateTime.Now is environment-dependent and non-deterministic. Moreover, the Date-Time.Now property is static, so it is not possible to use virtual method overriding to supply a different implementation at test time. This problem is symptomatic of the isolation issue in unit testing: programs that directly call into the database APIs, communicate with web services, etc., are hard to unit test because their logic depends on the environment.

If .NET allowed us to redefine the meaning of static methods at runtime, we could easily solve this testing problem by replacing the computed value of DateTime.Now with something else.

```
// does not compile: DateTime.Now cannot be set
DateTime.Now = new DateTime(2000, 1, 1);
```

Moles enables this scenario. *Mole types* provide a mechanism to detour any .NET method. When a method is detoured, all invocations of that method get forwarded to an alternative implementation, and the original method is never actually invoked.

To this end, the Moles code generator creates a type MDateTime which has a settable property NowGet. This property can be set to an instance of a delegate which doesn't take parameters, and returns a DateTime value. C# 3.0 allows one to write a function inline within another method.

```
// attach delegate to the mole property to redirect DateTime.Now
// to return January 1st of 2000
MDateTime.NowGet = () => new DateTime(2000, 1, 1);
Y2KChecker.Check();
```

After setting MDateTime.NowGet, all calls to the property getter of DateTime.Now are detoured to the user-supplied delegate. This is realized by code instrumentation. To enable the code instrumentation when using the Visual Studio Unit Test framework, the attribute [HostType("Moles")] must be added to instruct the Visual Studio Unit Test framework to run the test under the control of the Moles instrumentation framework.

```
[TestMethod]
[HostType("Moles")] // run with code instrumentation
```

```
public void Y2kCheckerTest() {
  ...
}
```

The `[TestMethod]` annotation identified the above method as a unit test.

Pex, an automated white-box test generation tool for .NET, enables Parameterized Unit Testing [19]. The following method is identified as a parameterized unit test by the `[PexMethod]` attribute. It states that for all possible parameter values, the test should succeed (and not terminate with an uncaught exception).

```
[PexMethod]
public void Y2kCheckerTest(DateTime time) {
  // hook to the method to redirect DateTime.Now
  MDateTime.NowGet = () => time;
  Y2KChecker.Check();
}
```

By symbolically tracing the test inputs through the C# compiler-generated closure, the delegate, and the detoured invocation of `DateTime.Now`, Pex discovers the path condition `time == new DateTime(2000,1,1)` where `time` is the test input. As a result, Pex generates two traditional unit tests such as the two unit tests shown below, one where the path condition is fulfilled, and one where it is not.

```
[TestMethod]
[HostType("Moles")]
public void Y2kCheckerTest01() {
  Y2kCheckerTest(new DateTime(1, 1, 1));
}
[TestMethod]
[HostType("Moles")]
public void Y2kCheckerTest02() {
  Y2kCheckerTest(new DateTime(2000, 1, 1));
}
```

Without Moles, Pex would not have been able to construct test cases that cover all cases in the code, as the actual implementation of `DateTime.Now` relies on system calls to query the current machine time, which is outside of the semantics of .NET, and therefore outside of the scope which Pex can analyze. The resulting test cases can be executed in isolation, only relying on Moles to make the execution deterministic by circumventing the environment-facing components, without requiring symoblic execution with Pex.

3 Background: Delegates, Lambda-Expressions, and Closures

This section gives an overview of .NET delegates, C# anonymous methods, lambda-expressions, and closures, which the Moles framework leverages.

In .NET, *delegates* allow the representation and invocation of function pointers as values, in a fully type-safe manner. In addition to the actual function pointer, a *delegate value* may also contain an object reference, which serves as the first argument of the target function, usually the receiver object of an instance method. A *delegate type* specifies the return type and the parameter types of a method call. Delegate types are named. For example, the following declaration defines a delegate type named D with two integer parameters and a string return type. (As you can see, C# requires the specification of parameter names, but they are semantically irrelevant.)

```
delegate string D(int x, int y);
```

Consider a class with the following method.

```
string Compute(int x, int y) {
   return (x+y).ToString();
}
```

Creating an instance of a delegate is written similar to a constructor call in C#; the parameter is the name of a method, qualified with an expression holding the object reference that should serve as the receiver object for an instance method (and which is omitted when referring to a static method):

```
D d = new D(this.Compute);
```

In C#, the syntax to invoke a delegate is similar to the syntax for invoking a regular method. For the example above, the delegate invocation d(23,42) will in effect invoke this.Compute(23,42).

   C# supports so-called *anonymous methods* starting with version 2.0. This allows the inlining of the above Compute method:

```
D d = delegate(int x, int y) {
   return (x+y).ToString();
};
```

Starting from version 3.0, C# supports so-called *lambda-expressions* which allow further abbreviating the code to the following equivalent code:

```
D d = (x, y) => (x+y).ToString();
```

An anonymous method or a lambda-expression may refer to local variables defined in the scope of the outer method.

```
int offset = 42;
D d = (x, y) => (x + y + offset).ToString();
```

In this case the C# compiler will generate a closure class which will hold all the referenced local variables as fields, and the C# compiler will take care of redirecting all accesses to an instance of the closure class. The following code represents the equivalent code generated by the C# compiler:

```
Closure c = new Closure();
c.offset = 42;
D d = new D(c.Body);

class Closure {
   public int offset;
   public string Body(int x, int y) {
```

```
  return (x + y + offset).ToString();
  }
}
```

In C#, the body of the anonymous method or lambda-expression may mutate the captured local variables, and the changes will be visible to all other references to the same variable. In other words, closures in C# capture variables, not just values.

4   Our Approach: Moles

4.1   Code Instrumentation, and Low-Level Detours Library

The Moles framework builds on top of the Extended Reflection code instrumentation framework to realize the detouring of method calls. Extended Reflection is also used by Pex and CHESS[11]. The details of the code instrumentation are hidden from the user who interacts only with the generated high-level *mole types* described in Section 4.2.

The instrumentation is done as follows. At the beginning of each method some code is inserted. This code queries a low-level detours library as to whether any detour was attached to this particular method. If so, then the detour delegate is invoked, otherwise, the normal code is executed.

For example, consider the following method.

```
string Compute(int x, int y) {
  return (x + y).ToString();
}
```

After instrumentation, the code will be similar to the following pseudo-code.

```
string Compute(int x, int y) {
  // obtain identifier of this method
  Method thisMethod = this.GetType().GetMethod(
    "Compute", new Type[]{typeof(int), typeof(int)});
  // query if a detour has been attached
  Delegate detour = _Detours.GetDetour(this, thisMethod);
  if (detour != null) {
    // pseudo-code; actual implementation avoids boxing
    return (string)_Detours.InvokeDetour(
      detour, this,
      new object[] { x, y });
  }
  // else execute normal code
  return (x + y).ToString();
}
```

The above code uses a low-level detours library shown in Figure 1, which manages all attached detours, and provides facilities to query and invoke detour delegates.

While the above code accurately reflects the behavior after code instrumentation has been applied, note that our actual code instrumentation results in more efficient code that avoids casting and boxing by using (potentially) "unsafe" .NET instructions (which are guaranteed to be "safe" in the particular way they are used by Moles), in effect simply passing through the values. This is possible as the instrumented code may bypass type-safety checks at test time.

```
public class _Detours {
  // attaching and detaching
  public static void AttachDetour(
    object receiver, Method method,
    Delegate detourDelegate) {
    ...
  }
  public static void DetachDetour(
    object receiver, Method method) {
    ...
  }
  // quering and invoking
  public static Delegate GetDetour(
    object receiver, Method method) {
    ...
  }
  public static object InvokeDetour(
    Delegate detour,
    object receiver, object[] args) {
    ...
  }
}
```

Fig. 1. Detours library used by Moles

4.2   Mole Type Generation for Type-Safety

When attaching and detaching moles via our general detours library shown in Figure 1, type-safety cannot be guaranteed at compile time: The AttachDetour method takes a method identifier, and a delegate of type Delegate, which is the base type of all delegate types. In order to enforce that attaching (and detaching) of moles is always done in a type-safe manner, the Moles framework generates specialized code. Besides type-safety, the specialized code also frees the developer from constructing method identifiers using the .NET reflection API, and it enables Visual Studio editor support for automatic code completion when attaching or detaching moles.

In the following, we discuss the details of the Moles code generator, which systematically covers static methods and constructors, as well as instance methods, in an instance-agnostic and an instance-specific way.

For every type t, a mole type Mt is generated. For every method in t, including the implicit getter and setter methods for .NET properties, and adders and removers for .NET events, settable mole properties are generated as explained in the following. The generated type M*t* is placed into a sub-namespace of type *t*; the suffix `.Moles` is added to the namespace of *t*. The generated types are placed in a separate *assembly*, which is a collection of types in .NET that can be addressed independently.

Static Methods and Constructors. For each static method in type *t* with parameter types $T_1, T_2, \ldots, T_n$ and return type U, a settable static property in type M*t* is generated, with a delegate type `Func` similar[1] to the following:

$$\text{delegate } U \text{ Func } (T_1, T_2, \ldots, T_n)$$

The same applies to instance constructors, where the implicit `this` argument becomes the first parameter T_1. The name of the property starts with the name of the static method, appended by short type names of the parameters, and possibly a number to make all generated property names distinct. This allows distinguishing different overloads with the same method name.

Example: The following pseudo-code illustrates the generated implementation of `MDateTime.NowGet` that we used in the motivating example in Section 2. (The first argument to `AttachDetour` and `DetachDetour` is `null`, as `DateTime.Now` is a static property that does not require any instance.) The code uses the low-level detours library shown in Figure 1.

```
static Func/*delegate DateTime Func()*/ NowGet {
  set { // property setter has implicit 'value' parameter
    Method method = typeof(DateTime).GetMethod("get_Now");
    if (value == null)
      _Detours.DetachDetour(null, method);
    else
      _Detours.AttachDetour(null, method, value);
  }
}
```

Instance Methods (for all instances). For each instance method in type *t* with explicit parameter types $T_1, T_2, \ldots, T_n$ and return type U, a settable static property in the nested type M*t*.`AllInstances` is generated, with a delegate type `Func` similar to the following:

$$\text{delegate } U \text{ Func } (t, T_1, T_2, \ldots, T_n)$$

Note the first parameter type, which represents the previously implicit `this` argument of the instance method.

Example: The following pseudo-code shows the implementation of the generated static property `ComputeInt32Int32` for the `Compute` example earlier in this section. Note that the name consists of the original method name, `Compute`, appended by `Int32Int32`, which represents the two `int` parameters (whose canonical .NET type name is `System.Int32`):

---

[1] Instead of generating a separate delegate type for each moled method, generic delegate types are instantiated. However, to simplify the exposition, we do not discuss .NET generics in this paper.

```
static Func/*delegate string Func(int,int)*/ ComputeInt32Int32 {
  set { // property setter has implicit 'value' parameter
    Method method = typeof(ComputeType).GetMethod("Compute",
      new Type[] { typeof(int), typeof(int) });
    if (value == null)
      _Detours.DetachDetour(null, method);
    else
      _Detours.AttachDetour(null, method, value);
  }
}
```

The first argument to `AttachDetour` and `DetachAttach` is `null`, indicating that this detour should apply to all instances.

Instance Methods (for a specific instance). As an alternative to detouring all calls to instance methods regardless of the implicit `this` parameter, detouring can dispatch to different detour delegates depending on the value of the `this` parameter. To this end, the low-level API maintains a mapping of receiver-object and method pairs to detour delegates.

The high-level mole types allow binding to specific receiver objects by making Mt instantiable, associating each instance of Mt with an instance of t, and by a providing settable instance properties on Mt for all instance methods of t.

For each instance method in type t with parameter types $T_1, T_2, \ldots, T_n$ and return type U, a settable instance property in type Mt is generated, with a delegate type similar to the following:

$$\texttt{delegate } U \texttt{ Func } (T_1, T_2, \ldots, T_n)$$

Note that unlike the static property in the nested `AllInstances` type, there is no provision to pass on the implicit `this` argument of the instance method. (However, it could be captured in the closure object of the detour delegate.)

The Mt type has an instance property called `Instance` to access the associated t instance. The Mt type also defines an implicit conversion operator to t.

Example: The following pseudo-code shows the implementation of the generated property `ComputeInt32Int32` for the `Compute` example earlier in this section.

```
Func/*delegate string Func(int,int)*/ ComputeInt32Int32 {
  set { // property setter has implicit 'value' parameter
    Method method = typeof(ComputeType).GetMethod("Compute",
      new Type[] { typeof(int), typeof(int) });
    if (value == null)
      _Detours.DetachDetour(this.Instance, method);
    else
      _Detours.AttachDetour(this.Instance, method, value);
  }
}
```

The first argument to `AttachDetour` and `DetachDetour` is `this.Instance`, indicating that this detour should apply to only to the specific instance associated with the current mole instance.

4.3   Formalization

We discussed the code instrumentation and the generated type-safe mole types, and illustrated our implementation using the low-level _Detours library. The Moles framework was motivated by Pex [18,14], an automated white-box test generation tool, which uses dynamic symbolic execution [4]. Pex tracks precisely the control- and data-flow of program executions, in order to gather *path conditions* describing the condition, expressed as a formula over the test inputs, under which the program takes a particular execution path. Variations of such path conditions are then solved by an automated constraint solver, in order to compute new test inputs that will exercise a new execution path. Symbolic execution requires a precise model of the semantics of the operations of the executing program in order to build exact path conditions. In effect, Moles adds new and modifies existing operations of the execution environment, which must be modeled precisely: Moles adds the ability to attach and detach detour delegates, and Moles modifies the meaning of a method call: If a detour delegate is currently attached, control is transferred to the detour delegate, otherwise the method executes normally.

Detour delegates are effectively a pair, consisting of a closure object, and a pointer to a function. If the detoured method takes a receiver object argument, then a detour can either apply to all receiver objects, or only to a particular one.

In the following, we describe the meaning of some basic operations, attaching and detaching detour delegates, method calls and call returns.[2]

We consider the following operations. All instructions belong to the sort $INSTR$, the names x, y, $y_1, y_2, \ldots, y_n$ refer to local variables of sort VAR, and M and N are method identifiers of sort $PROC$.

General computation, assignment and conditional control flow:[3]

- Assigning a value computed by a built-in function f:
    assign $x := f(y_1, y_2, \ldots, y_n)$
- Conditional branching:
    if(x) goto PC

For attaching and detaching moles:

- Attaching a mole closure (y, N) for a method M:
    mole $M := (y, N)$
- Attaching a mole closure (y, N) for a specific instance x and its method M:
    mole $(x, M) := (y, N)$
- Detaching a mole for a method M:
    unmole M
- Detaching a mole for a specific instance x and its method M:
    unmole (x, M)

---

[2] We ignore many details of the execution engine which are not relevant here, including object allocation, object field accesses, virtual method resolution, etc.

[3] We include these instruction for illustrative purposes; they are not necessary to understand the behavior of Moles.

For calling and returning:

- Calling a method M with arguments $y_1, y_2, \ldots, y_n$ and storing the result in x:
  $$x := \mathtt{call}\ M(y_1, y_2, \ldots, y_n)$$
  (Note in this operation, any initial `this` argument is made explicit.)
- Returning from a method call with value y:
  $$\mathtt{ret}\ y$$

A program P has a function $start_P : PROC \rightarrow \mathcal{N}$ which maps a method to the offset of its first instruction, and a function $instr_P : \mathcal{N} \rightarrow INSTR$ which maps each offset to its associated instruction. A program starts at offset 0.

The program semantics are described by the constant $init_P : HEAP \times STACK$, which represents the initial program state, together with the function $step_P : HEAP \times STACK \rightarrow HEAP \times STACK$ which represents the execution of a single instruction by transforming the program heap and stack. The heap maps values to values, and the stack is a sequence of stack frames, where each stack frame is given by a pair of a current program counter, and a mapping of local variables of sort VAR to values. While in general the heap may hold other objects or global state, we only use it to model the globally active attached detours. Every method has a special set of local variables for incoming arguments: $arg_1, arg_2, \ldots$

We use standard notations for maps and sequences. We write $\{\mapsto\}$ for the empty map, $\{x \mapsto y\}$ for the map with one entry that maps x to y, $M \oplus N$ for the combined map where N takes precedence over M, and $M \setminus x$ for the map that is M except that it does not contain index x, and $\{x \mapsto y : p\}$ for map that maps x to y wherever p holds, and $x \mapsto y \in M$ holds if the map contains the given mapping, $M(x)$ represents the value of M at index x. We write $[x]$ for the sequence holding one element x, and $x \mathbin{+\!\!+} y$ for the concatenation of sequences x and y.

Initial program state:
$$init_P = (\{\mapsto\}, [(0, \{\mapsto\})])$$

General computation, assignment and conditional control-flow:
$$
\begin{aligned}
&step_P(H, R \mathbin{+\!\!+} (PC, L)) \\
&\quad \text{where } (instr_P(PC) = \mathtt{assign}\ x := f(y_1, y_2, \ldots, y_n)) \\
&\quad = (H, R \mathbin{+\!\!+} (PC + 1, L \oplus \{x \mapsto \hat{f}(L(y_1, y_2, \ldots, y_n))\})) \\
&\quad \text{where } \hat{f} \text{ is the built-in function computing } f \\
&step_P(H, R \mathbin{+\!\!+} (PC, L)) \\
&\quad \text{where } (instr_P(PC) = \mathtt{if}(x)\ \mathtt{goto}\ PC') \\
&\quad = \begin{cases} (H, R \mathbin{+\!\!+} (PC', L)) & \text{if } L(x) \text{ is true} \\ (H, R \mathbin{+\!\!+} (PC + 1, L)) & \text{otherwise} \end{cases}
\end{aligned}
$$

In words: If the current instruction is an assignment, then it does not change the heap, it increments the current program counter, and it assigns the value, computed over the local variables values, to a local variable. If the current instruction is a conditional control-flow operation, it evaluates the given condition with the current local variables assignment, and if it evaluates to `true`, the program counter changes to the specified target, otherwise it is incremented by one.

For attaching and detaching moles:

$step_P(H, R \text{ ++ } (PC, L))$
  where $(instr_P(PC) = \text{mole } M := (y, N))$
$= (H \oplus \{M \mapsto (y, N)\}, R \text{ ++ } (PC + 1, L))$
$step_P(H, R \text{ ++ } (PC, L))$
  where $(instr_P(PC) = \text{unmole } M)$
$= (H \setminus M, R \text{ ++ } (PC + 1, L))$
$step_P(H, R \text{ ++ } (PC, L))$
  where $(instr_P(PC) = \text{mole } (x, M) := (y, N))$
$= (H \oplus \{(x, M) \mapsto (y, N)\}, R \text{ ++ } (PC + 1, L))$
$step_P(H, R \text{ ++ } (PC, L))$
  where $(instr_P(PC) = \text{unmole } (x, M))$
$= (H \setminus (x, M), R \text{ ++ } (PC + 1, L))$

The above instructions basically add moles to or remove moles from the global state, represented here as H.

For calling and returning:

$step_P(H, R \text{ ++ } (PC, L))$
  where $(instr_P(PC) = \_ := \text{call } M(y_1, \ldots, y_n))$
$= \begin{cases} (H, R \text{ ++ } (PC, L) \text{ ++ } f_{v,N}^{\text{One}}) & \text{if } (L(y_1), M) \mapsto (v, N) \in H \\ (H, R \text{ ++ } (PC, L) \text{ ++ } f_{v,N}^{\text{All}}) & \text{if } M \mapsto (v, N) \in H \\ (H, R \text{ ++ } (PC, L) \text{ ++ } f) & \text{otherwise} \end{cases}$
  where the new frame $f_{v,N}$, f_N or f is defined as follows:
    $f_{v,N}^{\text{One}} = (start_P(N), \{arg_1 \mapsto v\} \oplus \{arg_i \mapsto L(y_i) : 2 \leq i \leq n\})$
    $f_{v,N}^{\text{All}} = (start_P(N), \{arg_1 \mapsto v\} \oplus \{arg_{i+1} \mapsto L(y_i) : 1 \leq i \leq n\})$
    $f \quad = (start_P(M), \{arg_i \mapsto L(y_i) : 1 \leq i \leq n\})$
$step_P(H, R \text{ ++ } (PC, L) \text{ ++ } (PC', L'))$
  where $(instr_P(PC) = x := \text{call } \_(\_) \quad \wedge \quad instr_P(PC') = \text{ret } y)$
$= (H, R \text{ ++ } (PC + 1, L \oplus \{x \mapsto L'(y)\}))$

In words: If the current instruction is a call operation, it is checked if an instance-specific mole, an instance-agnostic mole, or no mole has been attached. In any case, a new stack frame is added. In the case of an instance-specific mole, the stack frame $f_{v,N}^{\text{One}}$ points the mole method, the first argument is the mole closure, the instance is dropped, and all other arguments are passed on. In the case of an instance-agnostic mole, the stack frame $f_{v,N}^{\text{All}}$ points to the mole method, the first argument is the mole closure, and all other arguments are passed on, but are shifted by one. Otherwise, a regular new stack frame is created, whose initial local variables arg_i map to the specified local values in the current stack frame. If the current instruction is a return operation (and the instruction in the previous stack frame is a call operation), the current stack frame is removed, and the current result value is stored in the previous stack frame.

5   Case Study

5.1   Introduction to SharePoint Unit Testing

We applied Moles and Pex to test a Microsoft SharePoint application. Microsoft Share-Point Foundation [10] provides a platform for comprehensive content management,

```
public void UpdateTitle(SPItemEventProperties properties) {
  using (SPWeb web = new SPSite(properties.WebUrl).OpenWeb()) {
    SPList list = web.Lists[properties.ListId];
    SPListItem item = list.GetItemById(properties.ListItemId);
    string contentType = (string)item["ContentType"];
    if (contentType.Length < 5)
      throw new ArgumentException("too short");
    if (contentType.Length > 60)
      throw new ArgumentOutOfRangeException("too long");
    if (contentType.Contains("\r\n"))
      throw new ArgumentException("no new lines");
    item["Title"] = contentType;
    item.SystemUpdate(false);
  }
    }
```

Fig. 2. SharePoint code-under-test

enterprise search, collaboration, communication, and more. SharePoint Foundation provides an API that allows building applications on top of the platform. It is often difficult to create unit tests for such applications as it is impossible to execute the underlying SharePoint Object Model without being connected to a live SharePoint site that runs the SharePoint server software. For that reason, most of the "unit tests" that have been written in the past for SharePoint applications are actually integration tests because they need a live system to run. As a result, those test take a long time to run which defeats the goals of unit testing: the tests should run fast, test only one component, and be completely reproducible.

Furthermore, most test cases induce some state change in the SharePoint server, which either means that state-dependent test cases are unreliable, or that the SharePoint server and its database must be restarted and reinitialized after every individual test case, which again contributes to long running test cases.

The SharePoint Object Model, including classes such as SPSite, SPWeb, ..., does not allow the tester to inject fake service implementations because most of the SharePoint classes are sealed types with non-public constructors. We will show how to use the Moles framework for detouring and to inject a fake service implementation.

5.2   The Code-under-Test

In this case study, we will test a simple SharePoint application that updates a field in a SPListItem instance, after performing some validation of the supplied values. The method shown in Figure 2 performs the actual work.

The above UpdateTitle method presents the typical challenges of unit testing with SharePoint Foundation: it connects to a live SPWeb through a SPSite. Unfortunately, it is not possible to provide a fake implementation of SPSite since this class is sealed.

The method under test is encapsulated into a SPItemEvenReceiver implementation, shown below.

```
public class ContentTypeItemEventReceiver
  : SPItemEventReceiver {
  public override void ItemAdded(
    SPItemEventProperties properties) {
    this.EventFiringEnabled = false;
    this.UpdateTitle(properties);
    this.EventFiringEnabled = true;
  }
  ...
}
```

5.3   The (Parameterized) Unit Test with Moles

The choice of contentType is critical to test the implementation of the UpdateTitle method, as different values take different code paths in the application. Pex is a tool that automates the process of finding relevant test inputs in a systematic way. Pex executes the code-under-test while monitoring every instruction executed by the .NET code. In particular, Pex records all the conditions that the program checks along the executed code path, and how they relate to the test input. Pex gives this information to a constraint solver, which then crafts new inputs that will trigger different code paths. Explaining how Pex works in more detail is beyond the scope of this paper, so we refer the reader to the Pex documentation for further details [14,18].

We write a parameterized unit test, shown in Figure 3, that states that the method under test should work correctly for all values of listItemId and contentType. The test constructs moles in a fashion mirroring the usage of the SharePoint classes in the code-under-test: First, the WebUrl property is queried from an SPItemEvent-Properties instance (and later the ListId and ListItemId properties). Then the constructor of SPSite is called, and then its method OpenWeb, and so on. We use the C# 3.0 *object initializer* syntax, where T t = new T(); t.P = x; can be abbreviated to new T() { P = x; }. Also note that the names of the mole properties for the indexer accesses _[_] in the code-under-test are ItemGetString and ItemSetString.

The contentType parameter is passed through (via closures), until it is returned by ItemGetString, and we also implemented logic to assert that the correct string is set in the call to ItemSetStringObject, and we maintain state in the titleSet variable to check later on that this call actually happened. The assignment titleSet = true is done in a nested anonymous method, and it is only due to the fact that closures in C# capture variables, and not just values, that we can query this modification in the assertion at the end: Assert.IsTrue(titleSet).

While the test case seems to be quite long, this has to be seen in relation to effort it takes to setup and maintain a SharePoint server with appropriate test data.

5.4   Evaluation

We let Pex explore the parameterized unit test code together with the code-under-test. Within seven seconds[4], the following six (non-parameterized) unit tests are generated.

---

[4] Pex and Moles version 0.21, Intel Core Duo P9500 with 2.53Ghz, 4GB RAM.

```
[PexMethod]
public void UpdateTitle(int listItemId, object contentType) {
  //// arrange ////
  string url = "http://foo";
  Guid listId = new Guid();
  var properties = new MSPItemEventProperties {
    WebUrlGet = () => url,
    ListIdGet = () => listId,
    ListItemIdGet = () => listItemId
  };
  bool titleSet = false;
  MSPSite.ConstructorString = (site, _url) => {
    new MSPSite(site) {
      OpenWeb = () => new MSPWeb {
        Dispose = () => { },
        ListsGet = () => new MSPListCollection {
          ItemGetGuid = id => {
            Assert.IsTrue(listId == id);
            return new MSPList {
              GetItemByIdInt32 = itemId => {
                Assert.IsTrue(listItemId == itemId);
                return new MSPListItem {
                  InstanceBehavior =
                    MoleBehaviors.DefaultValue,
                  ItemGetString = name => {
                    Assert.IsTrue("ContentType" == name);
                    return contentType;
                  }, // ItemGetString
                  ItemSetStringObject = (name, value) => {
                    Assert.IsTrue("Title" == name);
                    Assert.IsTrue(contentType == value);
                    titleSet = true;
                  } // ItemSetStringObject
                }; // new MSPListItem
              } // GetItemByIdIn32
            }; // new MSPList()
          } // ItemGetGuid
        } // new MSPListCollection
      } // new MSPWeb
    }; // new MSPSite
  }; // MSPSite.New
  //// act ////
  var target = new ContentTypeItemEventReceiver();
  target.UpdateTitle(properties);
  //// assert ////
  Assert.IsTrue(titleSet);
}
```

Fig. 3. Parameterized Unit Test for UpdateTitle

	listItemId	contentType	Summary/Exception	Error Message
1	0	null	**NullReferenceException**	**Object reference not set to an instance of an object.**
2	0	""	ArgumentException	too short
3	0	"\0\0\0\0\0\0'		
4	0	"\r\r\r\r\n"	ArgumentException	no new lines
5	0	new string('\0', 61)	ArgumentOutOfRangeException	Specified argument was out of the range of valid values.Parameter name: too long
6	0	object	**InvalidCastException**	**Unable to cast object of type 'System.Object' to type 'System.String'.**

Pex Exploration Results - stopped - 2 failed, 6 runs- 33/33 dynamic coverage
UpdateTitle(Int32 listItemId, Object contentType) ... Views ... Ask A Question
Review bold issues: All Tests | 2 Failed Tests | All Events

Fig. 4. Screenshot of the Pex tool with generated test cases

Figure 4 shows a screenshot of the Pex tool with the results. In the table, there is one row per generated test case; the input data for each generated test case is shown in the columns `listItemId` and `contentType`. (In addition to the table, Pex also generated C# code for the test cases.) When an exception occurred, then the `Summary/Exception` and `Error Message` columns are filled. We configured Pex to treat an `Argument...` `Exception` as permissible behaviors. All tests cases but two are passing: One failing test case causes a `NullReferenceException`, and the other an `InvalidCast` `Exception`. Those are unexpected exceptions. In addition to revealing the two unexpected exceptions, the generated test suite covers all explicit branches in the code, and as a consequence all basic blocks, in the test case as well as the code-under-test, We confirmed this result via the coverage reports that Pex generates as a side effect, as well as independently using the Visual Studio code coverage analysis.

While test generation in isolation with Pex and Moles took seven seconds, starting a live SharePoint server, and bringing it and its database back to a well-defined initial state for unit testing purposes takes about an order of magnitude longer.

5.5   Reproduction of Case Study

A detailed tutorial to reproduce the results of this case study can be found on the Pex website [15].

6   Related Work

The basic idea of dynamic detouring for testing purposes is not new. For .NET, a commercial tool is TypeMock Isolator [20]. Several detouring frameworks are available for Java, notably JMockit [7]. However, both TypeMock Isolator and JMockit focus not on providing basic or systematic detouring functionality, but instead they are *mocking* frameworks. This means that they provide powerful APIs that allow stating expectations, imposing verification checks, and adding annotations to existing methods. Moles in contrast simply provides a light-weight delegate-based detouring facility, which other mock frameworks do not provide. Simplicity is paramount for automated test generation via dynamic symbolic execution, as the semantics of all operations must be modeled precisely.

General detour mechanisms, which are not specialized for unit testing, exist for other platforms as well, e.g. for Win32 [6]. While our Moles framework has been implemented for the .NET framework, the idea of generating type-safe attachment points can be applied to any other platform where a general (untyped) detour mechanism is available.

Moles enables effective stubbing of legacy code [2], requiring a developer or tester to manually write code. There are several approaches to automatically turning slow system tests into focused unit tests [17,21,1,8,12]. They all require existing system tests, and are strictly capture and replay approaches. Some are implemented as a program transformation at the bytecode level, other at the source code level. But in any case, they do not provide an easy mechanism to attach custom behaviors in user-written test code to the detoured environment interactions.

Some approaches to represent mock objects are based on instrumentation via aspect-oriented programming (AOP) [16], which can also be used to automatically turn slow system tests into focused unit tests [13]. While AOP can certainly be used to realize the instrumentation necessary to detour method calls, the syntax and semantics typically employed by general-purpose AOP languages add a considerable complexity to the semantics of a unit test.

Isolation for testing is related to the idea of encapsulation, which in principle should allow the treatment of components as black boxes which can be swapped out at test time. Encapsulation is a key principle of the object-oriented software paradigm [9], and was already proposed earlier in the form of abstract data types [5]. While a consequent application of these ideas should make the problem of mocking for unit testing go away, legacy code does exist that violates those principles.

7   Conclusion and Future Work

We have developed a new lightweight framework called Moles which allows one to isolate unit tests by detouring calls to environment-dependent methods via .NET delegates. The changes to the operational semantics of a program are easy to model formally, which enables automated program analysis. We have performed a case study where we applied Moles and Pex, an automated test generation tool based dynamic symbolic execution, on code that uses the SharePoint Foundation API. After isolating all dependencies, multiple test cases were automatically generated in seconds, while starting and resetting a real SharePoint server takes an order of magnitude longer. Moles is part of Pex, an incubation project for Visual Studio developed at Microsoft Research. Pex is available for academic use and for commercial evaluation.

Unlike traditional mock-based unit testing, unit tests with Moles do not impose a simple capture-replay structure where expectations and verification conditions on method calls are stated sequentially, without the ability to programmatically simulate the detoured behavior, or to maintain or manipulate state across method calls. Instead, by using delegates and C# anonymous methods, Moles makes it easy to write light-weight and reusable *models* of the original detoured methods. Closures in C# capture variables, not just values, which enables writing stateful models. Future work includes adding facilities to Moles which further simplify writing models by a skilled tester or developer.

References

1. Elbaum, S., Chin, H.N., Dwyer, M.B., Dokulil, J.: Carving differential unit test cases from system test cases. In: Proceedings of the 14th ACM SIGSOFT international symposium on Foundations of software engineering, pp. 253–264. ACM, New York (2006)
2. Feathers, M.: Working Effectively with Legacy Code. Prentice Hall PTR, Englewood Cliffs (September 2004)
3. Fowler, M.: Refactoring: Improving the Design of Existing Code. Addison-Wesley, Reading (1999)
4. Godefroid, P., Klarlund, N., Sen, K.: DART: directed automated random testing. SIGPLAN Notices 40(6), 213–223 (2005)
5. Guttag, J.V., Horning, J.J.: The algebraic specification of abstract data types. Acta Informatica 10, 27–52 (1978)
6. Hunt, G., Brubacher, D.: Detours: binary interception of win32 functions. In: WINSYM'99: Proceedings of the 3rd conference on USENIX Windows NT Symposium, Berkeley, CA, USA, pp. 14. USENIX Association (1999)
7. JMockit developers. The JMockit testing toolkit (January 2010), http://jmockit.googlecode.com/svn/trunk/www/about.html
8. Joshi, S., Orso, A.: SCARPE: A technique and tool for selective record and replay of program executions. In: Proceedings of the 23rd IEEE International Conference on Software Maintenance (ICSM 2007), Paris, France (October 2007)
9. Micallef, J.: Encapsulation, reusability and extensibility in object-oriented programming languages. Journal of Object-Oriented Programming, 12–36 (April/May 1988)
10. Microsoft. Windows sharepoint services 3.0. (January 2010), http://technet.microsoft.com/en-us/windowsserver/sharepoint/default.aspx
11. Musuvathi, M., Qadeer, S., Ball, T., Basler, G., Nainar, P.A., Neamtiu, I.: Finding and reproducing heisenbugs in concurrent programs. In: OSDI, pp. 267–280 (2008)
12. Orso, A., Joshi, S., Burger, M., Zeller, A.: Isolating relevant Component Interactions with JINSI. In: Proceedings of the Fourth International ICSE Workshop on Dynamic Analysis (WODA 2006), Shanghai, China, May 2006, pp. 3–9 (2006)
13. Pasternak, B., Tyszberowicz, S., Yehudai, A.: GenUTest: a unit test and mock aspect generation tool. Int. J. Softw. Tools Technol. Transf. 11(4), 273–290 (2009)
14. Pex development team. Pex (2008), http://research.microsoft.com/Pex
15. Pex development team. Unit testing SharePoint Foundation with Microsoft Pex and Moles (April 2010), http://research.microsoft.com/pex/pexsharepoint.pdf
16. Rho, T., Kniesel, G.: Uniform genericity for aspect languages. Technical report, Needs, Options and Challenges, Special issue of L'Objet. Hermes Science Publishing (2004)
17. Saff, D., Artzi, S., Perkins, J.H., Ernst, M.D.: Automatic test factoring for Java. In: ASE '05: Proceedings of the 20th IEEE/ACM International Conference on Automated Software Engineering, pp. 114–123. ACM Press, New York (2005)
18. Tillmann, N., de Halleux, J.: Pex - white box test generation for .NET. In: Beckert, B., Hähnle, R. (eds.) TAP 2008. LNCS, vol. 4966, pp. 134–153. Springer, Heidelberg (2008)
19. Tillmann, N., Schulte, W.: Parameterized unit tests. In: Proceedings of the 10th European Software Engineering Conference held jointly with 13th ACM SIGSOFT International Symposium on Foundations of Software Engineering, pp. 253–262. ACM, New York (2005)
20. TypeMock Development Team. Isolator, http://www.typemock.com/learn_about_typemock_isolator.html
21. Xu, G., Rountev, A., Tang, Y., Qin, F.: Efficient checkpointing of java software using context-sensitive capture and replay. In: ESEC-FSE '07: Proceedings of the the 6th joint meeting of the European software engineering conference and the ACM SIGSOFT symposium on the foundations of software engineering, pp. 85–94. ACM, New York (2007)

Encoding Ownership Types in Java

Nicholas Cameron and James Noble

Victoria University of Wellington, New Zealand

Abstract. Ownership types systems organise the heap into a hierarchy which can be used to support encapsulation properties, effects, and invariants. Ownership types have many applications including parallelisation, concurrency, memory management, and security. In this paper, we show that several flavours and extensions of ownership types can be entirely encoded using the standard Java type system.

Ownership types systems usually require a sizable effort to implement and the relation of ownership types to standard type systems is poorly understood. Our encoding demonstrates the connection between ownership types and parametric and existential types. We formalise our encoding using a model for Java's type system, and prove that it is sound and enforces an ownership hierarchy. Finally, we leverage our encoding to produce lightweight compilers for Ownership Types and Universe Types — each compiler took only one day to implement.

1 Introduction

Ownership types describe the topology of the heap in the program source code. They come in several varieties (context-parametric [16], Universes [17], Ownership Domains [3], OGJ [27], and more) and have many practical applications, including preventing data races [6,18], parallelisation [15,5], real-time memory management [4], and enforcing architectural constraints [2].

Ownership types usually require large, complicated type systems and compilers, and their relation to standard type theory is not well understood. We give a simple encoding from ownership types to standard generic Java by extending the previously identified relationship between ownership types and parametric types [26,27]. This previous work encoded ownership parameters as type parameters, but treated the current object's ownership context (the this or This context) specially; we treat it as a standard type parameter, hidden externally by existential quantification [13]. With this technique we can encode ownership types (with generics and existential quantification), Ownership Domains, and Generic Universe Types. Furthermore, by unpacking the This parameter we can support a range of extensions, including inner classes [7], dynamic aliases [15], fields as contexts [12], and existential downcasting [31], within the same standard type system.

Contributions and Organisation. The contributions of this paper are: a thorough discussion of how various flavours and extensions of ownership types can be

J. Vitek (Ed.): TOOLS 2010, LNCS 6141, pp. 271–290, 2010.

encoded in a standard type system, such as Java's (Sect. 3), a formal type system which captures these concepts (including variations and extensions) and a soundness proof for this system which demonstrates that our encoding enforces the ownership hierarchy (Sect. 4), and compilers for Generic Universe Types and Ownership Types (Sect. 5).

Our work is of benefit to theoreticians and implementors: it provides an element of the fundamental underpinnings of ownership types and a shorter path to the implementation of languages with ownership types. We do not introduce new features or make existing approaches more expressive. We do not envisage that programmers would use a language like our encoding directly.

Additionally, we give background on Java generics and ownership types in Sect. 2 and conclude and describe future work in Sect. 6.

2 Background

In this section, we describe ownership types and features of the Java type system used in our encoding.

2.1 Java Generics and Wildcards

Java has featured parametric and existential types since version 5.0, in the form of *generics* and *wildcards* [20]. Java types consist of a class name and a (possibly empty) list of actual type parameters, for example, we can describe a list of books as List<Book>, this requires a class (or interface) with formal type parameters, e.g., class List<X> {...}. The formal type parameters (e.g., X) may be used in the body of the class; outside the class body they must be instantiated with actual parameters (e.g., Book).

Generic types must be *invariant* with respect to subtyping. However, it is sometimes safe and desirable to make generic types co- or contravariant. To support this, Java has wildcards [28]: an object of type List<? extends Book> is a covariant list of books, that is, a list of some subtype of book. To remain sound, covariant lists must be read-only and contravariant lists (indicated by lower bounds, using the **super** keyword) write-only; wildcards enforce this. Formal models of Java typically use bounded existential types to represent wildcards [11]: our covariant list is denoted $\exists X \to [\bot \; Book].List<X>$ (we use [L U] to denote lower and upper bounds on type variables; $\bot$, the bottom type, indicates no lower bound).

A wildcard *hides* a type parameter; for example, we can store (due to subtyping) an object of type List<Book> in a variable of type List<?>: the wildcard hides the witness type Book. Java does allow the type to be temporarily named, but only as a fresh type variable, this is known as *wildcard capture* and corresponds to *unpacking* an existential type[1]. For example, List<?> can be *capture converted* to List<Z>, where Z is fresh; however, the type system does not know of any relationship between Z and Book.

---

[1] Subtyping of concrete types to wildcard types corresponds to *packing*.

2.2 Ownership Types

At their most abstract, ownership types [16] are a mechanism for organising the heap into a hierarchy of contexts. The type system ensures that objects' positions in the hierarchy are reflected in their types. This soundness property allows contexts to be used to specify encapsulation properties (for which ownership types are famous), such as owners-as-dominators [16] and owners-as-modifiers [17], or to specify effects [15] or invariants [24]. Several mechanisms for reflecting the ownership hierarchy in types have been proposed; these can be separated into parameter-based systems, where types are parameterised by contexts (such as 'vanilla' ownership types [16,15], multiple ownership [12], and ownership domains [3]) and annotation-based systems, where types are annotated to describe relative position in the hierarchy (such as Universes [17]).

There have been several syntactic (but semantically equivalent) variations in the way ownership types are denoted, in our source language we prefix an object's type with its owner and parameterise it with actual context parameters. A class is declared without an explicit owner (only context parameters) and the `owner` keyword is added to the language for use as an actual context parameter (similarly to the `this` keyword); for example:

```
class List<d> {
    this:Node<d> first;
}
class Node<d> {
    owner:Node<d> next;
    d:Object datum;
}
```
——— Ownership types

Here, a list object owns all of its nodes and the context parameter `d` holds the data in the list. We will use this list as a running example.

Encapsulation and Effects. Most ownership systems consist of a descriptive part (describing the topology of the heap) and a prescriptive part, which uses the described topology to specify an encapsulation policy or effect system. Encapsulation properties can restrict aliasing (e.g., owners-as-dominators, associated with vanilla ownership types [16]) or access (e.g., owners-as-modifiers, from Universes [17]). An effect system describes how objects are accessed, rather than restricting access. In this paper we concentrate on the descriptive aspects of ownership and so we will not describe these policies in detail.

Universes. Universes [17] are an annotation-based ownership system. Types may be annotated with `rep` (denoting that objects of this type are owned by `this`), `peer` (objects are in the same context as `this`), or `any` (objects are in an unknown context). Generic Universe Types [19] support both type parametricity and universe modifiers; the programmer can write types such as `rep List<peer Book>`, which represents a list (owned by the current object) of books in the current context. Universe types and ownership types describe the same hierarchies [9]. Universe types are simpler to write than ownership types, but less expressive. The

above list example is expressed using Universes below, the data in the list can
be described more precisely (as in ownership types) if we were to use generics.

```
class List {
    rep Node first;
}
class Node {
    peer Node next;
    any Object datum;
}
```
——————————————————————————————— *Universe* ——

2.3 OGJ

Ownership types and generics can be combined in an orthogonal fashion [19,10],
giving the benefits and flexibility of both systems. They can also be integrated,
as in Ownership Generics Java (OGJ [27]); the benefits of both systems are
still gained, but with only a single kind of parameter: type parameters are used
to represent context parameters. The only extra ingredient in OGJ (beyond
standard Java generics) is a This type parameter which represents not a type,
but the current context. This type parameter is treated specially by the formal
type rules.

Our list example can be written in OGJ:

```
class List<D, Owner> {
    Node<D, This> first;
}
class Node<D, Owner> {
    Node<D, Owner> next;
    Object<D> datum;
}
```
——————————————————————————————— *OGJ* ——

The syntax is almost identical to the standard ownership types version, other
than the owner of a type is specified as the last type parameter. The semantics,
however, are different: all parameters are treated as type parameters by the type
system, the usual rules for type checking Java are applied, rather than special
ownership types rules. The exception is in dealing with the This owner of first,
here, special rules must be applied.

Featherweight Generic Confinement (FGC [26]) uses the same representation
of contexts as type parameters, but without any support for the This context.
The result is encapsulation within static packages, but not within dynamically
allocated objects.

3   Encoding Ownership Types into Java

In this section we describe how we encode source ownership types programs
into Java. As in FGC [26] and OGJ [27], we represent the owner of a class

and its context parameters with type parameters. Actual context parameters are encoded as actual type parameters. We create a formal type parameter to represent the this context [13], bounded above by Owner. The inside relation (context ordering) is encoded by subtyping (as in OGJ). Since this cannot be named outside its class declaration, we must hide the corresponding This type parameter in types, which is done using Java wildcards; conveniently, the wildcard will inherit the bound declared on This. Our basic ownership types list example (Sect. 2.2) is encoded as:

```
class List<D, Owner extends World, This extends Owner> {
    Node<D, This, ?> first;
}
class Node<D, Owner extends World, This extends Owner> {
    Node<D, Owner, ?> next;
    Object<D, ?> datum;
}
```
———— *Java* ————

Actual context parameters are either World (which represents the root context) or formal context variables (either quantified or with class scope). The inherited or explicit bounds on these type variables produce a partial ordering on type parameters corresponding to the ownership hierarchy[2]. Because there are no concrete types representing contexts (other than World), the hierarchy is an illusion: an omniscient type checker would know that all context-type variables ultimately hold World. The opacity of existential types ensures that the illusory hierarchy is respected during type checking.

Type systems must treat existentially quantified variables as hiding unique types; this gives the correct behaviour for ownership types in our encoding by treating each This context as unique. If we did not always hide the This parameter, ownership typing would not be effective[3]:

```
List<World, World, X> l1 = new List<World, World, X>();
List<World, World, X> l2 = new List<World, World, X>();
l1.first = l2.first;        //OK, but should be an error
```
———— *Java* ————

Universes. Generic Universe Types can be encoded into ownership types [9], and then into Java using the above scheme. The only obstacle is that the universe modifier any corresponds to an existentially quantified owner (see below); any can be encoded as an unbounded wildcard. The translation of the Universes basic list is given below. It is simpler than the ownership types version because we do not need to encode the context parameter; note the owner of datum is a wildcard, which encodes any.

---

[2] There are effectively two subtype hierarchies: one of real objects with Object at its root, and one of ownership contexts with World at its root.

[3] In this section we will use wildcards in new expressions, this is not allowed in Java and we describe how to avoid this in Sect. 5.

```
class List<Owner extends World, This extends Owner> {
    Node<This, ?> first;
}
class Node<Owner extends World, This extends Owner> {
    Node<Owner, ?> next;
    Object<?, ?> datum;
}
```
Java

The extension to Generic Universe Types is straightforward, type parameters remain in the encoding, upper bounds are encoded in the same way as other types.

Ownership Domains. Ownership domains [3] support more flexible topologies and a more flexible encapsulation property than ownership types. Topologically, ownership domains allow for multiple contexts (called domains) per object; objects can belong to any of these contexts and all contexts are nested within the object's owner.

To support multiple contexts per object in our encoding we allow multiple parameters in place of the single This parameter. All these parameters are given the upper bound of Owner and all must be hidden with wildcards to create the phantom ownership hierarchy. Types are encoded in the same way as for ownership types.

For example, the following class with two domains and a single domain parameter,

```
class C<domP> {  domain dom1, dom2;  }
```
ODs

it is encoded as the Java class,

```
class C<DomP, Owner, Dom1 extends Owner, Dom2 extends Owner> {}
```
Java

3.1   Extensions to Ownership Types

There has been much work on making ownership types systems more descriptive and more flexible. Generally the underlying ownership hierarchy is unchanged, but it can be described more precisely in the source code, usually combined with a relaxation of encapsulation properties in certain circumstances. In this section we describe several extensions to ownership types and how they can be encoded.

Bounds. Context parameters may be given upper and lower bounds [15,10] with respect to the ownership hierarchy. These are usually denoted inside and outside, respectively. For example, class C<a outside owner, b inside a>.

Upper bounds on context parameters can easily be replicated using upper bounds on the corresponding type parameters (e.g. B extends A). The encoded bounds are with respect to the subtype hierarchy, within which the ownership hierarchy is encoded. Lower bounds cannot be encoded in Java without changing the type system to support lower bounds on type parameters.

Context Parametric Methods. Methods may be parameterised by contexts [14,30] in an ownership system in the same way as they can be parameterised by types in Java. This allows for better code reuse. For example:

```
<a,b> a:Node<b> next(a:Node<b> n) {
    return n.next;
}
```
Ownership types

This method will work for all possible nodes; without context-parametric methods, such a method could not be written.

Context parametric methods are easily encoded as type parametric Java methods, upper bounds on context parameters can be handled as above:

```
<A,B> Node<B, A, ?> next(Node<B, A, ?> n) {
    return n.next;
}
```
Java

Inner Classes. Ownership types systems can be made more flexible by giving inner classes access to the this and owner parameters of the surrounding class [7]. This increases the descriptiveness of the type system because more contexts can be named inside an inner class. Owners-as-dominators can be relaxed to allow instantiations of inner classes to hold references to their surrounding objects (e.g., curNode field in the following example). This allows iterators to be implemented in an owners-as-dominators system, an early obstacle to acceptance of ownership types systems. We extend our list example:

```
class List<d> {
    ...
    class Iterator {
        List.this:Node<d> curNode;
        d:Object next() {
            d:Object val = curNode.datum;
            curNode = curNode.next();
            return val;
        }
    }
}

class Client {
    void m(this:List<world> l) {
        this:Iterator i = l.new this:Iterator()
        world:Object first = i.next();
    }
}
```
Ownership types

Inner classes must be able to name the context of their surrounding class; this happens naturally in Java, an inner class can name type parameters of

its surrounding class. We must be careful to avoid hiding the generated type
parameter by adding This parameters for both inner and outer classes. This is
easily accomplished by prepending the name of the class to the names of the
Owner and This parameters (we elide some bounds):

```java
class List<D, Owner, This extends Owner> {
    ...
    class Iterator<It_Owner, It_This extends It_Owner> {
        Node<D, This, ?> curNode;
        Object<D, ?> next() {
            Object<D, ?> val = curNode.datum;
            curNode = curNode.next();
            return val;
        }
    }
}

class Client<Owner, This extends Owner> {
    void m(List<World, This, ?> l) {
        Iterator<This, ?> i = l.new Iterator<This, ?>();
        Object<World, ?> first = i.next();
    }
}
```
Java

Dynamic Aliases. An alternative solution to the iterators problem under
owners-as-dominators is to allow *dynamic aliases* [15], that is allow variables
on the stack to reference objects which break owners-as-dominators, and only
enforce owners-as-dominators on the heap. Dynamic aliases achieve this by allowing local variables to be used as contexts. Extending the original list example:

```
class Iterator<d> {
    owner:Node<d> curNode;
    d:Object next() {
        d:Object val = curNode.datum;
        curNode = curNode.next();
        return val;
    }
}

class Client {
    void m(final this:List<world> l) {
        l:Iterator<world> i = new l:Iterator<world>();
        world:Object first = i.next();
    }
}
```
Ownership types

The variable 1 cannot be named outside of m, and so the dynamic alias to i (owned by 1) cannot be stored in the heap. It is only sound to use final variables to name contexts.

An object's context is represented by its hidden This argument; therefore, encoding dynamic aliases in Java requires naming that argument using a fresh, temporary type variable which is introduced as an extra type parameter to a method. Unpacking the hidden This argument to the named variable is achieved by wildcard capture:

```
class Iterator<D, Owner extends World, This extends Owner> {
    Node<D, Owner, ?> curNode;
    Object<D, ?> next() {
        Object<D, ?> val = curNode.datum;
        curNode = curNode.next();
        return val;
    }
}

class Client<Owner extends World, This extends Owner> {
    void m(List<World, This, ?> l) {
        this.mAux(l)
    }

    <L> void mAux(List<World, This, L> l) {
        Iterator<World, L, ?> i = new Iterator<World, L, ?>;
        Object<World, ?> first = i.next();
    }
}
```
Java

The wildcard which hides 1's This argument is capture converted to the fresh type variable L when mAux is called. Using 1 as an owner in the source program is encoded to using L as an owner. L can only be named within the scope of mAux, and this corresponds to the scope of 1.

Our example is simple because it does not require other state to be passed to mAux. In a more realistic example we would need to pass any data accessed in m to mAux, and back again if it is not passed by reference. A simpler encoding is to modify the original method so that the This argument of 1 is captured by calling m (rather than when mAux). The simpler encoding only works if the variable being used as a context is an argument rather than a local variable. Note that the call-sites of m do not have to be modified, despite the extra type parameter, due to Java's type parameter inference:

```
class Client<Owner, This> {
    <L> void m(List<World, This, L> l) { ... }   //body as mAux
}
```
Java

Fields as Contexts. Similarly to local variables, final fields can be used to name contexts [12], this again improves flexibility. We can extend the list example:

```
class List<d> {
    final this:Node<d> first;
    first:Object f2;     //owned by a field
}
```
Ownership types

Paths of final fields may also be used as contexts [12], e.g., one could allow the type f3.first:Object, where f3 is a final field of type List.

We encode fields used as contexts by adding their hidden This parameters to the class's parameter list:

```
class List<D, Owner extends World, This extends Owner,
          First extends This> {
    final Node<D, This, ? extends First> first;
    Object<First, ?> f2;
}
```
Java

Instantiating this class requires that the value of first is passed into the constructor, wildcard capture is used to name First and then both this and First are hidden by wildcards.

Existential Quantification. Just as type variables may be quantified existentially, so may context variables [10]. This gives existential ownership types such as ∃o.o:Object or ∃o.this:List<o>. Such quantification has two benefits: context variance, that is subtyping which is variant with respect to the ownership hierarchy, and expressing partial knowledge about contexts (e.g., an unknown context or some unknown context within another known context). Existential quantification is the mechanism which underlies a number of proposals involving some kind of variance annotations on contexts [23,8].

Existentially quantified contexts can be encoded as wildcards. Since wildcards are syntactic sugar for existential types, this is not surprising. Both upper and lower bounds can be straightforwardly encoded. The only difficulty is if quantified contexts have both upper and lower bounds, which is not supported by Java wildcards. This should not be a problem, however, because quantification is usually provided by variance annotations or wildcard-like syntax.

Existential Downcasting. Downcasting is a common feature in programs, especially those that do not use generics. When downcasting from type A to type B, if B has context parameters which A does not, these must be synthesised. Wrigstad and Clarke propose the use of "existential owners" to handle these introduced context parameters [31]. For example:

```
void m(this:Object x) {
    this:List<d> l = (this:List<d>) x;
    d:Object first = l.first.datum;
    l.first.datum = new d:Object();
}
```
Ownership types

Here x is cast from type this:Object to this:List<d>, the d context is a fresh context (an "existential owner") that can be named in the scope of the method and allows operations on l to take place. Objects owned by d cannot be stored in the heap, outside of the original data structure, since d can only be named locally. Note that there is no explicit quantification, although "existential owners" correspond to unpacked context-existential types [8].

We can cast x to a type where D is hidden by a wildcard, although we cannot cast directly to a type containing D because D is not in scope. We must split the method in order to name D using capture conversion:

```
void m(Object<This, ?> x) {
    this.mAux((List<?, This, ?>) x);
}
<D> void mAux(List<D, This, ?> l) {
    Object<D, ?> first = l.first.datum;
    l.first.datum = new Object<D, ?>();
}
```
Java

Owners-as-Dominators. The owners-as-dominators property specifies that all reference paths from the root of the ownership hierarchy to any object pass through that object's owner: owners dominate reference paths. The property is enforced by restricting which contexts can be named: if only contexts outside the current context can be named, then no references can exist *into* contexts other than the one owned by the current this object.

We have previously sketched how owners-as-dominators can be supported in an encoding of ownership into Java [13]. This approach can be duplicated here with the same drawback: owners-as-dominators can only be guaranteed if the Java compiler is modified, it cannot be supported as a pre-processor step like the rest of the encodings discussed. The modifications are not major: a small change to the well-formedness rules for classes and types to ensure that context parameters are outside the declared owner (the usual requirement for ownership types to support owners-as-dominators). The issue is that at intermediate steps of computation the compiler might allow the This parameter to be named in types: this is not a problem for descriptive ownership because it is only temporary, but it can allow owners-as-dominators to be violated.

4   Formalisation

To show that our encoding does in fact demonstrate the behaviour of an ownership types system, we extend a model for the Java type system with elements of our encoding and runtime ownership information. Our formalisation (Tame FJ$_{Own}$) follows the approach of OGJ [27], in representing context parameters as type parameters, but, by supporting existential types, we do not need any special machinery to deal with ownership issues.

The bulk of the formal system is relatively standard or follows Tame FJ [11]. Differences from Tame FJ to model ownership are highlighted in grey . We also add field assignment, null, a heap, and casting (to model dynamic downcasts), and make some small improvements elsewhere, these changes are not highlighted. For the sake of brevity, we do not describe the parts unchanged from Tame FJ. Parts of the operational semantics, well-formed environments and heaps, auxiliary functions, and rules for using the heap as an environment are relegated to the appendix.

e	::=	γ | null | $e.f$ | $e.f = e$ | $e.<\overline{P}, \overline{\mathcal{P}}>m(\overline{e})$	*expressions*
		| new C$<\overline{\mathcal{T}}, \star>$ | $(T)e$	
v	::=	ι | null	*values*
Q	::=	class C$<\overline{X \lhd T}, \overline{0 \lhd \tau}, \text{Owner} \lhd \tau, \text{This} \lhd \tau > \lhd N \{\overline{T f}; \overline{M}\}$	
M	::=	$<\overline{X \lhd T}, \overline{0 \lhd T} > T m (\overline{T x}) \{\text{return } e;\}$	*method declarations*
N	::=	C$<\overline{T}, \overline{\tau} >$ | Object$< \tau, \tau >$	*class types*
R	::=	N | X	*non-existential types*
T, U	::=	$\exists \Delta.N$ | $\exists \emptyset.X$ *types*	$\mathcal{T}$ ::= T | τ *types and contexts*
P	::=	T | $\star$ *method type parameters*	$\mathcal{P}$ ::= $\mathcal{T}$ | $\star$ *method parameters*
$\mathcal{X}, \mathcal{Y}$	::=	X | 0 | v *type parameters*	τ ::= World<> | 0 | v *contexts*

Δ	::=	$\overline{\mathcal{X} \rightarrow [B_l \; B_u]}$ *type environments*	x, this	*variables*
B	::=	T | $\bot$ *bounds*	X, Y	*type variables*
Γ	::=	$\overline{\gamma:T}$ *variable environments*	0, Owner, This	*context variables*
γ	::=	ι | x *locations or variables*	ι	*locations*
$\mathcal{H}$	::=	$\overline{\iota \rightarrow \{N; \; \overline{f \rightarrow v}\}}$ *heaps*	C, Object, World	*class names*
			f, g	*field names*
			m	*method names*

Fig. 1. Syntax of Tame FJ$_{Own}$

Syntax. The syntax of Tame FJ$_{Own}$ is given in Fig. 1. For convenience, and following OGJ [27], we syntactically separate types and type parameters used to represent contexts from regular types: we use τ to denote types which represent contexts, T to denote regular types, and $\mathcal{T}$ to denote either type; likewise for parameters, we use O to denote type parameters which represent context parameters, X for regular type parameters, and $\mathcal{X}$ for either kind. Importantly, the two kinds of type are treated almost identically by the type system. We can do without this convenience by examining the type's top supertype: contexts will be bounded by World, other types by Object.

We allow values (v, which are addresses and null; the latter corresponds to World) to be context (and thus type) parameters at runtime so that we can prove enforcement of the ownership hierarchy (see Sect. 4.1); values are not allowed as parameters in source code.

We use a few shorthands for types: C for C<>, and R for $\exists\emptyset.R$.

Well-formed types: $\boxed{\Delta \vdash B \text{ OK}, \ \Delta \vdash \mathcal{P} \text{ OK}, \ \Delta \vdash R \text{ OK}}$

$$\frac{\mathcal{X} \in \Delta}{\Delta \vdash \mathcal{X} \text{ OK}} \quad \frac{}{\Delta \vdash \text{World<> OK}} \quad \frac{}{\Delta \vdash \bot \text{ OK}} \quad \frac{}{\Delta \vdash \star \text{ OK}} \quad \frac{\Delta \vdash \Delta' \text{ OK} \quad \Delta, \Delta' \vdash \mathbb{N} \text{ OK}}{\Delta \vdash \exists \Delta'.\mathbb{N} \text{ OK}}$$

$$\text{(F-Var)} \qquad \text{(F-World)} \qquad \text{(F-Bottom)} \qquad \text{(F-Star)} \qquad \text{(F-Exists)}$$

$$\frac{\Delta \vdash \overline{T}, \overline{\tau}, \tau_o \text{ OK} \quad \overline{\mathcal{T}} = \overline{T}, \overline{\tau}, \tau_o, \tau_t \quad \Delta(\tau_t) = [\bot \ T] \quad \text{class } \text{C}<\overline{\mathcal{X}} \lhd \overline{\mathcal{T}_u}> \lhd N\{\dots\} \quad \Delta \vdash \overline{T} <: [\overline{T/\mathcal{X}}]\overline{\mathcal{T}_u}}{\Delta \vdash \text{C}<\overline{\mathcal{T}}> \text{ OK}}$$

$$\text{(F-Class)}$$

$$\frac{\Delta \vdash \tau_o \text{ OK} \quad \Delta(\tau_t) = [\bot \ T]}{\Delta \vdash \text{Object}< \tau_o, \tau_t > \text{ OK}}$$

$$\text{(F-Object)}$$

Fig. 2. Tame FJ$_{Own}$ well-formed types, type environments, and heaps

Well-formed Types. Well-formed types are defined in Fig. 2. In F-Class and F-Object, we do not check that the type parameter in the This position is well-formed. Instead we check that it is in the environment and is bounded below by bottom. This ensures that it is always an in-scope variable (in fact it is usually a quantified variable, although this does not need to be enforced) and that no other type can be derived to be a subtype of it (as would be the case if it had a lower bound). This ensures that the This context cannot be named by using subsumption.

Type Checking. Selected type rules are given in Fig. 3. Object creation (T-New) does not take any (value) parameters (i.e., we don't have constructors, at runtime all fields are initialised to null). This requires null and the T-Null rule. Initialising objects in this way is necessary so that fields owned by This can be initialised. The actual type parameter in the This position of new

Expression typing: $\boxed{\Delta; \Gamma \vdash e : T}$

$$\frac{\Delta \vdash T \text{ OK}}{\Delta; \Gamma \vdash \texttt{null} : T}$$

$$(\text{ T-Null })$$

$$\frac{\Delta; \Gamma \vdash e : \exists \Delta'.N \qquad fType(\texttt{f}, N) = T' \qquad \Delta; \Gamma \vdash e' : T \qquad \Delta, \Delta' \vdash T <: T'}{\Delta; \Gamma \vdash e.\texttt{f} = e' : T}$$

$$(\text{T-Assign})$$

$$\frac{\Delta \vdash \overline{T}, \mathcal{T} \text{ OK} \qquad \Delta \vdash \exists \texttt{0} \rightarrow [\bot \ T].\texttt{C}<\overline{\mathcal{T}},\mathcal{T},\texttt{0}> \text{ OK}}{\Delta; \Gamma \vdash \texttt{new } \texttt{C}<\overline{\mathcal{T}},\mathcal{T},\star > : \exists \texttt{0} \rightarrow [\bot \ T].\texttt{C}<\overline{\mathcal{T}},\mathcal{T},\texttt{0}>}$$

$$(\text{ T-New })$$

Class typing: $\boxed{\vdash Q \text{ OK}}$

$$\frac{\begin{array}{c} \Delta = \overline{\texttt{X} \rightarrow [\bot \ T_u]}, \texttt{Owner} \rightarrow [\bot \ \tau_o], \texttt{This} \rightarrow [\bot \ \texttt{Owner}], \overline{\texttt{0} \rightarrow [\bot \ \tau_u]} \\ \emptyset \vdash \Delta \text{ OK} \qquad \Delta \vdash N, \overline{T} \text{ OK} \\ \overline{\mathcal{X}} = \overline{\texttt{X}, \overline{\texttt{0}}, \texttt{Owner}, \texttt{This}} \qquad \Delta; \texttt{this}:\texttt{C}<\overline{\mathcal{X}}> \vdash \overline{M} \text{ OK in C} \\ N = \texttt{D}<\overline{\mathcal{T}}, \texttt{Owner}, \texttt{This}> \qquad \Delta \vdash N <: \texttt{Object}<\texttt{Owner}, \texttt{This}> \end{array}}{\vdash \texttt{class } \texttt{C}<\overline{\texttt{X} \lhd \ T_u}, \overline{\texttt{0} \lhd \ \tau_u}, \texttt{Owner} \lhd \ \tau_o, \texttt{This} \lhd \ \texttt{Owner} > \ \lhd \ N\{\overline{\texttt{T f};} \ \overline{M}\} \text{ OK}}$$

$$(\text{T-Class})$$

Fig. 3. Selected Tame FJ$_{Own}$ expression and class typing rules

expressions must always be $\star$, so no actual parameter is named at initialisation. New objects are given existential types, with the This parameter existentially quantified (bounded above by the Owner parameter), which ensures that the actual This parameter can never be named directly. The extra well-formedness premise in T-New is stricter than the usual well-formedness premise and ensures that the type parameters are well-formed without the extra, quantified parameter in the environment.

We add a rule for casting (T-Cast), which is standard. Unlike in Featherweight Java, we do not distinguish between up-, down-, and stupid casts.

In T-Class we enforce that the declared upper bound of This is Owner[4]. The last two premises ensure that declared classes fall under the Object hierarchy and are not subtypes of World, which means they cannot be used as context parameters, and that the Owner and This parameters are invariant with respect to inheritance. The latter is an important sanity condition of our encoding of ownership and corresponds to the well-known condition on inheritance and ownership [15]. We assume that Object is declared with parameters Owner and This with the usual bounds.

---

[4] The re-ordering of type parameters is a hangover from supporting owners-as-dominators, where the lower bound of each 0 is Owner.

Operational Semantics. Operational semantics are mostly defined in the appendix; the most interesting change from Tame FJ is in object creation:

$$\frac{\iota \notin dom(\mathcal{H}) \qquad fields(\texttt{C}) = \overline{\texttt{f}}}{\mathcal{H}' = \mathcal{H}, \iota \to \{\texttt{C}{<}\overline{T},T,\iota{>}; \overline{\texttt{f}{\to}\texttt{null}}\}}{\texttt{new } \texttt{C}{<}\overline{T},T,\star >; \mathcal{H} \rightsquigarrow \iota; \mathcal{H}'}$$

(R-New)

A new object's runtime type (stored in the heap) is formed by replacing the $\star$ used in the program source by the new object's address. Together with the usual rules of substitution (in method invocation), occurrences of both this and This in class declarations are replaced by the instantiation's address (ι), unifying the two representations of the object. Together with the quantification in T-New, objects are, in effect, packed into existential types, with the object's address as witness 'type'.

4.1 Discussion

Ownership types are intrinsically dependent because they reflect objects' positions in the heap. We have shown that ownership types can be encoded as parametric types in a Java-like type system, reminiscent of *phantom types* [21]. Phantom types are parametric types where type parameters are never used as types[5]. Phantom types are used in Haskell to simulate values in types, without the complexity and decidability issues of full dependent types [21]. This is exactly what our system is doing with respect to ownership information. We conclude then, that ownership type systems are, in some sense, no more complex than standard parametric type systems such as Java's. Despite their dependent character, the full power of dependent types is not required to support ownership type systems. However, we should not overstep the mark and assume that type parametricity is the only, or even the best, foundational model for ownership types.

Most of the ownership features described in Sect. 3 can be accommodated in Tame FJ$_{Own}$. Inner classes require encoding and are discussed below. Paths of final fields cannot easily by encoded in our formal system. Generic Universe Types [19] can be accommodated after encoding. Ownership domains would require a small extension to the formal system, which we have avoided for the sake of simplicity: each class has a list of This type parameters rather than a single parameter. Each parameter represents a domain. Since this change merely changes This to $\overline{\text{This}}$, we expect very few changes to be necessary to accommodate it.

The extensions to support ownership domains and inner classes (below) are fairly superficial changes, modifying only the restrictions on type parameters and which type parameters are hidden in T-New.

---

[5] More precisely, phantom type parameters are not used on the right hand side of the definition of a type constructor.

Inner Classes. Encoding inner classes in Tame FJ_{Own} would require a small extension to our formalisation. References to the surrounding object and the type parameters of the surrounding object must be made available to objects of the inner class. Extending Tame FJ_{Own} could be done by adopting a nesting of classes and objects in the class table and heap or by adding a field to each class pointing to the surrounding object, and type parameters for the surrounding classes' type parameters; object creation becomes more complex, but otherwise the calculus is not changed too much. The iterator as inner class example from Sect. 3.1 is encoded as (we elide bounds):

```
class Iterator<D, L_Owner, L_This, It_Owner, It_This> {
    List<D, L_Owner, L_This> out;
    Node<D, L_This, ?> curNode;
    Object<It_This, ?> privField;

    Object<D, ?> next() {...}
}

class Client<Owner, This> {
    <LT> void m(List<World, This, LT> l) {
        Iterator<World, This, LT, This, ?> i
            = new Iterator<World, This, LT, This, ?>();
        i.out = l;
        Object<World, ?> first = i.next();
    }
}
```
—— *Java* ——

We must use (a presumably capture converted) type variable (LT) for the This parameter of l, provide l's type parameters to i, and must instantiate the out field of i.

Type Soundness. We have proved type soundness for Tame FJ_{Own} in the usual way [29] by proving progress and preservation theorems. For the most part, our proofs follow those of Tame FJ [11]; they can be downloaded from [1].

In standard existential type systems, witness types are known at runtime, and type soundness guarantees that no type errors involving witness types occur, even though the type system has only partial knowledge of these types during type checking. Taking this approach with Tame FJ_{Own} would not be very informative, since all witness types (according to T-NEW) will be $\star$. Our static types hold *more* information (the ownership hierarchy) than is represented by the 'witness types'. Our soundness result proves that Tame FJ_{Own} does enforce the ownership hierarchy, i.e., Tame FJ_{Own} enforces not only strict type soundness (well-typed programs won't access non-existent fields or methods), but also that objects reside in the context described by their type. Ownership information is represented at runtime by storing the object's address into it's This position (in

R-New), the address propagates into other ownership positions by substitution (in R-Invk).

In proving type soundness for Tame FJ_{Own}, we have proved that a one-stage type checker (corresponding to an integration of our pre-processor and the Java type checker) is sound, rather than proving that a two-stage type checker (corresponding to pre-processing and then Java type checking, as in our implementation) is sound. Our approach is theoretically more direct and reflects what we envision to be the long term use of our techniques.

5   Implementation

We have implemented compilers for Java with ownership types and Generic Universe Types by using the techniques described in this paper. Our implementations are simple source to source translators which translate source code to plain Java; the Java compiler is then used to type check and compile the code. Most type errors are caught by the Java compiler, only a few are handled by our translators. Our translators are extensions to the parser and AST elements of the JKit Java compiler [25]. We encode one class at a time and do not need to be aware of the whole program. Generated classes will behave well together, but will be incompatible with plain Java classes[6].

Our approach supports ownership and universe types on top of nearly the entire Java Language, including generics, arrays (including the various kinds of array initialisers; we only support ownership information on the elements in an array, the array itself (like primitive types) is not considered to have an owner), interfaces, inner classes (but not anonymous classes), statics, and wildcards.

Our implementations are very much prototypes, an industrial strength compiler would integrate the encoding with Java type checking, as opposed to our two-stage process. Integration would allow for meaningful error messages and support for effects and encapsulation properties. Furthermore, to be usable, a language requires more than a compiler, libraries must be supported, either by support for non-ownership aware classes (currently, all classes must be written with ownership types) or by producing a set of ownership annotated libraries (or a combination of the two approaches). Our compilers can be downloaded [1].

5.1   Ownership Types

Our source syntax is mostly similar to that used throughout this paper. We support owners, context parameters, orthogonal generics, context- and type-parametric methods, final method parameters as contexts (for dynamic aliases), existential quantification in the form of context wildcards, and inner classes with access to the contexts and context parameters of the surrounding object. We do not support local variables (other than method parameters) or fields as contexts. We support standard casting, including to wildcard owners, but do not directly

---

[6] Strictly, since we generate plain Java, one could write classes which behave well with the generated classes, but not in a way which behaves nicely with the source classes.

support "existential owners". Since Java implements generics using erasure [22], the runtime checks on casts do not ensure correctness of ownership parameters; with respect to ownership types, casting merely ensures that a program can type check at compile time. This is not a problem in our formalism, because we do not erase type parameters in the operational semantics.

The obvious function of our compiler is to strip owners and context parameters and replace them with type parameters, this is done both in class declarations and in types; in the latter case, using wildcards in the This position.

Java does not allow wildcard parameters when objects are instantiated: to get around this we use the Owner type parameter in the This position (because it is the only type parameter which satisfies the declared bound) and immediately cast to the required wildcard type (which inherits the upper bound),

```
new world:Object()                                      //source syntax
new Object<World, ?>()                                  //pseudo-Java
(OwnedObject<World, ?>) new OwnedObject<World, World>()   //Java
```

Note also that, as in OGJ, we have to add an OwnedObject which extends Object at the root of our class hierarchy to take the encoded ownership parameters. All classes must extend this class (rather than Object, which may happen implicitly) and all uses of Object changed to OwnedObject. In the source syntax, the object's owner is implicit in the extends clause, and so translation of the superclass type must be treated differently from other types. Because we add OwnedObject and World to our runtime, we must import these classes into each encoded class file.

5.2   Generic Universe Types

The source syntax is pretty standard for generic universes, e.g., rep List<any Object>. The translation is much simpler than for ownership types since we do not have to translate context parameters, only types. Most of the issues faced are similar, and simpler, than in the ownership types case: we must check for universe modifiers on all types (but not in extends clauses, because ownership is invariant with respect to inheritance, that is superclasses must be peers), Object is translated to OwnedObject, and care must be taken with array types. As with our ownership types implementation and Java, casting is unsafe and allows for Universe modifiers to be changed improperly; Universes usually requires safe down-casting.

6   Conclusion and Future Work

In this paper we have shown how ownership types, Generic Universe Types, Ownership Domains, and a range of extensions to ownership types systems can be encoded using Java Generics and wildcards. The key concepts are the representation of context parameters as type parameters, the reification of this as a type parameter, the hiding of `this` using wildcards, and the phantom ownership hierarchy thus created. Our developments shed light on the type-theoretic foundations of ownership types and offer a route for practical compilers constructed upon existing technology.

Future Work. The main thrust of future work will be in supporting owners-as-dominators, and other encapsulation polices and effects, in our formal work and compilers. This would require integrating our translating compiler with an existing Java compiler, which would also allow for better error messages and more efficient type checking. We would also like to encode libraries with ownership type information for use with our compilers. An alternative would be to develop our encoding so that encoded classes and the un-annotated Java libraries can interact together.

References

1. Accompanying webpage, https://ecs.victoria.ac.nz/Main/Encoding
2. Abi-Antoun, M., Aldrich, J.: Ownership Domains in the Real World. In: International Workshop on Aliasing, Confinement and Ownership in object-oriented programming, IWACO (2008)
3. Aldrich, J., Chambers, C.: Ownership Domains: Separating Aliasing Policy from Mechanism. In: Odersky, M. (ed.) ECOOP 2004. LNCS, vol. 3086, pp. 1–25. Springer, Heidelberg (2004)
4. Armbruster, A., Baker, J., Cunei, A., Flack, C., Holmes, D., Pizlo, F., Pla, E., Prochazka, M., Vitek, J.: A Real-Time Java Virtual Machine with Applications in Avionics. Transactions on Embedded Computing Systems 7(1), 1–49 (2007)
5. Bocchino Jr., R.L., Adve, V.S., Dig, D., Adve, S.V., Heumann, S., Komuravelli, R., Overbey, J., Simmons, P., Sung, H., Vakilian, M.: A Type and Effect System for Deterministic Parallel Java. In: Object-Oriented Programming, Systems, Languages, and Applications, OOPSLA (2009)
6. Boyapati, C., Lee, R., Rinard, M.C.: Ownership Types for Safe Programming: Preventing Data Races and Deadlocks. In: Object-Oriented Programming, Systems, Languages, and Applications, OOPSLA (2002)
7. Boyapati, C., Liskov, B., Shrira, L.: Ownership Types for Object Encapsulation. In: Principles of Programming Languages, POPL (2003)
8. Cameron, N.: Existential Types for Variance | Java Wildcards and Ownership Types. PhD thesis, Imperial College London (2009)
9. Cameron, N., Dietl, W.: Comparing Universes and Existential Own- ership Types. In: International Workshop on Aliasing, Confinement and Ownership in object-oriented programming, IWACO (2009)
10. Cameron, N., Drossopoulou, S.: Existential Quantification for Variant Ownership. In: Castagna, G. (ed.) ESOP 2009. LNCS, vol. 5502, pp. 128–142. Springer, Heidelberg (2009)
11. Cameron, N., Drossopoulou, S., Ernst, E.: A Model for Java with Wildcards. In: Vitek, J. (ed.) ECOOP 2008. LNCS, vol. 5142, pp. 2–26. Springer, Heidelberg (2008)
12. Cameron, N., Drossopoulou, S., Noble, J., Smith, M.: Multiple Ownership. In: Object-Oriented Programming, Systems, Languages, and Applications, OOPSLA (2007)

13. Cameron, N., Noble, J.: OGJ Gone Wild. In: International Workshop on Aliasing, Confinement and Ownership in object-oriented programming, IWACO (2009)
14. Clarke, D.G.: Object Ownership and Containment. PhD thesis, School of Computer Science and Engineering, The University of New South Wales, Sydney, Australia (2001)
15. Clarke, D.G., Drossopoulou, S.: Ownership, Encapsulation and the Disjointness of Type and Effect. In: Object-Oriented Programming, Systems, Languages, and Applications, OOPSLA (2002)
16. Clarke, D.G., Potter, J.M., Noble, J.: Ownership Types for Flexible Alias Protection. In: Object-Oriented Programming, Systems, Languages, and Applications, OOPSLA (1998)
17. Cunningham, D., Dietl, W., Drossopoulou, S., Francalanza, A., Müller, P., Summers, A.J.: Universe Types for Topology and Encapsulation. In: Formal Methods for Components and Objects, FMCO (2008)
18. Cunningham, D., Drossopoulou, S., Eisenbach, S.: Universe Types for Race Safety. In: Verification and Analysis of Multi-threaded Java-like Programs, VAMP (2007)
19. Dietl, W., Drossopoulou, S., Müller, P.: Generic Universe Types. In: Ernst, E. (ed.) ECOOP 2007. LNCS, vol. 4609, pp. 28–53. Springer, Heidelberg (2007)
20. Gosling, J., Joy, B., Steele, G., Bracha, G.: The Java Language Specification, 3rd edn. Addison-Wesley, Boston (2005)
21. Hinze, R.: The Fun. of Programming, pp. 245–262. Palgrave Macmillan, Basingstoke (2003)
22. Igarashi, A., Pierce, B.C., Wadler, P.: Featherweight Java: a Minimal Core Calculus For Java and GJ. ACM Trans. Program. Lang. Syst. 23(3), 396–450 (2001); An earlier version of this work appeared at OOPSLA'99
23. Lu, Y., Potter, J.: On Ownership and Accessibility. In: Thomas, D. (ed.) ECOOP 2006. LNCS, vol. 4067, pp. 99–123. Springer, Heidelberg (2006)
24. Müller, P., Poetzsch-Heffter, A., Leavens, G.T.: Modular Invariants for Layered Object Structures. Science of Computer Programming 62, 253–286 (2006)
25. Pearce, D.: Jkit compiler, http://www.ecs.vuw.ac.nz/~djp/jkit
26. Potanin, A., Noble, J., Clarke, D., Biddle, R.: Featherweight Generic Confinement. J. Funct. Program. 16(6), 793–811 (2006)
27. Potanin, A., Noble, J., Clarke, D., Biddle, R.: Generic Ownership for Generic Java. In: Object-Oriented Programming, Systems, Languages, and Applications, OOPSLA (2006)
28. Torgersen, M., Hansen, C.P., Ernst, E., von der Ahé, P., Bracha, G., Gafter, N.: Adding Wildcards to the Java Programming Language. Journal of Object Technology 3(11), 97–116 (2004)
29. Wright, A.K., Felleisen, M.: A Syntactic Approach to Type Soundness. Information and Computation 115(1), 38–94 (1994)
30. Wrigstad, T.: Ownership-Based Alias Managemant. PhD thesis, KTH, Sweden (2006)
31. Wrigstad, T., Clarke, D.G.: Existential Owners for Ownership Types. Journal of Object Technology 6(4) (2007)

Visualizing Dynamic Metrics with Profiling Blueprints

Alexandre Bergel[1], Romain Robbes[1], and Walter Binder[2]

[1] Pleiad Lab, DCC, University of Chile, Santiago, Chile
http://bergel.eu, http://www.dcc.uchile.cl/~rrobbes
[2] University of Lugano, Switzerland
http://www.inf.usi.ch/faculty/binder

Abstract. While traditional approaches to code profiling help locate performance bottlenecks, they offer only limited support for removing these bottlenecks. The main reason is the lack of visual and detailed runtime information to identify and eliminate computation redundancy. We provide two profiling blueprints which help identify and remove performance bottlenecks. The *structural distribution blueprint* graphically represents the CPU consumption share for each method and class of an application. The *behavioral distribution blueprint* depicts the distribution of CPU consumption along method invocations, and hints at method candidates for caching optimizations. These two blueprints helped us to significantly optimize Mondrian, an open source visualization engine. Our implementation is freely available for the Pharo development environment and has been evaluated in a number of different scenarios.

1 Introduction

Even though computing resources are abundant, execution optimization through code profiling remains an important software development activity. A CPU time profiler is a crucial tool to identify bottlenecks – program elements that take a large part of the execution time. Today, it is inconceivable to ship a programming environment without a code profiler included or provided by a third party.

However, when we retrospectively look at the history of code profiler tools, we see that tool usability and profiling overhead reduction have steadily improved, but that the set of offered abstractions has remained constant. For instance, gprof, which appeared in 1982, offers a number of textual reports focussed on "how much time was spent executing directly in each function" and call graphs[1]. JProfiler essentially produces the same output, using a graphical rendering instead of a textual one[2]. Most of the research conducted in the field of code profiling focus on reducing the overhead triggered by the code instrumentation and observation. The abstractions used to profile object-oriented applications are very close to the ones for procedural applications.

---

[1] http://sourceware.org/binutils/docs/gprof/Output.html#Output

[2] http://www.ej-technologies.com/products/jprofiler/screenshots.html

J. Vitek (Ed.): TOOLS 2010, LNCS 6141, pp. 291–309, 2010.

The contribution of this paper is to apply some visualizations that have been previously used in static software analysis to display dynamic metric for profiling purposes. We propose a visual mechanism for rendering dynamic information that effectively enables comparison of different metrics related to a program execution. *Structural distribution blueprint* and *behavioral distribution blueprint* are two visualizations intended to identify bottlenecks and propose hints on how to remove them. The first blueprint represents the distribution of the CPU effort along the program structure. The second blueprint directs the distribution along method invocations and identifies methods prone to one class of optimization, namely caching. The work presented in this paper aims at complementing existing profilers with new visualizations that help specific optimization tasks.

We obtained the results presented in this paper using Pharo[3], an open-source Smalltalk-dialect programming language. Nothing in the visualizations we propose prevents one from using them in a different setting.

We apply our techniques to the visualization framework Mondrian[4] [MGL06], our running example. We first describe our blueprints (Section 2). Subsequently, we identify and implement opportunities for optimization in Mondrian (Section 3). We then review related work (Section 4) and conclude (Section 5).

2   Profiling Blueprints

2.1   Profiling Blueprint in a Nutshell

Time profiling blueprints are graphical representations meant to help programmers (i) assess the time distribution and (ii) identify bottlenecks and give hints on how to remove them for a given program execution. The essence of profiling blueprints is to enable a better comparison of elements constituting the program structure and behavior. To render information, these blueprints use a graph metaphor, composed of nodes and edges.

The size of a node hints at its importance in the execution. In the case that nodes represent methods, a large node may say that the program execution spends "a lot of time" in this method. The expression "a lot of time" is then quantified by visually comparing the height and/or the width of the node against other nodes.

Color is used to either transmit a boolean property (*e.g.*, a gray node represents a method that always returns the same value) or a metric (*e.g.*, a color gradient is mapped to the number of times a method has been invoked).

We propose two blueprints that help identify opportunities for code optimization. They provide hints to programmers to refactor their program along the following two principles: (i) make often-used methods faster and (ii) call slow methods less often. The metrics we adopted in this paper help finding methods that are either unlikely to perform a side effect or return always the same result, good candidates for simple caching optimizations.

---

[3] http://www.pharo-project.org/home
[4] http://www.moosetechnology.org/tools/mondrian

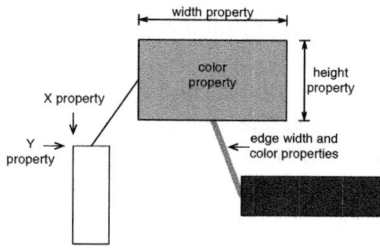

Fig. 1. Principle of polymetric view

2.2   Polymetric Views

The blueprints we propose are graphically rendered as *polymetric views* [LD03].
A *polymetric view* is a lightweight software visualization enriched with software
metrics. It has been successfully used to provide "software maps" intended to
help software comprehension and visualization. Figure 1 depicts the general aspect of a polymetric view.

Given two-dimensional nodes representing entities, we can map up to 5 metrics
on the node characteristics: position (X and Y), size (width and height), and
color:

- *Position.* The X and Y coordinates of the position of a node may reflect two
  measurements.
- *Size.* The width and height of a node can render two measurements. We
  follow the intuitive notion that the wider and the higher the node, the larger
  the associated metric.
- *Color.* The color interval between white and black may render one measurement. The convention that is usually adopted [GL04] is that the higher
  the measurement, the darker the node. Thus light gray represents a smaller
  measurement than dark gray.

Edges may also render properties along a number of dimensions (width, color,
direction, etc.). However, for the purpose of this work, all edges are identical.

2.3   Structural Distribution Blueprint

The execution of an object-oriented program yields a large amount of information [DLB04] (*e.g.,* number of objects created at runtime, total execution time of
a method). Unfortunately, all these dimensions cannot be visually rendered in a
meaningful fashion. The *structural distribution blueprint* displays a selected number of metrics indicating the distribution of the execution time along the static
structure of a program (*i.e.,* classes, methods and class hierarchy). Table 1 gives
the specification of the *structural distribution blueprint*. The blueprint renders
a program in terms of classes, methods and inheritance relations. Each method
representation exhibits its corresponding CPU time profiling information along
three metrics:

- *number of different receivers*: amount of different object receivers the method has been invoked on. Due to implementation limitations, this is at the moment a lower bound estimate.
- *total execution time of a method*: time for which a call frame corresponding to the method is present on the stack at runtime. The precision depends on the underlining profiler used to collect runtime information.
- *number of executions*: number of times the method has been executed, independently of the object receiver.

Actual metric values, and additional information, are accessible through a contextual popup window.

Table 1. Specification of the structural distribution blueprint

Structural distribution blueprint	
Scope	full system execution time
Edge	class inheritance (upper is superclass of below)
Layout	tree layout for outer nodes and gridlayout for inner nodes (inner nodes are ordered by increasing height)
Metric scale	linear (except for node width)
Node	outer node is a class, an inner node is a method
Inner node color	Number of different receivers
Inner node height	total execution time of a method
Inner node width	number of executions (logarithmic scale)
Example	Figure 2

Example. Troughout this paper, we use the graph visualization framework Mondrian as a case study. The blueprints described in this paper are also rendered using Mondrian. An example of the structural distribution blueprint is given in Figure 2. Four classes are represented: MOGraphElement, MOViewRenderer, MONode and MORoot. This figure is a small part of a bigger picture obtained by evaluating the following code snippet, which renders a simple visualization of 100 nodes, each containing 100 nodes:

```
ProfilingPackageSpy
      viewProfiling: [
            | view |
            view := MOViewRenderer new.
            view nodes: (1 to: 100)
                  forEach: [:each |  view nodes: (1 to: 100)].
            view root applyLayout ]
      inPackage: 'Mondrian'
```

The code being profiled is indicated using a **bold font** in the example source code. The profiling is realized from the perspective of one package, Mondrian in our case. MOGraphElement inherits from MONode, MORoot from MOGraphElement, and MOViewRenderer from Object. Since Object does not belong to Mondrian (but to the Kernel package), it is not rendered in the blueprint.

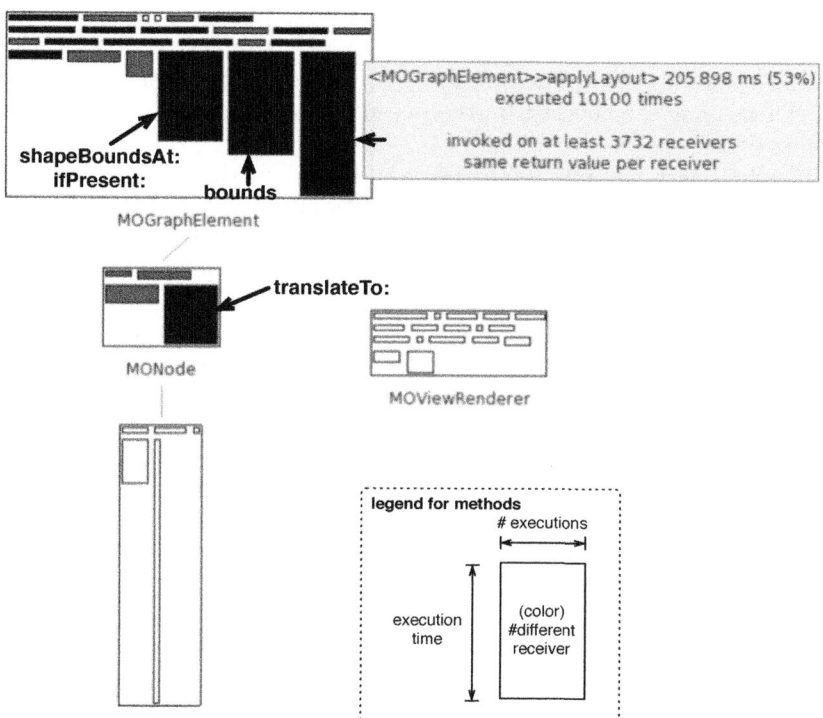

Fig. 2. Example of a structural blueprint

The height of a method node is proportional to the total execution time taken by the method (*e.g.,* 53% of the code execution is spent in the method applyLayout and 38% in bounds). The width is proportional to the number of times the method has been executed. A logarithmic scale is used. The method node color represents the number of different objects this method has been executed on (more than 3 732). The scope of the blueprint is global, which means that the darkest method corresponds to the method that has been executed on the greatest number of object receivers, system-wide.

Moving the mouse over a method node pops up additional contextual information. In the example, the contextual window says that the method applyLayout defined in the class MOGraphElement has been executed 10 100 times, and has been executed on more than 3 732 distinct receiver objects (*i.e.,* instances of MOGraphElement or one of its subclasses). It is also indicated that this method returns always the same value for a given object receiver. While the blueprint emphasizes the three metrics indicated above, the contextual information provides useful data when one wants to know more about a particular method.

Within a class, methods are ordered along their height. This helps quickly spot the amount of costly methods. For example, it is clear that among MOGraphElement's methods, 3 are dominating with respect to execution time.

Interpretation. Classes represented in Figure 2 illustrate part of a scenario that totals 11 classes. Among the 111 classes that define Mondrian, these 11 classes are the only classes involved in the code snippet execution given above. Only classes that are covered by the execution, even partially, are depicted in the blueprint.

MOGraphElement contains "many large and dark" methods. This indicates that this class is central to the code snippet execution: these large and black methods consume a lot of CPU time and are invoked on many different instances. Almost all of MOGraphElement's methods are executed a large number of times: in the visualization, they are quite wide compared to methods in other classes. For most of them, this is not a problem because they are thin and horizontal: even if these methods are executed many times, they do not consume CPU time. On the left of applyLayout stands the bounds method. This method takes 38% of the CPU time and is invoked 70 201 times on more than 3 732 object receivers. The third costliest method on MOGraphElement, shapeBoundsAt:ifPresent: takes 33% of the CPU time. MONode contains a black and relatively large method: MONode>> translateTo: consumes 22% of the total CPU time. The method has been invoked 10 100 times on at least 3 732 receivers.

Comparing to MOGraphElement, we find that classes are not involved in the computation as much. The representation of MOViewRenderer quickly says that its methods are invoked a few times without consuming much CPU. Moreover, methods are white, which tells that they are invoked on few instances only. The contextual information obtained by moving the mouse over the methods reveals that these methods are executed on a unique receiver. This is not surprising since only one instance of MOViewRenderer is created in the code example given above.

MORoot also does not seem to be the cause of a bottleneck at runtime. The few methods of this class are not frequently executed since they are relatively narrow. MORoot also defines a method applyLayout. This method is the tall, thin and white method. The contextual information reveals that this method is executed once and on one object only. It consumes 97% of the CPU time. The method MORoot>> applyLayout invokes MOGraphElement>> applyLayout on each of the nodes. The relation between these two applyLayout methods is indicated by a fly-by-highlighting (not represented in the picture) and the *behavioral distribution blueprint*, described below.

All in all, a large piece of the total CPU time is distributed over four methods: MONode>> translateTo: (24%), MOGraphElement>> bounds (32%), MOGraphElement>> shapeBoundsAt:ifPresent: (33%), MOGraphElement>> applyLayout (53%). Note that at this stage, we cannot say that the CPU time share of these three methods is the sum of their individual share. We have $24 + 32 + 33 + 53 = 142$. This indicates that some of these methods call each other since their sum cannot exceed 100%.

2.4   Behavioral Distribution Blueprint

In a pure object-oriented setting, computation is solely performed through message sending between objects. The CPU time consumption is distributed along method executions. Assessing the runtime distribution along method invocations complements the structural distribution described in the previous section. To reflect this profiling along method invocations, we provide the *behavioral distribution blueprint*. Table 2 gives the specification of the figure.

The goal of this blueprint is to assess runtime information alongside method call invocations. It is intended to find optimization opportunities, which may be tackled with caching. In addition to the metrics such as the number of calls and execution time, we also show whether a given method returns constant values, and whether it is likely to perform a side effect or not. As shown later, this information is helpful to identify a class of bottlenecks.

Classes do not appear on this blueprint. Methods are represented by nodes and invocations by directed edges. The blueprint uses the two metrics described in the previous blueprint for the width and height of a method. In addition to the shape, node color indicates a property:

– the gray color indicates methods that return self, the default return value. When no return value is specified in Pharo, the object receiver is returned. This corresponds to void methods in a statically typed language. No result is expected from the method, strongly suggesting that the method operates via side effects.
– the yellow color (which appears as light gray on a black and white printout) indicates methods that are constant on their return value, this value being different from self.
– other methods are white.

A tree layout is used to order methods, with upper methods calling lower methods. We illustrates this blueprint on the MOGraphElement>> bounds method that we previously saw, a candidate for optimization.

Table 2. Specification of the behavioral distribution blueprint

Behavioral distribution blueprint	
Scope	all methods directly or indirectly invoked for a given starting method
Edge	method invocation (upper methods invoke lower ones)
Layout	tree layout
Metric scale	linear (except for node width)
Nodes	methods
Node color	gray: return always self; yellow: same return value per object receiver; white: remaining methods
Node height	total execution time
Node width	number of execution (logarithmic scale)
Example	Figure 3

Example. In the previous blueprint (Figure 2), right-clicking on the method MORoot>> applyLayout opens a behavioral distribution blueprint for this method. The complete picture is given in Figure 3. The picture has to be read top-down. Methods in this blueprint have the same dimensions as in the behavioral

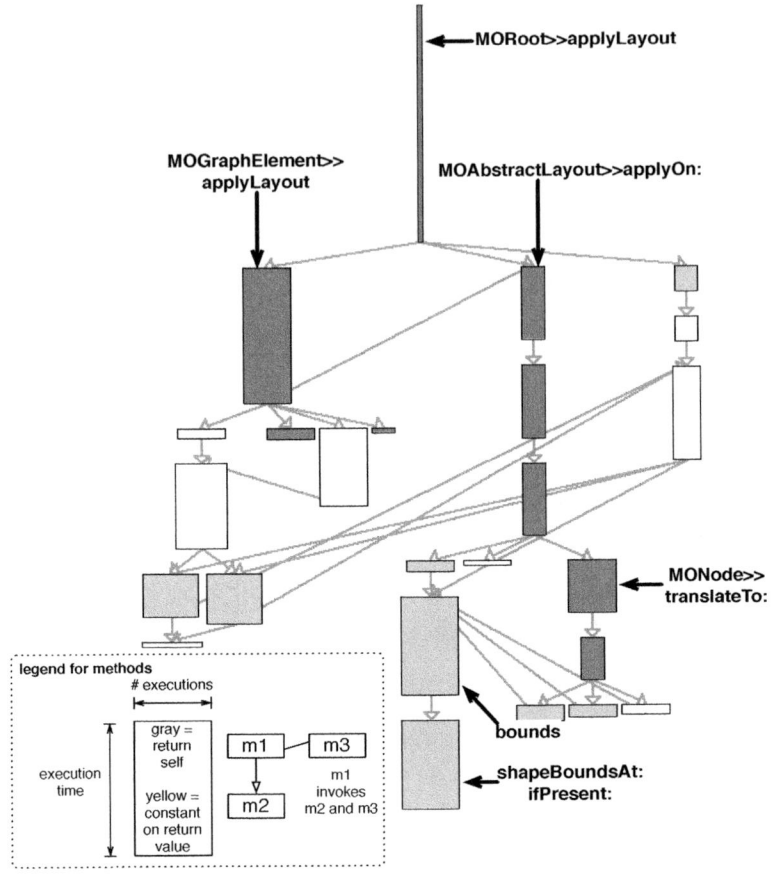

Fig. 3. Example of a behavioral blueprint

blueprint. We recognize the tall and thin MORoot>> applyLayout at the top. All methods in Figure 3 are therefore invoked directly or indirectly by MORoot >> applyLayout. MORoot>> applyLayout invokes 3 methods, including MOGraphElement>> applyLayout (labelled in the figure). MOGraphElement>> applyLayout calls MOAbstractLayout>> applyOn:, and both of these are called by MORoot>> applyLayout.

Interpretation. As the first blueprint revealed, bounds, applyLayout, shapeBoundsAt:ifPresent:, translateTo: are expensive in terms of CPU time consumption. The behavior blueprint highlights this fact from a different point of view, along method invocations. In the following we will optimize bounds by identifying the reason of its high cost and provide a solution to fix it. Our experience with Mondrian tells us that this method has a surprisingly high cost. Where to start a refactoring among all potential candidates remains the programmer's task. Our blueprint only says "how it is" and not "how it should be", however it is a rich source of indication of what's going on at runtime.

The return value of MOGraphElement>> bounds is constant over time, hence it is painted in yellow. This method is involved in a rich invocation graph (presented in Figure 3). In general, understanding the interaction of a single method is likely to be difficult when a complete call graph is used. The contextual menu obtained by right-clicking on a method offers a filtered view on the entity of interest.

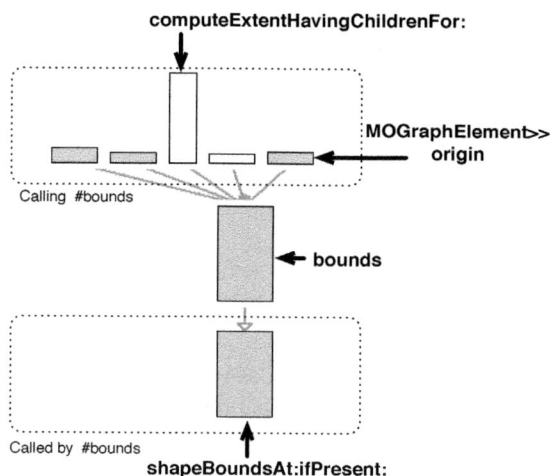

Fig. 4. Detailed view of MOGraphElement>> bounds

Figure 4 shows a detailed view of a behavioral blueprint, centered on MO-GraphElement>> bounds. This method is at the center of the picture. Above are located the methods calling bounds. Below, the unique method that is called by bounds. Among the 5 methods that call bounds, 3 always return the same value when executed. The method called by bounds also remains constant on its return value. Figure 4 renders bounds and shapeBoundsAt:ifPresent: with the same width. It is therefore likely that these two methods are invoked the same number of times. The contextual window indicates that each of these two methods is invoked 70 201 times. We can deduce the following:

- bounds belongs to several execution paths in which each method is constant on its return value. This is indicated in the upper part of Figure 4.
- bounds calls shapeBoundsAt:ifPresent:, which is constant on return value.
- bounds and shapeBoundsAt:ifPresent: are invoked the same number of times.

The following section addresses this bottleneck by adding a cache in bounds and unveils another bottleneck in Mondrian.

3   Optimizing Mondrian

The combination of the structural and behavioral blueprints helped us to identify a number of bottlenecks in Mondrian. In this section, we address some of these bottlenecks by using memoization[5], i.e. we cache values to avoid redundant computations.

3.1 Bottleneck MOGraphElement>> Bounds

As we saw earlier, the behavioral blueprint on the method MOGraphElement>> bounds reveals a number of facts about the program's execution. These facts are good hints that bounds will benefit from a caching mechanism since it always returns the same value and calls a method that is also constant. We inspect its source code:

```
MOGraphElement>> bounds
   "Answer the bounds of the receiver."
   | basicBounds |
   self shapeBoundsAt: self shape ifPresent: [ :b | ^ b ].

   basicBounds := shape computeBoundsFor: self.
   self shapeBoundsAt: self shape put: basicBounds.
   ^ basicBounds
```

The code source confirms that shapeBoundsAt:ifPresent: is invoked once each time bounds is invoked. The method shape is also invoked at each invocation of bounds. The contextual window obtained in the structural blueprint reveals that the return value of shape is constant: It is a simple variable accessor ("getter" method), so it is fast. bounds calls computeBoundsFor: and shapeBoundsAt:put: in addition to shapeBoundsAt:ifPresent: and shape. However, they do not appear in Figure 3 and 4. This means that bounds exits before reaching computeBoundsFor:. The block [:b | ^b], which has the effect of exiting the method, is therefore always executed in the considered example.

We first thought that the last tree lines of bounds may be removed since they are not executed in our scenario. However, the large number of tests in Mondrian indicate that these lines are indeed important in other scenarios, although not in our particular example.

We elected to upgrade bounds with a simple cache mechanism. Differences with the original version are indicated using a **bold font**. The class MOGraphElement is extended with a new instance variable, boundsCache. In addition, the cache variable has to be reset in 5 methods related to graphical bounds manipulation of nodes, such as translating and resizing.

```
MOGraphElement>> bounds
   "Answer the bounds of the receiver."
   | basicBounds |
   boundsCache ifNotNil: [ ^ boundsCache ].
   self shapeBoundsAt: self shape ifPresent: [ :b | ^ boundsCache := b ].

   basicBounds := shape computeBoundsFor: self.
   self shapeBoundsAt: self shape put: basicBounds.
   ^ boundsCache := basicBounds
```

---

[5] http://en.wikipedia.org/wiki/Memoization

There is no risk of concurrent accesses of boundsCache since this variable is set when the layout is being computed. This occurs before the display of the visualization, which is done in a different thread.

Result. Adding a statement boundsCache ifNotNil: [^ boundsCache] significantly reduces the execution time of the code given in Section 2.3. Before adding this simple cache mechanism, the code took 430 ms to execute (on a MacBook Pro, 2Gb of RAM (1067 MHz DDR3), 2.26 GHz Intel Core 2 Duo, Squeak VM 4.2.1beta1U). With the cache, the same execution takes 242 ms only, which represents a speedup of approximately 43%.

This gain is reflected on the overall distribution of the computational effort. Figure 5 provides two structural blueprints of the code snippet given in Section 2.3. The left blueprint has been produced before upgrading the method MOGraphElement>> bounds. Figure 2 is a part of it. The right one has been produced after upgrading bounds as described above. Many places are impacted. We annotated the figure with the most significant changes:

- the size of the bounds method and the methods invoked by it (C) have seen their height significantly reduced. Before the optimization, bounds used 38% of the total CPU consumption. After the optimization, its CPU use fell to 5%.
- the 5 methods denoted by the circle A and B have seen their height increased and their color darkened. The height increase illustrates the augmentation in relative CPU consumption these methods are subject to, now that bounds has been improved.

The evolution of the behavioral blueprint is presented in Figure 6. We can clearly see the reduced size of bounds and shapeBoundsAt:ifPresent: (Circle B) and the increase of the applyLayout method (Circle A).

3.2   Bottleneck in MONode>> displayOn:

We fixed an important bottleneck when computing bounds in Mondrian. We push our analysis of bounds computing a step further. We inspect the User Interface (UI) thread of Mondrian. Most applications with a graphical user interface run in at least 2 threads: one for the program logic and another in charge of receiving user events (e.g., keystrokes, mouse events) and virtual machine/OS events (e.g., window refreshes). Mondrian is no exception. The blueprints presented earlier focused on profiling the application logic.

Step 1. Figure 7 shows the structural profiling of the UI thread for the Mondrian script given in Section 2.3. The blueprint contains many large methods, indicating methods that received a significant CPU share. Among these, our knowledge of Mondrian lead us to absoluteBounds. This method is very similar to bounds that we previously saw. It returns the bounds of a node using absolute coordinates (instead of relative). The UI thread spends most of the time in MONode>> displayOn: since it is the root of the thread's computation.

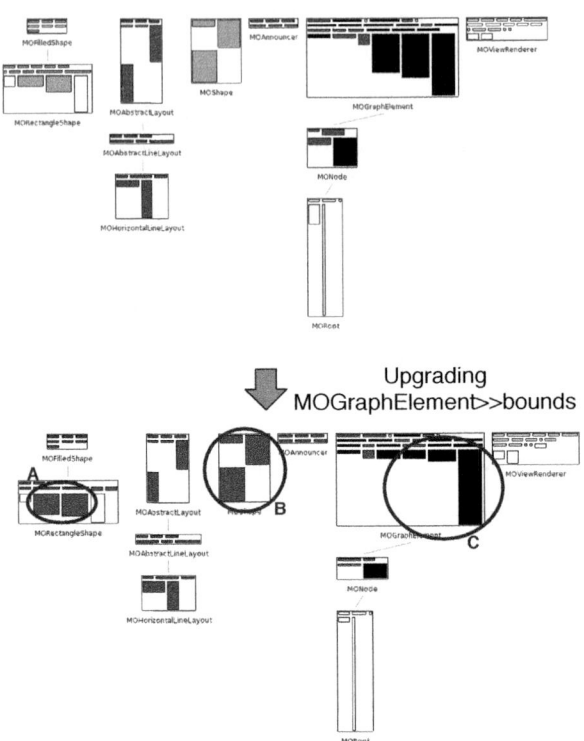

Fig. 5. Upgrading bounds has a global structural impact

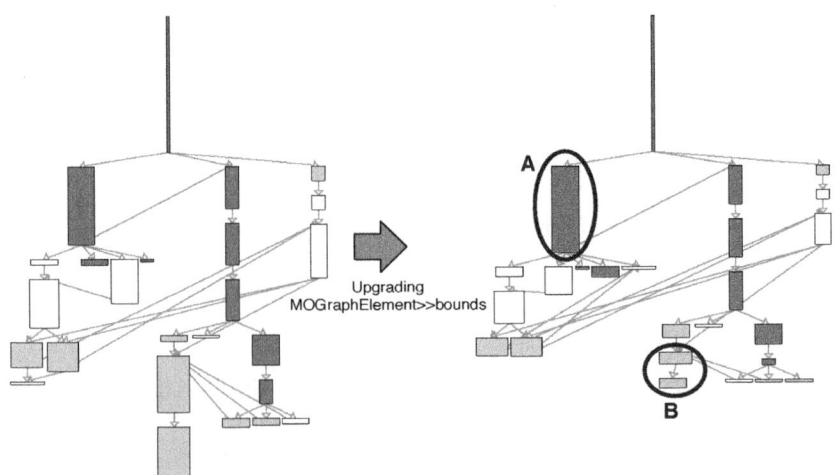

Fig. 6. Upgrading bounds has a global behavioral impact

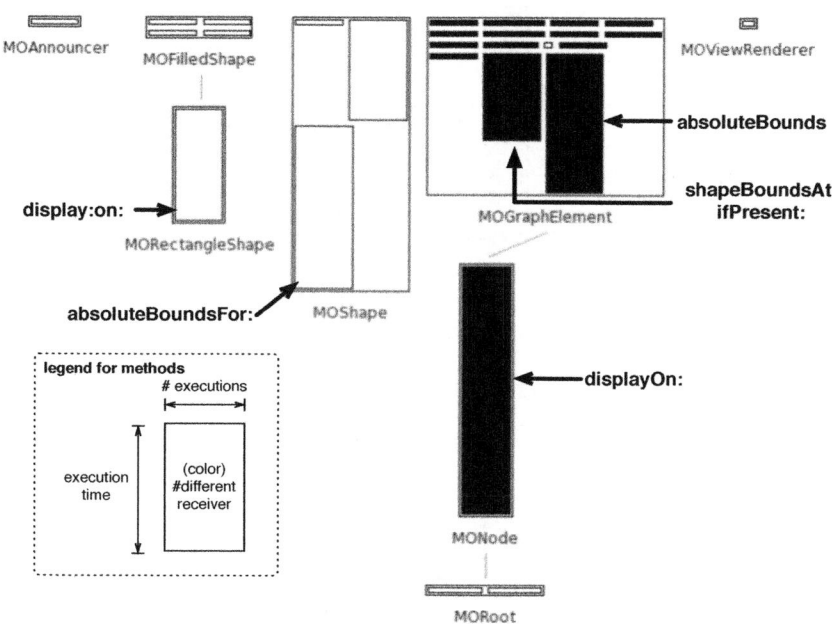

Fig. 7. Profiling of the UI thread in Mondrian

Figure 8 shows the behavioral blueprint opened on MONode>> displayOn:. The blueprint reveals that absoluteBounds and absoluteBoundsFor: call each other. Return values of these two methods are constant as indicated by their yellow color. They are therefore good candidates for caching:

```
MOGraphElement>> absoluteBounds
    "Answer the bounds in absolute terms (relative to the entire Canvas, not just the parent)."
    absoluteBoundsCache ifNotNil: [ ^absoluteBoundsCache ].
    ^absoluteBoundsCache := self shape absoluteBoundsFor: self
```

Result. Without the cache in absoluteBounds, the scenario takes 356 ms to run. With the cache, it takes 231 ms. We therefore gained 35% when displaying the visualization.

Step 2. By adding the cache in absoluteBounds, we significantly reduced the cost of this method. We can still do better. As shown in Figure 8, there is another caller of absoluteBounds. MORectangleShape>> display:on: is 85 lines long and begins with:

```
MORectangleShape>> display: aFigure on: aCanvas
    | bounds borderWidthValue textExtent c textToDisplay font borderColorValue ... |
    bounds := self absoluteBoundsFor: aFigure.
    c := self fillColorFor: aFigure.
    ...
```

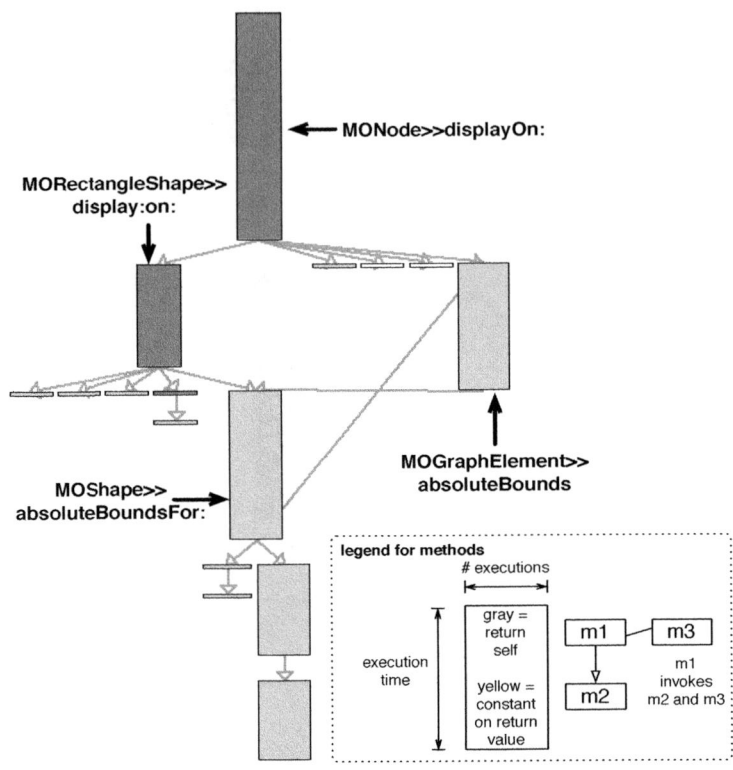

Fig. 8. Profiling of the UI thread in Mondrian

We saw in Step 1 that absoluteBounds calls the expensive and uncached absolute-BoundsFor:. Replacing the call to absoluteBoundsFor: by absoluteBounds improves performance further:

```
MORectangleShape>> display: aFigure on: aCanvas
  | bounds borderWidthValue textExtent c textToDisplay font borderColorValue ... |
  bounds := aFigure absoluteBounds.
  c := self fillColorFor: aFigure.
  ...
```

Result. The execution time of the code snippet has been reduced to 198 ms. A speedup of 14% from Step 1, and of 45% overall.

Blueprint evolution. Figure 9 summarizes the two evolution steps described previously. Differences with a previous step are denoted using a circle. The effect of caching absoluteBounds considerably diminished the execution time of this method. This is illustrated by Circle C. It has also the effect of reducing the size of MOShape's methods and increasing MORectangleShape>> display:on:. The share of the CPU consumption increased for this method. Step 2 reduced the

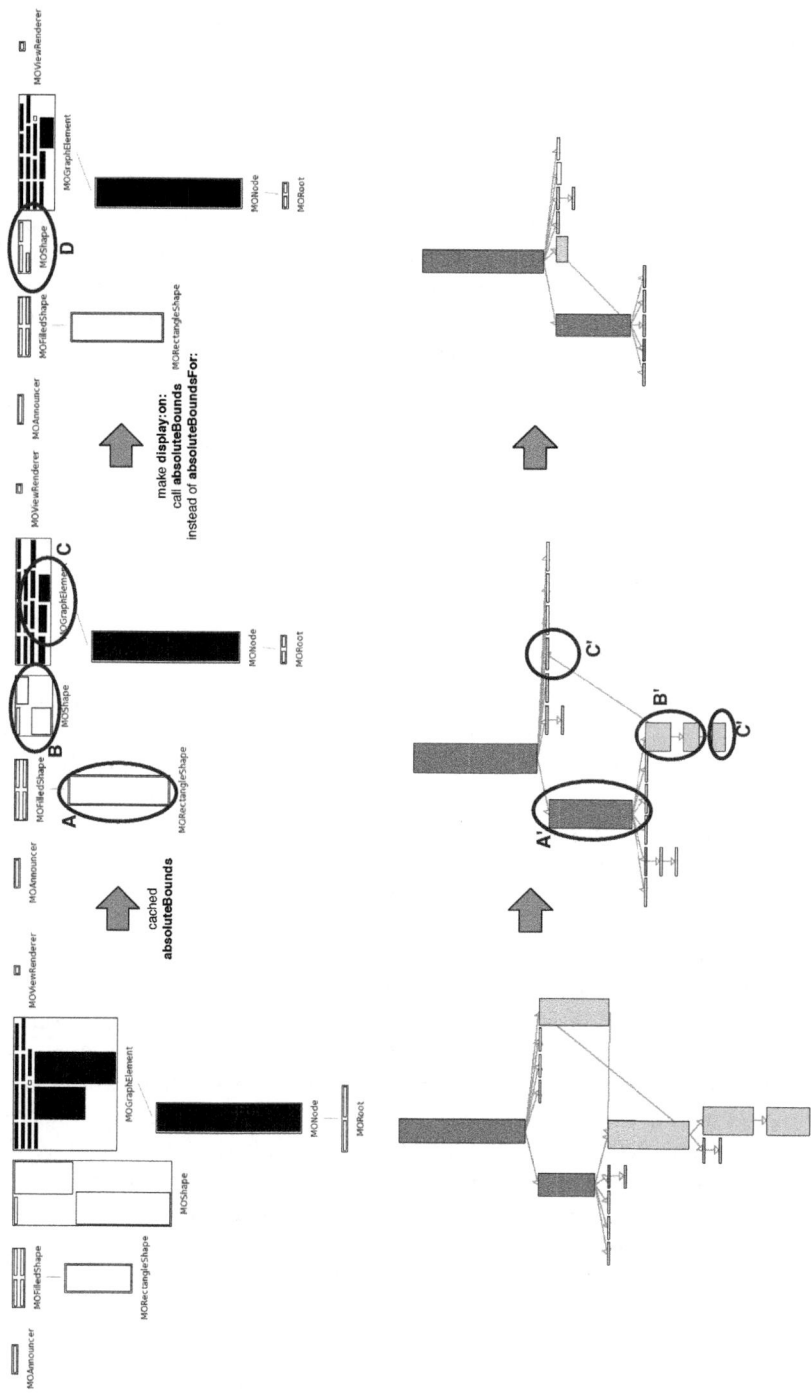

Fig. 9. Profiling of the UI thread in Mondrian

size of MOShape's method. Their execution time became so small, that it does not appear in the behavioral blueprint (since we use a sampling-based profiler to obtain the runtime information, methods having less than 1% of the CPU do not appear in this blueprint).

3.3   Summary

The cache value of MOGraphElement>> bounds (Section 3.1) is implemented and has been finalized in the version 341 of Mondrian[6]. The improvement of absoluteBounds and display:on: may be found in the version 352 of Mondrian. The complete experiment lead to a 43% improvement in creating the layout of a view, and of 45% in displaying the same view.

We identify and remove a number of bottlenecks. From this experience, it is tempting to identify and look after some general patterns that would easily expose fixable execution bottleneck. Unfortunately, we haven't see the opportunity to deduce some general rules. The visualization we provide clearly identify costly methods and classes, potentially being candidates for optimization. Whether the optimization can be easily realized or not depends heavily on a wide range of parameters (*e.g.*, algorithm, architecture, data structure).

4   Related Work

Profiling capabilities have been integrated in IDEs such as the NetBeans Profiler[7] and Eclipse's Tracing and Profiling Project (TPTP)[8]. The NetBeans Profiler uses JFluid [Dmi04], which offers a Calling Context Tree (CCT) [ABL97] augmented with the accumulated execution time for individual methods. The CCT is visualized as an expandable tree, where calling contexts are sorted by their execution time and can be expanded (respectively collapsed) in order to show (or hide) callees. However, as CCTs for real-world applications are often large, comprising up to some million nodes, an expandable tree representation makes it difficult to detect hotspots in deep calling contexts.

The Calling Context Ring Chart (CCRC) [MBAV09] is a CCT visualization that eases the exploration of large trees. Like the Sunburst visualization [Sta00], CCRC uses a circular layout. Callee methods are represented in ring segments surrounding the caller's ring segment. In order to reveal hot calling contexts, the ring segments can be sized according to a chosen dynamic metric. Recently, CCRC has been integrated into the Senseo plugin for Eclipse [RHV+09], which enriches Eclipse's static source views with several dynamic metrics. Our blueprints have a different focus, since global information is shown instead of providing a line-of-code granularity.

Execution traces may be used to analyze dynamic program behavior. Execution traces are logged events, such as method entry and exit, or object allocation.

---

[6] The source code is available at: http://www.squeaksource.com/Mondrian.html
[7] http://profiler.netbeans.org/
[8] http://www.eclipse.org/tptp/performance/

However, the resulting amount of data can be excessive. In Deelen *et al.* [DvHHvdW07] execution traces are visualized with nodes representing classes and edges representing method calls. Node size and edge thickness are mapped to properties (e.g., number of method invocations). A time range can be selected in order to limit the data to be visualized. Another approach to visualizing execution traces has been introduced in Holten *et al.* [HCvW07]. It uses the concept of hierarchical edge bundles [Hol06], where similar edges are put together to improve the visualization of larger traces. Execution traces allow keeping calls in sequences and selecting a precise time interval to be visualized, which helps understand a particular phase in the execution of a program. Blueprint profiling offers a global map of the complete execution without focusing on sequentiality in time. However, they offer hints about the behavior of individual methods that help to solve a class of optimization problem, namely introducing caches.

Tree-maps [JS91] visualize hierarchical structures. Nodes are represented as rectangular areas sized proportionally to a metric. Tree-maps have been used to visualize profiling data. For instance, in [WKT04] the authors present KCacheGrind, a front end to a simulator-based cache profiling tool, using a combination of tree-maps and call graphs to visualize the data. Our blueprint use polymetric view to render data. A tree-map solves a problem in a different way that a polymetric view would solve it. A polymetric enables one to compare several different metrics, whereas a tree-map is dedicated to showing a single metric (besides color) in a compact space.

5   Conclusion

In this paper we presented two visualizations helping developers to identify and remove performance bottlenecks. Providing visualizations that are intuitive and easy to use is our primary goal. Our graphical blueprints follow simple principles such as "big nodes are slow methods", "gray nodes are methods likely to have side-effects", "yellow nodes remain constant on return values". Our visualizations helped us to significantly improve Mondrian, a visualization engine. We described a number of optimizations we realized. For space reason, we couldn't describe all the optimizations. The last version of Mondrian contains an improved version of the applyLayout method, thus mitigating the bottleneck caused by this method. This improvement was recently publicly announced[9].

A number of conclusions may be drawn from the experiment described in this paper. First, bottleneck identification and removal are significantly easier when side-effects and constant return values are localized. Second, an extensive set of unit tests remains essential to assess whether a candidate optimization can be applied without changing the behavior of the system.

As future work, we plan to focus on architectural views by adopting coarser grain than methods and classes.

---

[9] http://www.iam.unibe.ch/pipermail/moose-dev/2010-January/003781.html

We used our blueprint visualizations on a number of case studies not described in this paper: Glamour and Moose, and O2[10]. Our visualizations and profiler are available in Pharo[11] under the MIT license.

References

[ABL97]   Ammons, G., Ball, T., Larus, J.R.: Exploiting hardware performance counters with flow and context sensitive profiling. In: Proceedings of the ACM SIGPLAN conference on Programming language design and implementation (PLDI'97), pp. 85–96 (1997)

[DLB04]   Ducasse, S., Lanza, M., Bertuli, R.: High-level polymetric views of condensed run-time information. In: Proceedings of 8th European Conference on Software Maintenance and Reengineering (CSMR 2004), pp. 309–318. IEEE Press, Los Alamitos (2004)

[Dmi04]   Dmitriev, M.: Profiling Java applications using code hotswapping and dynamic call graph revelation. In: Proceedings of the Fourth International Workshop on Software and Performance (WOSP 2004), pp. 139–150 (2004)

[DvHHvdW07]   Deelen, P., van Ham, F., Huizing, C., van de Watering, H.: Visualization of dynamic program aspects. In: Proceedings of the 4th IEEE International Workshop on Visualizing Software for Understanding and Analysis (VISSOFT 2007), June 2007, pp. 39–46 (2007)

[GL04]   Gîrba, T., Lanza, M.: Visualizing and characterizing the evolution of class hierarchies. In: Proceedings of the 5th ECOOP Workshop on Object-Oriented Reengineering (WOOR 2004)

[HCvW07]   Holten, D., Cornelissen, B., van Wijk, J.J.: Trace visualization using hierarchical edge bundles and massive sequence views. In: Proceedings of the 4th IEEE International Workshop on Visualizing Software for Understanding and Analysis (VISSOFT 2007), pp. 47–54 (2007)

[Hol06]   Holten, D.: Hierarchical edge bundles: Visualization of adjacency relations in hierarchical data. IEEE Transactions on Visualization and Computer Graphics 12(5), 741–748 (2006)

[JS91]   Johnson, B., Shneiderman, B.: Tree-maps: a space-filling approach to the visualization of hierarchical information structures. In: Proceedings of the 2nd conference on Visualization (VIS 1991), pp. 284–291. IEEE Computer Society Press, Los Alamitos (1991)

[LD03]   Lanza, M., Ducasse, S.: Polymetric views—a lightweight visual approach to reverse engineering. Transactions on Software Engineering (TSE) 29(9), 782–795 (2003)

[MBAV09]   Moret, P., Binder, W., Ansaloni, D., Villazón, A.: Visualizing Calling Context Profiles with Ring Charts. In: Proceedings of the 5th IEEE International Workshop on Visualizing Software for Understanding and Analysis (VISSOFT 2009), pp. 33–36. IEEE Computer Society, Los Alamitos (2009)

---

[10] http://www.moosetechnology.org/tools/, http://www.squeaksource.com/O2.html
[11] http://www.squeaksource.com/Spy.html

[MGL06]   Meyer, M., Gîrba, T., Lungu, M.: Mondrian: An agile visualization framework. In: Proceedings of the 3rd ACM Symposium on Software Visualization (SoftVis 2006), pp. 135–144. ACM Press, New York (2006)

[RHV⁺09]   Röthlisberger, D., Härry, M., Villazón, A., Ansaloni, D., Binder, W., Nierstrasz, O., Moret, P.: Augmenting Static Source Views in IDEs with Dynamic Metrics. In: Proceedings of the 25th IEEE International Conference on Software Maintenance (ICSM 2009), pp. 253–262. IEEE Computer Society, Los Alamitos (2009)

[Sta00]   Stasko, J.: An evaluation of space-filling information visualizations for depicting hierarchical structures. Int. J. Hum.-Comput. Stud. 53(5), 663–694 (2000)

[WKT04]   Weidendorfer, J., Kowarschik, M., Trinitis, C.: A tool suite for simulation based analysis of memory access behavior. In: Bubak, M., van Albada, G.D., Sloot, P.M.A., Dongarra, J. (eds.) ICCS 2004. LNCS, vol. 3038, pp. 440–447. Springer, Heidelberg (2004)

Author Index